THE HOLMES–EINSTEIN LETTERS

MR. JUSTICE HOLMES
from a photograph taken about 1902

THE
HOLMES–EINSTEIN
LETTERS

*Correspondence of Mr. Justice Holmes
and Lewis Einstein 1903–1935*

EDITED BY

JAMES BISHOP PEABODY

NEW YORK
ST MARTIN'S PRESS INC
1964

MACMILLAN AND COMPANY LIMITED
St Martin's Street London WC 2
also Bombay Calcutta Madras Melbourne

THE MACMILLAN COMPANY OF CANADA LIMITED
Toronto

ST MARTIN'S PRESS INC
New York

PRINTED IN GREAT BRITAIN

PREFACE

I used to dream of a final calm under old trees,
possibly, no — impossibly, in England or in the East.
But my life began and seems likely to end in war, and
one must grow one's trees in one's soul.— HOLMES
TO EINSTEIN, June 27, 1917.

ONE evening in February 1903, a young American scholar
was invited by Mr. Justice Holmes to dine at his home in
Washington. The meeting had been brought about by a
mutual friend, Lady Castletown of Doneraile, Ireland.

Lewis Einstein, then twenty-six years old, was about to be
appointed to his first diplomatic post as Third Secretary in the
American Embassy in Paris. Despite his youth, he was the
author of two scholarly books, the more important of which,
The Italian Renaissance in England,[1] he brought with him and
left with Holmes on the occasion of their first meeting.

Holmes, at sixty-one, was already a national figure. After
distinguishing himself in the Civil War, he had published his
great work on the common law,[2] served as Chief Justice of
the Massachusetts Supreme Judicial Court, and accepted in
1902 an appointment as an Associate Justice of the Supreme
Court of the United States.

Although a span of thirty-six years separated the two men,
their friendship, once formed, flourished undisturbed by war
or distance until Holmes's death, on March 6, 1935, two days
before his ninety-fourth birthday.

The record of this friendship is preserved in the letters
exchanged between them, now published for the first time.
The fact that there are two hundred and seven letters from
Holmes and only fifty-six from Einstein does not mean that
Holmes was the more faithful correspondent but only that he

---

[1] Published in London in 1902. His earlier work, *Luigi Pulci and the Morgante
Maggiore*, had been published in Berlin in the same year.
[2] *The Common Law*, Boston (1881).

was the more assiduous housekeeper. As Holmes confessed to Einstein in his letter of September 30, 1932, he made it a point to destroy illuminating documents relating to his personal life. It is to be regretted that the majority of Einstein's letters were almost certainly consumed in the course of these lamentable conflagrations ; those published here found a safe haven after the Justice's death with the rest of his extant private papers in the Harvard Law School Library in Cambridge, Massachusetts. Einstein, on the other hand, preserved all Holmes's letters and thoughtfully donated them to the Library of Congress in Washington. The present collection contains all the known, surviving correspondence between the two men with the exception of some invitations and incidental cards of no literary or historical importance.

The Holmes papers have already yielded four substantial volumes containing the Justice's correspondence with Sir Frederick Pollock and with Professor Harold Laski,[3] written in the same years and discussing many of the same subjects found in the letters to Einstein. Unlike Pollock, however, Einstein had little acquaintance with, and still less interest in, the law as a subject of human inquiry. This was an ignorance which the Justice was fully prepared to accept, as evidenced by his letter to Einstein of October 10, 1920 : 'If you ask me what a *certiorari* is, I must answer with Jeremiah Mason to a client : That is something your Heavenly Father never meant you to know.' And although Laski and Einstein were both considerably younger than Holmes, Einstein was successful in bringing out a warm and playful, almost Rabelaisian, side of the Justice's character which the Professor of Political Economy was not able to evoke. Holmes's frequent amusing references to Casanova in his letters to Einstein reveal an aspect of his character not wholly consistent with the austere judge's New England puritanism. Time and again in this correspondence one sees the Justice happily drawn away from the atmosphere of the courts, free to display his broad human qualities as he pricks the cosmos with an epigram, sketches a lively vignette of some illustrious friend, or 'regilds the illusions of life' before returning to the law.

[3] *Holmes–Pollock Letters*, Cambridge (1941) ; *Holmes–Laski Letters*, Cambridge (1953).

Obviously no ordinary correspondent could have provoked so lively a response from the august 'Yankee from Olympus', and Einstein's letters, even in the incomplete form in which they have survived, establish that he was no ordinary correspondent. Born in New York City in 1877, Lewis Einstein was tutored by Horatio Alger before entering Columbia University where he took his M.A. degree with honors in 1902. He then entered the diplomatic service. In 1904 he married Helen Ralli, daughter of a well-known Anglo-Greek family, and this long and happy marriage was terminated only by her death in 1949. Before the First World War Einstein served as Secretary of the United States delegation to the Algeciras Conference in 1906, at Constantinople, Peking and as Minister to Costa Rica. During the war he was sent again to Turkey and had charge of British interests in Bulgaria. From 1921 to 1929 he was United States Minister in Czechoslovakia. His subsequent retirement from the Foreign Service provoked Charles Evans Hughes's lament, reported in Holmes's letter of April 15, 1930.

As a diplomat Einstein is best known for his forecast of world events. Cassandra-like, he read the future correctly, and his prophecy of the First World War, published in 1913, was a document of unusual prescience.[4] The passage of time and the attention of scholars have more recently contributed to a better appreciation of his political insight. George Kennan, in a critical study of United States diplomacy in the first half of this century, has noted :

'In the winter of 1913 there appeared, anonymously, and in an English magazine (because no American magazine would take it), an article written by an American diplomatist of the time, Mr. Lewis Einstein. In this article Mr. Einstein drew attention to the storm clouds gathering over Europe, to the depth of the Anglo-German antagonism, to the danger that war might arise from some relatively insignificant incident, and to the effect that a war might have on the equilibrium and stability of Europe. He then went on to trace out the significance of such a European war for the

---

[4] 'The Anglo-German Rivalry and the United States', *National Review*, January 1913, formed the first part of a series of two essays which first appeared in London and were later published in book form in the United States with an interesting foreword by Theodore Roosevelt; see *A Prophecy of War* by Lewis Einstein, Columbia University Press (1918).

security of the United States.   He never doubted that we
would have to intervene to save England, if the alternative
were clearly her destruction.   But he warned against the
assumption that we would not be affected by any alteration
either way in the balance of forces in Europe.'[5]

Einstein's literary talent continues the tradition of the
diplomat-writer, represented in the United States by such
scholars as Irving, Motley, and Lowell.   During and between
diplomatic posts he found time to publish a study of American
foreign policy,[6] a description of events inside Constantinople
at the time of the ill-fated Dardenelles expedition,[7] a further
study of the Renaissance mind based on the ideals of the
sixteenth century,[8] a life of Theodore Roosevelt,[9] an original
account of Americans in England during the War of Independence,[10] a novel study of the philosophy of history,[11] articles in
French and Italian periodicals on art, an account of the Italian
School as represented in the Washington National Gallery of
Art, and two volumes of verses.

Einstein's diplomatic career and his scholarly accomplishments were not, however, the real basis of his thirty-two-year
friendship with Holmes, although the latter followed his young
friend's activities with sympathetic interest, as his letters show.
Rather it was the unique combination of talents and personality that so fascinated and pleased the Justice.   Einstein's
genuine appreciation of art and literature by no means excluded
a lively interest in people with all their strengths and foibles ;
a report of his discovery of Chinese designs on a door in San
Marco in Venice is followed by the latest *bon mot* of Margot
Asquith at dinner the night before.   Small wonder, then, that

[5] *American Diplomacy 1900–1950*, Chicago (1951), pp. 70-71. See also Arthur
Schlesinger Jr.'s comment concerning the United States' stumbling entry into
the First World War : 'People occasionally had flashes as to what it was all
about — Theodore Roosevelt, in certain moods, Admiral Mahan, Lewis Einstein
— but in general the key problems of foreign policy were misunderstood and
ignored.'—*Partisan Review*, November–December 1951, p. 707.

[6] *American Foreign Policy by a Diplomatist*, New York (1909).

[7] *Inside Constantinople: a Diplomatist's Diary during the Dardanelles Expedition*,
London (1917).

[8] *Tudor Ideals*, London (1921).

[9] *Roosevelt: his Mind in Action*, London (1930).

[10] *Divided Loyalties—Americans in England during the War of Independence*, London
(1933).

[11] *Historical Change*, Cambridge (1946).

Holmes was willing to take time out from a busy life to reply
to so witty and erudite a correspondent.

Since most of Einstein's adult years were spent abroad, the
two men were able to meet face to face only during Holmes's
summer holidays in Europe or on Einstein's infrequent return
visits to the land which, as he wrote to Holmes in his letter of
December 14, 1930, 'is at once home and yet not a home to
me'. On these occasions he could sense the rejuvenating effect
of the American atmosphere — 'that sort of national monkey
gland which quickens the pulse and makes the blood stream
faster' — but he never stayed for long. During the Second
World War he served in the American Embassy in London as a
Special Assistant to the Ambassador; at its close he moved to
Paris where his experience and abilities have since contributed
significantly to the improvement of Franco-American relations
during a difficult and agitated period of transition.

In addition to reintroducing Einstein to the reading public,
this correspondence also throws light upon a particular facet
of Holmes's character which has perplexed later students of
his life and thought. Many of his critics have never been
able to resolve the paradox presented by the skepticism of a
man whose views they regard as undermining the philosophical
and religious foundations of the society in which he lived and
yet whom they feel bound to honor as an undeniably great
human being. The Justice's letters to Einstein make it clear
that he was an essentially religious man even though he had no
easy explanation for that unshakeable faith in the moral values
of courage and personal sacrifice which shaped his life.

Skeptic but no cynic, agnostic but no atheist, Holmes rejected the more familiar symbols of the New England Calvinistic
religion of his forefathers without denying its essential values.
He could not accept the notion of God as a father image — a
concept he dismissed as the 'beard behind the cosmos' — nor
was he able to achieve the experience of the mystic, though
he often strained to hear what he described as the 'clang
behind phenomena'. He had a healthy respect for the subtle
tyranny of words which led him to reject any belief in the
dogmatic finality of verbal formulations in the domain of
philosophy or religion. Yet his was a skepticism devoid of
arrogance. 'Your phrase "the real humility of the sceptic",'

he wrote Einstein on May 26, 1926, 'hits me where I live. I always insist and believe that the sceptic is more humble than all the other devotees of the sects. He does not look at himself as a little God but recognizes his only significance as a part of the I know not what.' And later, on February 1, 1927 : 'It seems to me that the sceptic may well be the most truly religious as well as the most philosophical of men. I would undertake to defend that thesis.' Readers may well conclude from these letters that the great achievements of Holmes's life were indeed founded upon a stoic adaptation of the traditional religion of his ancestors,[12] and that this faith was tempered, through some felicitous quirk of nature, by a remarkably keen sense of humor, the reflected light of which still flickers joyfully across the following pages.

Four proper names have been suppressed in the letters so as not to embarrass living persons. Several guesses at illegible words have been indicated in the text. The difficulties of Holmes's handwriting, exceeded only by Einstein's script, are proverbial : 'It was as if a demented fly had followed the pen across the paper'.[13] The punctuation has been expanded and additional paragraphing introduced. It is hoped that the notes will assist and not detract. It is doubtful, however, that all the legitimate demands of that shadowy figure, the hypothetical reader, have been satisfied in this respect, and the editor pleads guilty in advance to manifold and obvious inadequacies. His primary aims have been to achieve accuracy in the text and to emulate as best he could the high standards set by his former teacher, Professor Mark DeWolfe Howe, in his monumental editions of the Holmes–Pollock and the Holmes–Laski letters.

[12] 'Holmes developed a unique combination of skepticism and mysticism which enabled him to formulate for himself a modernized version of Calvinism.' *American Thought, A Critical Sketch*, by Morris R. Cohen, New York (1954), p. 168.

[13] Introduction by Sir John Pollock to *The Pollock–Holmes Letters*, Cambridge University Press (1942), p. xvii.

CONTENTS

ILLUSTRATIONS

INTRODUCTION

TWENTY-NINE years have gone by since Justice Holmes died, and now he lives with the immortals. Francis Biddle and Justice Benjamin Cardozo have aptly remarked that he stands in the same company as the greatest in our history. His memory is now framed by the receding distance of years, and his image, instead of being blurred by time, stands out in sharper relief. For his character was of a piece in which some very different ingredients had been fused. Even his looks with their singular distinction seemed to grace his mind, for he had the courtly appearance and manners of an old-world cavalry officer. This went without any vanity on his part, for he remained seemingly unaware of his own handsomeness. Indeed whatever slight vanity his character contained became apparent only after he had coined a happy phrase or invented some fresh image which gave him satisfaction. Behind the Magistrate was always the man of letters who took pleasure in shaping a well-turned sentence that he could introduce into a legal decision or an argument. Highly fastidious for himself in his use of words, he was also highly critical of any carelessness in others, as I discovered to my cost when he took me to task for making a verb out of 'voice'. In fact slipshod English was almost the only sin to which he refused to extend his customary tolerance.

There was a slight touch of the pedagogue in the Justice, which he humorously would explain by dwelling on his fear at Judgment Day at being tripped up by his ignorance of some book. This pertained to the facetious side of Holmes's character, and indeed Judgment Day, perhaps, from his Puritan remembrance, entered into his scheme of humor in other ways. Once he invented a witty apophthegm which gave him considerable pleasure, for he related it on more than one occasion. It concerned the first John D. Rockefeller who, in Holmes's fancy, was supposed to appear before the Throne trembling at what he dreaded would be his fate. To his relief the man of wealth heard a voice say to him : 'You poor fool ! You have amassed the greatest amount of money any man has ever done in the belief that it was all your own when in reality you were only the portal through which it flowed to productive uses, and you yourself took from it only the smallest possible tax consistent with your manner of life. You need not be afraid. Take a seat, but pretty low down.'

It is unusual for any man's life to be divided so sharply yet so unevenly in its span as that of Justice Holmes. He passed through two periods of very unequal duration. The first was spent as a soldier during three years of the Civil War, and the second, which was taken up with the law, lasted for seventy years to his dying day. Seemingly soldier and jurist have little in common, yet it was impossible to spend an hour with Holmes without realizing how great an impression these early experiences of war had left on his character. He told me that after the Civil War the world never seemed quite right again. Once when I called, he reminded me that it was the anniversary of his wound at Ball's Bluff. Cervantes was prouder of the arm lost at Lepanto than of Don Quixote, and the Justice, I believe, would never have exchanged his battle memories for his seat on the Bench. Yet, oddly enough, the cause for which he had fought meant little to him, certainly later in life, and once he remarked to me that he was not sure if, from a constitutional point of view, the South was not in the right. To him the real significance of soldiering came from some very different reasons than those of partisanship. In an early Memorial Day address he has said that since life is action and passion a man must share the passion and the action of his time at peril of being judged not to have lived. Yet the very conditions of the Bench made for safely ensconcing him as far away as possible from any opportunity to display either passion or action. He had to take refuge in these early memories in order to find again in the recollection of his years as a soldier the fulfilment of smothered desires and hidden tastes which the course of his subsequent life rendered impossible. New satisfactions came to him from the mind and were stimulating in their way, but somehow they lacked *panache* for a man who discovered his hero on the battlefield. More than once he remarked that the finest thing a man could do was to die for a cause in which he didn't believe. This came close to reducing a paradoxical ideal to the borderland of absurdity, but it contained more than a grain of his conviction. In a less abstract sense the experience of war left him with the difficult task of harmonizing in his mind the fervent faith in the merit of action with a no less profound skepticism regarding the purpose of that action.

Holmes has expressed this feeling in his magnificent address, 'The Soldier's Faith'. He would frequently refer to this speech in current talk so that probably it conveys his intimate conviction. The following passage certainly helps to explain this curious dualism in his character between skepticism and faith :

> 'I do not know what is true. I do not know the meaning of the Universe. But in the midst of doubt, in the collapse of creeds, there is one thing I do not doubt, that the faith is true and adorable which leads a soldier to throw away his life in obedience to a blindly accepted duty, in a cause which he little understands, in a plan of campaign of which he has no notion, under tactics of which he does not see the use.' [1]

His opinion never changed in this respect although it did in certain others. Toward Lincoln he admitted that his early estimate had been mistaken, and that after all he may have been a great man. Yet the memory was still vivid in his mind of a night passed in the trenches conversing with some Harvard classmates as to whether the Civil War had produced a great man, and when one of these feebly suggested Lincoln the others had laughed him down. The lesson which the War left stamped on his character was one of duty performed, of confidence that came from readiness to face danger and accept sacrifice, and of willingness to sink his own personality in a loyalty to something greater than himself. More than once he related that he had cried with rage as he lay wounded in a hospital near Fredericksburg because he could not be with his regiment on the day of that grim assault. And he would add, 'If I had been I would probably not be here today'. Army experience disciplined his character — but also

---

[1] 'The Soldier's Faith', an address delivered on Memorial Day, May 30, 1895, at a meeting called by the Graduating Class of Harvard University. See *Speeches by Oliver Wendell Holmes* (1913), p. 59.

B

contributed to the skeptical attitude he displayed toward any pedestaled authority which rested on something unreal that did not satisfy his own exacting test of merit.

Another circumstance may have contributed to the somewhat disparaging opinions he was prone to express regarding many men of supposed eminence. Much too long he himself had been regarded merely as his father's son. True enough he was never quite able to overcome certain youthful inhibitions which dated from that time — and he always thought of the house he lived in at Boston as his father's in contrast to the one in Washington which was his own. I see no reason to accept the opinion that Holmes disliked his father, but I think the Justice was often riled at the early imputation that his chief claim to attention came because of his relationship. The feeling subsided only when his own reputation grew so enormously in the latter years of his life.

Except for the memories of the Civil War Holmes was never very prone to speak of his early days, but he did remark that his father's friends, with whom he had spent his youth, held themselves in far higher esteem than he was disposed to concede to their talents, and he certainly refused to place them on the top shelf. I suspect that he found it hard to forgive something he was aware of in himself which linked him with that self-exalted circle. Not unnaturally he felt proud of the association. Yet still another secret pride led him to express quite a fictitious hatred for the 'children of culture', though he would qualify this prejudice by restricting it to those 'whose fuel is piled high in the backyard instead of being in their furnace'. Once he quoted Emerson at his own expense. This happened when, still an undergraduate at Harvard, he had written an essay criticizing Plato as being a superficial thinker. With youthful conceit he had shown this to Emerson who promptly rebuked him in one short sentence that he had never forgotten : 'When you strike at a King you must kill him'.

Deep down Holmes felt real pride in his native tradition, and there was a note of inward satisfaction whenever he showed one of his father's manuscripts, which were carefully put away. This pride was also mingled with not a few annoyances from the distant past and not a little stifled criticism of a too great assumption of eminence on the part of his father's set. The Justice, in fact, found Boston to be cultivated but provincial just as later he found Washington uncultivated but national. The gap which separated him from Dr. Holmes's coterie and generation was not only one of years and habits of thought but also dated from his Civil War experiences. Whoever has served America knows the sudden growth of a feeling within the heart which acts almost at once to reduce in scale every local value before the immensely expanded horizon of the nation. It would have been easy for Holmes after the Civil War to step into the ready-made groove that had been prepared for him by his father and then to identify himself with the New England sages instead of being prone to regard these as somewhat second rate. He refused to follow this easy way. War had taught him that Boston was only one American city, and somehow its significance was no longer quite the same after he had fought for the United States.

Established in the Capital, the Justice's interest in political life never went far. When he first came to Washington he had been on very friendly terms with Theodore Roosevelt, to whom he owed his appointment to the Supreme Court. But after Holmes delivered an opinion unfavorable to the government in the *Northern Securities Case* their relations were no longer the same as before. Holmes never complained of this nor did he criticize the President. The latter's picturesque qualities always interested far more than they impressed him. He liked to compare Roosevelt's many-sidedness to the multiple talents of Casanova, who is known principally for a single aspect of his adventurous life which had nothing in common with T.R. Once the Justice repeated to me a remark which had tickled his fancy about Roosevelt just then being very popular with Congress because 'he didn't care a damn about the law'.

I had the feeling that the Justice disliked Woodrow Wilson, particularly before we entered the First World War. Holmes, who had said that the very name of gentleman was 'built on the soldier's choice of honor rather than life', was no pacifist, and he made no secret that he regarded as most unfortunate such remarks of the President as being 'too proud to fight'. Political bickerings, however, left him indifferent and somewhat amused from the height of his Olympian eminence. The

Justice professed complete ignorance of all politics that did not touch the Court, and as he never read the newspapers this was no mere affectation.

Like Disraeli, Holmes enjoyed talking to women and delighted in feminine society. He relished the opportunity for a conversation which gave him occasion to employ a courtly if somewhat baroque phraseology that was redolent with the faint aroma of distant, very distant, romance. He had many warm friends among women, and more than once he mentioned that it was principally to Mrs. Lodge that he attributed his own appointment to the Supreme Court. Oddly enough certain women on whom he called regularly in Washington or with whom he corresponded in England were by no means of an intellectual or even of a distinguished type, but their talk provided him with a facile medium for the flow of his own ideas which must often have risen far above their heads. The swift gyrations of the Justice's rapier-like brain were sufficient in themselves not to require a come-back from his listener. He far preferred the silent sympathy of their acquiescence to the drooling platitudes and lengthy pomposities which he complained that he was obliged to listen to from certain of his fellow judges on the Bench.

I owed my own introduction to the Justice to the late Lady Castletown. The Judge used often to stay with her at Doneraile Court in Ireland where he had made friends with the village priest, Father Sheehan, who was also something of a mystic. No one was ever less mystical than the skeptical rationalist Holmes, but there was enough common humanity between the Irish priest and the New England judge for a warm friendship to spring up between them. Lady Castletown had asked me to call on Holmes just after he moved to Washington. I remember going to see him early in 1903 when he lived in a rented house in Lafayette Square which was hung with fox-hunting prints that seemed particularly incongruous. After dinner I sat talking to him on philosophical topics till long past midnight, or rather I listened while he talked and reduced metaphysical concepts into familiar language. Shortly after this midnight talk I was appointed a third Secretary at our Embassy in Paris. I don't recall how or why, but I wrote him from Paris, and he answered me promptly. Then for nearly thirty years we exchanged letters. All the Justice's letters to me, with some insignificant exceptions, are now in the Congressional Library in Washington and are reproduced in the following pages. As the reader will discover he spares me the legal disquisitions which fill so much of his correspondence with Sir Frederick Pollock, for I was no lawyer. Yet not infrequently he alludes to his work on the Bench, if only to express a dislike for the so-called great cases which appeared to him far less important than many smaller ones that might set in motion principles and influences which could shape the thought of future generations. The law meant to him something that men desired sufficiently to make them erect it as a compelling force which they accepted as a guide for their conduct. Jurisprudence interested him, I think, less in the abstract than as a great human document, for no jurist ever treated legal values more from a social standpoint. He would say half as a joke, half seriously, that he would like to see the Ten Commandments written into the Constitution.

On other occasions he would hold forth on the Universe and deliver some scathing criticisms of Hegel whose genius he respected but whom he hated for always trying to identify the King of Prussia with God. The Justice had a decided taste for philosophy, but he delighted in employing unphilosophical images like 'holding the world by the tail' in order to explain abstract ideas. I think that he would as gladly have discussed the immortality of the soul with a taxi driver as with a philosopher. He had the New England trait of passing easily from the pedestrian to the astral and connecting the two by some quip that allowed him to descend rapidly to earth. He was particularly pleased when he invented the word 'bettibilitarian' which signified, in his mind, a kind of pragmatic betting to oneself that if one believed some particular assumption to be true one ought to act accordingly.

At other times he would hold forth on literature to display with critical discernment the wide range of his scattered reading. Men of letters, he observed facetiously, were like billposters who put up their names everywhere, for he found their glory exaggerated. Praise from him was infrequent but it was generous, and I still recall the pleasure he gave me by acquiescing in some views I had published before the First

World War that for our own protection we could not allow England to be crushed. I think that Holmes valued concision in style more than imagination or descriptive power. That was why he relished Anatole France's books — although mildly scandalized by that writer's occasional lewdness. Yet Holmes who had a real fondness for Rabelais could at times also be Rabelaisian. The Justice had a good classical foundation and kept his ability to enjoy the Ancients. He told me that he had read Dante through although he knew no Italian. Outside the law and the philosophy of law his interests were catholic, and in later days he developed, half apologetically, a taste for detective stories.

During the many years of our correspondence I went from one diplomatic post to another in different countries and to different continents. Always he seemed interested in what I did with that friendly interest in younger men which was one of his most endearing traits, and whenever I returned to Washington he would welcome me as an old friend. Justice and Mrs. Holmes had a pleasant custom of keeping an extra place at their table for the chance visitor who might drop in, so that often I enjoyed a quiet meal with them. The fare was good although plain, and the Justice's longing for the exquisite would occasionally make him express a wish to sit down to one perfect repast. Mrs. Holmes would tease him for any such flights of fancy, just as she always liked to tease him. Then, after dinner, she would sit in her rocking chair by the fireside in the back drawing-room and take up her knitting while the Justice played his customary game of patience. Social life bored her ; she did her strict duty but no more, and the Justice who liked some of his new friends had always to see them pass through the fire of her comments. Mrs. Holmes certainly acted as a damper on the Justice's feminine enthusiasm. She enjoyed twitting him though, really, encouraging these harmless little flirtations. Nor would she ever accompany him on the yearly visit that he paid to England up to the time of the First World War. She knew how much he enjoyed these journeys, for he relished social amenities, and she knew also that if she went with him his movements would be less free. In England he was always a welcome guest in many country houses, but after a brief stay he would return early from abroad to spend with her the rest of the summer in their house on the North Shore.

Mrs. Holmes cared for very few people, though she tolerated her husband's friends and enjoyed their talk when it was good. Occasionally she would interject some remark, humorous or critical, and often derogatory. I recall her dubbing a 'common little Yankee' one of the greatest of the land. She had a caustic tongue which respected the mighty even less than did her husband. Holmes was rather proud of the fact that among his wife's ancestors had been one of Charles the First's judges, and she followed her forebears' example by sentencing many people of eminence to extinction. But beneath the dried-up surface of old age there was an acute sensitiveness that made her suffer when her husband was criticized and also some unsuspectedly warm humanity in her character. Once she related to me an episode which, though it had happened before the Civil War, had left in her memory a vivid impression. At the school which she attended she had known a girl, supposedly a Cuban and the daughter of a wealthy planter. One day the girl had received a telegram that her father was dead and she must return at once to his plantation in Louisiana. Then a few weeks later news reached the school that she also was dead. The girl had gone back to the planter's family only to be told that her place was in the slave quarters with 'the niggers'. Turned out from her father's home after years passed in a fashionable New England school, she had killed herself.

Mrs. Holmes spoke also with far more feeling than one would have suspected of having known a Miss Aaronsohn, a Zionist, who in the First World War had become a spy for the Allies in Palestine, and when caught by the Turks had killed herself. And Mrs. Holmes added, 'It is worth living to have known such people'.

I was far away when Mrs. Holmes died. The Justice answered my letter of sympathy barely saying much more than that it was better that she should have died before him. Then he passed to other things. No outward sign of the shattering blow would he permit to ruffle the serenity of surface which he presented to his friends. After her death he no longer sat in the back drawing-room and would receive me in his upstairs study behind a wide old-fashioned desk. The walls were lined with books and occasionally he produced an early edition which he had just acquired. As a collector his taste went more to engravings, and he took pleasure in some occasional purchases of prints, preferring line to the sensuousness of color.

Holmes found a certain companionship in inanimate things, but he had trained himself to lead an almost Spartan existence. Though he welcomed occasional relaxations and distractions these never formed a necessary part of his life. In spite of his indifference to creed, in spite of absorbing much German philosophy, French rationalism, British tolerance, and a taste for the social amenities, Holmes remained at heart a Puritan faithful to Plymouth Rock. Perhaps he came nearer to being a great Roman stoic, for he was not religious in any orthodox sense. He did not believe in personal survival nor did he find it desirable. In his creed he attached a kind of religious meaning to his own agnosticism, regarding this in the light of proper humility before the great mystery which could never be fathomed. The assumption that eternal truth had been established seemed to him to imply a kind of arrogance, and arrogance was the only sin he could never forgive. His own lack of belief was very far from being a mere negation. It carried with it the thought that life was in itself an end, but that real life must always wrestle in a struggle either of the mind or of the body, for nothing that one came by easily was ever worth having. No man despised materialism more, and he felt little sympathy for any future world that was 'cut up into five-acre lots and having no man upon it who was not well fed and well housed' unless this future world was also prepared to understand 'the divine folly of honor . . . the senseless passion for knowledge', and the pursuit of ideals that could never be achieved but which made life worth living.

Invariably the Justice would counter any query about the Universe by asking what kind of a world one wanted to build. He was not particularly impressed either by the importance of human life or of human achievement, and was always fond of saying that no man's splash ever amounted to much or lasted for very long. His taste for philosophical speculations was probably responsible for his writing down most accepted values to a remarkably low cosmic figure, and those who found merit in his eyes had to qualify by his own Olympian standards.

His skeptical attitude became in this way the groundwork of his own modesty, for he felt that when a man had done his utmost it amounted to very little. Modesty perhaps is more frequently met with among the cultivated who have gazed at other men's attainments in other ages and measured their own talent accordingly than it is among self-made men. I fancy that Holmes's opinion about himself was not unlike that of the Frenchman who remarked that he was in despair when he examined himself but elated after comparing himself to others. Once in a London drawing-room his hostess had observed of Sir Alfred Lyall, who was among her guests, that there were no longer any men of his caliber. 'Nonsense,' said Holmes, 'there are plenty quite as distinguished in this very room.'

The Justice was not unconscious of his own worth though he gave little indication of this attitude. He told me once as a joke on himself that being impressed by a book on sociology he had just read and learning that the writer lived in Washington he had called on him, mentioning by way of introduction that he was a Judge. To his amusement the sociologist asked him of what court.

For Holmes triumph came only in later years. The criticism he had met with in his earlier life when he told me that he was regarded in Boston as 'a dangerous young radical' was then heard no more. No one was ever less of a radical than Holmes, and the famous opinions which he delivered on the Bench were inspired far more by his own philosophy of liberal skepticism than by any doctrinaire belief in the value of economic nostrums. Indeed he remarked that there was nothing he enjoyed so much as enforcing a law of which he thoroughly disapproved.

The inroads of time were slow and Holmes retained his full abilities almost to the last. Only an occasional regret would he ever express at his advancing years. When he was well over eighty he remarked to me more than once that he watched himself most carefully and was prepared to leave at the first intimation that his faculties were no longer undimmed. Even then he related a story about himself. To some woman who asked him when he proposed to retire, as there were several candidates who would like his seat, he had replied,

'You'll have to ask the undertaker'. He felt that the end could not be far off, although he still hoped to reach ninety on the Bench. He took no interest in the New Supreme Court Building. He knew he would not sit there and merely remarked, 'We have done some pretty good business in the old place'.

It was the good fortune of his last years that fresh currents of American opinion flowed more and more along the channels he long ago had traced. His fame suddenly grew by leaps and bounds and recognition fortunately came to him when he could still enjoy it. The honors which were showered on him, the requests he then received to allow his portrait to be painted, gave him real pleasure even if he knew that these were the gifts and greetings for a departing traveler. Often he related that as a boy he had gazed admiringly on some venerable survivors of the Revolution riding in a military procession, and had then felt that to be carried in triumph as an ancient veteran of a long past war was the most enviable lot that could befall any man. Now that America had suddenly awakened to his greatness he discovered that he had become that ancient veteran for he, too, was being carried in triumph.

LEWIS EINSTEIN

1964

PART ONE

1903–13

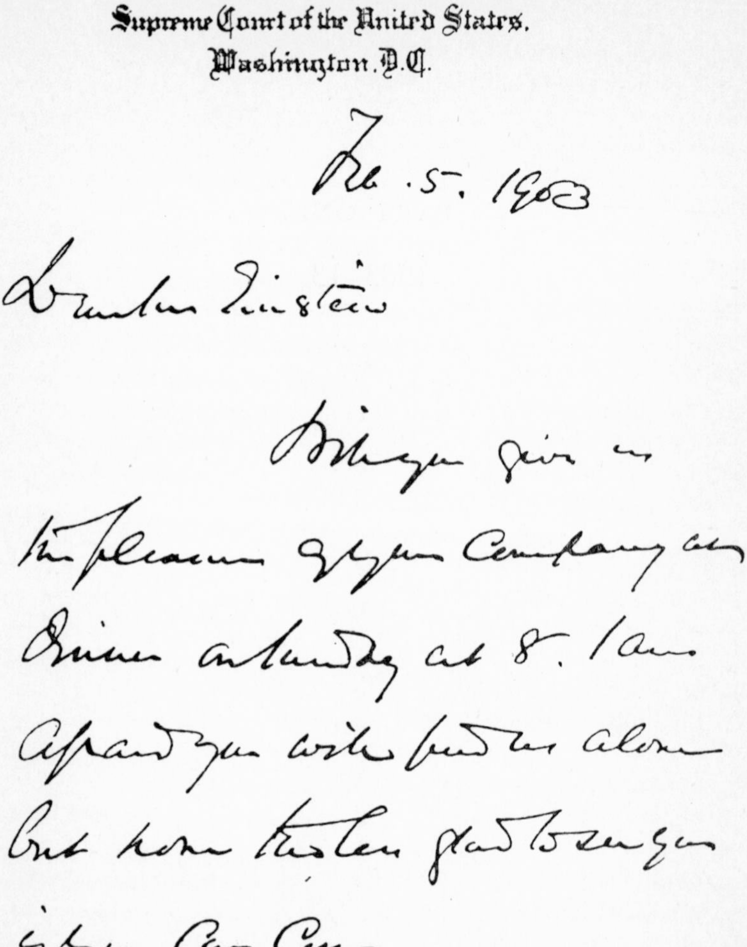

Feb. 5. 1903

Dear Mr. Einstein

[handwritten text, largely illegible]

Sincerely yours

O. W. Holmes

Specimen of handwriting of Justice Holmes

From a letter to Einstein of February 5, 1903

Supreme Court of the United States, Washington, D.C.

Feb. 5, 1903

Dear Mr. Einstein :

Will you give us the pleasure of your company at dinner on Sunday at 8? I am afraid you will find us alone but none the less glad to see you if you can come.

Very truly yours,

O. W. Holmes

Supreme Court of the United States, Washington, D.C.

Feb. 21, 1903

Dear Einstein :

Your beautiful book [1] was delivered to me and I began it at once. I wrote before I have got far in it because otherwise I shall not catch you before you go, my time for reading it being, or at least having been, very short. I am delighted with it as the rest of the world has been, and find that I have embarked upon a most interesting story thanks largely to the way in which you tell it. I should think that possibly your language about the introduction of the Roman Law by Tiptoft [2] on pp. 26/27 was a little large. So far as I know the

Editor's Note: Einstein has mentioned in his Introduction Holmes's fastidiousness about language. Holmes writes with some scorn of 'reporter's English', of the politician's 'meaningless polysyllabic adjectives and adverbs', of misuse of words. The letters, usually written at top speed, have many examples of his skill in constructing sentences that express complex ideas without punctuation. It is to be noted also that he disregards distinctions between British and U.S. spellings and punctuation. In the same letter may be honour and honor, centre and center, quotation marks before or after the period. No details of this nature were permitted by Holmes to interfere with the delightful spontaneity of his letters.

[1] *The Italian Renaissance in England* (1903) ; a comprehensive survey of the influences of the Italian Renaissance upon English life.

[2] John Tiptoft, Earl of Worcester (1427–70) ; Constable of England, prominent member of Yorkist faction during the Wars of the Roses, friend and patron of learned men, and cultivated traveler.

Year Books, which report the judicial decisions during that period, pursue their way undisturbed. The Common Law pursued its development (mainly from Frankish sources, I think, except in the matter of wills and some minor details) in a pretty unbroken course. I should guess, without knowing about it, that the would-be innovation might have consisted in trying to maintain the Roman *quod principi placuit legis habet vigorem*, which technical statement presented itself to the mind of Fortescue [3] (again if my memory does not deceive me) as the great feature and as the parent of tyranny. I don't suppose that anyone could have made any serious impact on the great body of common law customs except by starting some unperceived source of interstitial change. At all events it did come down pretty straight and less changed I imagine than anywhere else. But this is an unjustified preachment on my part. You say nothing that I mean to criticize, and I was addressing myself rather to what I imagined your attitude of mind than to the printed words. I congratulate you on your success and am glad I have had the chance of talking with you. I wish it might be longer.

Sincerely yours,
O. W. Holmes

Supreme Court of the United States, Washington, D.C.

May 10, 1903

My dear Einstein :

You give me real pleasure by remembering me and by the way in which you do it. I like your essay [4] and heartily agree with its motif as far as it goes. I suppose that to one who thinks that thinking means the study of cause and effect it would occur that ideals themselves although causes when they exist also are effects and not mystic ultimates. I do not mean

---

[3] Sir John Fortescue (1394?–1476?) ; Chief Justice of the King's Bench and legal writer.

[4] 'The Relation of Literature to History' appeared in the *Journal of Comparative Literature*, Vol. 1, No. 2 (1903). It appealed to historians, increasingly enamored of scientific interpretations of history, not to abandon considerations of style or the study of literature as embodying the ideals of human history.

that you say the contrary, but possibly you hesitate a little in your implications. I sympathize with you in your emphasis of the internal element. It does not follow because consciousness appears, even if inevitably, when the mysterious understream joins a certain eddy, that consciousness is a fifth wheel to the coach. What we mean by matter, or force, or the understream, is a thing that does produce consciousness, that is conscious, when it clashes in a certain way. If I may quote as parallel what I once printed, the way in which the inevitable comes to pass is through effort, even if the two have not been adjusted perfectly as yet.

I think I get more inward sustenance from Windelband's [5] *History of Philosophy* than from Brooks Adams's [6] *Civilization and Decay*, although the latter is incomparably better reading for immediate pleasure. The internal inevitable is more moving than the external, although the latter presents itself as controlling the former and accounts for man as the most cunning of the animals moved like the rest by his greeds and his fears.

Happily for the world and yourself you still are young, and therefore can stand a little criticism and possibly may profit by it. The old who will are rare. I venture to suggest that you still have something to learn in the way of style, a matter of which you speak. You use some words that I think not allowable because they are reporters' English. I notice especially 'voiced' or 'voice' of which you seem fond. Put it away from thee, my son. I think that gradually you will diminish somewhat your use of words of latin derivation. A sentence gets its force from short words. That is all. You have given me real pleasure and I thank you.

Sincerely yours,

O. W. Holmes

You may say, why this preciosity? Doth not even Charles Francis Adams [7] the same? I answer he does, and he will be damned for it. Style at bottom, of course, is a question of totals not of single words. It is the personal equation of the

[5] William Windelband (1848–1915); Professor of Philosophy at Strasbourg.

[6] Brooks Adams (1848–1927); historian, boyhood friend of Holmes, and descendant of American Presidents.

[7] Charles Francis Adams (1835–1915); benefactor, reformer, writer on railroads, brother of Brooks and Henry Adams.

writer. You have not quite reached yours yet. Your writing is not quite pure spontaneous glee. When the Style is fully formed if it has a sweet undersong we call it beautiful, and the writer may do what he likes in words, or syntax; the material is plastic in his hands to image himself, which is all that anyone can give.

I sent this to N.Y. supposing that it will reach you, but I hear that you are in London — where I expect to be before the end of June.

The New Willard, Washington, D.C.

Nov. 23, 1903

My dear Einstein :

I was very glad to hear from you, and I take the only moment I have, while smoking after dinner at this tavern, to answer.

I suppose we shall go over to my house (1720 I Street; address, however, always Supreme Court, U.S.) tomorrow or the next day. And having dashed off three little masterpieces in the way of my share of decisions last week, it now being an adjournment, I have worked from 10 a.m. to 7 p.m. with half an hour out for luncheon, in arranging books. Oh the heavenly joy! It always is joy to see order where was confusion, and when the subject matter is books, and for the first time in one's life one can see what one has, it is *fecundissimus*. I have found incunabula which I didn't know I owned. I have some little shelves for little Alduses [8] and Elzevirs.[9] I have a family shrine over one of the fireplaces in the two rooms which make my library where I have put all the works of my two grandfathers and my father and myself and presentation early copies of the local illustrious, Emerson, Hawthorne, Longfellow *et alteri*, and things that belonged to forgotten great-granddaddies, and little

---

[8] Aldus Manutius (1450–1515) ; founder of the famous Aldine press in Venice. The Aldine editions of the classics published in the sixteenth century are considered unsurpassed for the beauty of their typography.

[9] Elzevir ; name of a celebrated seventeenth-century family of Dutch printers of French Huguenot descent. The Elzevir editions of the classics are still highly prized by collectors on account of their elegance of design, excellent type, and the outstanding beauty of their paper.

precious trifles of one sort and another—and generally have disported myself as if I didn't hate the children of culture. Don't be alarmed. The only ones I hate are those whose fuel is piled in their backyard instead of being in their furnaces; it doesn't hit you.

It is the devil of a job to transport all one's belongings five hundred miles when one is over sixty, but it is vitalizing; you get rid of dead matter, and the circulation is improved. That is the great problem: to keep alive. One has continually to throw off excreta if one wants to feel the blood to one's finger tips. But the satisfaction is to have one's own surroundings about one instead of another feller's. I debated with myself this very p.m. whether I should put your books downstairs with the poetry and art and pretty things or up in the library proper, with the law, philosophy, anthropology, and all the rest that make my proper personality. There are weighty arguments both ways and I left it undecided at seven.

Mrs. Holmes got tired out working like a cart-horse, and for ten days she has been resting here; but she is nearly all vigour again if only she won't do too much once more. She was at the house to-day. I really think you would say it was a pleasant place in a modest way, and the sun streams in at the back, and I feel that I am settled for good in a place which is mine. The Boston house never ceased to be my father's.

Nov. 27. We are in my house, and I've been so constantly at my job of clearing up that I am afraid I have missed this mail. I shall give it a chance when we go to dinner, for though we sleep in my house we don't dine here until Monday.

I am much interested in what you say you are doing and shall look forward to seeing the results. I thank you so much for your offer as to novels and plays. I don't quite know what would be the wise thing to do. I am tempted to try to keep just a little *au courant*, but I have hardly read a book except yours and what's her name's *Claudine s'en va*,[10] for a year. Yes, one of Ely's [11] economic books dedicated to me by that

---

[10] A novel by Colette Gauthier-Villars (1873–1954); popular French novelist known as Colette.

[11] Richard T. Ely (1854–1943); American political economist whose *Studies in the Evolution of Industrial Society* (1903) was dedicated to Holmes ' in appreciation of the enlightened philosophy so conspicuous in his opinions, which is laying a firm foundation for a superstructure of industrial liberty '.

admirable and enlightened man.   I took the *Mercure de France* [12] for a time which seems to give one a notion.

Au revoir.   I wish it might be here.

Sincerely yours,

O. W. Holmes

My compliments to your parents.

Supreme Court of the United States, Washington, D.C.

Dec. 30, 1903

Dear Einstein :

I have not time to write as a rule, as I have my nose on the grindstone from morning till night, but I snatch a moment of all too unusual leisure to thank you for your letter and to wish you a happy New Year.   Whenever you have nothing better to do I am delighted to hear from you, although, as I say, there is little chance that I shall be able to reply.   I don't know Paris, and I am much interested by what you say.   One had imagined their ticketing propensity, but I had not felt sure that the prepossession with matters of sex was not a purely literary phenomenon, which one might have assumed not to be likely.

I think of what you kindly suggested before in the way of keeping me up a little with what is published.   But I don't quite know how to manage it.   If you could once in a while let me know of anything in the way of light literature, philosophy, or law that I really ought to see I can send for it through Brentano and I should be infinitely obliged.   I hardly ever have time to read a book unless and until I resume reading before going to bed which I have avoided of late years.   But I must do something.   I can't dry rot into uncivilization.   However at my age a man has his final formula made up, and my cosmos goes into a pretty small package.   It is not likely to

---

[12] *Mercure de France*;   literary revue founded in 1890 by a group of symbolist writers.

change its contents very much, or to let in either Hegel or the Catholic Church.

The season is beginning with its incessant dinners. I like them as a rest and change.

Do you ever see Paul Viollet [13] of the Institute? He must be an old man if, as I hope, he still is alive. If you do, remember me to him. We have interchanged one or two letters, and he is an able and learned man.

I am distracted even in this day of what I called leisure with an approaching tea in this house; a sort of first opening, bells ringing continuously, and there is no peace. I wish you could see the place. I think you would think it a change for the better. I am very happy in it although my wife has been nearly worn out with the work of getting in. My compliments to your parents.

Sincerely yours,

O. W. Holmes

Supreme Court of the United States, Washington, D.C.

Jan. 26, 1904

Dear Einstein:

Many thanks for *L'Adversaire* [14] which I have opened this moment. I shall read it at once, with my wife if possible; if not we will read it separately. I have not time for a letter for I must work on my cases. I shall be much obliged if you will mention anything especially needing to be read when you have nothing better to do. But I have mighty little time until the summer. Your book was almost the only one I read last year in Washington. It repaid me as you know. Of course I am not hinting that you send me other books.

Sincerely yours,

O. W. Holmes

[13] Paul Viollet (1840–1914); French legal historian whose major work *Droit public: histoire des institutions politiques et administratives de la France* (3 vols., 1889–1903) was greatly esteemed by Holmes.
[14] A play by Georges de Porto Riche.

Hotel Somerset, Commonwealth Avenue, Boston

June 7, 1904

My dear Einstein :

Your welcome letter has just reached me here and I have to answer it from a hotel on hotel paper. It gives me real pleasure and high hopes for your happiness.[15] A man as well as a woman finds life enlarged and glorified by marriage. The adjustment of personality is easy to people who think nobly, and I feel confident that you will reach a new and higher plane of life. I wish that there was a more individual prospect of seeing you both, but I hope it will come before very long. Meantime we both send you our best wishes and I especially send you my warmest remembrances. Please give my compliments and felicitations to your parents. If I knew the lady I should whisper some good prophecies in her ear.

Sincerely yours,

O. W. Holmes

Supreme Court of the United States, Washington, D.C.

Nov. 27, 1904

My dear Einstein :

Thanks for your letter. While you are gathering aesthetic impressions I am trying to enrich the philosophy of law by occasionally suggesting a vista in an opinion. So we both are pursuing the path of education which is the multiplication of prejudices and the diminution of beliefs.

I am glad to think of you in your new happiness, and I hope that I am now presented to your wife and shall be some day in proper person.

I read Boissier's book [16] some years ago but could not stand an examination on it I fear. I remember it as very pleasant.

---

[15] Lewis Einstein married Helen Ralli, February 17, 1904. Mrs. Einstein died June 25, 1949.

[16] *La Fin du paganisme en occident* in two volumes by Gaston Boissier (1823–1908); Professor at the Collège de France and at the École Normale Supérieure.

You speak of my stoic calm. Just now it is a Hegelian flurry. That is, I read, O rarity in Washington, a Hegelian account of the development of society as exhibited in the law, and that turned me to rereading Hegel's *Philosophy of Law*. I haven't quite finished it (3rd. time) and I have to steal quarter hours to open it, but I got more of an impression of his being great after all than I ever did before. But I doubt if he was quite as intimate with God as he thought. There are many deceptions on that score for which I think it only fair to say that the Deity is not responsible.

Admirable youth! To be able to say: 'I know the collections, and long to get away!' I wish I knew anything; this is not chaff. However I most enjoy suggesting paths when I get a chance and letting others travel there.

I have just met the French Ambassador [17] at lunch. He says Barrett Wendell [18] is having a success in Paris of which I am glad. I don't know when I shall see you again unless you come here. As yet I make no plans for foreign travel.

My homage to Madame and believe me,

Sincerely yours,

O. W. Holmes

Supreme Court of the United States, Washington, D.C.

Feb. 15, 1905

My dear Einstein:

On these days I am slave of the lamp and the pen, and the only writing I can do is of opinion or memoranda pointing out the error in the opinion of others. As a correspondent I am not a success. However I have a breathing space of a day or two and hasten to remind you that I still live.

I even have read a book or two, and just now am reading one which would interest you. A privately printed quarto by Henry Adams on Mont St. Michel and Chartres. The quarto

[17] Jean Adrien Antoine Jules Jusserand (1855-1932). See page 339.
[18] Barrett Wendell (1855-1921); American educator and author who had been appointed Exchange Professor at the Sorbonne.

form, the absence of name of author or even printer enhance the kind of tragic feeling one has with regard to him. You know the story of his wife? She killed herself. And you may have seen that figure by St. Gaudens, one of the most impressive and beautiful creations of modern art, which he set without inscription in the hedged-in square where she lies. The statue, a seated woman whom you hardly declare woman, defies epithets as the Universe, as the End defies them. It is not despair. It is not hope. It is the Unspeakable. The End. Well, in this book Henry Adams, usually cynical in speech, discloses in writing his hidden enthusiasm and reverence. He makes you feel with the first cathedral builders — and the *Chanson de Roland* — and the great world passion for the Virgin — and, much more, his assuming the attitude of a lost soul who understands and reveres the 'queen long dead, who died there young.' There is a touch of Adams in it all, but so much learning and feeling, and the subject so stirs one's blood that for the moment I am out of the world of Washington and ready to declare that melodrama and the unreal are better than drama and the real.

A daughter of Mrs. John Rodgers dined with us the other day and said she used to know you and that your mother was very kind to her, on the Nile I think. Mrs. Rodgers is a friend of mine by an odd sort of contradiction seeing that she spends much time on bridge and the like which I know not and care not for. But temperaments are quite as important as intellectual sympathies. I don't see much of anyone, however, except the young sportsmen in whose company I hunt the law. I feel appreciably older since I have taken to playing with them. After all it is time; but perhaps it is just as well not to think on such themes.

I don't know Metchnikoff,[19] whom you mention, except by name.

[19] Élie Metchnikoff (1845–1916) ; Russian zoologist and microbiologist, Nobel Prize (1908), disciple of Louis Pasteur. His chief contribution to science was the recognition of the importance of phagocytosis in protecting the body against infection. Metchnikoff won approval at Madame Duclaux's salon (widow of the former head of the Pasteur Institute and herself a poet of merit writing under her maiden name of Mary F. Robinson) for remarking that the first fifty years of a man's life should be devoted to the passions, the next fifty years to the cultivation of some art or science, and the third fifty years to the service of the State. See page 13.

Please present my respectful compliments to Madame and believe me,

Sincerely yours,

O. W. Holmes

Supreme Court of the United States, Washington, D.C.

April 7, 1905

Dear Einstein :

I am in Court listening to an argument. My only chance to follow my own thoughts this week ! So I snatch the moment to thank you for the last book.[20] I haven't read it yet of course. But I have read through to see how deeply interested I am. I find myself thinking : When shall I get a chance to read another page or two ? It belongs to the class of things which I study when my leisure permits. I shouldn't have heard of the book but for you and I am truly obliged.

I am hacking and sweating like *Cœur de Lion* at the siege of Front de Bœuf's Castle. Now dissenting and trying to overcome dissent, now attending to arguments when I have made up my mind, reading the records of many cases, and so forth and so forth, and in spite of Lent dining out a good deal of nights. I am beginning to feel the fatigue of the whole business a little and shall not be sorry when the time comes to shut up shop for a while.

My wife has let me in for the painting of my portrait in a few days. It is very difficult to get one's hair cut decently, as a preliminary. They mostly make one look like a rustic Solomon, with a survival on some parts of one's head of the Southern liking for long locks. However my secretary took me to a good man last night.

I hope you like your London appointment.[21] I suppose it is what you would have chosen. I don't quite know whether to direct to London or to Paris.

Sincerely yours,

O. W. Holmes

[20] *Études sur la nature humaine; essai de philosophie optimiste* by Élie Metchnikoff (1903).
[21] Lewis Einstein was appointed Third Secretary to the United States Embassy in London early in 1905.

Beverly Farms

April 26, 1905

Dear Einstein :

I received a very pleasant letter from you yesterday, and am tempted by it to wander further in historical patter. I yesterday finished Rhodes's [22] book about this country between '50 and now — so far as he has finished it, 5 Vols. As I never read the newspapers I thought it about time to pick up the rudiments of events in which I have taken part.

I should not suppose that the French would be very sympathetic interpreters or very seer-ious prophets of our institutions and fate. After one has just been seeing what extraordinary power was in Mr. Lincoln's hands, one can't help feeling that we know so well that we would knock the head off of anybody who tried to turn power to his own uses that we feel pretty safe. Still, our friend Brooks Adams thought that if the Northern Securities [23] case had been decided as I thought it should be we should have a despotism in a very short time.

I never have had the chance to be Mediterranized, but I understand it from the glimpses I have had of Italy. The first was when I was mountaineering with Leslie Stephen [24] in '66 and we came down into Val d'Aosta by chestnut trees and fragments of Roman ruins and dark eyed women who suggested that although not beautiful they came of a beautiful race. It would have been enough to see a dirty little Italian girl skipping down Chestnut Street in Boston to realize that this is a people capable of a grace and charm that the cleverest Gautier that ever was born might gaze at with impotent wonder. I never pass a street vendor of fruit without inwardly taking off my hat to suggested potentialities.

[22] James Ford Rhodes (1848–1927) ; American historian whose major work, *History of the United States from the Compromise of 1850*, was published in seven volumes between 1893 and 1906.

[23] *Northern Securities Co.* v. *United States*, 193 U.S. 197 (1904), held that the formation of the Northern Securities Company with the purpose of holding the stock of competing railroads was a violation of the Sherman Anti-Trust Act. The case attracted considerable public interest in connection with President Theodore Roosevelt's trust-busting policy. Holmes's dissent in the case incurred the President's displeasure ; see pages 277 and 279.

[24] Sir Leslie Stephen (1832–1904) ; English philosopher and man of letters, president of the Alpine Club (1865–68), and father of Virginia Woolf by his second wife.

Does the French interest in Russia partly account for a heightening of adverse criticism of us? Naturally they would not like us any more than they would like Englishmen or Germans.

I am idle and empty of ideas. I must turn from history to philosophy or, better, letters or something that will stir me up a bit; although it is curious how much one is stirred and how nervous one gets in reading a story of which one knows the end, like that of our war.

I was interested, by the by, as an illustration of how little fame is a measure of the power of men, to read of Lewis B. Parsons,[25] whose name I never heard before that I remember, who was superintendent of rivers and railroad transportation from the beginning to the end of the war, 'Never delaying for a moment any military operation dependent upon you' as Grant wrote to him. One readily imagines what Grant said in substance: that no General did more important work and probably few if any did work requiring so much intellect and force. Yet we all know of Sheridan and who knows of Parsons? I surmise that the great business men are the Greatest; but they are forgotten while the author [26] of the *Burial of Sir John Moore* survives. I used to say to my father that literary men are the bill stickers and take deuced good care to see that their own names are in large letters on the bills. That was when I was trying to make it pleasant all round. Well, I must shut up; idleness has many occupations and I must yield myself to some of them.

My compliments to your parents and, if you permit, to your wife.

Sincerely yours,

O. W. Holmes

Supreme Court of the United States, Washington, D.C.

June 1, 1905

My dear Einstein:

This is just a word in recognition of your moving and to thank you again for the Metchnikoff book.[27] It is one of the

[25] Lewis Baldwin Parsons (1818-1907); American soldier and lawyer.
[26] Charles Wolfe (1791-1823).
[27] See page 13, note 20.

half dozen that I have had to make time to read since I have
been here.   Scientific men rarely shine when they touch the
speculation, and I think he, like the rest of us, a trifle soft
in his qualities.   Neither do I particularly believe or warmly
respond to his programme for our future aspiration : the substitution of physiologic for pathologic data with possible
horizons of joyful demise.   But the pleasure of suggestions does
not depend upon their acceptance, and this one pleases me
as at least a programme.   I think his illustration from the
Ephémères [28] is most happy.   Also I am tickled by his brusque
statement that all intelligent men have chucked the notion of
future life and his summary account of all religion and philo-
sophies.   I even rather agree with him.   Perhaps I should add
to his account of the philosophers Brooks Adams's statement to
me, that they were hired by the comfortable classes to prove
everything is all right.   I yesterday read in *Mind* [29] some pother
of Wm. James [30] and others about their 'Humanism' — which,
if I didn't believe they were using for theologic ends to sneak in
the miraculous at the back door, I should think was tending
towards the right way.

I mean by truth simply what I can't help accepting.   Now,
as I have taken one jump of faith and decided to bet that I am
not God and that the world is not my dream but that you exist
in the same sense that I do, the consequence follows as a prob-
ability that in some sense, I know not what, I came out of the
Universe, whatever it may be, rather than it out of me.   If so
my limits, my can't helps, come from it and are not necessarily
its limits.   Therefore I know nothing about absolute truth, but
do my job sufficiently when I to the best of my power reduce
my world to unity.   Philosophy is one of the ends of life, but it
must recognize its limits ;   and professors as a class, like the

---

[28] *Ephemerids* ;   order of slender, delicate winged insects, some species of which
are known as the Mayfly.   Metchnikoff chose their life cycle as best illustrating
one of the rare examples of natural death.   After passing two or three years in the
mud of streams the winged forms emerge from the larval state with no organs
capable of maintaining life.   Their few hours of aerial life are devoted to love,
and death comes the moment their sexual instincts are satisfied.

[29] See *Prof. James on 'Humanism and Truth'* by H. W. B. Joseph at p. 28, Vol.
XIV of *Mind* (1905), where the author criticizes James's 'Humanism' as leading
'to the paradox of saying that what is intellectually satisfactory is untrue if it does
not help us practically'.

[30] William James (1842–1910) ;   American philosopher, friend of Holmes, and
older brother of Henry James, the novelist.

clergy, dogmatize on unrealities. To illustrate that my can't helps are not necessarily cosmic can't helps even my universe, which of course I don't suppose to be *the* universe, is indifferent between port or ditchwater — while I can't help preferring port. Such have been my tenets for a long time, but I suppose the humanists would despise them as much as Bradley,[31] and I make up for it by no longer caring a damn what they think, although philosophy is the supreme playground of their intellect.

Adieu.   My compliments to your wife.

Sincerely yours,

O. W. Holmes

Beverly Farms, Massachusetts

Sept. 18, 1905

My dear Einstein :

Your charming letter has just come and I answer it at once.   After I get to Washington, where I am due at the beginning of next month, I have no time for writing.   I am struck by the contrast between our vacations.   While you have wandered in enchantments of which I hardly know even the names I have been in the laboratory of a severer magic.   I have been closeted with Hegel, a black beast whom may you never know.   His logic is the hardest thing going, and, as the English-man said about the Chinese language, it is the devil and all to learn and not worth a damn when you have learned it.   It reads to me like an international mystification.   I can't believe that anyone would think his reasoning serious, and yet you surmise that he is a great man.   I came on *aperçus* and sugges-tions which make *esprit* and common sense seem small.   So I

[31] Francis Herbert Bradley (1846–1924) ; English philosopher and one of twenty-two children sired by his nonconformist father, the Rev. Charles Bradley. Promi-nently connected with the Absolute Idealist movement, Bradley's thought represents a trend away from the utilitarian empiricism of the English school toward the monistic idealism of the German school.   His *Appearance and Reality* (1893) dis-appointed his disciples, who had expected a revelation of the spiritual nature of the universe but were presented with a treatise on first principles and a lesson in doubt.   He is read today less for his conclusions than for his methods in reaching them.

went on to his *Philosophy of History* where you see the great man realized. Old as it is and behind the times in detail I know no such picture of the movement of the intellect to completed self-consciousness. One sees that it is a seed book. His talk about heroes gives you Carlyle in a page ; and I think he even made my friend Brooks Adams possible. His picture of Greece might be read with profit by the Japanese. He makes you hear the Wagnerian note of tragic change when Socrates asked what is virtue of a people not ready for conscious choice. When scepticism comes in with the other modern improvements and the Japanese soldier asks why should I die for the Mikado a worse crisis than Russia will come — or at least it seems to me that it may. I remember before the war Takahira [32] meditating on that theme said to me that he was inclined to introduce Protestant Christianity ! I recommended him to read Lecky.[33]

But after all Hegel has been but an episode, though a large one, and now I am trying to pick up a little of the small change of intellect and reading *belles lettres* at random. Some of our modern novelists take themselves so seriously that they bore me, and I go back to Dickens. I contentedly assume the bourgeois attitude and want to be amused or touched. I don't care for art if it does not fulfil the end of art for me by pulling the trigger of an emotion.

I have an occasional glimpse of some pleasant women but not many. In the main I live in a happy *solitude à deux*. My wife and I read aloud together so far as her eyes and my voice let us. Do you know the value of that to make you enter into books which would be tiresome to read alone ? And I play solitaire and poke about a little on my wheel. I have had a great rest which is the main thing, and so I think has my wife, who has had a hard three years in the move to Washington and getting settled in new ways and a new home. She seems better than she has for a long time. She would join me in messages but she has gone to town. I must follow her in a

[32] Baron Kogoro Takahira was Japanese Ambassador to the United States from 1900 to 1905.

[33] William E. H. Lecky (1838–1903) ; distinguished Irish historian and essayist esteemed for purity of style, clarity of thought, and soundness of judgment. His *History of Rationalism* (1865), referred to here, *History of European Morals* (1869), and *The History of England in the XVIIIth Century* (8 vols., 1878–90) are his best known works.

few minutes. I think while I am there I will buy Rabelais. I just have been reading about him and should rather like to read him. He is different from the run of medieval stories which are like the naif talk of dirty little boys and bore one to death. Even the *Moyen de Parvenir* [34] did that for me last summer, though that also had seeds floating; and I wish I could pick up a good store of driftwood in the remaining two weeks. Meditation on the universe as a whole makes one dull, and almost verifies Hegel's pure being is pure nothing.

Adieu. My compliments to your wife.

Sincerely yours,

O. W. Holmes

Supreme Court of the United States, Washington, D.C.

Oct. 22, 1905

My dear Einstein:

I have time only for a line, for now I am at it from Monday morning till Sunday night in one way or another. I delight in your letters. You have a strain of knowledge that otherwise I should miss; and permit me to add that, perhaps not uninfluenced by your wife, you are becoming a stylist (a word I should not use except with a smile).

I have no doubt I should be interested by Boutmy, [35] but I have rather given up international comparisons and digging up our national brain to see if it has begun to take root. I read a book of S. Reinach, [36] *Cultes, Mythes et Religions* with interest before I came on here and was wondering when your letter arrived whether it was worth while to send for his *Répertoire de Peintures du Moyen Âge et de la Renaissance*, vol. 1, Leroux. Do you know it, and if so had I better get it? Also do you ever read the *Mercure de France* or Rémy de Gourmont? [37] I used

---

[34] *Le Moyen de parvenir* by Béroalde de Verville (1610).

[35] Émile Boutmy (1835–1906); French political writer and co-founder of l'École Libre des Sciences politiques in Paris.

[36] Salomon Reinach (1858–1932); French archaeologist and philologist who wrote many learned books on abstruse subjects.

[37] Rémy de Gourmont (1858–1915); French author and polymath of vast erudition and critical acumen. Member of the symbolist circle, he became one of the chief contributors to the *Mercure de France* after being cashiered as Librarian at the Bibliothèque Nationale in 1891 for having written *le Joujou patriotisme*.

to with amusement.   The periodical was like a nest of squirrels with an eternally alternating contagion of electric shocks of ideas.   But most of the French, like B. Shaw, are rational in their negations but irrational and dogmatic in what they affirm.   Wherefore I can't imagine taking Bernard Shaw seriously or those Mussoos who are like him in the respect mentioned.   All the same R. de G. is a very knowing chap if you don't demand too much.

My wife appears and I must go forth for good.   She desires to be remembered.   Goodbye.

Sincerely yours,
O. W. Holmes

1720 I Street, Washington, D.C.

Nov. 12, 1905

Dear Einstein :

As usual your letter gives me great pleasure and I am especially interested in your characterization of Reinach, which essentially backs up the impression I had derived from his book. I was seized with an apprehension after I last wrote lest you should think I was hinting at your sending the volume I asked about, but it did not occur to me until too late so I did not write again.   Of course I did not mean anything of that sort.

I did receive your diplomatic address.[38]   Forgive me for not thanking you.   I always am interested in what you do.

What you say about Bismarck reminds me of what I have felt in past years in talking with successful English lawyers.   I have done it as a wholesome correction of dwelling in a fool's paradise.   When in the course of their speculation you come up smack against a 'That is not the law of England' as a finisher you feel that the horizon is not infinite; but you realize with Hegel that the absolute is infinitely determined, and that you can do *this* only by being not *that*.   I praise the finite even if I rebel.

I am in full blast and have fired off one decision which gives

---

[38] *Napoléon III and American Diplomacy in the Civil War* was delivered at the Société d'Histoire Diplomatique in Paris in 1905.

me pleasure although it did not quite satisfy me in point of form. One cannot be perfectly clear until the struggle of thought is over and you have got so far past the idea that it is almost a bore to state it; but decisions can't wait for that, and writers usually *won't*. Therefore I do not regard perfect luminosity as the highest praise. An original mind really at work is hardly likely to attain it. Those who are perfectly clear are apt to be nearer the commonplace.

Adieu, *mon ami*, I have a dozen things which I must do in half an hour.

Sincerely yours,

O. W. Holmes

Supreme Court of the United States, Washington, D.C.

April 8, 1906

My dear Einstein :

Your letters give me a special pleasure as I have told you before. This time I am malevolently amused at your *ennuis* at Algeciras.[39] It certainly is a surprise, I think an agreeable one, when one finds that important people in other countries are just as finite as the illustrious of one's own. I have realized it by flashes from time to time with inward comfort.

I do not recognize the name of Bowdoin as that of an acquaintance here, but I might have taken her to dinner and not be able to recite — such a worm am I with regard to any fact that I could get along without. However, I will keep my eye peeled. There are lots of people who have some interesting gifts or experience, but it is a mere chance whether an official continually dining with officials meets them.

As usual I have read but little. One truly civilized and, I am happy to say, American book: Ross, *Social Control*, Macmillan Co., sold for $1.25, which indicates that it expects to be read by the general public, another encouraging circumstance. It is a study of the forces and devices by which man is made to behave, with sidelights of many knowledges. It could

---

[39] Einstein was Secretary to the American delegation to the international conference on Morocco held at Algeciras in 1906.

not have been written until within twenty-five years, which
makes me a Philistine and leads me to say as such, that give me
the books of the last fifty years and you may destroy the rest.
Do I get a rise out of you? What time did I not waste or half
waste when young on the great men of the past. How much
better equipped I should have been had I known where to
look in the present. The present has our emphasis; the past
has not. And it is only when our questions are answered that
one can afford to bother with dead interests. Leslie Stephen in
his '*Thought in the XVIIIth Century*', a philosophical book, can
spend time on the Bangorian Controversy. It is just as real as
Plato when you don't read modern ideas into him.

Well, I must stop to call on the Chief Justice; [40] and I
think I will not leave this open for later additions but just send
it with my sincere regards to remind you that I am,

Sincerely yours,
O. W. Holmes

Beverly Farms, Massachusetts

June 12, 1906

My dear Einstein :

Here I am for a quiet summer vacation, and your last
most interesting letter shall wait no longer for an answer. But
what have I to tell to one in such moving surroundings ? [41] 'All
my migrations from the blue bed to the brown', if I remember
my Vicar of Wakefield correctly. My chief interest is reading
in fact and in prospect. I shall read some sociological books —
with great delight to find so much talent, civilization, and good
writing in American authors. Lester Ward [42] is the leader ; an
original thinker of no mean degree. He has lived in Washington, but leaves to take a professorship. I called on him to
express my appreciation and was delighted to have him ask
what Court I belonged to and express a polite surprise that
any member of our Court should read his books. The implica-

---

[40] Melville Weston Fuller (1833–1910) ; Chief Justice (1888–1910).

[41] After the conference at Algeciras, Einstein was posted to Constantinople
where he served as Secretary of the United States Embassy and later Counsellor
and Chargé d'Affaires.

[42] Lester E. Ward (1841–1913) ; American geologist and sociologist.

tion was obvious.   Another man is Ross, *Social Control*, $1.25, indicating a popular audience which again is encouraging; a biting work, and there are others.

I like to multiply my skepticisms as against the judicial tendency to read into a Constitution class prejudices naïvely imagined to be eternal laws.

But just now I am fearing a lapse into a vacancy of mind which I suppose is the best thing for a man after a long, hard pull.   I notice I am having that lapse as I sit here with the paper before me and feel no throng of ideas struggling for utterance.   I am out of focus with my recent occupations and hardly have got into a new one.

I have a different sort of book: Jernigan, *China in Law and Commerce*, which was recommended to me by a clever man. But China is off my beat, and one gets a narrow-minded feeling that one is wasting time when one leaves one's regular track. Law, Philosophy, with slight detours into Science and Art, and with pauses for an occasional Can-Can in the way of some French indecency, make my itinerary.   When one has been absorbed in untying specific knots for many months the discussion comes hard, and it seems like wasting time; while at the same moment one feels a sting of envy at those who are free to utter generalities as their regular job.   'Whichever you do you will repent it' is of wide application and truer than [its application] to marriage.

I have a horrid misgiving whether this will reach you.   I am not quite confident that Constantinople is the right address, but I will risk it.   The doubt looming sudden and large stops my pen.

Sincerely yours,
O. W. Holmes

Beverly Farms, Massachusetts

July 23, 1906
Monday

Dear Einstein :

Your welcome letter has arrived, and I answer at once. It is not yet half past eight, but I breakfasted early to see off Bob

D

Barlow,[43] a son of the late General and much resembling him, with whom I have jawed continuously from his arrival till 12 Saturday night, from 11 a.m. till 12 p.m. Sunday, and this morning. He really likes to talk about literature, drama, and life, and has reasoned opinions. I have time to talk and write here as I am a man of leisure and really am taking a rest. At Washington I have no chance. I am sorry that I did not send the little book on Social Control. I would have, had I thought that you would like it, as I hope you will. (This sentence is inaccurate but you will see my meaning.)

After a sociological riot I read Aristotle's Ethics with some pleasure. The eternal, universal, wise, good man. He is much in advance of ordinary Christian morality with its slapdash universals : (*Never* tell a lie. Sell *all* thou hast and give to the poor etc.). He has the ideals of altruism, and yet understands that life is painting a picture not doing a sum, that specific cases can't be decided by general rules, and that everything is a question of degree.

I read a little law to alleviate Rabelais whom I keep on hand as a *pièce de résistance*, not that I don't delight in gusto. I came on an immortal page the other day.[44] Picrochole's advisers are laying out the conquests of the world to him with that delightful, large handling which one has witnessed in people who never could make a dollar but who propose some great financial scheme, or who never went through the school for soldiers but are ready with a plan of campaign. '*Passez la mer Picrocholine* (it has received that name because in their plan he has just mastered it,) *voicy Barberousse qui se rend votre esclave. Je, dist Picrochole, le prendray mercy.*' I think that naïf acceptance of the picture as an accomplished fact is for all time ; or at least for as long as French is spoken and the universal language is not yet a fact. It has the germ of all possible Uncle Tobys, and seems to me a new note.

Just now I am taking up Euripides, spurred to it by Verrall's book [45] which insists on and develops what I am never tired of talking about : the necessity of realizing beliefs which for nearly two thousand years have been dreamed impossible

---

[43] Robert Shaw Barlow (1869–1943) ; Boston lawyer and friend of Holmes.
[44] *Gargantua*, chapter xxxiii.
[45] *Euripides the Rationalist* by Arthur Woolgar Verrall (1895).

before you can be sure that you don't 'dilate with the wrong emotion.' I feel by no means sure that Verrall has accomplished the conditions. Most of us can't understand anything that is more than a hundred miles away or a hundred years back. However, Barlow, who is a more accurate critic than I, insists that the great things keep their greatness and defy the effect of repetition of the motif; that Homer would give the same delight if the Iliad were written to-day. It does to him. To me it is a feeble joy. I prefer the modern and complex. I read the other day G. Droz, *Tristesses et Sourires*,[46] and was struck with the thought that it was impossible that the book should have been written within twenty years. It is the reflection of an old lady who doesn't believe in the new, as very likely you remember. But in spite of the fictitious impersonation I doubt if anyone now could go through the job of elaborating opinions to which the answers are so obvious or which, as Lecky says about miracles, are not so much disproved as outgrown.

Well, I have told you no events. I have none to tell — 'And all our migrations from the blue bed to the brown', as it says in the Vicar of Wakefield. Yet I gather that my surroundings are more inwardly stirring than yours!

Sincerely yours,

O. H. Holmes

Beverly Farms, Massachusetts

August 27, 1906

My dear Einstein:

You are an enviable youth with your Florentine villa [47] and all. I think that would suit me, if I could keep my work. But after all to use our energies, to function, is the end and joy of life, as I observed in one of my speeches which I think you have, and the first thing is to be where you can live in that sense.

I am still as quiet as ever, and just have finished an admirable French book on the Roman Law.[48] It has all the modern

[46] *Tristesses et sourires* by Gustave Droz (1884).
[47] The Villa Schifanoia was the residence of Mrs. Einstein's mother. It was given to the Pope when the German army was approaching Florence during World War II. It is now occupied by nuns and used as a school of art and music.
[48] *Manuel élémentaire de droit romain* by Paul Frédéric Girard (1895).

improvements, electricity, telephone, and an automobile at the door. Less metaphorically it presents the subject in the full light of modern knowledge at once as a growth and a whole. It is written by one Girard, professor of the University of Paris. If I thought he could read English I should be tempted to write to him and even to send him my book on the Common Law, which I make bold to believe had some ideas, now well known, before they had been distributed on the Continent.

But this does not interest you. Now for some French indecency to restore the tone of my mind. Lord, what a lot of time one spends in reading books to fill gaps in useless knowledge and even, as I did Hegel last summer and Karl Marx recently, merely to be able to state articulately why one doesn't believe them. But, as I said to a feller the other day, I am getting old and I have to think of the day of Judgment. I shouldn't like to be asked a question in Aristotle's Ethics, for instance, on that day, and have to sit down because I never had read the book.

I think I have met Woodberry.[49] He used to call on my father; but I fear that his interest is less in a follower of the law. I haven't met him to my knowledge for a long time, and I have no particular excuse for hunting him up. Apropos of poetry, I was reading in the September (*Scribners'* I think) the Phi Beta poem of Lodge,[50] son of the Senator, who takes his soul rather solemnly. Rightly enough, as he said to me, he can get more out of himself in that way. It seemed to me a mass of literary echoes. Walt Whitman for the *fond*, and all the moderns for his adjectives. I suppose after all it slightly aggravates me to hear a man make such a toot about devotion to truth when I don't see that he has any bills to pay for it. A man augustly intimates that he doesn't believe in God and regards Jesus Christ in rather a brotherly way and looks at you out of one corner of his eye to see if you won't please be shocked. I want to say Hell! What of it? Devotion to truth means hard obscure work not wrapping oneself in a toga and talking tall. But I like the lad, and I think he has some talent. I only doubt whether he will account for himself by his poetry.

[49] George Edward Woodberry (1855–1930); American poet and literary critic.
[50] George Cabot Lodge (1873–1909); American poet and father and son of a Henry Cabot Lodge.

I am afraid that my items are not very interesting, but they and more of this kind are all I have.

Sincerely yours,

O. W. Holmes

Supreme Court of the United States, Washington, D.C.

October 21, 1906

My dear Einstein :

My work has begun and after that I am a bad correspondent. Even this Sunday, on which day I generally avoid work on principle but find my time fully occupied, even today I must read papers and get ready for the new week. I hope it will not prevent you writing if I halt in answering.

Today is the anniversary of Ball's Bluff where I was hit farther up this river forty-five years ago. I was asked to a reunion of Confederate soldiers there which I regretted being unable to attend.

No more reading now. No ideas outside the law. However one popped into my head within half an hour that I am so tickled with that I think it worth setting down. One sometimes (*vide* your reflections on Brown's gratitude for food) thinks it a theme for melancholy that the greater part of most men's time is spent in the interests of food and sex. But all our ideals are derived from the three functions of nutrition, reproduction, and locomotion. Hence, when we proclaim the superiority of intellectual interests we merely are giving the preference to the motor machinery over that belonging to the other two activities. All thought is only a preliminary to action, and when one says, as I did in the last speech in my little volume,[51] that the true end of life is the exercise of one's faculties, so far as I did not in intention embrace all three, one is saying in a roundabout way I prefer the kitten when it chases its tail to when it laps milk. I was talking to this effect to my wife at luncheon just now, and on rereading your last letter I found a text for repeating what I said to you. I think it rather a chuckly cynical formula — *hein*?

---

[51] Speech at a dinner given to Chief Justice Holmes by the Bar Association of Boston on March 7, 1900, reprinted in *Speeches by Oliver Wendell Holmes* (1900).

We dined at the White House the other day and found the President [52] in his most agreeable humor. But he generally is; although I infer that he has his periods of private melancholy. Apart from that we are still in the quiet of first arrival, diversified as I have implied by a great volume of work to be done by me, to which I shall turn before turning this page.

If, under your difficulties, you hear of any new, interesting book, mention it that I may note it for any leisure that may be on the horizon. I read part of Swinburne's *Essay on Blake* the other day with a good deal of pleasure not unmixed with amusement at the attempt of the artist to present in rational terms the claims to faculties transcending reason, *quod non credo*.

Sincerely yours,

O. W. Holmes

Supreme Court of the United States, Washington, D.C.

Jan. 20, 1907

My dear Einstein :

A thousand thanks for your beautiful Leonardo,[53] and your striking introduction. Leonardo always has been a haunting and perturbing mystery. You give me a better notion of how to conceive him.

I can't write now; my work is so incessant that I have time only for a gasp as I emerge from one plunge to take a second. I hope that my silence will not silence you. I think there is some chance of my coming over in June, but I fear that I shall not reach Constantinople if I do. As you know I don't get beyond London, or at least haven't for twenty years.

All good wishes for this New Year.

Ever sincerely yours,

O. W. Holmes

[52] Theodore Roosevelt (1858–1919); President of the United States from 1901 to 1909.

[53] Einstein was General Editor of the Humanists' Library, a series published by the Merrymount Press, which had just issued a selection translated by Maurice Baring from the writings of Leonardo da Vinci entitled *Leonardo da Vinci — Fragments*, Humanists' Press (1907).

Doneraile, Ireland

August 24, 1907

My dear Einstein :

Lady Castletown [54] and I were talking of you, not to your disadvantage, last night, and I follow it up with a line this morning. I have been paying a visit of affection to England, seeing old friends, and not bothering about making new ones, and I am winding up here. On Sept. 3 I leave for home. I took in about a month of the season, and then made a visit or two in Paris before coming to Ireland. I doubt if I come over again unless I can persuade my wife to come with me, and then we should not seek society but pictures, country, and repose.

Naturally I have not been reading much, although I did amuse myself the other day at Newtown (Cumb.) with a translation of the *Mémoires* of the Comtesse de Boigne. I have in my portmanteau *Prolegomena to the Study of Greek Religion* [55] which would count as one vol. on my list of books read if I had read it. Jane Harrison I think is the author's name. I imagine her an admirer of the Golden Bough and Salomon Reinach, but she seems to be a scholar on her own hook.

Lady Castletown asks me to send her kind regards to you and Mrs. Einstein, and to say that she has received pretty post-cards from time to time but didn't know how to thank you as she didn't know where you were. I should join in the first if I might consider myself presented to Madame.

This is a reminder of my existence and a partial atonement for my necessary slackness in writing when I am in harness.

Sincerely yours,
O. W. Holmes

Beverly Farms, Massachusetts

Sept. 26, 1907

Dear Einstein :

One whack more before Washington and business. Your letter came yesterday and intensified the rather sad

[54] Lady Castletown (1853–1927) ; Irish lady, elder daughter of the Fourth Viscount Doneraile. It was to Lady Castletown that Einstein owed his introduction to Holmes.
[55] *Prolegomena to the Study of Greek Religion* by Jane Ellen Harrison (1903).

impression I got of your experiences at Constantinople. I am glad you are to have a vacation. I now am idling and trying to get a little rest. London is not rest, and even Ireland hardly so. You are under a kind of tension in other people's houses. I don't even try to improve my mind except by talking to any amusing woman I may meet. I mean to go to call upon one this morning and possibly another in the p.m.

When I was on the boat coming back I found myself in such a perfectly respectable society of Boston people (it was a Boston boat) that I did read a bit. Jane Harrison's *Prolegomena to the Study of Greek Religion* and Demolins' *Comment la route crée le type social*.[56] The former acute, original, and suggestive, but somewhat chastened by a style of Ruskin and water with a dash of Swinburne to hearten it up. Emotional rhetoric apropos of Greek religion hardly moves. I don't care a damn except in the way of intellectual curiosity whether their cult was high or low, and 'lovely' and 'ugly' seem to me out of place. Also she does not handle the phallus with the humpy indifference of a man bent on science. She puts on the gloves of a dead language and blushingly shrinks. The other book is suggestive. At least semi-convincing in the simpler cases. In more complex ones like Greece and Rome I feel as if the reasoning was more or less based on adjectives, and adjectives are free. I was interested to find that the influence of routes seems to be an old story in France, and then to get on to see the curves of Brooks Adams, who has worked the theme. He is so august that you never can tell whether his ideas are the result of ten years' study or were told to him by a feller in the street just before you met him. I have learned a lot from him, but I always wonder on this point, as he is quite capable of saying that he wishes to impress upon your mind something that you have told him within half an hour.

Bob Barlow (son of the General) has just left here. I delight in his talk. He really studies literature with an unobstructed eye and seasons the results with most improving slang. For instance, talking of a man who seemed to find life empty he said, 'If he really finds it empty I should think he'd eat something'. I thought of victuals and was slow to take the hint

[56] *Les Grandes Routes des peuples, essai de géographie sociale. Comment la route crée le type social* by Edmond Demolins, 2 Vols. (1901–1903).

as poison. It is a great privilege to be allowed to associate with the (relatively) young on equal terms.

I shall send this to Florence but with misgivings as to your getting it — especially as I can't be sure I read the address. I shall try to imitate your MS.

You speak of Tolstoy. Barlow and I agreed last night in putting him above all others of the century, but I must read more of him. I have not read *Resurrection*. I may have mentioned that I have been so long in the habit of untying knots, that, unless books present a certain amount of what an average reader would call difficulty, I soon feel cloyed and therefore should find it hard to pursue a course of *belles lettres* unless I made my own difficulty out of them by trying to find a formula of some kind. I am proud that you find any merit in the style of my letters. Of course in letters one simply lets oneself go without thinking of form. But in my legal writing I do try to make it decent, and I have come fully to agree with Flaubert. He speaks of writing French; but to write any language is enormously hard. To avoid vulgar errors and pitfalls already is a job. To arrange the thoughts so that one springs naturally from that which precedes it and to express them with a singing variety is the devil and all.

I hope I may see you in Washington.

Sincerely yours,
O. W. Holmes

I shall not say L. E. Esq. for fear of puzzling the Post.

Supreme Court of the United States, Washington, D.C.

Jan. 6, 1908

My dear Einstein :

I have been hoping to hear from you, to learn where you were, and to thank you for your last book, the *Erasmus against War*,[57] as well as again for the Leonardo, which I read the other day with equal admiration at three or four wonderful prognostics and pungent sayings and surprise at the drool that

[57] *Erasmus against War*, Humanist's Library (1907).

makes up the body of the book and which he seemed to take pleasure in repeating.

At the risk of being too personal I must felicitate you on the growth of your power of expression. Perhaps you have been helped by the critical taste of your wife, but certainly your writing is a different thing from what it was when I first knew you. You have grown to your own style, and I only hope I may have many like the last. Forgive my freedom and set it down to the real interest I feel in all that concerns you.

I have not read any of the books you mention, but under your leadership I have recurred to Anatole France and the works you recommended, with the result that I have got more pleasure from him than ever before. He has some of the wisdom of scepticism although he, like other Frenchmen, (as we agreed in our talk) is a dogmatist at bottom. The Mussoos never seem to realize that cosmic criticism changes the critic's relation to the object fired at only by the kick of the gun. When one damns the weather he only signifies that he is ill adjusted to his environment, not that the environment is bad. And when A. F. makes his M. Coignard talk on the baseness of mankind, one says to oneself pray do you regard yourself as a little God outside of the Show? Where do you get your $\pi o\nu\ \sigma\tau\hat{\omega}$, your criterion to condemn the whole?

Since I wrote the last word I have had my day in Court, fired off my decisions, and been bored with listening to those of others. We waste two thirds of the day in solemnly spouting our views and our differences, when it all goes into print and the real audience is the 'vide-ence' that reads. But it is usage and not without a touch of pompous impressiveness. The custom was established before the days of intellectual breech-loaders and magazine guns. And once in a while it rather tickles one to have something imperturbable and slow. The Chief twigs things as well as another, but you don't get him to change what has been, one jot. The man who puts my robe on to my shoulders did it for Taney thirty years ago. In the same way when I went on the bench in Massachusetts twenty-five years ago and said I wanted a quill pen, the old messenger (who had been on Lafayette's guard of honor when he returned to the U.S.) took a bunch from a drawer and said, 'If you don't mind cutting them here are some that Chief Justice Shaw left.' C. J. Shaw had been dead for a quarter of a century.

But I must dress and go out to dine. A happy New Year to you and yours.

Sincerely yours,
O. W. Holmes

Supreme Court of the United States, Washington, D.C.

Feb. 10, 1908

My dear Einstein :

I feel as if our communication was less remote than it commonly seems on getting your letter with a reference to Anatole France, for I still have his *Vie Littéraire* on hand for my odd minutes. I do delight in his purely personal way of taking criticism, in his disbelief in the absolute and recognition that what he writes must stand on our interest in the way of feeling and thinking of a man whom we find agreeable. I have the promise of some leisure during the next two weeks and shall snap up the rest of him pretty quickly unless I have the self-control to save him a bit and tackle some dull improver of my mind. I call Dicey [58] light reading. But Lord, what big books I have read simply to make sure that they had nothing to say (to me). Then, as I may have told you, I read nowadays a certain amount for the day of judgment. It would be so mortifying to be had up on final examination with a question on the Nicomachean Ethics and have to sit down because one never had read it. It is proper that a gentleman should have read certain books before he dies. I don't know that that may not even include Gibbon; but history, other than technical, like that of law, economics, or philosophy, is always a desperate resource. I have got so accustomed to a degree of strain on my attention in the law that I really think many books seem easy that are hard to those who have had a less strenuous experience.

One of the advantages of growing older is that one grows also more contented with ignorance. One knows how little one can know. I dissented in the Employers' Liability Cases,[59]

[58] Albert Venn Dicey (1835–1922); Vinerian Professor of English Law at Oxford and legal author.
[59] *The Employers' Liability Cases*, 207 U.S. 463 (1908).

little as I liked the Act. I think most of the government meddling with the organization of the world which is happening outside of and in spite of Government is probably noxious; but, of course, I don't say so. To lay the main emphasis on the incidental frauds or cruelties seems to me like estimating Napoleon or Frederick solely from the point of view of private ethics. A very able man once said to me apropos of the asphalting of Washington that no great improvement ever was accomplished without some abuses.

As to socialism I think it drool. The practical question, as no doubt I have repeated *ad nauseam*, is who consumes the annual product, not who owns the instruments. If under the illusion of self-seeking the head of a trust directs labour in a direction to produce the greatest return for the next year, which, of course, is what he tries to do, he is doing the thing that is wanted; and I think it plain that never before was production so exclusively directed to the needs of the crowd. I was tickled at a speech by an accountant who said he had had to study the figures of all sorts of enterprises from trusts to government offices, in which he contrasted the ability and honesty of private enterprise with Government and gave figures and diagrams to show how railroad building had stopped since the Interstate Commerce Act. Well, I talk of what happens to be in my mind, or part of it. I don't discourse on Indian claims about which I have been writing a bothering case.

Sincerely yours,

O. W. Holmes

Beverly Farms, Massachusetts

June 17, 1908

My dear Einstein :

After too long a delay I am at last here to write to you. I was much harassed during the latter part of the term and in no condition to expatiate. Now I am fairly settled here for the summer. My worries and anxieties are over — (the last of them disposed of by paying a bill that I thought discreditable with a letter written, as Stevenson says, with the hope of giving pain ;

s that can be pene-
My only remaining
rest of the week in
e an opinion or two

g Balzac, I blush to
of translations down
house left unoccupied
l opinion of the great
giving. I delight in
of the cultured class,
e story of the thirteen

saving devices, includ-
mean talk after work,
you out of the law and
iy wheel. But I don't
i Washington, and the
ome days I want to do
ay solitaire. My only
week ago was to have
a little volume as I do
i is not closed. Then it
ionths of life in my hand
into anything that comes
near enough to fundamental   ities. And in my fool's
paradise I see a philosophy of law and some little touch of a
philosophy of life gradually unrolling itself as I write. I
remember reading of a man who had a passion for windmills
and committed a murder in the hope that he might be confined
in a place from which windmills were visible. He too was a
philosopher, but a little careless in his premises.

I heard the other day that you could tell a Bostonian (var.
Harvard man) anywhere but you couldn't tell him much.
Which pleased me.

I hear occasional echoes of William James's *Pragmatism*,
which I regard as an amusing humbug. He has the Irish per-
ception of varieties of human nature, but I don't think him
strong in speculation, and may have observed before that his

60   *Eugénie Grandet* by Honoré de Balzac (1833).

suggestion that prayer is answered in the subliminal consciousness was a true spiritualist's thought : a miracle, if you will
turn down the gas. So as to free will. And as to the will to
believe: why should he call on me to believe one thing rather
than another except on the postulate that I *must* admit the
premises, or the good of the end subserved by the belief, or
something. But as I have said before all I mean by truth is
what I can't help thinking. But my can't helps are outside
the scope of exhortation although I suspect they are inside the
cosmos, whatever that may be, and therefore not necessarily
limits to it. You tell me of politics and world affairs of which
I am ignorant ; I can only ramble among the generalities as
a poor reply.

Sincerely yours,
O. W. Holmes

Supreme Court of the United States, Washington, D.C.

March 22, 1908

My dear Einstein :

Your transpositions tickle my fancy greatly, especially
Abdul Hamid brought up as the son of a Baptist preacher at
Smyrna — and I like to hear of diplomatic intrigue and
interests, so foreign to my daily thoughts. Once in a while
even here I get hints that the diplomatists don't like each other
or feel a muffled hostility. I suppose it is part of their job.

My events are almost wholly internal writing decisions
for the Chief, and they hardly are interesting to tell about.

I received a book from a Catholic priest, a friend of mine.
Perhaps you know him ? Father Sheehan of Doneraile.[61]
This is *Parerga*, companion to *Under the Cedars and the Stars*, a
rhapsody on Nation and Life, in the light of his religion. He
is a beautiful spirit, a tender idealist, but hardly familiar with
the modern breechloading speculation. Carlyle and Emerson
represent to him the dark angels of unbelief. The notion of

---

[61] The Reverend Canon Patrick Augustus Sheehan, D.D. (1852–1913);
parish priest of Doneraile from 1895 who wrote essays and many novels.

anyone caring what either of those sages thought! Of course
I do not regard prophecy (professional) as the best guide to a
theory of the Universe, or spend much time in trying to get
to the backside of phenomena. If anyone wants to feel that
illusion I think Maeterlinck's [62] *Bees* will give it to him as well
as any book I know. But I should advise him to spend more
time on Karl Pearson, (*Grammar of Science*), Poincaré, or Stallo.

Also I received a work promising a panacea to the nation
in the shape of forty-nine prigs on a pinnacle; i.e. a Council
of the best and most gifted, to embody and express the national
consciousness, to give it its purpose, and to set an example. I
advised him to try a subdivision before he spent more time on
setting the whole thing right, and wonderful to tell he replied
gratefully. Authors don't send their books for anything but
praise, as I have experienced before now. But I have had no
time for reading anything except records.

The President of the Carnegie Institute wrote asking my
opinion as to a department of legal research. I am skeptical.
Originality is not produced by faculties. The law is a small
subject (though like all others it leads to all things), and the
tendency of professors is to overvalue antiquarianism. Of
course as a study of the human document antiquarianism is
valuable and delightful; but its bearing on the law of to-day
as a speculative force is mainly, to my mind, in the tendency to
produce a wide scepticism about the worth of various doctrines
by showing how they arose. That again is a very limited
sphere.

The dinners are beginning to abate and I am glad of it.
London coming in between last season and this I have had
enough and am glad to sit still. I passed another milestone
on the 8th. and am now sixty-seven. But as yet my interest in
life remains pretty keen, and as the doctor looked me over and
gave a good report a month or two ago, I shall hope to hang
on to the branch for a time longer when you young ones shake
it, ready to forget the fifth commandment.

Sincerely yours,

O. W. Holmes

---

[62] Maurice Maeterlinck (1862–1949); Belgian-French mystical dramatist
and poet. *La Vie des abeilles* (1901) is a striking mixture of natural history, philosophy, and pure fancy.

Beverly Farms, Massachusetts

Aug. 1, 1908

My dear Einstein :

Yours first received, interesting as usual, though I regret that you are not in a more bookish *milieu* from which you might send news to Boeotia.[63]

I have just had experience of the contrasts between the man trained in literature and the man of science. The latter seems to me to have the real substance of education, and I envy and admire ; but the former is easier to talk to. How large a part of life are the charms of personality and that in the sphere of literature ! My literary friend maintained that art was an end in itself and the rest all means ; but I asked him why I had not the same right to take an ultimate pleasure in the sequences that make a melody. I am of A. France's mind : What is an end in itself is a question for the individual, and no one has a right to dogmatize. The human mind is a strawberry plant and throws out roots at each joint. Less figuratively, means constantly become ends in themselves, and no one has a right to bully. We are more interested in statesmanship — the means — than in a man eating his dinner or travelling or begetting his species — the end. (Perhaps I should except the last if it were aesthetically displayed).

Just now I am reading law ; a lot of cases on the Anti-Trust Act. The U.S. judges of the lower courts (as of the higher) while intelligent are diffuse to a maddening degree. Also the usual able man slides along conventional grooves in a mechanical way. A current convention is that monopolies are against public interest, and the way this is repeated as if it were God's revelation makes me grin and grunt. How do they know? If I had to bet, I should bet that monopolies on the whole, i.e. the trusts and the like, were very much for the public interest ; and I feel sure that the popular prejudice stands on no reasoned grounds. Yet I read a very long decision this morning by our, I hope, future

[63] To the sophisticated Athenians of antiquity Boeotia was the land of uncultivated peasants.

President as Circuit Judge solemnly enunciating all the old saws in what is popularly called a masterly decision, and excluding the judgments of Courts from economic questions in detail on a fundamental economic postulate that I venture to say may as well be false as true for all that he knew. However this is only a private reaction after unwilling listening to long discourse.

I read Alfred de Musset's and George Sand's correspondence the other day. They thought posterity would care, and provided for posterity by a deposit of letters. I venture to think that in about ten years the last person who cared a sixpence about their rights and wrongs will be extinct. It looks as if his love were mainly passion, and when she wasn't feeling up to concert pitch he told her she was a bore, while she is a trifle too solemnly virginal in her fornications to suit me. At odd minutes I still tuck in Balzac. And I have read some philosophy hardly worth talking about.

Adieu,

Yours ever,
O. W. Holmes

Beverly Farms, Massachusetts

Aug. 30, 1908

Dear Einstein:

I have two things to thank you for: a mighty good letter telling me about the changes in Turkey, and another of your handsome books.[64] The latter pleased me all the more that it seemed to have come direct from you. As to the former my wife, who reads the papers, had been wondering that there was not more sympathy expressed with the changes,[65] but I suppose nobody knows enough to say anything. Your verses bring a blush to the cheek of innocence and display a new

[64] Probably *The Defence of Poesie* &c. by Sir Philip Sidney, Humanists' Library (1908).

[65] The Young Turk movement led by the Committee of Union and Progress caused a bloodless revolt in July 1908 which forced Sultan Abd ul-Hamid II to restore the Constitution of 1876.

E

claim to my admiration, but Ertogroul gets me.[66]   It sounds
like Rabelais.

I am working my quiet way along.   I forget how far I was
on my road when last I wrote.   Probably I talked about the
Lusiads [67] and a little philosophy I have read.   Since then I
have waded through over two thousand pages of longwinded
cases on the Anti-Trust Act, and read other rather unilluminat-
ing law.   The only book that has seemed to mark a point is
Crozier's [68] *Wheel of Wealth*, which has some and missed other
notions that I have had on political economy, and taught me
new ones.   He says, what seems plausible, that it is absurd to
suppose that any theory framed before the days of science and
evolution can be adequate; and proceeds to go for Adam
Smith and all the rest, rather to my glee.   It pleases me too,
as a sceptic, to have him come out a protectionist, even for
England.   The freetraders used at least to have a cockyness in
assuming that anyone who did not accept their conclusions
must be a damned fool.   That excited my hostility as their
success largely depended on the assumption of postulates in the
way of ideals that one is not obliged to grant.   I regard the
question as I do the present prejudice against big combinations
or as I do going to the theatre or buying a picture.   If you can
afford it and want it enough I have nothing to say except to
ask that the grounds of wanting be intelligent, which in the
matter of this prejudice I fear they are not.   As to protection
one may ask what do you want?   World prosperity or national
prosperity?   Or perhaps do you disagree with those who think
that war is a contingency that may be neglected, and prefer
relative independence to greater comfort?   I don't see why
one may not.   Crozier goes farther, and says that even from the

---

[66] . . . Byzance croule
    Et Stamboul te retrouve mosquée
    Où les fils d'Ertogroul *
    En conquérants dressent
    Remplis d'allégresse
    Sur des seins de négresse
    Les mâles minarets.

* Ertogroul (d. 1281); according to official tradition the father of Osman, the
first Ottoman Sultan of Turkey.

[67] *Lusiads*; a Portuguese epic poem written by Camoëns in 1572 recounting
the adventures of Portuguese voyagers.

[68] *The Wheel of Wealth* by John Beattie Crozier (1906).

point of view of national prosperity sale of the instruments of production, e.g. coal, should be discouraged; that you are better off for the moment but you are ruining yourself in the long run.

Just now I am in the 2nd. vol. of L. Lowell's [69] *Government of England*, a kind of literature I don't hanker for but readable and, I trust, counting in the way of general improvement. I think it rather encouraging and very intelligent. Also it has the merit of emitting ideas without making a row over them. Matthew Arnold used to cackle like a morning hen when he had laid an *aperçu*.

To complete my account of myself I have sent five or six volumes of my father's M.S. to the binder in addition to four that I had last year. I didn't know that I had any until my return from Europe. It is a work of filial piety and some personal interest.

I semi-occasionally see a scattering woman or two, but keep very much at home. I wish I had more to show for my leisure, but I seem unable to think of any of the things that will occur to me as soon as I get to work. It is a pity that one can't have two or three outlying workshops attached to one's brain, where one can work up material that doesn't seem entitled to occupy the main factory. I should like to read some more classics and reread Homer etc., but it always seems the time should be given to more living matter. One feels more at leisure perhaps when one has made up one's philosophical bundle, at least to the extent of deciding what speculations are vain. But then there is sociology and science and even law. There is always some law that I feel I ought to know more about. Naturally in my present place I care less for professors' law and more for the fighting article; but there is plenty of both on hand.

Life seems very short to the old, the past part of it, but the length of the future (*ici bas*) after all is but an induction; perhaps our case will be the exception. Newman I believe was less sure of the sunrise than of his faith. One may be wrong even in thinking one is a poor creature.

Sincerely yours,

O. W. Holmes

[69] *The Government of England* by A. L. Lowell, 2 Vols. (1908).

Supreme Court of the United States, Washington, D.C.

Jan 30, 1909

My dear Einstein :

A welcome letter from you a day or two ago, and earlier your cask of wine for which I am not sure that I have thanked you. I do sincerely.

I am and have been so hard worked that I have not been and am not fit to write to an intelligent man, unless he will let me put a point of law. I hope for a mitigation soon, but I have had a number of interesting but fighting cases and my hands have been busy in the attempt to keep my own head and now and then to break my neighbour's. Therefore my only general observations are those that occur to me at the dinner table when one forgets about law and tries to be a man of the world. I told a neighbour the other evening that morals were a contrivance of man to take himself seriously, and this notion took possession of me as soon as uttered. It is a sneer at the philosophers who are not content to treat morals like other conveniences of life as to be used but not thought or talked about more than necessary, but by making them an end in themselves and attributing to them cosmic worth try to strengthen their own position as personal friends of God and get in on the ground floor. When a man is after absolute truth he is driven to strange shifts and queer company. The truths I am engaged with just now are highly relative, but have got a lot of fight in them and are more fun than the absolute article to be had at the rival shop.

I am just back from a luncheon (I hate to be asked out on Sunday) at a new demi-palace looking over Sheridan Circle and the hero on horseback ; very pleasant but an unsparable two hours gone. However we adjourn for three weeks tomorrow, when I hope to get back breath, digestion, and philosophic calm if not a few ideas. I have those you gave me as if they were inborn and refer easily to our want of diplomatic education etc., sometimes hinting that we have a young man or two who knows his job and really is getting into the business. I think I told you that I mentioned my satisfaction at your advances to the President and that he said that was his doing.

I must cut this short because as I have indicated there are a dozen tasks with their mouths open looking at me, like the fish in Doré's illustration at Munchausen's bottom stuck into the hole in the ship. I was delighted with the slip from the paper you sent to me. I wondered if you wrote it? It was good anyhow.

I have among the books on my table *Les Immémoriaux* by Max Anély. Sandwich Islanders; the first chapters showing them with their feelings and their magic spells when the blessings of Christianity were dawning, and their attempts at exorcism. What more I know not. Noticeable but not quite charming. How rare is charm! Rarer than intellect, as Paul Crozier the other day said, was the extra energy that leads a general when his day's work is done to go out and see what he can discover on the outposts.

Goodbye. Regards and regrets that we can't talk.

Sincerely yours,
O. W. Holmes

American Embassy, Constantinople

26 February 1909

Dear Judge Holmes:

Your letters are always most interesting reading and I prize them especially for keeping me in touch with the larger world of ideas, or rather with the larger individuals, for Constantinople is hardly more sterile than elsewhere save on the surface, while even Parnassus, I fancy, would now be Paquinized.[70] But in place of ideas we have the daily changing spectacle of international politics to watch with the lottery chance of war thrown into the bargain, for the Serbs are again on the warpath. When at some future day, which I trust is as far off as possible, you are seated on the bench up there (James isn't the only Swedenborgian) you will have some very pretty problems of national responsibility to determine:

[70] Paquin was a fashionable dressmaker in the rue St. Florentin in Paris before 1914.

(1) The Servians were set on their feet by Europe though in a mutilated form. They try to regain the missing members and are at once accused of disturbing the peace and set upon by the powers who miscarried them at birth.

(2) The Turks were ruined by thirty years of misgovernment. They overthrew the tyranny, but the debts of the old generation are visited on the new, and a race with every military virtue is dragged down because of its financial vices.

I believe it was Cleanthes (?) who scaled down the Athenians' debts and was hailed as a savior. In our democratically opulent age credit has become the most sacred of creeds with the subsidized press as its Inquisition. I don't think I could ever be a socialist for the simple reason that it would make the world even more mechanically uniform than it now is, but I do understand their distaste for those who have erected as the highest virtues the eminently selfish ones. Our 'Captains of Industry' pose perhaps rightly as public benefactors, but after all their primary and usually ultimate consideration has been their own paunch.

The oriental conception of our struggle for life was rather epitomized the other night at dinner to my wife by Hassan Fehmi Pasha (the President of the Council of State). I must relate it in French. '*Ils appellent ça une République, mais il n'y a pas d'air* — (individual liberty: the Turkish 'Keif' [71]). *On entre dans un tram on vote; on sort d'un tram on vote; une femme tombe dans la rue tout le monde vote.*' All America was in his mind a vast voting match. Here action assumes a different form. Having lately sacked my Greek servant I have taken a Montenegrin one, and asking for references from his former master I was told that he was very devoted and very courageous. If I ordered him to kill any enemy of mine he would immediately do so without hesitation. Would you like such a man in Washington?

What a curious metempsychosis between Knox and Root! [72]

[71] 'Keif' is an Arabic word currently used throughout the Middle East for an agreeable rest.

[72] Secretary of State Elihu Root (1845–1937) resigned January 25, 1909, and was succeeded by Robert Bacon (1860–1919) for six weeks until the inauguration of President William Howard Taft on March 4, 1909, when Philander Chase Knox (1853–1921) became Secretary of State.

As Leishman [73] is the former's most intimate friend I am naturally very pleased; no more confidential circulars inquiring as to how we dress!

Have you read anything of interest? I am finding renewed delight in France's *Monsieur Bergeret* series.

Sincerely yours,
Lewis Einstein

March 26, 1909

Dear Einstein:

I snatch my first let-up to write. I have an adjournment and my work done. So now for friendship and culture. Let me pitch into you about the captains of industry. I don't believe their ultimate is their own paunch. I believe it is playing the game and, like the rest of us, making good their faculty. Also, looking at them aloof, for I hardly know any of them and don't frequent their society, I believe them to be economic benefactors, whatever other objections there may be to them. But, as I have observed before, people say damn Rockefeller who don't dare say the same about God so they can clothe their own lack of adjustment in the form of a perturbing tyrant. You will have to recognize my old thesis of the confusion in the popular mind between ownership and consumption, and the fact that, if the annual product is consumed by the crowd, ownership is merely a wheel of distribution.

I can't read the vital word in your Turk's epitome of America. Is it VOTE? I envy you your Montenegrin; but for the subsequent inconvenience I daresay I could find some uses for such virtues.

Outside of law I am at this moment perusing S. Reinach's Vol. 3 (*Cultes Mythes et Religions*) with great gusto. They are delightful volumes having pretty much all the virtues including that of some malice towards our holy religion.

---

[73] John G. Leishman (1857–1924); American businessman and diplomat. President Carnegie Steel Company (1886–97). Envoy Extraordinary and Minister Plenipotentiary to Turkey (1900–1906), Ambassador Extraordinary and Plenipotentiary (1906–9), subsequently Ambassador to Italy (1909–11) and to Germany (1911–13).

There are a lot of other books on my table from grave to gay. Did you ever read anything of Léon Bloy ? [74]   He writes now for the *Mercure de France* I think.   A Catholic *enragé* who for some reason excited the interest of my wife's nephew down here, a scientific gent.[75] of some renown.   He, Léon Bloy, publishes a journal from time to time, which seems to regard rich men as made mainly to fork out to him and so maintain a great master.   The story of his *La Femme Pauvre*, I think, moved me ; but he seems to me a beast.   However I have at my elbow *Celle qui Pleure*, an account of the appearance of the Virgin at La Galette in 1846, and I wish I hadn't.

I passed sixty-eight the other day.   I think one doesn't feel it as the approach of the end but as the finish of a race.   If one can keep the pace, do one's job in the superlative degree, and keep out of the Insolvency, Divorce, and Criminal Courts until one retires on a pension I call it a success.   All of which reminds me that I sent you a case in which I was much interested the other day.   On the criteria of property in the Philippines there is some fun up all the time.

I hope your affairs are all right.   I hear rumours that the Whites [76] are likely to come back and generally that Mrs. Taft's predilections are a governing power.   I know not.   I believe nothing on that or most other subjects.

Sincerely yours,
O. W. Holmes

March 28, 1909

Dear Einstein :
        In my letter the other day I forgot to say that the Belgian Minister (Baron Moncheur) who is shortly (i.e. within a year) to go to Turkey asked me to give him a letter to you, which I shall do.   The Baroness is a great friend of mine and seems to me to have a keener spiritual discernment than any of the others hereabout.   She has another side (fondness for

---

[74] Léon Bloy (1846–1917) ; French religious writer and proponent of a Catholic revival in France.

[75] Gerrit Smith Miller, Jr. (1869–1956) ; zoologist, son of Mrs. Holmes's sister, author of approximately four hundred scientific monographs.

[76] Mr. and Mrs. Henry White.

bridge etc.) to which I am a stranger. As she is also rather handsome I think I can promise that you will find the pair an addition. He is an amiable, pleasant man. I rather think more or less a student of economic problems.

Yours,

O. W. H.

Washington

May 21, 1909

Dear Einstein :

    I have a surmise that you may be in New York from something that my wife read to me, Oh God knows when — if in Constantinople so surrounded by events that a letter will seem out of place. So for various uncertainties this will be short.

    I have had your wine bottled, but as the man advised that it should be kept two years I have not drunk any of it. Also I have read S. Reinach's *Orpheus: Histoire Générale des Religions*, a keen little book sent to me by Fred Pollock [77] seemingly recently out. But I have been so busy that my literary wanderings have been only such as you would despise : *Masterpieces in Colour*. Little short accounts of various painters with surprisingly good cheap colored reproductions of six or eight of the paintings of each. For an odd half hour (deuced few I have had of them) they are a refreshment to one who is far from the originals.

    But now my work is done, barring the odds and ends of the finish, and I am feeling rather blank this rainy morning with the machinery still going inside and nothing for it to work upon. I sadly fear that I am industrious. If my fear is grounded it raises a strong unfavourable presumption. Personality needs long lapses of leisure. But then personality is an illusion only to be accepted on weekdays for working purposes. We are cosmic ganglia; so I believe as much as I believe anything. And personality is merely the gaslight at the crossroads with an accidentally larger or smaller radius of illumination.

[77] Sir Frederick Pollock (1845–1937) ; distinguished English jurist and intimate friend of Holmes with whom he corresponded for almost half a century; see *The Holmes–Pollock Letters*, 1874–1932, edited by Mark DeWolfe Howe (1941).

I will send you another case that may entertain you for a moment about the U.S. Fruit Co. [American Banana Company v. United Fruit Company (decided April 26, 1909) 213 U.S. 347]. I don't know that you mightn't be more amused by one about a lady whose portrait was published in connection with a certificate by a nurse that she constantly used somebody's whisky personally and for the patients whereas the plaintiff (thus portrayed) was not a nurse, was a teetotaller, and did not sign the certificate or authorize the sale of the portrait. We held that her action would lie and reversed the Courts below [Peck v. Tribune Company (decided May 17, 1909) 214 U.S. 185].

I must stop or I shan't keep my promise to be short. I really, I can't quite say why, save as above, feel a kind of uncertainty as to this reaching you. I expect to leave here June 3 or 4 and bring up at Beverly Farms in a few days thereafter, but a direction to Supreme Court of United States, Washington, D.C. always will reach me. Beverly Farms Massachusetts, also is safe.

Yours sincerely,
O. W. Holmes

Beverly Farms, Massachusetts

July 17, 1909

Dear Einstein:

I also have just returned from London and find your letter. I went to Oxford to receive the degree of Hon. D.C.L., made a three weeks visit to England, and now am back, happy there and happy to have returned. I don't know why, but I also have had no such predominating feeling of blood relationship as I suppose to be expected by the world at large. I reproach myself a little more broadly than that, however, for not loving my fellow men in general enough. I console myself by thinking that if one does one's job as well as one can one achieves practical altruism, and that it doesn't matter so much how one feels about it. But still it makes me uneasy; just as I say I don't believe in Hell but am afraid of it. I made that observation at luncheon in London and directly after took up

a paper in which Madame de Staël said the same about ghosts.
I couldn't but fear that my hostess would credit me with
copying when I thought the form of expression was first-hand.

Now I expect a little rest and sleep. I need them. To
help the latter, I mean to read a new history of law. Also
Wells has sent me his book about America.[78] He is a pet with
the ladies who frequent Taplow,[79] and I must say impressed me
as carrying off his part with a perfect manner — spontaneous
and unconscious — in spite of coming from a different stratum.
For some reasons I rather wanted to think him a light weight,
but as far as I have got in him and his book he rather impresses
me.

I don't believe we ever get a real clang from behind
phenomena. The poetical clan suggests if it does not assert
that it sounds one. So I am in a way down on them. They
have no intellect and I believe in intellect. But once in a while
a book or a hint or a phrase gives one a shudder of doubt
whether one needs to reconstruct one's universe. It is 51 to 49
with me; but I bet 50 to 1 that the balance won't shift in my
lifetime unless I am scared out of my wits. Goodbye.

Yours ever,
O. W. Holmes

Don't get massacred.[80]
I should miss you too sadly.

Beverly Farms, Massachusetts

Aug. 19, 1909

My dear Einstein :

I am delighted at the thought that we shall see you
probably in Washington, where we arrive soon after Oct. 1st.
I suppose that on the whole you will be glad to leave Constantinople, and I wish you luck for your next destination.

[78] *The Future in America* by H. G. Wells (1906).

[79] Taplow, Buckinghamshire, was the country seat of Lady Desborough.
See page 147, note 53.

[80] On April 25, 1909, Constantinople was occupied after five hours of severe
fighting by the troops of the Committee of Union and Progress, thus ending the
counter-revolution and resulting in the deposition of Sultan Abd ul-Hamid II two
days thereafter.

The chaffing at the giving of degrees has grown less I am told. One lad sang out, while the Latin speech in my honour was being made : 'Can you translate it, Sir ?' but that was all. I grinned to signify yes, but in fact I didn't follow it and only read it since I last wrote. I think I found to my surprise a sentence or two that really pleased me as the thing I should like to hear said.

France's book I have, but have not yet read : *La Chemise*. I am in a cultured atmosphere now. Even before this moment I had been reading some philosophy (Royce and Münsterberg) which I didn't believe in its postulates but did in its results ; and also had been doing a law job. But now Sir Frederick Pollock and his son are with me. He is diabolically clever and appallingly well informed, and the air has a peaceful hum of ideas and facts.

Before he came I also had read Henry James's *The Ambassadors*. All the characters as usual talk H. James, so that I regard it rather as a prolonged analysis and description than as a drama. It brought up Paris to me ; but more especially, by a kind of antagonism that it provoked, made me reflect, contrary to Münsterberg's book, (*The Eternal Values*), how personal are our judgments of worth. If a man debates for half an hour whether to put his right or left foot forward while he stands in a puddle, he will think me stupid when I prefer to *brusquer* the decision. For all I know the fate of the cosmos may hang on it, but I think him stupid as to the growth of ideas, or the law, or whatever my hobby may be. I was struck as usual by the exclusiveness of his criteria and interests. He lives in what seems to me rather a narrow world of taste and refined moral vacillations ; but in them he is a master. I can't help preferring him in description and criticism, but he has a circle that thinks him great as a novelist. My general attitude is relatively coarse : let the man take the girl or leave her. I don't care a damn which. Really, I suppose, he, like his brother and the parsons, attaches a kind of transcendental value to personality ; whereas my bet is that we have not the kind of cosmic importance that the parsons and philosophers teach. I doubt if a shudder would go through the spheres if the whole ant-heap were kerosened. Of course, for man, man is the most important theme ; but it makes a difference whether one thinks one is in relation or not with the absolute. As I probably have written before I define truth as the system of my limitations, and don't talk about the absolute except as a humourous bettabilitarian (one who treats the Universe simply as bettable). Man of course has the significance of fact; that is he is a part of the incomprehensible, but so has a grain of sand. I think the attitude of being a little god, even if the great one has vanished, is the sin against the Holy Ghost. Like other grounds of salvation this one is intellectual not moral. Man is damned, and I should like to see him executed for being inadequate. All of which I have probably said before, but as you have forgotten it, it does no harm to preach the gospel again.

I don't see the prospect of as much reading as I like for this season as I expect soon after the Pollocks leave that a lady may arrive, and when she goes we shall begin to pull our tent pins. I took the Ps to call upon the President [81] yesterday afternoon and found him very amiable. Today they have gone to town, and I snatch the moment to talk with you. Now I will tackle Münsterberg whom I have not finished.

Sincerely yours,
O. W. Holmes

I saw Lady Castletown in London, and we had friendly talk of you.

Beverly Farms, Massachusetts

Sept. 27, 1909

Dear Einstein:

I am just leaving this place for Boston, New York, Washington, and I can't read the name of your villa; two circumstances unfavorable to the writing and receipt respectively of this letter. Still I shoot off the last word of my quasi-leisure time. I don't remember how far I had got in my last one, but latterly I have not had much to talk about.

At first we had Sir Frederick Pollock and his son, and then

---

[81] President Taft spent the month of August 1909 in Beverly, Massachusetts.

my late London hostess, Mrs. Leslie Scott, with us, and I have had no chance to read and develop new ideas. I have just got hold of Tylor's [82] *Anthropology*, the kind of book I delight in, giving a mighty good picture of how we came to be what we are, the races, languages, implements, institutions. Such books give me more feeling of real gain than any others I think. But in spite of it I am afraid I shall have to turn to my old ideas and try to pass them off with a swagger for new this winter.

As I could not hope to humbug you I am afraid that Cosmic themes must slumber. I may mention however that I was amused by an article by William James on what he thought, or rather for the moment thinks, about the occult (Spiritualistic Manifestations). He concludes that there is something in it, no one knows what. Meantime he adopts a very patronising tone towards the sceptics, talks of 'the good Huxley,' and as I am one of them I naturally make counter-criticism. It is quite true that you can't safely say *falsus in uno falsus in omnibus*; but when you find a person who is cheating as far as you can see, whose general attitude is fraudulent, (and remember how many juggler's tricks you can't explain), the matter becomes quite different. And when it is said that there must be a significant residuum in such a mass of stuff I think it a fair reply that the mass is insignificant compared with the mass of events that give no hint of extra phenomenal causes for phenomena. I can't but note W. J.'s confession of how he helped out a scientific experiment, for I noticed the same thing when the first so-called mind-reading experiment was on, though then it was unconscious, no doubt. I note too that I have known of cases that were pronounced crucial beforehand and said nothing about when they failed. In other words he longs to have the business succeed in the interest of religion. He is eternally trying to get devout conclusions from sceptical premises, which I think very possible; but I think he takes the wrong road. He believes in miracles if you will turn down the lights. Free will and answer to prayer in the subliminal consciousness — a somewhat from a universal consciousness [sic] in table-tipping etc. I think scepticism should be humble and be content with saying the universe has consciousness, significance, etc. *inside* of it, for it has *us*; but the chances are that it transcends them in some unimaginable way. All of which no doubt I have said before twenty times.

A man sent me an interesting account of Verlaine the other day with sketches etc., and I am charmed with Mistral's [83] book of personal recollections that gave me a reflection. You artistic and poetical gents are apt to treat poetry as hurt by truth, and to lament the fables of youth. But it only means that the poets who so lament have not lived out of the fables and into the truth. Poetry is emotional presentation. You can't present what you don't realize. With which shot I leave you sending many good wishes for the future.

Sincerely yours,
O. W. Holmes

Beverly Farms, Massachusetts

July 23, 1910

Dear Einstein:

Your letter from Peking [84] (I never heard of the g before) has just this moment come and gladdened me in my retreat where I am awaiting the doctor and just recovering from a little pull-down after rushing to Sorrento, Maine and Chicago upon the death of the Chief Justice.[85]

I sympathize with your remarks about platitudes, but venture to refer to an observation in one of my speeches: that when an admitted truth is realized in life it is rediscovered and therefore has its day with each of us. For instance I am gradually rediscovering that life is short. The fact intensifies my Puritanical feeling that I should make the most of time, and that therefore I am not doing what I should unless I have some serious and more or less difficult work on hand for reading in the summer time. But it is delightful when one's conscience

---

[83] Frédéric Mistral (1830–1914); poet of Provence and founder of the *Félibrige*, a movement dedicated to the prescription of regional costumes and local dialects.

[84] Einstein had been appointed First Secretary to the United States Legation in Peking in December 1909.

[85] Melville Weston Fuller (1833–1910); Chief Justice (1888–1910).

is put to rest and, as yesterday, one can get upon a lounge with half a dozen unimproving books and dip and doze. I had Gray's letters, a translation of *Aristophanes*, unfortunately without the Greek, a new book of letters and life of Lothrop Motley, by his daughter, reviving old and giving some new impressions, *Ma Fille Bernadette*, by Francis James, an example of the innocence of Frenchmen who know better, *La Maternelle*, by Léon Frapié, illustrated by Steinlen, and sympathetic with his feeling for the ugliness and tragedy of the poor, and others that I didn't look into. Before that I had given two or three days to Bancroft's *History of the Constitution*, a not very succulent work, and before that had been absorbed in the philosophical work of Henri Bergson, *Membre de l'Institut, Professeur au Collège de France*, and creator of his own world poem, which is better than most, but I incline to think as arbitrary as Hegel though more fundamental. His criticisms of his predecessors seem to me good as showing their inadequacy; but you come to a personal equation when you reach the question how far you shall believe your ultimates to be cosmic ultimates. The fashion or a fashion of the moment seems to be to believe that there is more or less of a God with limited powers who is doing his best and needs the philosophers. I take modest views of our importance, but I like to hear what the lads say, and sample each new panacea. Also I get a lesson from their intellectual enthusiasm, and when I see each man so filled and satisfied with his own product, I learn to smile at myself when I shave having yielded to similar illusions. Of course I yield to them still when I am at work; but it is wholesome to have the ironic reaction.

Being better today, I am just ready for a book I sent for: Croly, *The Promise of American Life*, which I was told had something to say about monopolies, a subject on which I want to read. As far as I have got I disbelieve the current opinions as to their economic evil, although I have received voluminous letters from a gentleman who appealed to the universal belief from Greece to Queen Elizabeth! I replied that many almost universal beliefs interested me mainly for their place in the history of superstition. He rejoined that it was one of the strongholds of our belief in God. I surrejoined that I thought we understood each other's point of view. How early you reach the undissolved in most minds, at least of our fellow countrymen. Of course we all begin dogmatically, if only with our faith in reason. In practical life it is necessary. But Bergson says intellect is secreted in the *élan* of life merely for purposes of action, to open a larger choice, that it is not a speculative instrument, and that life overflows those narrow boundaries. He plays variations on that air with a good deal of effect so that you almost seem to hear a clang from behind phenomena, as sometimes, more often, with the poets; an illusion, I suspect, but stimulating. Incidentally one gets new vistas.

Well, as you stopped for luncheon I do for a drive, and as I haven't been out for two or three days I am glad to do it. Apropos of your culinary pleasures I often refer to such as illustrating the absurdity of speaking as if a pleasure could not be real if one had had it before. A spontaneous intellect and the appetites are abiding joys.

Ever yours,
O. W. Holmes

Beverly Farms, Massachusetts

Sept. 20, 1910

Dear Einstein:

This is adieu from Beverly Farms and carries my thanks for your letter with the Imperial Edict. How interesting it always is to realize what different things present themselves as ultimate realities to different men, not only individuals but masses! What more can the skeptic ask than a few such simple facts to prove my dictum that certitude is not the test of certainty?

I am refreshed for the day. I need it, for the President dined here last night (only eight out of consideration for the dining room), and although I was moderate in all things it made my head ache. There was a lady stopping with us and we sat up late after the illustrious had gone, so that altogether I am a trifle pale.

I haven't much to show for the latter part of my vacation.

F

A succession of deaths made it sober, and induced reflections that didn't feel quite as much as if I were posing to myself as sometimes when I try to realize the approach of *finis*. But no one quite fully believes that he will die.   It is but a generalization and involves the postulate of faith that one is not God ; so that after all one may be wrong when he prophesies that he also will disappear like the other apparitions of his dreams. Also I think it foolish to spend much time or energy in thinking about it.   To live greatly one must disregard the limit and have his picture end like a Japanese drawing outside the frame.

I have amused myself with a few novels and one thing or another.   I forget whether I sent you the result of reading the Greek dramatists and *Highways of Progress* by James Hill, the great railroad man ?   The main point was that if we were soon to exhaust our resources it would mean a thinner population, that the Greeks could not have supported New York, that with less quantity we might think more of quality, and, in short, that a drop from Jim Hill to Aeschylus would have its compensations.   Yesterday I read a book on the other side from Hill, *Why I am a Socialist ?* arguing as usual from dramatic contrasts, the man in the mine, mill, etc., and the palaces and yachts of the owners, but totally failing to realize the question of percentages, of what proportion the tax levied by the treasury for luxuries bears to the total product.   I don't believe it is one per cent.   Ownership is but a wheel of distribution so long as all the great products are consumed by the crowd.   The crowd has got all there is, and the howl against the rich is really a howl against the present possibilities of life.   Yet the writer seemed to be honest and convinced, as well as far from a fool. I like to hear suggestions as to the real causes of wars, e.g. financial interests in the Gold Mines of the Cape, or the coal of Alsace-Lorraine.   Whether true or not such explanations tickle one.   I must hurry to an end or interrupt my letter which I don't like to do.   My reflections on Hill and Aeschylus console me in my approaching duty to enforce laws I don't believe in.

I was interrupted in this last sentence by a telegram telling me of another death.   My old first sergeant, afterwards Captain in our Regiment and then in the regular Army, and the man who did all the clerical work of our firm ; a man I was very

fond of. I can't think of other things now. Though I finished
the sentence I was broken in upon. Dear me, they drop very
fast as one is reaching seventy.

Goodbye. Many kind and pleasant thoughts of you ; but
I am sad.

Yours ever,
O. W. Holmes

Supreme Court of the United States, Washington, D.C.

Dec. 19, 1910

Dear Einstein :

It is almost impossible to write from here the pressure of
work is so insistent, and even if one can snatch a half hour as I
do now one's mind is so cramped to what it has been working
on that it loses the spontaneity necessary for a letter. But I
would not willingly lose yours, and therefore as soon as may
be try to give you the last tag and make you It. (I trust you
remember the games of childhood.)

I suppose that White [86] will be sworn in this morning as
Chief Justice. I think it was the best thing that could be done,
although it took everybody by surprise, as until it was announced it was supposed that Hughes [87] had it. That would
have been politics ; this is, relatively speaking, law, as it should
be. White is a very able man, and the fact that he thinks more
as a legislator than as a pure lawyer is no objection when there
are a lot of other judges who have an equal voice. He is a
great friend of mine, and, although I am debating whether I
ought to impart certain criticisms to him, he is a big, high-
minded man, worthy of the place. My own ambitions are so
wholly internal that such events move me personally but little,
except that when I read the newspapers the total absence of
any critical appreciation tends to make me gloomy, as when I
was named it made me very blue, although then and now the

[86] Edward Douglas White (1845–1920) ; Chief Justice of the United States from
December 18, 1910, until his death on May 30, 1921. See page 195.
[87] Charles Evans Hughes (1862–1948) ; American jurist. See page 138.

talk was and is friendly. One has a despairing sense that popularity or popular appreciation is to be had only by the sacrifice of ideals. But what of it? After all the meaning of an ideal is comparative solitude. And too, just when one thinks one is most secretly alone some little chap pops up who has had his eye on what was doing and has twigged. I have found that happen time and again in matters that I supposed were hidden deep.

By the by, I forget whether I have had a chance to tell you that I got an encouragement out of the blue that really pleased me the other day in the form of an honorary degree from Berlin.

I read few books here for the same reason that I don't write. The last one, *Six Oxford Thinkers* by Cecil, sent to me from London, somewhat charmed and moved me by its Oxford mixture of Little Pedlington and the exquisite. Probably neither you nor I would think the Oxford Movement a fact of world significance or regard Newman as an immeasurably great man; but it is pleasant to read about him and Church and Pater and Froude at the hands of one who takes them all very seriously.

Later. White has taken the oath and is C.J. — Poor old Harlan,[88] who is superseded, looks sad and aged. He has been presiding and now that excitement is off I shouldn't be surprised if he caved in. He is too old for work. We are to have two new men who have not put in an appearance yet, and with the New Year I suppose they will be re-arguing all their damned 'Great Cases.' I loathe great cases. They are not half as important as many small ones that involve interstitial developments of the law, but they make talk for the newspapers.

Have you heard anything about the Castletowns? Lady C. you very likely know had trouble about one eye and wrote rather hopelessly about it, and then added that she supposed I had heard about Barney's smash and that they were reduced to poverty. I don't know what it means, but it makes my heart ache. Other friends are in trouble, and altogether I am almost ashamed to be well and in good condition. However,

[88] John Marshall Harlan (1833–1911); Associate Justice, United States Supreme Court (1877–1911).

if one stopped to realize one couldn't live, and luckily to realize the condition of others is primarily their business and certainly is beyond our power. Whence the futility of the command to love one's brother as oneself.

Merry Xmas. Goodbye.

Yours ever,

O. W. Holmes

Beverly Farms, Massachusetts

June 24, 1911

Dear Einstein :

Your letter arrived two days ago. I am more than glad that the family matter promises settlement. I feared very much the result of the fight, and deeply regretted that you should have such a cloud always hanging in your mind. So you give me very great pleasure by your news.

We are settled quietly here till October, and I am at my usual business of trying to improve my mind in semi-indolent fashion. This week brings an interruption as I have to make a little speech for my Class at Commencement (Harvard College) apropos of its being fifty years out ; but that is a trifle. The point that I have in view is continually to deepen and broaden the channels for the great forces that lie behind every detail. After a man has a working knowledge of his job it is less important to read the late decisions of other Courts, which generally are but the small change of thought, than to let in as much knowledge as one can of what ultimately determines those decisions ; philosophy, sociology, economics, and the like. I am not an expert in those matters ; but I open as many windows on them as I can, and fondly hope that in some way the habit of trying to see the particular in the light of the universal will tell in one's writing. I never was more pleased than by a letter I got on my last birthday from a leading legal writer indicating that he discerned that in my decisions judicial sociology is apt to be nothing but hypostatizing the social prejudices of the judge.

As to the tobacco and oil cases ; I was not satisfied but took the best I could get, and am very happy that they and some other troublesome matters are out of the way. It has been the most bothering term I have known or expect to know.

I must get Wells' book.[89]   I have heard others praise it. He impressed me a good deal personally, not only by his knowledge and insight, but by his dignity and unconsciousness in a society to which he was not born. His socialism struck me as of the fangless, aesthetic sort not to be taken too seriously.

I shall be interested to hear what you think of *Jean Christophe*.[90] It annoys some people and perhaps even bores them; but I think that a great wind blows through it and whisks away French *chic* like dead leaves. I was a good deal interested by Judith Gautier's *Wagner at Home*, (unfortunately in a translation). It seems as if some points of *Jean Christophe* might have been got from him, though I have heard it said that it was more or less autobiographic. I took opinion paper to write upon because notepaper cramps my thoughts and I intended to be longwinded; but there are people downstairs whom I must see. Also I am not quite sure that this will reach you.

Sincerely yours,
O. W. Holmes

Beverly Farms, Massachusetts

July 27, 1911

Dear Einstein :

This will be an unworthy return for your letter, because I am feeling hurried with no adequate reason. It is partly made up for by the fact that I sent a little speech to you the other day, which I count for half a letter. I am delighted to think that we may see you and your wife in October. Our servants will not be there, but I expect we shall by the course of the first week, and venal ravens will furnish food to the prophets. The New Willard represents the ravens *pro hac vice*.

[89] Possibly *The New Machiavelli* by H. G. Wells (1911).
[90] *Jean Christophe* by Romain Rolland (1905–9).

I have been improving my mind with a little philosophy
and economics, but have now turned to *belles lettres*. For the
moment I am full of Fairfax's translation of Tasso. I wish I
had your book by me to see if you speak of his Elizabethan
English. There are surprisingly good and some surprisingly
modern things in him. One characteristic of the times is that
having published the book recently in rather handsome form
they must needs stick in a picture or two. They preface it
with a portrait from Kaulbach! And insert an absolutely
irrelevant miniature illustrating the 81st. psalm from a XVth.
century illumination. So I remember in an edition of Montes-
quieu, to which I wrote an introduction, I found to my horror
a photogravure of a picture of a race in the circus, and God
knows what else. I shall hope to see Kant's *Critique* illustrated
by pictured leg pieces. We hardly have a stomach for black
letter folios in double columns illuminated after the initial
letters.

I read a play or two by Brieux [91] the other day which
seemed to me to have classically modulated wit and intelligence,
and among them his *Petite Amie* — a fine tragic touch at the
end. The son of a man milliner has got one of the girls in the
family way; would marry her but his parents won't let him;
she tells him that he must leave her; he says, '*J'aimerais mieux
mourir.*'; she puts her hands on his shoulders and says, '*Veux-
tu?*', and so *finis* in *au revoir*. I think the sudden seizing
on the abstract suggestion *mourir* and turning it to actuality
striking. Don't you?

I will get Willy's book if I can remember it long enough.
The devil of it is that when I am in the library I remember
that there are lots of things that I have been wanting a chance
to read, but I can't think what they are. While at the booksellers one is at the mercy of chance suggestion. I have half a
mind to re-read a part of Dante as soon as I finish Fairfax;
a short job, but I dunno. It is hard not to feel a surmise of
wasted time in reading anything that is more than twenty-five
years old. I like to read with a philistine touch.

Yours truly,
O. W. Holmes

[91] Eugène Brieux (1858–1932); French dramatist, member of the French
Academy.

Villa Schifanoia, Via Boccaccio

4 Aug. 1911

Dear Judge Holmes :
    Many thanks for remembering to send me your speech.
I have always envied your great war experience. There is
always something fine in being mixed up in something bigger
than oneself particularly when one brings to it all one has,
and to me at least the Civil War has seemed our epic period.
I have in my room the portrait of a grand-uncle killed at the
head of his regiment on the Southern side. I dug out his
record once while stopping at Gettysburg and felt vicariously
proud of it. I understand Cervantes was prouder of his arm
lost at Lepanto than of Don Quixote, and I understand the
thrill it must mean to you to think of those old times. It
makes me damn the pensions. They have succeeded almost in
degrading the finest thing in our history — something ever so
much finer than that twaddle about 'no taxation without
representation'. I should have made a poor revolutionary and
perhaps a Tory, but the Civil War makes me feel all there,
and I envy you having had it in your blood.

Ever sincerely yours,
Lewis Einstein

Beverly Farms, Massachusetts

August 20, 1911

Dear Einstein :
    Your letter suggests reflections — mainly of agreement
in what you say about the war, less than formerly about the
pensions (I do not receive one) ; for I suppose the real cause
was largely the outside interest to involve the Government in
large expenditures so as to secure a high tariff, and as I see
here in the country, for instance, the privates who receive them
I always feel that the war gave them a romantic spark that
has not been quenched. Brooks Adams said to me once that
formerly you gave a lady a flower, it was beautiful and it cost

nothing, but that money had vulgarized even that so that a girl when she received a bouquet incidentally knows how much it had cost. I don't think that money has succeeded with the soldiers, though no doubt the most audible of them are apt to be the men who were less conspicuous in the field. And though it is odious to see them posing as heroes I always feel like explaining, if I refer to the war in a speech, that I feel free to do so because that was not the spear of my vocation, and that my appreciations are for men of a different type. Of course the experience is part of me and I don't know what I should have been without it. In that as in other things it almost humiliates me to think of my luck. However I always say that the only things a man has a right to be proud of are those that are no credit to him — (his inborn faculties, etc.)

I have been spending my vacation largely on economics and a little philosophy, although the books that I have had would not make a very long list. The last was re-reading Bergson's *Creative Evolution* to fix the points. He comes near to the profound line in *Rejected Addresses* : 'Thinking is but an idle waste of thought,' and suggests that we truly live only when we are reduced to an inarticulate yawp. But he is suggestive, and more or less justifies my conjectured formula that the Universe is a spontaneity taking an irrational pleasure in a moment of rational sequence. This last week I have left those themes and have been re-reading the *Purgatorio* with the necessary translation alongside as I don't know Italian. It is very easy to construe and confirms my former impressions, although of course it is no longer the excitement that the first reading was. I think I told you of Fairfax's (Elizabethan) translation of Tasso. But for things that hit you where you live you must go to the last twenty-five years. I recur to that. I don't know but it would be better if I could be a little more thoroughly idle.

As I seem to be repeating my old sayings in this letter I will repeat another, that those who make the most of themselves don't make much. However my account is drawing to a close, and I dare say it doesn't greatly matter whether I am idle or busy. The abstract man misses much, but he gains something. His life is internal.

I have just been receiving communications, by no means the

first, from a man who thinks he has done more than Darwin and as much as Copernicus — who really, I believe, has done something. I think he originated weekly crop reports etc., but whom thus far I have vainly asked to make me understand what precisely it is that warrants his large claims. I have a weakness for cranks who suggest that they may be prophets; but one feels a big, warm, lifting, lifting, and then, as one expects the break, it seems to sink away underneath and nothing happens. I have had that experience more than once. I tell my friend that I am perfectly willing to be a disciple and to believe, but that I should like to know what. I suppose that this will reach you before you start for our shores.

Au revoir.
Ever yours,
O. W. Holmes

October 21, 1911

Dear Mrs. Einstein:

A word last night was not enough to thank you for your exquisite thought and expression.[92] Believe me I feel and appreciate it much more than the poor word told. I felt a sort of shame that my mention of what I thought might interest you should have had such a result, but that does not make my thanks the less warm.

Ever sincerely yours,
O. W. Holmes

November 30, 1911

Dear Einstein:

Your letter of the 18th. has just arrived. What a long time of transit! It amuses and makes me sigh. I am sorry for the difficulties; but you are still young, and, as a chap once wrote to me, the real path is the path of most resistance. That is what brings out a man's inward force. I am more

[92] Holmes had been severely wounded at the battle of Ball's Bluff fifty years before this letter.

sorry for your wife and Miss Marguerite; [93] but they also may find their account in the experience in unexpected ways. Do give our best remembrances to them. Since their charms have ceased to bewilder me I have been absorbed in the law and have written some decisions that I have been rather pleased with. I sometimes think that the main purpose of an opinion is to show that the Judge can dance the sword dance; that is he can justify an obvious result with stepping on either blades of opposing fallacies. A literary amusement for a public ready to scoff.

I met a clever man, Zimmern,[94] at Bryce's [95] the other night, and he dined with us the next evening. Then, departing he sent us his book, *The Greek Commonwealth*, which I am devoting my few moments of leisure to reading with much joy. All that is best worth reading is the product of the last twenty-five years. (I see Madame turn up her nose at this.) Such a book would have been impossible earlier. It combines a training in economics and archaeology, literary and aesthetic sensibility, familiarity with the places from having lived there, and a general sense of life. It is an inspiring lesson in detachment. It helps one to realize that most of our necessaries are superfluous to the root of the matter, and leaves me calm to contemplate even the substitution of Mongolian for European ideals. To understand the old Greeks he says: 'We must learn how to be civilized without being comfortable.' For he says we are apt unconsciously to credit them with the material blessings and comforts in which we moderns have been taught and are now trying to teach Asiatics and Africans to think that civilization consists in. Good, hein? He praises another book, which caused me to rush off last evening to our leading booksellers, the dry goods man (The Boston Store), to see if I could get, and which I found there: Graham Wallas's, *Human Nature in Politics*. It seems to have some rationality in it. But I haven't much time for literature, and if I were to talk realities I should let out slack on the arcana of the law of conspiracy, my refinements in which give pause to some of my brethren.

---

[93] Marguerite Ralli (1894-1944); daughter of Mrs. Einstein.
[94] Sir Alfred Zimmern (1879-1957); English political scientist and author of *The Greek Commonwealth* (1911).
[95] James Bryce (1838-1922); see comment on page 198.

I hope to make them swallow the dose, however, even if there is a dissent.

This being Thanksgiving Day we are going out to Friend-ship, the John McLanes's place, to what I suppose will be a crowded and noisy luncheon with a touch of the picturesque and the reasonable proportion of pleasant people. A most good play. 'Would 'twere done',[96] as Christopher Sly says if my memory is right. I actually have ventured on the anomaly of ordering a taxi, seeing that it is cold and I dread a slow jog-trot of half an hour. Meantime the orchids that your wife gave us on the anniversary of Ball's Bluff still stand in the little middle room downstairs. They have dried on their stems and are pretty even in death. That is about all I have to tell.

Keep up your heart, my lad. The fight never ends until one becomes a non-combattant. I go up and down as I did forty-five years ago, at one moment on an intellectual throne at another a worm at its foot, but I don't let it bother me very much, having the advantage, to be sure, that there always is something to be done. But the problem for all of us and the test of the fires in our belly is to turn the inorganic into the organic; to digest the indigestible and make it into a flower or good hard muscle. I trust the metaphor is not unduly mixed. I enclose one of my pronunciamentos, which may amuse you.

Ever sincerely yours,
O. W. Holmes

March 27, 1912

Dear Einstein :

Your letter has arrived this moment, and as it is also one of about three minutes of leisure before I jump in again, I take it to reply. [Many] reverences and salutations to the ladies. I fear now that my younger charmer [97] has by this time forgotten her aged admirer as she flits volatile from the poesy of Costa Rica to the song of Italy. Alas, on the 8th. I reached seventy-one; a different thing from seventy. It is breaking a

96 *The Taming of the Shrew*, Act I, Scene i, line 259.
97 Marguerite Ralli; stepdaughter of Lewis Einstein, who accompanied him to Costa Rica where he served as United States Minister.

new package, with the chances against there being another underneath it. But give the child my love.

Secundo: You give a different number (115) on the Via Boccaccio. Formerly you gave 91. Have they given you a bigger number because of steam, heat, and electricity?

Tertio: Things in general. An impressive moment the other day over the bones of those who went down in the Maine.[98] It made me say: Well — there is one thing you can't do through your hat. You come down to truth in War. Woman's Suffrage, T.R., the referendum and the recall, the iniquity of Capital and the wrongs of Labor, all can be waged on cant. But when I saw the caissons and the strings of horses, and heard the jingle of the sabres and the short command of the bugles I felt as if I touched the blue steel edge of actuality for half an hour.

The usual dining season has come and mostly gone. I have had enough of it. One weekend my friend Mrs. Clifford (British writeress of novels) turned up, and on Sunday A.M. I whisked her in a motor over to Arlington, then round by Rock Creek Park and the military road to Fort Stevens where in '64 I saw my General walking up and down the earthworks and President Lincoln standing within it and the big guns going and the skirmish line over on the opposite slope going up to the closest approach to the city that was made; then round again through the Soldier's Home and back all in two hours before luncheon. I had not realized before what these new contrivances make possible.

I am reading almost nothing nor have been since your ladies took my heart to Italy. Writing little masterpieces of judicial discussion has been all my joy and taken all my time. I have had my share of irritation and annoyance in that business, but nothing worth telling and all now is serene. In one opinion I gave a puff to Monsieur le Professeur Paul Frédéric Girard (University of Paris) for a most admirably good book on the Roman Law. Then I bethought me to send the opinion to him without remark whereupon by return mail came a later edition of his book and a very flattering letter

[98] The sinking of the U.S. battleship 'Maine' in Havana harbour as a result of an explosion on February 15, 1898 was the incident which led to the Spanish-American War of 1898.

indicating that he knew mine, which of course I ordered to be sent to him.[99]   Also I hope the German translation of my book is nearly finished by now.   I got the first sheets a good while back, but haven't heard since.

I still live in the future while I see the enemy gradually creeping up and occupying little vantage ground after little vantage ground.   Now this, now that, not quite so strong as once;   but still everything seems to be in fair working order for a little longer.

Adieu for the moment.   There are still some odds and ends to finish up and a dinner out tonight.

Yours ever,
O. W. Holmes

Washington, D.C.

April 25, 1912

Dear Einstein :
    Your letter arrived on a beautiful spring morning, and finds me having had a good night's sleep and with half an hour free ;   so that I am not inclined to meditate on age but rather, were it not for having to go to Court to listen to presumably bores, I could go forth like a young man seeking whom I might devour.   I can't read the name of Mademoiselle Marguerite's new friend, but tell her I hate him.   I don't mind S. Reinach and am glad that he does homage.

We have been having some dreadful State rate cases (Railroads) involving fundamental questions and possibly endless figures for the wretches who have to write them ;   a matter not yet decided.

Altogether I have had no time to read, though I have managed to slip in *Present Philosophical Tendencies* by a young man, Perry,[100] which is very good.   It is amusing to see philosophy working round to very near what plain people think.   But there is just that little difference (like a hump on a wheel that takes the place of complex machinery) that marks two thousand years of speculation.   I was reflecting this morning, apropos

---

99   *The Common Law* (1881).
100   Ralph Barton Perry (1876–1957) ;   American philosopher.

of the law, but the same thing is true of philosophy, how ideas become encysted in phrases and thereby lose all motive power and become no better than dead. Indeed, after the first enlightenment that comes when a new refinement is expressed in a vivid phrase, the phrase becomes a positive obstacle to further progress for all time.

I am interested by your reflections and prospective writing on our diplomatic shortcomings. I also am interested in the political and social situation all over the world. As Col. Thompson [101] said to me a night or two ago, civilization at a certain stage seems to develop a toxic poison that threatens its life. Of course I believe that a great deal of discontent is due to the crowd not knowing, perhaps not being able or willing to know that it has all there is, now. I have been in the habit of saying that the luxuries of the few couldn't be more than one per cent of the annual product, and Thompson told me that he had figured that eighty-five per cent was consumed by people with incomes under $1000, the expenses of government coming out of the other fifteen. If he is right it shows that what I feared might some day be a more serious controversy than the great fortunes, moderate comfort could not be made much of a grievance. Mr. T. said he would like to see a democrat elected and then a campaign of education like that about greenbacks and free silver. But as yet I find people who ought to know better treating ownership as a terminus and not as a gateway, and not realizing that so far as Rockefeller reinvests and does not go in for luxuries he simply is a wheel of distribution. But it makes me sad to see a gospel of hate preached and a lot of papers indicating that nothing would give them more pleasure than to prove that my brethren and I are damned rascals. I hardly think that such papers represent the real tone of the country or of the working man, but they make me sad.

At this point I had to leave, and I finish in Court. Please give my best and pleasantest remembrances to your wife. It was a very great pleasure when I met those delightful ladies here. But now, alas, I hear only the voice of the advocate.

Yours ever,

O. W. Holmes

[101] Colonel Robert M. Thompson, U.S. Army, friend of Holmes.

Beverly Farms, Massachusetts

Sept. 2, 1912

Dear Einstein :

It is ages since I heard from you or indeed wrote to you and I want to. Of course, the impulse seizes one at a moment when for some reason or another one is in a hurry. So this is just a twitch to remind you and prove that I exist.

Exist very quietly at present reading little odds and ends of small books in the Home University Library on such varied themes as Insanity and Crime, Psychical Research, the History of England, Anthropology, Architecture, etc. etc. They give a fillip to the mind, and once in a while suggest a new idea or impart a new fact. At worst they keep one exercised on varied themes. You who despise everything but hyperaesthetics and diplomacy will not quite sympathize with my velleities in the direction of philosophy and economics. So I omit the former, on which to be sure I have done nothing to speak of, and the latter, except to say that I read a German book and also Sainte-Beuve on Proudhon with some instruction and more *ennui.*

Men with definite and final formulas or issues soon become bores. My most definite one is that, or are those, that set a limit to our speculation. Coupled with them is one agreeable result of age : that many of the infinities of youth have become finites, and that one discerns that anxieties that once would have covered the sky and aims that once filled the mind have both but a limited scope. I get to contemplate, without dismay, the stripping of a continent, the possible predominance of Mongolian ideals, nay, the ultimate repose in sleeping motion [sic] of the extinction of man. You remember Carlyle's comment on Margaret Fuller's 'I accept the Universe' — 'Gad, she'd better.' Well, in spite of that obvious retort I am inclined to repeat her phrase. If I really should achieve a serene old age I should think better of myself.

This last reminds me that my portrait has been painted for the Massachusetts Bar Association. In a way this has that effect on me. I don't think it is flattery in any ordinary sense. They say it makes me look older than I am. But the painter got some insides as well as outsides, and I can't but be pleased that any one should see me as he seems to have.

We shall be here till the end of this month and then work on to Washington, via Boston and New York as usual. Please remember me most warmly to the ladies. Tell the *jeune Mademoiselle* that she has broken my heart by forgetting me in her later conquests, but that I am trying to show courage in adversity. I was tremendously tempted to try to get a glimpse of you this summer, but there were too many reasons on the other side.

Ever sincerely yours,
O. W. Holmes

Beverly Farms, Massachusetts

Sept. 28, 1912

Dear Einstein :

Your letter gave me great pleasure after the long silence. The piece on Chinese painting [102] that you mention I probably shall find in Washington as only letters are forwarded. That means I probably shall see it soon as I start on a deliberate journey, three days in Boston and three in New York next Thursday. I scorn your suggestion that small considerations kept me from coming over. It was a balancing of large considerations, as there are many claims on one, and there was thrown into the balance our being kept later in Washington than usual with the result that London was more difficult if not impossible.

Just now I have been receiving several pats of a friendly kind, that I take as evidence that I really am getting to be an old fellow, though I can't realize it, but that at the same time causes me to anticipate some speedy let down, as I have observed that fate is not slow to teach one humility if for a moment we are puffed up. The last was last night when they gave me a dinner at a College Club at Cambridge where were the President of Harvard College, the Dean of the Law School

---

[102] Lewis Einstein had written an article entitled, 'Some Notes on Chinese Painting' that appeared in the *Burlington Magazine*, Vol. XXI, July 1912.

etc. and a lot of clear-eyed lads. They really did what they could to make me think myself a great man. However in the main I have continued my course of mild reading and am content if I carry away one articulate idea from a volume.

I am glad you have resumed your studies and writing because, though I should be sorry to have the country lose your services, diplomacy is hardly a certain career with us, and I want to see you secure full recognition of your knowledge and talents. But I notice that you are turning to the world for the moment. How I hate that damned bridge! I will whisper in your ear that the most potent reason is my inward conviction that I couldn't learn to play it well if I tried.

I did read *Les Dieux ont Soif* and was much more interested than I usually have been by A. F.'s stories. I have no scruples of course, but I didn't see how he helped his tales by such scenes as the chap with the dirty double-boned farm girl in the garret. The other books you mention (*Pierre Mille*) with more or less illegible names I never heard of but note. Dear me, how many books there are nowadays that I want to read. I mean late books, for it always seems like a waste of time to read old ones, though I have done my share. I saw Fraser's [*sic*] *Golden Bough* in a shop this morning — now, it seems, swollen to many volumes. I don't believe I shall ever find time to go through it, but I should like to.

I have had thoughts whether it would not be a good thing to do some gardening on an infinitesimal scale in one's old age. You have begun prematurely. But I take life from month to month and don't bother too much, perhaps not enough, about resources as one's powers grow less.

Don't forget to remember me to Mademoiselle Marguerite as well as to your charming wife. Your wife will be kind to me as your friend, but the young one will have forgotten me in her later conquests. This time I haven't broken loose on any theoretical point such as occurs to me apropos of my reading, perhaps because I still am echoing a little from last night. I regret the Roosevelt manifestation,[103] which has carried away some of my young men, because it seems to me

[103] On February 25, 1912, Theodore Roosevelt 'threw his hat in the ring', and on August 7 he was nominated for President by the Progressive Party in the coming election.

to touch all the sore points of the social consciousness and to make vague and sweeping suggestions of cures to come by legislation, which I believe to be blatant humbug.

Goodbye, my dear lad. Don't forget me.

Yours ever,

O. W. Holmes

Washington

Oct. 11, 1912

Dear boy:

I have just read your article in the Burlington Magazine with renewed admiration for your diversified knowledge. And aren't you a lardy dardy swell with your specimens 'taken rather at random from the writer's collection!' It is most interesting, and fills me with despair. Also permit me to compliment you on your style. It shows how you have grown.

I have just got here and am trying to get order into accounts and cubic yards of paper and books piled up during the summer. Therefore I only write this line of acknowledgment. I wrote more at length from Beverly Farms. Now that my work is beginning don't be too *exigeant*, but remember that my interest is keen in everything that concerns you or that you do, also that I highly appreciate your letters.

Please renew my homage to the ladies and believe me,

Ever sincerely yours,

O. W. Holmes

Supreme Court of the United States, Washington, D.C.

October 28, 1912

Dear Einstein:

Yours has arrived within the hour and must be answered at once, were it only for the important news it brings.[104] I send you all my felicitations, and I add every good wish and

[104] Marguerite Ralli married William Hay, 11th Marquess of Tweeddale in 1912.

happy prophecy for the charming creature who, I am sure, always would be a brilliant star whatever her place in the heavens. Give her my love. I could not be more pleased, assuming as I do from your letter that you like the man. It is hard to write about anything else but I will when I turn the page.

You are wrong in thinking that I am even an unbelieving Rooseveltian. I agree with Mr. Dooley [105] that the country in the main will pursue its destinies no matter who is president; but even presidents can do harm. And I think the most harmful thing that can be done is done by such of the Rooseveltian manifestos as I have seen. For they touch and irritate the sensitive points of the social consciousness and suggest in a vague and shocking way that something would happen if only they got in; whereas I should like to see the truth told, that legislation can't cure things, that the crowd now has substantially all there is, that the sooner they make up their mind to it the better, and that the fights against capital are simply fights between the different bands of producers only properly to be settled by the equilibrium of social desires. But I won't repeat all the commonplaces I have bored you with before now. If I had a vote I should vote for Taft in spite of the fact that he like the rest of them seems to believe in the present legislative tendencies, anti-trust etc. etc. that I believe to be noxious humbug. Perhaps I told you of a conversation with him in which I said that of course I carried out in good faith these damned laws (perhaps I didn't say damned), and that if they could make a case for putting Rockefeller in prison I should do my part; but if they left it to me I should put up a bronze statue of him. All this *entre nous* of course.

We are in full blast now and I am stealing time from duty to write even this short letter. My blood is up and I am out for slaughter. Things seem more satisfactory than they did at the end of last term. My own opinions have cleared up at least a number of important matters. Hesitation and doubt are the most uncomfortable feelings of the mind, and though *au fond* I believe almost nothing I generally can settle my conclusions as to a practical course, I mean in my own job. If my

---

[105] Irish saloon-keeper and philosopher character created by American humorist Finley Peter Dunne (1867–1936).

wife should consult me as to the household I should be an imbecile. My function there is that of God, a terrific idol to be appealed to on condition that it remains dumb.

Yours ever,

O. W. Holmes

Supreme Court of the United States, Washington, D.C.

November 24, 1912

Dear Einstein:

It seems uncertain from your letter whether this will reach you, so I cut it short. I am delighted at what you say about the young'un and her prospective, and philosophically disgusted to find you on the side of T.R. I knew him and liked him personally very much, as much as it was possible to like a man that you knew would throw over the friendship he professed the moment one allowed one's own understanding of one's judicial duty to prevail over what he wanted. But as I think I did not say to you, but did say to someone, the Bull Moose Manifestos struck me as exhibiting a strenuous vagueness that produced atmospheric disturbance without transmitting a message. And as I regard the party as only meaning T.R., so far as articulate, and regard him as perhaps unconsciously but wholly cynical in self-seeking, I naturally feel no enthusiasm for it. Even your quotation seems a trifle vague as to what there may be behind the new person. The thing I see most plainly is a vast amount of more or less real social discontent based on economic superstition and ignorance of what is possible. Everything in our literature and speech favors the squashy, and T.R. is the last man to stand up to the crowd and say: 'Stop whining. Stop thinking you can have something for nothing. Stop churning the void for cheese. You have got all there is. Now be men or else die like dogs.'

However there are a lot of young men who think with you. And although as yet I have not extracted any definite proposition from any of them (except an ignoble fear of something worse from one more intelligent than most of the rest) I admit in words and, so far as humanely may be, in my heart that they may have the message of the future in their belly. I find it dreadfully hard to think there is much chance that they have, thinking as I do that all the strange currents that I see in legislation etc. are wrong to the point of being ridiculous.

To return to what you quote from your unpublished MS, it smacks of a yearning for Socialism, qualified or not. I have read a good many things or rather some leading books on that theme and as yet have found none that did not repose on the confusion between ownership and consumption of which I have written before. I think the great body of our wealth is administered socially now. Of course I have no *a priori* objection to socialism any more than to polygamy. Our public schools and our post office are socialist, and wherever it is thought to pay I have no objection except that it probably is wrongly thought. But on the other hand I have as little enthusiasm for it as I have for teetotalism. Well, I never wrote so much politics before, but it is a pleasure to let out a little irresponsible slack in the hope of giving pain (as R.L.S. says).

My love to you all,

Yours ever,

O. W. Holmes

Supreme Court of the United States, Washington, D.C.

March 20, 1913

10⁴⁰ AM

Dear Einstein :

The telephone tells me that I was just five minutes too late to catch you for a last word. I am so sorry that I have seen so little of you, but it has not been my fault. I have been so busy with my duties (and some previous engagements) that I could not help it. Perhaps you will be coming back here before going to Europe? I hope that you may get what you want and that if you don't literature may profit by your disappointment. You are a man of ideas, and you must not allow indolence or lesser preoccupations to prevent your contributing your share. From every one according to his faculties if not to every one according to his needs. I like your contemplated theme, and you have proved in your early books that you could handle it with learning and ability. So I have every hope that whatever happens it will turn out all right. If I don't see you again goodbye. With real regret at not having seen more of you, and my best remembrances to your wife.

Sincerely yours,

O. W. Holmes

Ritz-Carlton Hotel, New York

22 March 1913

Dear Justice Holmes:

There is no one whose counsel is more appreciated than yours by me, and your lines of the other day are an ever welcome reminder of how much I owe you, perhaps without your knowledge, in the various little circumstances which go to make up my patchwork of life.

I envy you in having found such an appropriate equation for your abilities where your Olympianism can blend serenely with an always indulgent skepticism. What there may be in store for me I know not, and my official career has become a matter of indifference — or at least I try to persuade myself that it is. I am promised news by the Peerless One [106] in another fortnight and, though I do not believe it, I shall at least look forward to a brief refreshment at the 1720 Eye Oasis.

With respectful homage to Mrs. Holmes who gave me solace while you were plunged in legal mysteries.

Ever sincerely yours,

Lewis Einstein

May 18, 1913

Dear Einstein:

Last night a card dropped out of *Barnavaux et quelques femmes* [107] and I had legal notice that it came from you. Before

---

[106] William Jennings Bryan (1860–1925); American lawyer and political leader; Secretary of State 1913 to 1915.

[107] *Barnavaux et quelques femmes* by Pierre Mille (1908).

that I had not, and, though I had little doubt, I hung up writing as I was very busy.   But two days ago I wrote my last case and took the same time to tumble on my knees and be laid up to make sure no harm was done.   Hence leisure and amused perusal.   The man has not the sting of Kipling's genius ; but he is good and has an atmosphere of his own.

I expect to go to England August 11 — Mauretania — assuming that my knee is not going to make trouble.   Morgan my banker, and my first hostess Mrs. J. R. Green, 36 Grosvenor Road, S.W., then Sir F. Pollock, 21, Hyde Park Place, W. ; but I have inward doubts whether I shall be as free as if I had rooms of my own and may break for them.

I shall come back towards the end of August — so it will be a hurried visit.   If you are there we will hobnob.   This is a hasty bulletin as I sit with my leg up.

Compliments to the ladies.

Yours as ever,
O. W. Holmes

Beverly Farms, Massachusetts

September 12, 1913

Dear Einstein :

Your letter has just arrived.   I hope before this that all has turned out well.   What Mrs. Einstein told me left some anxiety in my mind for the dear expectant, but I infer from the tone of what you wrote that all promised well.   You leave me in some doubt as to how I should direct this, but I shall rely on its being forwarded if you have left Scotland.

I don't regret that you got no further appointment, as Bryan was right in saying that (under existing practice) diplomacy is not a career.   My wife read an article in some paper on our folly in giving up men trained to the business and putting in novices which it illustrated by you.   Since we are so foolish I am well content that you are out of it.

But because you are out of it you must not sink into comfort and sloth.   You must make for yourself a regular occupation, presumably literary, and keep your nose to the grindstone.

It is astonishing what a lot one can accomplish even with an hour a day. The Chancellor (Haldane), with whom I crossed and sat at table, gave me a belly-ache with the account of the work he does, ending up at midnight with an hour's reading of philosophy. (I have just been reading a very able Hegelian book that he recommended, and not believing it.) The result is that he seems an old man before sixty. Without emulating him one can do a good deal. As I probably have said before one of the pleasures of old age after a life of work is the recognition that begins to grow more frequent and ungrudging. So crack ahead, and go at your English Civilization or the downfall of ours or what you like, only hit it a sound whack. It is not enough to be a very refined dilettante. Yet why not? After all I am simply expressing my own temperament. If you would be happy in accomplishment and equilibrium without further achievement I don't see that I could criticize. The most I could say would be that I should want to see some result outside myself. Of course it is true that one sees disintegrating tendencies. As it says in *Jean Christophe*, (*Le Buisson ardent*), ideas don't conquer the world as such but by virtue of some vital radiation that comes from them at certain moments. When they become a religion reason is vain for the time. All that one can do, as I said to the C.J. apropos of Catholicism, is to bet on science and reason for the long run. If we lose the bet we shan't know it, and we shall have done our part.

I was very sorry not to go to Scotland, but it was impossible in July which I spent in London continuously lunching and dining with old friends whom I could not neglect. After that it was too late. I went first to the Castletowns in Ireland, then back to England, and, having failed in a scheme of dashing over to France, I went to Lincoln (Lord Monson's), and then wound up with L. Scott at Brackley, Northants — neighbourhood of the Cotswolds and many charming little churches as well as agreeable people. Lincoln also was delightful. In London and at the Castletowns there were saddening elements of tragedy. C. is still not wholly recovered from his breakdown, and my friend, Canon Sheehan, whom I went to see every day, considered himself a dying man. It makes one feel wicked to be happy when so near to misery, but I suppose it is normal. To love 'one's brother as oneself' means to realize his consciousness as vividly as one's own, and so is a vain exhortation to have more imagination than is given to man.

Lord, how the Hegelian logic chopping does rile me! All this means that the old beast had such penetrating *aperçus*. My love to yours.

As ever,
O. W. Holmes

Beverly Farms, Massachusetts

Oct. 2, 1913

Dear Einstein :

Your letter reaches me on the eve of departure for Washington by easy stages. (The blot above was caused by the tyrant of the house, a white kitten, jumping from a chair to my lap and thence to the table and walking across my paper. He is fond of doing it, and when I am reading Fabre (*Souvenirs entomologiques*) to my wife of an evening he hops up and sits on my book.)

I have read something of Birmingham's [108] whom you mention. It rather amused me, but not violently.

My friend among the Irish priests is Canon Sheehan, whom I probably have mentioned to you, the parish priest of Doneraile. When I read it I thought his *Under the Cedars and the Stars* one of the finest pieces of rhapsodical English in the language. I recommend that in return. He thinks he is dying, and, although I am not fully convinced of it, I fear it is true. I went to see him every day after luncheon when I was there. He asked me to take a book from his library, so I carried off a folio, Suarez, *De Legibus*, as he thought Suarez to be an original thinker on the law, concerning which I am lawfully sceptical until convinced by inspection. He also handed me to read on my voyage, as I did, the selected correspondence of Macvey Napier, once editor of the Edinburgh and also of the *Encyclopædia Britannica*. It isn't the kind of thing I naturally read, but it was rather amusing to see what a firebrand Brougham was and how he seemed to bully everybody. The letters of the other men of that time, Macaulay, Carlyle, the Mills etc. have

[108] George A. Birmingham was the pseudonym of a prolific British novelist, the Reverend James Owen Hannay (1865–1950).

a pale interest, but the book illustrates my general theories. Our emphasis has changed, and I imagine that Brougham's books would strike us as hopelessly thin if we ever dreamed of looking into them. However all this is going back to before my last letter.

I think you talked about the President's Mexican policy to me. Someone did in the same sense as your letter. In my ignorance your view seems to me sound.

How queer for you to be on Arthur Young. I thought he belonged to the Economists. I didn't know of the prophecy you mention, but he is said to have prophesied the French Revolution I remember. I think, since I wrote, I have read a volume of Lady Burghclere's *Life of the Duke of Ormonde*. The Irish seem to have been insoluble then as now. That also is off my beat, but she gave me the book. Do you read John Masefield's poetry? No truth about actuality with him; but I daresay you would regard a good deal of it as hardly within the sphere of legitimate art.

I mention a book or two; but I have been pretty idle since I got here and haven't much to tell about. My most serious preoccupations have been a small investment adding about two thousand feet to my place here, by purchase from a neighbour, and little improvements to the house and barn.

I am glad and relieved to hear that Lady Tweeddale has come out all right. Please give my kindest remembrances to your wife. I fear that I may be a bad correspondent this winter. When the work is on I find it almost impossible to let go. At this point my wife laid the enclosed work of art on my table and I pass it on.

Yours ever,
O. W. Holmes

Supreme Court of the United States, Washington, D.C.

Nov. 9, 1913

Dear Einstein:

The dangers of classic allusion in equivocal MS were illustrated by your letter, speaking of my being restored to my Areopagus. I read it at first oesophagus, thought I saw a delicate reference to my trouble with my insides on getting home, and said to myself I had not thought that oesophagus meant the lower gut!

What you say of living in an old civilization is curiously parallel to what I was writing lately as to the lesson of Washington, where in my eleven years I have seen so many great men rise, be mighty, vanish, and be forgotten. In the devitalized Sunday afternoon thought of contemplating man's solemnity in his way of taking himself is ridiculous enough. It is a different matter, of course, when he has got the blood in his head and is fighting. A man must be serious for practical purposes; but when it comes to being the friend that God had to create in order to realize that he exists, excuse *me*. (Slang.) I think even a better warrant for a smile is to notice how large a part of the fighting faiths of men depend on men having been shaped by them for a considerable time before they even heard these questions. You know my formula that friendship, property, and truth have a common root in time. Man is like any other organism, shaping himself to his environment so wholly that after he has taken the shape if you try to change it you alter his life. All of which is all right and fully justifies us undoing what we can't help doing and trying to make the world into the kind of a world that we think we should like; but it hardly warrants our talking much about absolute truth. I wonder if there is such a thing. What I mean by it is that body of propositions that I think in the long run can compel the assent of people as intelligent and educated as you and I; the *can't helps* that are common to what we consider the better part of the human race, without inquiry whether the universe or some possible different form of life might transcend them without at the same moment passing out of my world and becoming nonexistent *quod hoc* for me. The true type of the cosmic philosopher, perhaps of the cosmos, was furnished me when in college by a youth of other antecedents; a form of the endless '*ménagerie*', that dance of death that has gathered so many aesthetic motifs from the people. It was as follows :—
'This, gentlemen, is the Chihioo Ching or Chinese Fox. This *hanimal* when closely pursued by the Harrabee'an 'orsemen *is known* to creep up its own fundament and thence to smile in scorn upon its baffled pursuers.'

Since I wrote the last words I have made two afternoon calls, and my mind is purged of unholy thoughts. I have been working like the devil the last ten days or so under the drawback of lumbago, now happily vanishing. For one or two days I could not get up when the Court rose without help. But it is the most companiable and least disintegrating of pains. How different from the toothache or the bellyache.

I know little of current politics. I believe that I don't sympathize with anything that is being done; but as I don't quite know what *is* being done I walk softly before the law. *Claudite nunc rivos pueri sat prata biberunt* if I may quote the Latin Grammar of youth.

My homage to your wife and Lady Tweeddale.

Ever yours,

O. W. Holmes

December 5, 1913

Dear Einstein:

A very pleasant letter from you comes this morning. Also I am in no condition to make a wordy answer because I am under the continuous pressure of sometimes almost maddening work. So make allowances if during the winter I am not prompt, as well as for dullness, when I write.

Let me thank you for the delightful volume (Humanist Library) of A. Dürer.[110] I read it with much pleasure, which I never attempted except in little patches when I only had the original.

Secundo: I saw or rather F.[111] read to me an extract from a paper indicating that you had had litigation. I hope it does not mean that things are in worse condition. I thought you had compromised the matter. My anxiety is diminished by the serene tone of your letter.

In the evenings, when I neither work nor write, I have just read aloud (translation) Farrère, *La Maison des Hommes Vivants*.

[110] *Journey to Venice and to the Low Countries* by Albrecht Dürer, Humanists' Library (1913).

[111] Fanny Dixwell Holmes; wife of Holmes.

Rather a good modern form of the Vampire. Boucicault [112] used to freeze my blood as a boy by acting a play of that name. When you see him first it is in the time of Elizabeth, and then the same glittering eyes enter a Queen Anne drawing-room. Every century a maiden must be sacrificed, and every month he must stretch himself to receive the rays of the rising morn on the fine new canvas mountain of the Boston Theatre. Oh, it was soul filling! But when I asked him why he never tried it in the time of our only conversation more than twenty years ago he said it wouldn't do nowadays. But M. Farrère does pretty well with it; varied. For the most part I only hypnotize myself with solitaire after the day's work, as yet not having dined out much and not wanting to.

Last week while we were adjourned and my work being done I read with a great deal of admiration Santayana's '*Winds of Doctrine*'. Wonderful knowledge and easy criticisms of systems with many *aperçus* that I have shared without owing them to him. I said (considering his possible retention of his membership in the Catholic Church) that he stood on the flat road to heaven and buttered slides to hell for all the rest, so well does he state the fundamental scepticisms without committing himself.

I am much interested by what you tell me of Lady Tweeddale. My love to her and your wife. I must stop and go to Court in a few minutes.

Ever sincerely yours,
O. W. Holmes

[112] Dion Boucicault (1822–90); Irish playwright and actor who achieved prominence in the United States.

PART TWO

1914−18

Supreme Court of the United States, Washington, D.C.

Jan. 29, 1914

Dear Einstein:

(In answer to yours) of course higher up the tango is closer than the terza rima because in people who from circumstance if not from nature are more susceptible to the movement of the wave of dominant interest fashion is a law of life. So Cowley, who once delighted the world, is dead, and many kings have reigned in his place. So legal arguments that would have been serious *temp. Eliz.* now would be answered with a smile. So Wagner already has waned. So the man in vogue is a neo-somethingism; the neo being the essential part.

My most important piece of news is that I have filed my income tax return.[1] My dear delightful secretary[2] made it out for me, and little know I about the difficult mysteries it involves. I am and have been very hard at work at opinions before and after going to Court, but we adjourn on Monday and I shall be able to draw the first long breath for six weeks. I am up with my work, but it has meant strenuous days. So I have read nothing. But my wife got the other day a reprint of some poems by one Holmes, an American, dead, the work originally published in London, called '*Under a Fool's Cap is Song*', being variations on Mother Goose running from tragedy through midsummer night dreams to the grotesque that have a smack of genius. He and the distinguished maker of pies in Washington, (I see Holmes's pie wagons everywhere), will preserve the name for a day.

Some time back my wife read Wells's *Marriage* to me. It seemed to me pretty near to being a great novel. I think his thinking superficial, not unbecoming in a born artist, who gives

---

[1] The Sixteenth Amendment to the Constitution permitting the enactment of a federal income tax was adopted in 1913, and the income tax was inaugurated with a provision fixing a top rate of 6 per cent on incomes in excess of $500,000 a year.

[2] George L. Harrison was Holmes's secretary 1913–14.

you the big, serious, tender feelings that accompany great situations, for he does give these. And, although the solution of the latter-day difficulty by going to Labrador is rather mechanical, still being there they do talk, the hero and the heroine, adorably about victuals, and the tale ends with a snack.

As a hardened jurist I do smile, though as a friend I sympathize with them, at your complaints at publicity. Remember, my friend, that every good costs something. There is nothing that could not be destroyed if it were enough to point to an incidental evil; and your aged uncle has had occasion to point out in decisions the mistake of rushing on that ground to a general negation. In the particular matter publicity is a safeguard against corruption and arbitrariness. It sometimes fails, but you may bet there would be a good deal more if we didn't have to do everything in broad daylight. I remember a divorce case in which a woman had to go into the most private details. I said that I should make no order, but that if out of respect for delicacy the reporters saw fit to draw out of hearing I should think it very proper, and they did. But I should not have felt right in requiring it. Don't forget that to have anything means to go without something else. Even to be a person, to be *this* means to be *not that*. Forgive my lecture but I must say a word for my job.

I remember reading Gobineau before you were born, but I have forgotten all except the pleasure at a(n ex) ? diplomat writing so well. All you write is pleasant to my ear, and your suggestion as to visiting the Tweeddales has my thanks; not this summer, however, at least. Kindest remembrances to your wife.

Ever yours sincerely,
O. W. Holmes

March 8, 1914

Dear Einstein :

This can be but a bulletin. I am seedy with a cold that has kept me indoors today. It is my birthday. I have had many messages and flowers to acknowledge, and later we have a little dinner. So I am a long worm that has no turning. The only observation of recent date is that Gilbert Murray's *Euripides and His Age*, in the Home University Library series, seems to me charming; more so than his translations regarded as such. People think they are getting Euripides and get Swinburne and water. I am a little sceptical at the complete modernization and humanizing of any Greek. I guess there were insensibilities in the best of them upon some points as to which we feel. And I doubt if even a scholar when he finds a Greek fill his bill so completely does not sometimes 'dilate with the wrong emotion'. But it is vain for me to attempt today to do more than to send you friendly remembrances and my homage to your wife and Lady Tweeddale. There are times when I can't write.

Yours ever,

O. W. Holmes

April 17, 1914

Dear Einstein :

Your delightful letter came yesterday, and first it reminded me via Casanova of a talk with the Russian Ambassador the other day. He said that a lot of letters from women to Casanova had been published in Italy within a year or two (I commend them to you on spec.) among others from Manon Baletti (I forget whether there are two l's, I think not) and he remembered having seen a description of a portrait of her by Nattier in theatrical costume with a mask and one bosom bare. What was his amazement to see the portrait the other day, here, on the walls of Mrs. ——— ———. She knew nothing about it, he said, except that it had been bought for her by a *Commissionaire*. And he thought it a sad fate for the poor Manon to have to look on while the lady (he used a somewhat stronger phrase) danced the tango with Mrs. ——. (Neither of those two lacks *embonpoint*).

My literature is confined to the effort to make it in the form of judicial decisions, and I occasionally manage to slip a phrase past the negative vigilance of my brethren.

I have listened while playing solitaire to portions of H.

James's second autobiographical volume.[3]   He gives the impression that he seeks to, in spite of his style, which shows that the medium does not matter if you can do the trick.   I mention it because it recalls the time when we were intimate.   I knew well Minnie Temple some of whose remarkable letters he prints (she died young) and his father whose letters are perhaps the most vivid things in the book.   It recalled the total impression of the family, with its moral refinement, its keen personal intuitions, the optimistic anarchising of the old man, (a spiritual, unpractical anarchism) its general go-as-you-please but demand-nothing, apotheotic Irishry.   One had to invent a word to hit it.

This week too I have learned of the death of my oldest friend, Colonel Hallowell.[4]   A savage abolitionist, a fighting Quaker who blushed at his own militancy, intolerant of criticism or opposition, but the most generously gallant spirit and I don't know but the greatest soul I ever knew.   We had ceased to have much intercourse.   We were separated in space, and our intellectual development had not been the same ; but his death leaves a great space bare.   We were classmates, officers in the same regiment, lay on the field wounded side by side, and he gave the first adult impulse to my youth.   It is not exactly a loss to me but a blank.

I dined last night with Charles Adams.   We mentioned that Howells, he and I were the three or three of the four oldest men now living of the Saturday Club in Boston.   We are so near the edge of the void that we can spit into it.   But though I say so I don't feel or realize it except by the dropping of leaves from the tree between us and the sky.

I wish I could have seen your *fête*.   It must have been beautiful.   By the by, unless I mislaid it on opening your letter, you didn't send the second half of the newspaper account.   My part says continued on page four, which I regret.   I always envied the Venetian Costumes.   At this moment my intelligent secretary points out that the continuation is on the back of the slip.   I was stupid.   Well, I turned seventy-three on March 8th. and have a right to it.   Perhaps this is one of what I call the Lilliputian decrements of time.

---

[3] *Notes of a Son and Brother* by Henry James (1914).
[4] Norwood Penrose Hallowell.

In five minutes I must start for Court to hear the continuation of the argument in the case of *Virginia v. West Virginia*.[5] I wrote a decision two or three years ago in favor of the former State on the main point, the principle of division of the old State Debt which West Virginia still is trying to avoid bearing any share of; but they are trying to reopen fundamental questions in a new form on the ground of facts just discovered. So I must fly before I fill this sheet, but it will bear my kindest remembrances to you and yours, my dear lad.

Ever yours,
O. W. Holmes

Villa Schifanoia, Via Boccaccio, Florence

May 6, 1914

Dear Justice Holmes :

I enjoyed reading and rereading your letter which seemed so full of truth. And though you offer to spit into the void I envy you your youth. I never knew Colonel Hallowell, but felt after your lines that I too had lost a friend. Somehow the men of your generation seem more generous than our prating social service lot. They talked less and had fewer theories, but I fancy the Civil War brought out more humanity than that of our hard-boned professional altruists.

I have written to Wilson volunteering my services in any capacity he may see fit to employ them over Mexico,[6] but have little expectation of acceptance. I am not a little disgusted over the whole thing with its blundering diplomacy attached to catchword formulas culminating in virtual piracy. It takes a convinced pacifist to begin wars on such a pretext. The worst of it is there is nothing to do now save to support him.

Yes, I have the letters of women to Casanova, which Rava found at Pillnitz.[7] But the few I have read including Manon

---

[5] *Virginia* v. *West Virginia*, 234 U.S. 347 (1914).

[6] The occupation of Veracruz by United States troops on April 21, 1914 following the refusal of President Huerta of Mexico to comply with an official demand that the United States flag be saluted had led to the severance of diplomatic relations between the two countries.

[7] *Lettere di donne a Giacomo Casanova raccolte e commentate* by Aldo Rava, Milan (1912).

Balletti's are dullish in their incoherent and illiterate sincerity. I would trade them all for another adventure in the original. Bye the bye the new poem of Sappho which I read in the morning 'Times' is an astounding discovery and makes one wonder what the new Oxyrinchus find will be.[8]

I have been rather seedy all spring and unable to do little more than potter in the garden and stand over my slaving artists which makes me feel rather like a Renaissance Cardinal minus the mistresses. A monumental stairs and grotto with sporting dolphins stand as my constructive achievement. I must not forget the roses whose pruning and budding have kept me busy for months past till when finally they flower I half forget to look at their opulence. Truly the French are great, for the new Lyon roses (Madame Edouard Herriot, Beauté de Lyon etc.) are dreams of unsuspected tints. How I regret you are not in the garden with me now, for I should take all the grower's pride (and that is not a little) showing you the rounds for your expected admiration.

Yesterday the Tweeddales and I motored over to Siena, and on Saturday we cross the Apennines to Ravenna. Were you here on what excursions would we not go ?

My wife joins me in warm remembrances to Mrs. Holmes.

Ever yours,

L. E.

Supreme Court of the United States, Washington, D.C.

May 21, 1914

Dear Einstein :

Your letters always are delightful, this one more than ever, except that you say you have been seedy which grieves me.

I am much interested at the new poem by Sappho (of which I have not heard otherwise), for at the moment I am reading with much pleasure R. W. Livingstone's [9] ' *The Greek Genius and its Meaning to Us.*'

[8] Under the heading 'Romance in Archeology' *The Times* had published the complete Greek text as emended by Mr. J. M. Edmonds of a poem by Sappho recently discovered by Dr. B. P. Grenfell and Mr. A. S. Hunt at Oxyrhynchus, Egypt. See col. 1, page 5, *The Times*, May 4, 1914.

[9] Sir Richard Winn Livingstone (1880–1960) ; eminent English classicist and educator.

Apropos of the Greek directness, seeing things as an intelligent child would see them, with none of Ruskin's 'Pathetic Fallacy' I often have remarked that the Choruses have the manners of the poor. They look at you and say: You are looking awful thin. Livingstone excellently points out how with that directness we should lose much Latin and XVIIIth and XIXth century English poetry, but forgets to mention that we also should lose *Mona Lisa*, *Hamlet*, *Tristam Shandy*, and *Faust*.

But I am all on the Greek side in their rationality as to what Christians call sin and they called error. I daresay I have made to you a remark that I have thought of in these later days, that morals are imperfect social generalizations expressed in terms of feeling, and that to make the generalization perfect we must wash out the emotion and get a cold head. The retail dealers in thought will do the emotionalizing of whatever happens to be accepted doctrine of the day. *Nous autres* will permit them that. In fact, if we have got to hate anything, I don't see why we mightn't as well invert the Christian saying and hate the sinner but not the sin. Hate being a personal emotion naturally falls on the obstacles to our making the kind of world we like. It imports no judgment. Disgust is ultimate and therefore as irrational as reason itself — a dogmatic datum. The world has produced the rattlesnake as well as me; but I kill it if I get a chance, as also mosquitos, cockroaches, murderers, and flies. My only judgment is that they are incongruous with the world I want; the kind of world we all try to make according to our power.

I am afraid I also should find it hard to get on with the Greeks. We want the infinite, which Livingstone says they disliked. We want the reflection of the reflection, the looking-glass at both ends of the room. We are thankful to be corrupt, if not to be first intentioned is to be so; and I would rather read Livingstone (though I fear he is a Christian and hates sin) than Plato. But I prefer Socrates to the prophets even with the very great gain they got by being translated into English by people who only partly understood them, but, being convinced that they meant something pretty tall, achieved effect transcending the simple inspiration of Jehovah. There is an intelligible rational sequence even in inspired thought when you get its real meaning; but that destroys the divine non-sequence of the English version, and by becoming comprehensible ceases to be sublime. Were it not tedious I could illustrate by chapter and verse.

This is only a subdivision of my excursions on translation in general and 'dilating with the wrong emotion'. Which reminds me to say what I desire to mention to everyone who by any chance may lift up a voice, that the excellent plan of the Loeb Classical Library seems to me nearly ruined in the example that I have by the translators attempting to recommend their wares by poeticising them instead of giving the most intelligently accurate translation opposite the text that they can achieve.

Forgive me if I've said this before. I don't remember what I have written. I won't repeat apologies for repetition it can't be helped if one has hobbies, favorite thoughts, and doesn't write gossip — (for the same reason that one doesn't play bridge: it requires intelligence, or, not to be unnecessarily modest, intelligence of a kind I don't possess). If I have said nearly everything in this letter before, at least it will show that I am thinking of and to you, and asking you to sit in my well-worn furniture.

My compliments to your dear people including the baby if within reach. In about a month I expect to be in Beverly Farms, but Supreme Court is always the safest address until I notify you otherwise.

Sincerely yours,
O. W. Holmes

Villa Schifanoia, Via Boccaccio, Florence

7 June 1914

Dear Justice Holmes:
I am in one of these languid moods when one feels more inclined to stretch than to write; but your letter with its tabloid Emersonianism (forgive this misappropriateness for I cannot come closer to the bone) invites my gratitude in its

expectation of the future reply. I love the paradox of your
Hellenism. St. Thomas Aquinas plus Plymouth Rock prepare
you for nymphs and satyrs and fields of asphodel, while you
intellectualize instinctive vascular responses to appeals of sense.
I don't think our Northern minds can ever really grasp the
Mediterranean spirit, be it in Greece or Rome. Only yesterday a Sicilian friend was relating to us his mother's system
of education. She wanted her children to be brilliant in
everything, and when they were deficient she had only one
word of censure ' *Tu brutta*' (you are ugly). Even at this day
there is a directness and a simplicity and a common plain-
ness about the Italian mind which is puzzling, for in spite of
its simple directness it is astonishingly distrustful and self-
contained. But Italy makes a straight appeal to the sensuous
aspects of our nature, which, like at school, excuses you for the
day.

I am glad to find my own laziness is not an idiosyncracy.
I have spoken to many workers and they all tell me the same.
Yesterday a clever woman writer was here, the canoniste (how
else will you translate '*chanoinesse*'?) Cécile de Tormay, a
Hungarian novelist whose books have been translated into
most European tongues. She was remarking how where so
much beauty exists one does not feel the need of creating it.
Practically translated this means she is lazy while in Italy.
Yet one stores up a reservoir of impressions and feelings. I often
think admiringly of you doping out Hesiod (to bring Milton
to date) when there is so much to enjoy until I think of my
own stupid wish to put my head into a halter again. Madame
de Tormay (for, though unmarried, like cooks in England she
enjoys the courtesy title of 'Mrs.') related a pretty tale of an
old man daily buying a bird from a bird-catcher till the latter's
curiosity excited caused him to follow the purchaser to find
him freeing the bird. Angrily he clutches the old man's throat
and asks him how he can dare to be the cause of his risking
his life daily for nothing, and is answered: 'The important
thing is that you shall work; what becomes of you later is
immaterial'. I wish I could narrate an even prettier tale
about a Corinthian Lass which she narrated, but it is too long
for today.

Helen sends her warm greetings. The Tweeddales and

baby would likewise had they not left us, I am sorry to say, a fortnight ago.

> Ever yours,
> L. E.

June 22, 1914

Dear Einstein :

It is a pleasure to hear from you that someone else beside myself is languid.

Today we deliver our last opinions and adjourn, and when one gets off the race track there comes a kind of collapse that I have anticipated in the days when my work seemed finished. However nothing is finished till all is done. Our Conference was Saturday night as usual at the end of the term with a little supper after it. On Thursday a judge came to see me with suggestions that had to be complied with to get a majority for my most important case, and that necessitated rewriting it. I got it done, read it to the Chief Justice, sent it to the printer about noon Friday, and distributed it that evening. At the interview the C.J. asked me to take another case, which I wrote and distributed by Saturday noon. So you see the supposed end of my labor when my cases had been written was an illusion. But I don't expect anything more, and if, as I anticipate, I finish all that I have today, I shall have nothing more to do. We leave for Beverly Farms, Massachusetts, on Wednesday, and there I expect to remain during the summer. That will be my address.

In such moments as this Casanova is a blessing.

I interrupted the reading of *La Femme et le Pantin* by Pierre Louÿs to write to you. There is something coldly perverse about that gent to my mind, that one felt especially in *Aphrodite*.

As I have no ideas except possibly a few legal ones I take this opinion paper to write on ; the larger sweep of the arm gives greater freedom to the mind and inspires a deceptive hope.

You amuse me with your insults at my attempts to grasp the Mediterranean spirit. Ruskin, poor forgotten man, long ago remarked the contrast. But if a worm may turn why are not the spontaneities and pleasures of the intellect as legitimate, as human, (since some men feel them, including my inter-locutors,) as those of the senses? I might be ridiculous if I tried to make a statue; but I have a right to think about one. The sublime and beautiful, to use the old-fashioned phrases, are both confined to the visible. You can find the infinite in the law, perhaps the greatest human document, as well as anywhere else. If the universe can be thought about, which is a compulsory postulate, any fact exhibits it as much as any other if you can see how; and the universal is the only sublime. My pleasure in the law, apart from that found in the exercise of the faculties which is the fundamental one, is just in trying to exhibit some hint of horizons, even in small details.

You have charm in a letter, an easy achievement; but I hope without the aid of Italy to be lazy ere long and to forget the ever imminent feeling that I am neglecting some duty when I am idly amused. Another touch of Plymouth Rock you will say. Perhaps so, but also the result of being under pressure for a long time. Please continue your ironic smiling in articulate form as and when you feel like it, and be sure of such apprecia-tion as is possible to this poor Calvinist gone wrong.

Many messages to your wife.

Yours ever,
O. W. Holmes

Beverly Farms

July 20, 1914

Dear Einstein:
    Your letter has come, welcome as usual. I don't get the allusion when you say don't play at Tiberius. Apropos of Casanova and Louÿs — those books were a momentary relief from the strain in Washington. Since getting here I consider improvement as well, but got a good deal of amusement out of George Moore's *Hail and Farewell*. He can write. He has no general point of view that a white man is bound to respect, but he depicts himself with I doubt not great veracity — as to intervals at least. I am told that he has done unspeakable things in the way of describing women identifiably; and

indeed in this book, before I had heard that, I couldn't but wonder whether, if he was telling facts as he seemed to be, the dame could not be picked out. Perhaps that is part of his conscience as an immense admirer of Manet. I used to say that a philosopher couldn't be a gentleman, and vice versa, because a philosopher must hold in solution the dogmatic self-assertion or pride that is essential to his other character. Perhaps also on slightly different grounds easily stated an artist can't be.

Well, I have read a volume of Bergson that had escaped me, with no profit or belief beyond the greater or less stimulus to be found in him, and I am engaged with Freud on *The Interpretation of Dreams* of which I have heard talk. I think it must suffer very severely even in the substance of the argument from translation, but it is interesting. Ladies should be warned not to tell very innocent sounding dreams in public. An umbrella, unlike its behaviour in day life, generally is an instrument capable of begetting offspring. And going upstairs — well — there you are. The remoteness of the pictures from what Freud says they mean is amazing. He is a doctor, I think of great experience, and I don't doubt knows what he is talking about, but his statements and arguments in the translation, it seems to me, have to be taken a good deal on faith.

I also picked up along with him two others when I last went to Boston. *Echalote et ses Amants* by Jeanne Landre, I suppose the authoress's real name, a woman who practises the most modern directness of speech, but I have read only a few chapters. It is rather base and not lewd, whereas in such works I prefer the opposite. I don't care much about pocky Montmartrians, but this seems clear and very likely well observed. In a month more I hope to be a gentleman of cultivation, ready to give a light touch to the latest philosophy and to take the dust from the tongues of the last hatched butterflies of literature and art. I have forgotten my work which already is far behind.

Do you ever read Santayana? I thought his last book *Winds of Doctrine* delightful; and he ran a rapier through Bergson in a way that made it at the same time a porous plaster to my back.

All my compliments to your ladies.

Yours ever,

O. H. Holmes

Beverly Farms

Sept. 2, 1914

Dear Einstein :

We are only less anxious than you, and I think there is no doubt that the general hope of the country is the same as yours. The German Ambassador is loud in his complaints; but I should think had done, or rather, must have done his cause more harm than good by his talk. The assumption of an innocent air and saying the war was forced on them do not seem to fit the facts.

Everybody seems to be in trouble over there. I had a letter from a lady saying that she and her mother received no remittance and were hard up, and that their Hotel at Cadenabbia was talking of closing as no one could pay. I am conscious of a heartache underneath, but it hasn't prevented my reading some philosophy.

To my shame I never had read the *Nicomachean Ethics*, and I was surprised what a seed book it was — the foundations of stoicism, the formula of equality, doctrines of law that have shaped English discussion, and even the ideas in our Massachusetts Constitution that I used ignorantly to attribute to John Adams, 'that this may be a government of laws and not of men.'

After that came Descartes, Berkeley, Ricardo, and Malthus; much to my profit. I was delighted with Malthus and his quiet, English, unemphatic way of expressing penetrating thought over which a modern German sociologist or Matthew Arnold would have cackled for half a volume. But men don't believe what they don't want to, and humbugs that he exploded a century ago still live in the mouths of the politicians and labor leaders.

Various lighter works have amused me, but nothing new that I can recall. We were lucky and pleased to get some Alsatian humorous illustrations, and then *Mon Village* and *L'Histoire d'Alsace* par l'Oncle Hansi for which I believe the artist is now in prison.

I ought to tell you that an intelligent ex-Secretary of mine who had some business in Washington is reported to me as saying that he found Bryan knew more and was more efficient than all the rest, which from a strong anti-Bryan man is worth noting.

I am afraid my talk on other matters will seem to you unreal and empty, but if I don't speak of them I shall be reduced to ejaculations. It is not heartlessness that enables me to keep on thinking on abstract matters but simply an avoidance of futility. If men die so shall I. It is not a sufficient reason for not using one's time. But I think sadly and almost constantly of you all and of this march of Tamerlaine. If he can subdue civilization we must make over many notions.

Best remembrances to your wife.

Ever sincerely yours,
O. W. Holmes

Supreme Court of the United States, Washington, D.C.

Oct. 12, 1914

Dear Einstein :

If one could forget the war for a moment in the beginning of our term today your letter would be enough to bring back one's feelings in the most poignant form. I grieve for you all, and have a heartache underneath even when I am thinking of other things. Poor, dear, little Midge, if I may borrow the name in talking to you. I hate to think of suffering beginning so early for her.

As to the bearing of German success upon us, I don't know enough to feel convinced that it will be worse than the possible effects of Russian ascendancy. My sympathies are determined without regard to a calculation of relative advantages or disadvantages, although in national matters it may be that they should come first. At least I am so uncertain on that point that I leave it out of my account. I believe in 'my country right or wrong', and next to my country my crowd, and England is my crowd. I earnestly long to see her keep on top, and yet I shall grieve if, as I hope, Germany is crushed. I suppose the war was inevitable, and yet whatever the event, it fills me with sorrow, disinterested sorrow, apart from its effect upon us and from my personal sympathy with England.

But it shows us that classes as well as nations that mean to be in the saddle have got to be ready to kill to keep their seat; and that the notion that all that remained for the civilized world was to sit still, converse, and be comfortable was humbug. It even makes one wonder whether Flinders Petrie's rather inadequately backed up conception of cycles, say of a thousand years, for civilization to rise and fall, is going to come true for now. I don't mean that I believe it. While the trouble is on we always exaggerate its magnitude and import, as, indeed, I suspect you exaggerate the bloodiness of the fighting. My impression has been that, although a good many men have been killed and wounded because of the great number engaged, tested by the proportion of regimental losses (killed and wounded, by official reports) it has not been very severe. But my knowledge is nothing, only a conjecture from occasional figures.

I had to stop here to go to Court, see McReynolds sworn in *vice* Lurton, deceased, and make an annual call on the President. I have the impression that he has gained with the country. The war withdrew attention from Mexico, the death of his wife brought him sympathy when he kept on at his work, and I suppose that even the drooling business of suggesting prayers for peace meant votes from Methodists and Baptists. As I was saying to someone, prayers are like nettlerash — anything from heat to champagne may bring them out.

I was pleased to be told by a man who had seen the German Ambassador that he had changed his note very much and was nearer to talking peace than of going to Paris. But I should think that this would have to be fought nearer a finish than it is now. It seems as if Russia was going to be more of a factor than at least I realize it to have been so far.

If you know of a regiment that authentically has lost in killed and wounded (missing not counted) a quarter of its number, I should like to know it. If one has lost a half it is entitled to speak of a very bloody fight. Except in exceptional circumstances I think the improved weapons mean smaller losses. The great ones used to come when troops stood within a few paces letting into one another. To some of my English friends I can write on other themes, but with your letter before me it seems impossible.

Dear me, from the time of the Civil War to now it seems to me that some great anxiety has hung over life.

Affectionate remembrances to your two.

Ever yours,

O. W. Holmes

Washington, D.C.

Dec. 10, 1914

Dear Einstein :

Your welcome letter makes me sympathize with your grounds for sadness ; but I suppose that on the whole you are glad to compromise on Tweeddale's wound, especially if it keeps him from returning to the field.

I am in such a patch of things to be attended to that, as I have warned you heretofore, I am no good for a correspondent in winter time.

Some of our young men here write books well worth reading : Croly, *Progressive Democracy* ; Lippmann, *Drift & Mastery* ; but they seem to go more into social questions than aesthetics or philosophy. I take great pleasure in the company of such as I see.

Your account of losses is striking, but being of losses in the campaign doesn't give an impression of the severity of particular actions. The 2nd. Army Corps during the campaign from the Wilderness to Petersburg, *ex rel.* Walker, the Chief of Staff, starting with 12 Brigades and 25,000 men had lost 23 Brigade Commanders killed and wounded, and 25,000 men when we got to Petersburg.

I have just received your article within a day or two, and it lies on my table, but I have had no time to read it yet. I shall before a week has gone.

We were fairly quiet here. I believe the Ambassadors, or some of them, won't dine at a house to which those on the other side have been invited on a previous occasion, which seems pressing it rather far. I have received communications from several other learned and more or less eminent Germans since Gierke [10] wrote. You see the official impulse, but still the tone is just as convinced and just as noble as that of any Englishman could be. It makes my heart ache to think of them being beaten, as I hope they will be. And they are rather cocky about German achievements. I do not know that they are any worse than the stupidly arrogant English you often see, but they are a little more remote from us.

I am glad you are writing. Keep at it. My affectionate remembrances to your ladies.

Yours ever,
O. W. Holmes

10 Westbourne Street, W.

27 Dec. 1914

Dear Justice Holmes:

Your welcome letter finds me in London where we have taken a house for the winter at 3 Seymour Street, Portman Square, and meanwhile are staying with my niece whose husband was lately killed. Gifford [11] comes up for his medical examination Tuesday but I don't think he will be passed as he still is unfit. Another nephew, however, is leaving for the front the same day much to our anxiety. The war seems to have dried up all other thoughts for one can think of nothing else. The odd thing is that people impress one as more nervous and panicky and gullible here than in France. Around Edinburgh everyone was jumpy fearing invasion and all along the East coast I hear it is even worse. The spy mania is widespread and there is no radical who isn't supposed to be one. But if war 'rend bête et méchant', as Flaubert wrote in '70, it brings out

[10] Otto Friedrich von Gierke (1841-1921); eminent German jurist. A story about German propaganda published in the London *Times* of October 23, 1914, on page 6 (more than a week before Holmes received his letter from Gierke) containing an extract of a long letter from Gierke to Holmes dated September 26, 1914, of which an English lady was purported to have received a copy from an acquaintance in Berlin, indicated that the official impulse behind the letter was not unimportant. See *The Holmes-Pollock Letters*, Vol. 1, pp. 222 and 223.

[11] William Hay carried the second Tweeddale title, Earl of Gifford, from birth.

I

fine sides as well. I admire the calm courage of the women who have already suffered and the lack of militarism of even professional soldiers who frankly don't like it but of course want to do their duty. One poor chap who hobbles in here on crutches very often to play bridge was describing the fight at Villers-Cotterets where only a country road separated them from the Germans, and where he had to argue with a few of his men (the Grenadiers) who were inclined to straggle, that they had far better be shot by Germans than by their own people.

Some day when all is over I suppose that people will feel thrilled at having lived through it, but now that the first excitement is gone the dull monotony of the background, which is all I have seen at first hand, most impresses me, and from what I have heard it is only exceeded by the dull monotony of the front. Gifford came back most impressed by the absence of all the romance of war.

The smart thing here now is to pretend one is a bit deaf from the shrieking of the shells. There are comic glimpses like that of Colonel Seely (late Minister of War) who demands a V.C. for his chauffeur and, when the reason is asked, replied that he had accompanied him wherever he went. Then there is the story of the first gifts sent out with a painted card 'from Mary Regina and the ladies of the Empire', and the Subaltern who said he thought he knew most of the Empire ladies but who the hell was Mary R. And I like the perfectly true tale of a young English officer who after delivering a message under heavy fire to a French general was kissed by him on both cheeks, and could only find to say, '*Doucement, Mon Général, doucement*'.

Then there are the rumors: whispered rumors of battleships sunk, or army corps landed, impending surprises, or secret explanations of victory and defeat, intercepted wireless, and all the [?] apparatus of occult influences and female spydom. I think of Seward who answered an indiscreet question with, 'Madame, if I did not know I would tell you', for I suppose that the same things have happened in every war.

I am enclosing a letter regarding a dispatch quoting lengthily from the 'Washington Post'. Do you know the reason for its anglophobe attitude, and does it still belong to Mrs. Dewey's family? I shall try to do a little newspaper writing on diplomatic matters for I cannot remain inactive, and the XVIth Century seems too dead in times like these to wade through its texts.

Helen and Midge both send their love and all New Year wishes to you both.

Ever yours,
L. E.

Washington, D.C.

Jan. 15, 1915

Dear Einstein :

Many thanks for your delightful letter and your sensible communication to the paper. Incidentally I am pleased to have verified by what you tell the thing I said in one of my speeches, that war while you are at it is horrible and dull. Other letters corroborate it ; but I have had a copy of one that gives a different impression. It was from the eldest son of Lady Desborough [12] and tells of going out, creeping out to the edge of the German trenches and potting Germans on three successive occasions exactly as if it were stalking deer. I didn't know which to admire most, the young man who wrote with such almost impersonal *bonhomie* and *sangfroid* or the mother to whom a son could write in that way of getting leave to hang his life on a hair. I take off my hat and shut up.

It seems as if one must apologize for seeking amusement here, yet last night I went to a dull play and coming away we fell in with some young people and we took them to the New Willard and gave them a little modest blowout with a bottle of champagne, which in these days is a solemnity. It is pleasant to play the benevolent old uncle to young ones who are working for their living but have the spirit of larkiness.

I don't get much chance to read. I believe that is my usual refrain, and when I have the law cramp I don't do much in the way of outside ideas, and my preoccupation, unlike yours, is not interesting to write about. I am immensely

[12] See page 147, note 53.

interested myself, but hardly could expect you to be, for instance, in the question whether a District Court of the United States could levy a tax to pay defaulted county bonds on which a judgment had been recovered when the county officers refuse to do their duty. I can but repeat that anything is interesting that we understand and that calls out the energy of our personality.

I am feeling the sadness of age in seeing the leaves drop off. This morning brings me news of the death of a somewhat remarkable woman whom I knew and with whom I have had an occasional lark in former years. But, dear me, I have seen so many die that it seems as if I had lost something of my capacity for feeling.

I hope you will keep on writing. All that you have done in the diplomatic direction seems to be good and useful and wise. And let me express a sneaking hope that Lord Tweeddale may be just incapacitated enough not to be able to return. I hate to think of the anxiety of the little one, to whom I send my love.

By the bye, you leave it uncertain how I am to address my letter. I will fire two shots, or rather, put on an alternative address.

Do you know Alfred Zimmern? He wrote an admirable book, *The Greek Commonwealth*, and lately sent me a companion volume, *The War and Democracy*, to which he contributed.

I revere the people who seem to live in an atmosphere of moral exaltation, but I can't believe that mankind has changed much in these last fifty years. And, while I often feel like a worm when I read of men whose dominant motive is love for their kind, I console myself by thinking that most of the great work done in the world comes from a different type. I don't believe the gospel of love as the last or chief thing; and yet I revere it. I hope that at least there are other roads to salvation for temperaments to which that one is barred. Temperament, I read in the 'Sun' the other day, depends on the thyroid, the pituitary, and other ductless glands, if I am not misled by memory into talking nonsense about what I don't understand.

Please give my warmest remembrances to your wife also.

Yours ever,

O. W. Holmes

3 Seymour Street, Portman Square, W.

January 31, 1915

Dear Justice Holmes:

Your letter finds me like a gipsy about to pack and move. We had just settled here comfortably for the winter when a wire arrived two days ago from Bryan saying I was urgently needed at Constantinople and would I go as Special Agent. Only the day before I had been regretting my lack of active occupation in times like these and thinking of driving some ambulance. And now that it comes I cannot say that I look forward to it with pleasure or, in spite of the interest, without some misgivings — for my wife insists on going with me — and there may be trouble, whether through revolution or through scuttling; the latter I dread the most. It will be a wrench too leaving the family here, though Gifford is probably not going back. The medical board pronounced him unfit for two months, and then ordered light duty. But another nephew is in the Irish Guards who are now fighting. In one recent engagement the battalion lost 16 officers and 683 men, and the other day the Scots Guards and Grenadiers each lost the one seventy five percent the other sixty percent of their effectives — the trenches they occupied were blown up. One only sees greater losses ahead for the stiffest fighting will hardly come before April. The English will, I fancy, have over a million men at the front by that time as yet only drafts from the new armies have been sent over.

People here are very angry with us and the public is in ugly mood — full of irritation and suspicion and excitability. They especially resent our not protesting about Belgium, and only waiting, as they phrase, till our pockets are affected. The Government here means, I fancy, to be as conciliatory as they can, but they have to face a public only too pleased with a stiff attitude. Personally I think nothing as yet has passed of any intrinsic importance except this wretched ship purchase bill.[13] Irrespective of its other merits or drawbacks I cannot conceive

---

[13] An administrative measure designed by President Wilson to defeat the exorbitant charges demanded by the private owners. It was opposed for very different reasons both by the latter and by the Allies, England and France, who were then at war with Germany.

how Wilson can urge a measure likely to have permanent con-
sequences to cope with a purely temporary situation. But the
ways of Washington are like those of providence.

I have bought Zimmern and Croly and Lippman and others
but am without time to read anything beyond the papers.
They are all consuming nowadays even with censored news.
At Constantinople we shall be cut off from everything save
what the Germans allow to filter through since the place is
entirely in their hands.

I wish I could see some glimmer of the end but it is all too
far away, and on neither side do I realize where the elements
are which will bring it to a finish other than the slow pressure
of exhaustion. Kitchener,[14] I understand, thinks it will be
over by next winter. Perhaps if the Russians do their job,
but the latter doubtless say the same of the Western Allies.
My hope lies in Roumania and Italy. But even if Austria is
crushed Germany at bay will be a hard nut. I heard Kitchener
the other day make a speech at the opening of the Lords. He
disappointed me, not because of the commonplaceness of his
secretary-written speech, but his delivery did not give the
impression of great decision. Still his work as an organizer
has, I believe, been admirable. They sent eighty thousand
men to France last week and from now on, I gather, the army
there will be continuously increased. It is ticklish work with
German submarines in the Channel. Many people here are
very nervous over the Zeppelins, and the dark streets are most
dangerous. War is better in books than in reality, especially
now when the bright uniforms give way to drab — a war of
the unknown by the unseen, as one soldier termed it.

Many wishes.

Ever yours,

L. E.

My address had better be
   Villa Schifanoia,
      Via Boccaccio,
         Florence

[14] Horatio Herbert Kitchener, Earl Kitchener of Khartoum and of Broome
(1850–1916) ; British Field-Marshal and Secretary of State for War from August
6, 1914, until his death June 5, 1916, when the vessel which was carrying him to
Russia struck a mine off the Orkney and Shetland islands and sank.

Supreme Court of the United States, Washington, D.C.

February 14, 1915

Dear Einstein :

You have me at a disadvantage, a double one ; for you can talk interestingly about the war, and I can't ; and you know that your letter will reach me, whereas as to mine, I don't.

The only thing I have to tell outside my routine and apart from the law is of reading a new book by Bertrand Russell. But you don't care much for philosophy ; and, so far as I can judge from the first reading through, B.R. thinks he has the tail of the cosmos round a stump and is expounding a new true and only genuine philosophy, dispensing with all that has been done, thought, or written hitherto. I hardly see it, and am plugging on much the same as heretofore.

Many thanks for your letter to the papers. I revere your ease on themes upon which I am not at home.

I am delighted at the recognition of your value, and to have it come from Bryan. I feel sure that there can be very few who have the needed qualities that you possess, and I am not surprised to hear the country wants you now. I hope it will keep doing it, and that this is but a beginning.

I heard a newspaper man this p.m. giving out the opinion that the Germans were drawing to the end of their resources. It may be so, but I am skeptical of anyone's knowing it to be, as I am of outrages and pretty much anything else. I suppose the foresight of the Germans is exaggerated among other things, but the news today that the English trawlers are finding petroleum or gasolene or something of the sort at the bottom of the sea off the English coast stored there for future use by the German submarines is almost too good to be true. I mean by good amazing examples of preparation.

In view of my uncertainty and of having little to tell you that will amuse you at this moment I confine myself to this brief acknowledgment, but hope it won't discourage you from writing again.

Yours ever,

O. W. Holmes

American Embassy, Constantinople

March 14, 1915

Dear Justice Holmes :

Your letter has just reached me here and I hasten to answer it by tomorrow's pouch. We had an interesting enough journey through darkest Europe to reach here ; no great hardships but formalities and petty inconveniences smoothed over by my paraphernalia of official documents I carried and complicated by a French maid who accompanied my wife and whose passage through Austria and into Turkey required special dispensations. One has rather the sensation nowadays that Europe is on the operating table with all its ligaments cut. Trains and sleeping cars — those symbols of internationalism — stop at frontiers and, save for diplomats, the ordinary rank and file are searched on departure. Even in London tales exist of nude backs rubbed with lemon juice on the platform of Victoria lest they conceal secret writing. Half the world believes the other half to be spies and that in every land till I am sure I shall become one by suggestion. Yes, the dark ages have come again with bestiology as the highest science, and the tales of travellers from Cathay are not more extraordinary than what everyone believes of neighboring lands. In London we were firmly persuaded that Austria was at its last gasp — the hunger stricken population was rushing around in mad despair. But in Vienna there were no signs of war save the stale bread, and the streets were crowded with apparently able bodied men who found their duties elsewhere than at the front. Princess Windischgraetz told us solemnly there that Calais would be either English or German, and that Sir Edward Grey had written in his own hand a letter which the German Foreign Office possessed to arrange the murder of Casement ! [15]

Of course everyone we left expected a massacre to welcome our arrival, but even here there are practically no signs of

---

[15] Roger David Casement (1864–1916) ; retired British Consular Agent who was tried and executed for treason after sailing to Ireland in a German submarine in connection with an abortive rebellion to achieve Irish independence during the war.

war. Life is very much as usual though the allied fleet are daily bombarding the Dardanelles and half the population would be glad to see them here. All preparations for flight have been made by the Government, but meanwhile one sees them dining merrily at the Club and drinking champagne as if all were for the best — it is the modern form of theological disputation. My nephew lately wrote me from the trenches in Flanders that war seemed to him a ludicrous tragedy and it is much the same here. It seems like picnicking amid ruins which may fall on one at any moment. If only the Philistines were crushed!

It is hard writing at this desk with the Golden Horn beneath and the great mosques cutting the skyline opposite to realize that we are at the last gasp. I cannnot see it and yet I believe it. '*Credo quia altera non est possible*', and I feel sorry for these poor wretches who have smashed their own destinies so completely. A German officer (the place is, of course, full of them) was saying to me the other day: 'The Turks are no longer good soldiers. They have lost their military virtues, but they have one great quality in which they still lead — they know how to suffer.' Suffer they have and will till relief comes, but it is still far off. They could have kept out of war and they entered hypnotized by golden promises and the vanity of former conquest. One man dragged them in — Enver,[16] and the German Ambassador, Wangenheim, the latter an energetic, active, nervous, worn personality attentive to every detail, leaving nothing too slight for his attention, holding the Turks in rein and not fearing lest they elude his grasp. I rather fancy Germany will rue the day when she drove Turkey into war. It may prove a boomerang, and personally I believe it will. The old pot was too cracked for service. I feel as if I were the last of the Byzantines.

Ever yours,
L. E.

If you will send any letter for me to the State Department it will be put into the pouch for here — a much surer means.

---

[16] Enver Pasha (1881–1922); Minister of War, and virtual dictator of Turkey until the German collapse in 1918.

Supreme Court of the United States, Washington, D.C.

April 10, 1915

Dear Einstein :

Your delightful letter of March 14 arrived this morning.
You remember the French tombstone where the widow
inscribed 'I follow thee', and her own stone was dated thirty
years later. Someone wrote upon it, 'She took her time'.

I am afraid that our doings here would strike you as
Pedlingtonian in view of the interests by which you are surrounded; and before I say anything about them I will repeat
my satisfaction that when there is work to be done the Government was sensible enough to turn to a man who knows his
business. The policy seems to be to give a job to friends and
to help their incompetence by aid from outside. However I
know nothing of what your function is or of the competence or
incompetence of the regular appointees. I must confess, however, that if I may judge by what I see here my opinion of the
performance of one of its most important functions by the
Administration is not high. Of course there are exceptions —
'Even Shadwell deviates into sense.' (I am not sure I get
the name right.)

I have been in my usual routine. Some extras to relieve
others; a dissent as to which I feel a good deal, and which
seems to have delayed the prevailing opinion, as it went over
last Monday for modification, and I have heard no more about
it; [17] a little article [18] written at the request of my friend
Wigmore in which I turn out some of my philosophical chest-
nuts that I have written a good many times, but not printed;
all dotted with interviews with the dentist and some coughing
at night to be expected about this time. *Voilà.*

My events are all internal. They consist for the most part
in thinking of new formulas, e.g. to rest upon a formula is a
slumber that, prolonged, means death.

And meantime the spring is upon us and the magnolias are
beginning to be clothed in pink and white. Nothing more
marks one's increase in age than the swiftness with which the

[17] *Frank* v. *Mangum*, 237 U.S. 309 (1915); see *The Holmes–Pollock Letters*, Vol. 1,
p. 226.
[18] *Ideals and Doubts*, 10 Illinois Law Review 1 (1915).

terms of Court, the years, rush by. An amiable friend of mine, a lady who doesn't like growing old, suggested that one couldn't judge whether one was keeping the pace or not, a cheerful reflection for a veteran. But, unless in case of a sudden loss of wits, it seems to me that one ought to be able to tell with some accuracy. If we are willing to look facts in the face we can criticize ourselves better than others can. The turn of my reflections indicates that recently (March 8) I passed my seventy-fourth birthday.

Of one thing I can be certain, that whether my work is good or bad at least it is rapid, which I regard as an important element in decisions. I think that to let cases hang for months after they have been argued is discreditable, and that at least has never happened through me.

But enough of this. In the way of reading, apart from some philosophical matters in the watches of the night, I have lately kept by my bedside *Le Drâme de la Vie* [19] by Restif de la Bretonne, whose *M. Nicolas* interested me ages ago. It is very queer to read the bogus XVIIIth Century sensibility, like Greuze's innocence, the note of the coming revolution. But perhaps above all interesting is this feeling that notwithstanding all the talks and facts of tyranny and oppression and what not the poor were happy. That is all Münsterberg indicated and got pitched into for it, that there are waves and currents of feeling. Epidemics form opinion not corresponding to the situation so that probably there is more *feeling* of being wronged and unhappiness today among the poor than when they had a better case.

I must away to our Saturday Conference. When I fire at a bird on the wing, like you, it must be a snap shot. This is enough to tell you about myself and to send my love and compliments to you and yours. It seems as if all the issues of civilization were in the balance nowadays, and perhaps we are destined to shake down to a lower level than the one that has given delight to your life and mine. But I am not without hope.

Ever sincerely yours,
O. W. Holmes

[19] *Le Drame de la vie, contenant un homme tout entier: pièce en 13 actes des ombres, et en 10 pièces régulières* par Restif de la Bretonne, 5 vols. (1793) ; perhaps the unique representative of the literary genre of autobiographical drama as well as being among the longest plays ever written (1,252 pages). *Le Drame de la vie* is an excellent source for eighteenth-century conversation.

Constantinople

May 11, 1915

Dear Justice Holmes :

Your lines came from a quieter atmosphere than the one we are breathing here, and they speak of books and humanities and all the things which make life worth living, yet which are not life. Here we are rather in the struggle-for-existence stage, though I can not bring myself to realize it. I think of Wilde's *mot* that any fool can make history but it takes a wise man to write it. I suppose we are traversing a historic phase, though in principle I agree with Wells who taxes Americans with taking too aristocratic a view of the calendar.

At the Dardanelles only a few hours from here they have been fighting for more than a fortnight. Nearly twenty thousand wounded are already here, yet we have hardly any idea of what is going on there. Here in town there is almost a reign of terror ; Armenians, Greeks, monks, and nuns are arrested wholesale. We have our hands full looking after our *protégés* when and how we can, but it is not easy. Occasionally absurdities crop up to cheer one's existence. Thus the police come and seize leaden toy soldiers at the local *Bon Marché* and the next day ask the director to sign a paper in which he acknowledges that French uniforms and supplies had been seized on his premises. Another tale I have just been told also amused me. There are two English submarines in Marmora now. One of them called at Rodosto the other day, having put up the Turkish flag, and the Commandant believing the officers to be Germans gave them all they asked for in petrol and provisions. But most of our homely tales are of suffering and misery — gratuitous, intentional suffering — till one wonders if there is any order or justice in the world. The Councillor of the German Embassy just came up to me to speak of the 'Lusitania' and to expound the legal view — damn it. The Germans can see no view other than their own and believe that with a few arguments they can talk away the lives sent to the bottom. The whole thing is too sickening to dwell on, but I hope there is some red blood in Wilson's veins. We shall probably linger in ignorance here for weeks since nothing percolates through save what the Germans want and news is travestied in every garb.

I suppose there is no end to human misery and the mills of the Gods have gone on a strike. One's head swims in the moral fog ahead. I tell everyone that as neutrals we have become diplomatic eunuchs, but I at least chafe in my restlessness.

I take up these lines where I left them last night for it is out of the question here to have more than ten minutes uninterruptedly of one's own, and yet life is no other than it was. Breakfast is the same, the sunshine is the same, even the bridge table is the same. Do you recall Charles Lamb's essay on the Middle Ages when everyone was supposed to be groping in the blackness of the night? Here, if one walked any afternoon in the *Grande Rue*, nothing seems amiss. Even the days when the Russians bombard the Bosphorus only ten miles off the crowd has the same indifferent look.

One must admire the German organization here, and now they have persuaded a somewhat docile but obstinate people to fight their battles. They certainly have a magnificent optimism and confidence. The tragedy lies in the same confidence existing everywhere — London and Paris, Berlin and Vienna. There's the rub. I wish though that on the German side it were accompanied by less systematic cruelty. Here they even object to our relieving the lot of a few English prisoners captured from a stranded submarine! *Deutschland über Allah!*

Our best messages to Mrs. Holmes

from yours always,

L. E.

Beverly Farms, Massachusetts

July 8, 1915

Dear Einstein:

Your letter of May 11 arrived this morning. Not a promising interval for a correspondence, and I feel so doubtful of this even reaching you that I shall make it little more than a bulletin. That is about all I am capable of, for, though I have

been here a week and one day (no more), I have had so many
details of business to attend to that as yet I haven't profited
much by my vacation except in the way of more sleep.

I did read a book the other day by John Dewey, (eminent
philosopher), *German Philosophy and Politics*, which shows in a
striking way the parallelism between German speculation and
practices and conditions incredible elsewhere. As he says you
would often find a Cavalry General deriving the need of
military preparation from philosophy and basing himself on
Kant's *Critique*. I have also been reading aloud and translating
A. France's *La Révolte des Anges* with a good deal of amusement,
more than I formerly got from him, though still I don't like
him except on literary themes. Unlike many French books I
think his are hurt by his indecencies. They seem dragged in
to make the book sell. I felt so as to '*Les Dieux ont Soif*' and
do here again. Also I have begun a German book on '*Soziologie des Rechts*.' [20] But I am rather slow with German, and
most of my time here so far has been taken up with writing
checks and affairs as I said. We didn't adjourn till late, all
pretty tired with the work, which when the weather is hot in
Washington is rather trying. Since I have been here it has
rained a good deal of the time (and is raining now) so that
there hasn't been much chance for outdoor doings, but as I
don't play outdoors any more than indoor games I don't mind,
except that it affects one's spirits.

You speak of the German organization where you are.
Certainly they have given the world an object lesson; and
taking them and the tendency of the trusts and labor unions
into account it looks as if whatever happens the old go-as-you-
please days were over and that everything and everybody had
got to be organized. It is less charming than the England or
even America that we have known; but I don't spend much
time in prophesying and, having decided that I'm not God,
don't lie awake at night with cosmic worries, as no doubt I have
remarked before.

As to our neutrality and behaviour as such I confess that I
should be willing to put our dignity in my pocket for a time,
if thereby I could secure an Army, Navy, and equipment that
would restore it. A nation's dignity is all right as soon as it is

[20] *Grundelung der Soziologie des Rechts* by Eugen Ehrlich (1913).

strong.   What the administration thinks or does on the matter I don't know, but I believe there are some signs of the country's waking up.   We don't all believe that the walls of Jericho will tumble if Mr. Bryan blows a blast of words or sings a psalm. I keep in my corner and do my work as hard and as well as I can without worrying as to what is to come of it all; that is not my affair.

I believe that your wife is with you.   Please lay my homage at her feet, and remember me to the younger charmer when you write.

Yours as ever,
O. W. Holmes

Beverly Farms

Sept. 11, 1915

Dear Einstein:
    Your welcome but saddening letter has come today, or rather last night.   I too, often have thought of Talleyrand's remark about France before the Revolution; [21] but I also reflect that usually things seem bigger and more ominous while they are going than afterwards, and that even I may live to regard this war also as an episode.   At all events there is no use in my talking about it to you.   Of course it has made the heart of my vacation melancholy, but so far as might be I have turned my mind to other things.

I forget how far I had got when I last wrote; probably I had finished the readings on the philosophy of law and the history of institutions that took me through July.   Perhaps also I had skimmed through Plato's *Republic*, which amused me and interested me by suggesting some reflections that I may have uttered and would risk repeating.   Since then I have browsed. I read a few books of the *Odyssey* with a pleasure that I don't often get from the old.   Like Dante, though in a less degree, the song of the words added to their sense seems sometimes to open a road to paradise.   And there are delightful human touches, and interesting suggestions of ancient institutions;

---

[21] See *Mémoires pour servir à l'histoire de mon temps* by Guizot, 8 vols. (1858–67), Vol. 1, p. 6: 'M. de Talleyrand me disait un jour: "Qui n'a pas vécu dans les années voisines de 1789 ne sait pas ce que c'est que le plaisir de vivre"'.

but I have had enough for the moment and have turned for amusement elsewhere. Rémy de Gourmont never seems to me profound and not often first rate, but some of his critical remarks strike one as instructive or just. I was pleased to see him repeat what I have often insisted on, that the secret of the success of a poet, (he says I should say of any *Littérateur*), is in the accord between his sensibility and the general sensibility of his generation. There is a law of fashion even in matters of pure intellect; witness the way they work totemism nowadays in archeological circles.

Do you like, despise, or amiably tolerate the man of reputation made in England strictly for home use and not for export such as Jowett or Stanley (the Dean)? I was just reading Stanley about Canterbury; [22] harmlessly pleasant until he gets the British note of 'our undoubting confidence in the superiority of Englishmen to all the world' when he almost makes one glad that they are paying for it now, not that I could be really glad, of course. But as, in the circumstances, I think the administration has been quite right to keep out of the fight I have to remember my affection for individuals and have my sympathies neutralized by their taunts and interestedly rotten talk, as of those entitled to point out the requirements of honor from a superior point of view. (There was a funny bit of chaff in Punch, Sept. 1st., about our neutrality with a picture of two chaps singing in a music hall).

At this moment I have some chapters of a '*Life of John Marshall*' that my neighbour, ex-Senator Beveridge, is writing to look over. They begin well.

I suppose that I am getting to be, am, one of the last leaves on the tree; but I am not made aware of the passing of time except in small secondary ways, and expect to return to my work at the beginning of next month in good condition for it.

I am sorry for your isolation and painful surroundings. I was thought unpatriotic once when at home with a wound for saying that war was an organized bore; but I am afraid my opinion has not changed.

Please give my kindest remembrances to your wife.

Yours ever,

O. W. Holmes

[22] Probably *Memorials of Canterbury* (1854) by Arthur Penrhyn Stanley.

American Legation, Sofia

November 15, 1915

Dear Justice Holmes :

Your letter of September 11 which I have just received has followed me twice across Europe and then back again.

I left Constantinople in mid-September disgusted with what went on, and as I was powerless to do anything there was no urgent reason to induce me to remain. A fortnight later I was at Yester, for it takes two weeks now to traverse Europe where once three days sufficed. We passed a happy week there in a family reunion. My nephew who had been shot through the stomach last May when two of the Guards battalions lost 800 men by machine gun fire in four minutes, was there and well again after his close shave. Then after six days there and while actually grouse shooting on the Lammermoors a messenger brought me a wire from Washington asking me to leave immediately for here to take charge,[23] for we have British interests to look after as well as our own. So once more I packed up feeling like a modern Ulysses. I left Helen in Scotland for she was too fagged after her long journey and needed rest. I hope she will join me later. I have come here alone.

I hardly know what to say about this place. There is little picturesqueness here save that of the Macedonian peasants, and little or nothing that is old, but the air is good (in the East one always scents the air) and the location fine. I lack the journalist's faculty of rapid and sensational impressions. Things impress themselves on me as strata of shapeless feeling difficult to visualize in descriptive form but which, like a spider's web, I spin or unravel from already formed secretion. And here all I have ever known about the new East stands out as a kind of pattern which throws the shadow of its design. The streets are spotless, (at least those in the center) the new houses are western, and there is a certain intense ambition to leave the Orient as far behind as possible ; yet it stands out and stands out too without its graces and its poetry and the atmosphere we associate with it in our mind's eye.

Here as elsewhere there is the oppression of war. The

[23] Einstein was appointed United States Diplomatic Representative in Sofia in October 1915.

K

whole of Europe is now betrenched and bewired, from Edinburgh to Sofia one is challenged by sentries, and only at Berne, in old Berne, in spite of a sentinel pacing in front of the hotel, I had the sensation of peace. At Sofia we hear the cannon in the distance, whether British or Bulgar, I do not know. And in the outstreets of the town I have seen Serbian prisoners mending the roads, while the hospitals as elsewhere are full. In one of these I saw in neighboring beds a French prisoner and a Bulgar. Each had bayoneted the other, but when all was done the Bulgar refused to leave the Frenchman for whom he had conceived friendship and in spite of various attempts to separate them insisted on being taken to the same hospital and occupying the next bed. Oh what a struggle of the nations is this, and nowhere more so than here in the Balkans and here in Bulgaria with its ambitious Czar.[24] In the Cathedral there is his portrait in mosaic garbed as a Byzantine Emperor and supporting the image of the Cathedral, and still another and greater portrait as the upholder of the temporal power with sword and cross opposite that of the two patron Saints Cyril and Methodius. It is said that his robes of an ancient Bulgarian Czar are already prepared in which he expects to be crowned Emperor of the Balkans.

The quiet activity of Washington seems far away. Have you many interesting cases ahead of you, or have you time for your memoirs? I earnestly hope the latter and that you will enrich the letters of the land as well as the law. I have little idea of what is going on at home though my interest is always green. But papers do not yet come through and mails are scarce.

My best compliments to Mrs. Holmes.

Ever yours,

L. E.

Washington, D.C.

January 1, 1916

Dear Einstein :

A happy New Year to you. It seems so doubtful whether a letter will catch up with your nomad steps that I

---

[24] Czar Ferdinand I (1861–1948) ; second son of Prince August of Saxe-Coburg and Princess Clémentine of Bourbon-Orléans, daughter of Louis-Philippe.

shall do little more than repeat to you what pleasure your letters always give. But for the hope of a return I hardly should venture to write. For while you are within the sound of the guns my external adventures are parochial and my internal ones so much confined to the law that they wouldn't interest you.

This New Year's day, it being rainy, I have given up the customary calls and have allowed myself an unwonted, delightful, dozy hour over the *Print Collector's Quarterly*, published by the Boston Art Museum. When I was a boy I used to collect what my small pocket money would allow. I knew all the old portfolios in Boston where I got one or two good things and more rubbish. Other portfolios containing what my father bought when a student in Paris were my starting point and gave me the first breath of a different atmosphere from that of the Boston of my youth. I remember the first station that was put up and conditions that recall Mr. Arnold's 'Unutterable Ennui' of the Middle Ages. Later I was thick with Theis [25] who made the Gray Collection and got me a few things that I could afford, mainly Dürer woodcuts. An old collector's feeling that I have discouraged in later years comes up as I read the pleasing details of this or that it may be quite second rate producer, like W. Hollar. I should like to make a small collection: Dürer, Rembrandt, some engravings by the pupils of Rubens, an etching or two of Vandyck's, one or two of the great French portraits and so on. Of Dürer I have perhaps enough. The Faust that I used to think a striking Rembrandt you don't see attributed to him in these days, though I wonder who has *droit* etc. I have little or nothing of his and almost nothing of the later ones I mention. But one's shell soon begins to feel personal to one, and my library has enough odds and ends to feel mine and not a library in the abstract or, as they are apt to become from too uniform good binding, an architectural adjunct.

I am talking this twaddle just to give you a whiff of difference. I wish that I could make it more vivid by a note of new French books, but on that theme I can't recite. A new psychology book starting from Freud, *The Freudian Wit*, impresses

[25] Louis Theis was curator of the Gray Collection of Engravings, Harvard University from 1862 to 1870.

my young friends of the new Republic rather more than it does me.

Last night my wife and I went to the New Willard to watch in the New Year and to watch the crowd. Dames divided well below the arm, (I think they show to meet the exigency), an agreeable suggestion of deliquescence, decadence, the Roman Empire, etc. and stimulating contacts in which I did not share ; but respectable, not a debauch.

Yours ever,

O. W. Holmes

American Legation, Sofia

3 Feb. 1916

Dear Justice Holmes :

Just this instant I receive your lines of January 1st. with their ever welcome wishes and their gambit of allusions from Durer prints to the New Willard which make me feel like the small boy rubbing his nose against the pastry cook's window. Think that I can see the wild Rhodope range almost from my windows; or, translated into modern terms, although the pavement is good and the electric light plentiful I passed two men lying freshly murdered on the sidewalk the other night going to dine at the Club.

This wretched diplomatic wanderer's life is as much a disease as any other. I hate it and yet would be wretched were I not doing something of the kind just now. But fortunately there is enough to keep busy. I have just had rather an interesting case which has delved me into international law. When the Entente arrested the Consuls of the Central Powers at Salonica these people at once tried reprisals by arresting the French consular official and attempting to get hold of Hurst, the English. But the latter came here to ask my protection, and I gave him asylum. I am living at a hotel kept by a German who since then has tried to eject me several times, while the government sent soldiers, police agents, and various kinds of gentry to get me to give him up. The crux of the

matter came over the hotel corridor, for this is an old fashioned
hotel and the rooms are separated. As natural causes would
make it imperative for Hurst to leave the Legation rooms at
certain times they intended to arrest him in the corridor and
placed soldiers for that purpose. So I wrote to the Prime
Minister that I should regard this as tantamount to a violation
of the Legation and requested him to withdraw his agents in
order to avoid an incident. But for a long while every time
Hurst had to go to the W.C. I used to stand watch outside to
see that the soldiers on duty did not nab him. The thing was
comical and the siege in one form or another lasted over a
month during which I had to send out for his meals, for the
hotel refused to serve them. But yesterday, after I had the
necessary guarantees, I saw him back to his former quarters in
the British Legation. I believe it is the first case of asylum in
Europe, (save for Turkey) in fifty years, and it has also some
other new points. I enclose the copy of a duplicate [26] on the
subject and would much welcome the impression of *Il maestro
di color che sanno* as to the points raised.

British interests are giving me a deal of worry for there are
already some five hundred prisoners to look after and, like a
fine Oriental land, they seem to regard these as a kind of
domestic property and my inquiry into their welfare as an
impertinence. Officially I am not allowed to see them though
in practice I can get at the wounded in the hospitals. But the
old Minister of War, the other day when I went to see him
and remarked that the practice of visiting was current in
Europe now, calmly told me that Bulgaria was unlike any other
country! One storms and fumes here without even getting
a reply, the government is invisible, and notes remain unanswered. I have heard of dollar diplomacy and of secret
diplomacy, but here it is constipated diplomacy.

Just as I write these words the Prime Minister has sent
around to say that he will see me today. It is over two months
since I have been to him.

I have been so nearly packing my trunk on various occasions

---

[26] Documents pertaining to the case of the British Vice-Consul at Sofia are
published in *Papers Relating to the Foreign Relations of the United States, 1916 Supple-
ment, The World War*, United States Government Printing Office, Washington D.C.
(1929) at pp. 825 ff.

of late (including a resignation triply tendered to Washington almost three months ago) that I have never wished Helen to come here, but now since it looks as if I were to stay I shall expect her before long. She is with Marguerite now who awaits a baby and looks forward to an heir.

My homages to Mrs. Holmes.

Ever yours,
Lewis Einstein

Supreme Court of the United States, Washington, D.C.

March 10, 1916

Dear Einstein :

How can a man who has Rhodope in the distance and murdered men in the foreground care for the modest divergondations of the 'Vicar of Wakefield'? Yet if I wrote about public affairs I should at once display my ignorance and be dull. I remember when I was in the army two reliefs were gossiping local letters from my cousin John Morse in Boston and Bryan and Carlton's brimstone matches from the same place. To be sure Johnny Morse wrote much more amusing letters than I could ever hope to do ; but the principle was the same, and I take courage from the remembrance.

My chief event of the last few days has been passing my seventyfifth birthday. I received some very pleasing letters, and the evening before, as the day was Ash Wednesday when Christians, I am told, will not be abroad, we had some few, quiet people in to dine. After they left, as a complete surprise to me, my wife had arranged to have all the young people (relatively young) who come and play with us on Monday afternoons gather here. The first I knew was hearing the house filled with the song of birds, as she had provided them all with bird calls, and there was a little supper and a pleasing bowl of punch. We giggled and made giggle, as Cowper says, till after midnight, and I was really touched and pleased. So that's that. I like the young, and these, at least, seem to be fond of me. We encourage each other.

March 11. I am afraid I can say nothing worth saying on your problem of asylum. I should think you had acted with the discretion and wisdom that I should expect. I am glad that the Government has sense enough to hang on to you. I don't remember when I last wrote; I mean whether it was in recess or before, but probably have had no adventures into literature since.

Did I tell you of meeting Paul Warburg [27] of the Federal Reserve Board? I merely had a short talk after dinner at Mrs. Hanna's, and at that time didn't know, to my shame, exactly what his functions were or more than that he was on some Government Board. But I haven't met anyone for a long time who so hit me where I lived. He gave me new courage; and he seemed to like me. I suppose he is German in his sympathies, and I believe that his brother is high in the German finance; but that doesn't affect one's personal impressions. I called on him a day or two ago, but he had just started with MacAdoo for South America. I saw his wife and found the German Ambassador there. She was very amiable and seems a cultivated and intelligent woman, but of course I was after him.

We have dined out a little as I imply; not very much however. Naturally things are rather quiet here, and I would rather stay at home than accept the run of invitations. I suppose that is age, not yet so pronounced that I don't like to go where there is a chance of agreeable company. I mean a little more agreeable than the average. The trouble with me now is that my head is full of my cases and that they permit no themes that would interest you.

In a few minutes I am off on our regular Saturday afternoon jaw, Conference, it is called, where, without discredit to my brethren, I expect to be bored.

Remember me most kindly to your wife and to the young one when you write to her. You are all still vivid impressions.

Yours ever,
O. W. Holmes

[27] Paul Moritz Warburg (1868–1932); American banker influential in the establishment of the Federal Reserve System in 1914 to overcome the disadvantages resulting from the lack of a central bank of issue in the United States.

American Legation, Sofia

9 April 1916

Dear Justice Holmes :

I love your celebration and wish I had been privileged to drink the midnight punch. The last time I was at Washington it was the fiftieth anniversary of your wound, and now it is your seventyfifth in years. May there be ten thousand more I would wish you Japanese fashion !

It is pleasant to think that in some part of the world there is festivity for I have had nothing but depression and endless rows and wrangling. We still have the political manners of the XVth century here and the Prime Minister would make a very creditable Malatesta or Visconti, minus the cultivation. He embraces his enemies in public, announces that harmony is restored, dines with them, and an hour after Parliament adjourns and the dinner is over has them arrested. 'I am very paternal with them' he said the other day to a colleague. 'Yes you will hang them paternally' was the answer. But the same colleague asked me to walk home with him the other night from the Club for he fears assassination.

He is furious with me just now because I have called things by their name to his face about the barbarous treatment of the English prisoners. They began by playing a trick on the Dutch Minister, who is in charge of French interests. After waiting for over three months and having a series of tempestuous interviews with the local Kitchener, who told me Bulgaria was unlike any other country, we at last had permission to see the prisoners who were to have been concentrated at Philippopolis. But the very morning of our arrival they whisked away all save a handful, and having cleaned up the camp intended us to report that this was in good order and everything was Candidian in its perfection. The French never returned, but I got back the English. Do you recall Kipling's '*The man who was*'? When they appeared and paraded before me never did I see more wretched mortals. All were in tatters, none had boots, they were emaciated and starved. The Bulgarian popular word for prisoner is the same as for slave, and they have been treated as such or rather worse, for there was the master's interest to keep the slave alive which is here not the case. They have been made to drudge on working parties under the whip with half a loaf of bread a day to eat and left sick and dying in barns without food or attendance. I asked how many were sick of those intended for this new working party and forty-seven out of one hundred and twelve stepped from the ranks. When I inquired why they had not gone into hospital I heard that the treatment received had been so bad that they preferred not to! I was revolted and furious and had no hesitation in writing the Prime Minister what I had seen and heard and sending a copy of my note to the Palace. And now they are wild at me and I have become the most unpopular person in the place. It is a matter of complete indifference to me.

What worries me far more is a wire I have just received from my wife who is lying seriously ill in a nursing home in London. I have cabled the Department to ask for leave and if, as I trust, it is granted will start immediately. Fortunately there is little on hand here and I think my rows about the prisoners will have done some good. Most of my other work has been about Servia and that is now a squeezed lemon as far as Americans and English are concerned. So I trust they will be able to send some Secretary from a neighbouring post here while I am gone. I have no notion how long it will be. I am most anxious to see my wife once more. She has been through very trying experiences with Marguerite's recent confinement — a second little girl to her mother's disappointment. Helen I fear has broken down under the strain of absences and trouble. She has been fretting terribly, but I am without details and lose myself in conjecture.

Ever yours,
L. E.

P.S. — Later. I have had better news of my wife and hope it may not be necessary for me to go just now at least. They would at once say here I had been forced out!

Supreme Court of the United States, Washington, D.C.

May 14, 1916

Dear Einstein:

This will not be long in view of your possibly having left Sofia before it gets to you. I grieve for your anxiety and perk up at your postscript which tells of better news from your wife and your probable stay. Your letter speaks of festivities here (as on my birthday), but they are very modest. I think there is a general recognition that such gaiety is impossible with things as they are. My main occupation has been writing opinions, the last two or three, it seems to me, with more gusto than the average perhaps because the end of the term approaches and my work is so well up, in fact all done to date. I don't believe they will find any falling off in the old man yet.

But I have had no time to read books or to do much else and have to rely on this summer to restore me to the ranks of the civilized. I saw Cabot Lodge yesterday for a moment, looking very old and tired. You know his wife died last summer. Also we went to a White House Garden Party a few days ago. I think the average democratic politician is even a more odious type than the inferior of republican stripe.

Brandeis's [28] matter hangs along, and I don't know what will happen. You met him at our house one night and I thought didn't fancy him, though of course you didn't say so. He always left on me the impression of a good man when he called, and I never have fully fathomed the reasons for the strong prejudice against him shown by other good men. Whatever happens it is a misfortune for the Court, for the time being. If he is turned down the proletariat will say only tools of the plutocrats can get in (though the ps. didn't favor me, you may bet). If he gets in many people will think that the character of the Court no longer is above question. Well, I always can hop off if I don't like it, but having kept on a good time so far I should like to keep it going until eighty.

[28] Louis Dembitz Brandeis (1856–1941); Associate Justice of the Supreme Court of the United States from 1916 to 1939. Appointed an Associate Justice of the Supreme Court by President Wilson, January 28, 1916, Brandeis was confirmed by the Senate Judiciary Committee only after much opposition to his appointment had been publicly expressed in the course of the protracted subcommittee hearings.

What do you know about Benedetto Croce?[29] An English-man the other day sent me a translation of his *Aesthetic* by Douglas Ainslee who professes to think him one of the great thinkers of all time. I doubt that, but have been pleased by what I have read and imperfectly understood.

I said I was going to write but a word, and as my doubt about you getting this is real I will shut up. I do hope that your next news from both the ladies will be good, and that you will have emerged into the sunlight of success.

Ever yours,
O. W. Holmes

Ritz Hotel, Piccadilly, London

8 June 1916

Dear Justice Holmes :

Your letter finds me in London for a recurrence of worries had brought me hither — fortunately so. My return has, I think, aided my wife to approach convalescence after a long and severe illness all the more troublesome because with-out fever. Though recovery is still distant and though she has painful moments I no longer feel anxious, but it will be months before she is herself again.

Otherwise I am pleased to be again in London ; at least the atmosphere differs from the one I have breathed this last year and a half in the Eastern end of the Central Powers. There is both depression and gayety. The very young have their nightly dances, and there are plenty of luncheons and small dinners, war food it is called, which only means one less course and an easier digestion. Kitchener's end came two days ago as a sudden fall. He had been mainly a symbol of late for the real man is the ex-footman Robertson,[30] who still drops his 'h's', but now that K is no more he will rise to the British Olympus. Everywhere one hears, 'What a pity it was not

---

[29] Benedetto Croce (1866–1952) ; Italian philosopher.

[30] Sir William Robert Robertson (1860–1933) ; British Field-Marshal and the first officer risen from the ranks to pass through the Staff College. Robertson was appointed by Kitchener Chief of the Imperial General Staff in December 1915 at the time of the allied withdrawal from the Dardanelles, which followed upon the reorganization of the Asquith ministry as a coalition and the resignation of Winston Churchill as First Lord of the Admiralty in May 1915.

Asquith' who has become the general whipping boy now that Winston is out of the way.

I had a very pleasant talk with Grey [31] yesterday. He treats the Foreign Office like a country house where he plays host. Some one said he reminded him of an English Bob Bacon.[32] Odd how Germans still regard him as the wiliest of schemers and find the finishing touch in his blandness. To me he is the perfect example of how the best parliamentarian makes the worst diplomatist and of how democracy demands the wrong test for those it exalts.

I have seen quite a number of people. I had breakfast the other day with Lord Reading [33] who tells me he gets through most of his work from six to nine in the morning. He was a sympathetic figure, but you know him. He wants me to meet Lloyd George to talk about Bulgaria. But if I have not yet seen the uncrowned King I had a pleasant private audience with the crowned one who thanked me for efforts in Bulgaria. He was quite animated and interested and not at all the lifeless wooden figure one used to see at levees in King Edward's time. I missed his profanity for they say he gets terribly profane talking of Germans, and he shows his dislikes with fierce emphasis.

I have found everyone here far more appreciative for my stewardship of British interests in Bulgaria than anything I had done has warranted. But a rather odd thing has happened. In a letter published in the 'Times' at the end of April and addressed by Lord Newton,[34] who is an Under Secretary to an M.P., my name was mentioned as being authority for the deplorable treatment suffered last winter by English prisoners in Bulgaria. All my reports about this had been confidential

---

[31] Sir Edward Grey, Viscount Grey of Fallodon (1862–1933); British statesman and eminent amateur ornithologist and dryfly fisherman. Foreign Secretary from December 1905 to December 1916, Grey was largely responsible after the outbreak of the war for cultivating relations with the United States which finally bore fruit when the United States entered the war in April 1917.

[32] Robert Bacon, (1860–1919); American banker, sportsman, and public servant. Bacon was Secretary of State for a short period in 1909 and Ambassador to France from 1910 to 1912.

[33] Rufus Daniel Isaacs, Marquess of Reading (1860–1935); Lord Chief Justice of England and later Viceroy of India, he was the first commoner to be created Marquess since the Duke of Wellington.

[34] Thomas Wodehouse Legh, Baron Newton (1857–1942); Controller of the Prisoners of War Department from 1916 to 1919.

and when the British Government asked me through Washington for permission to publish these I had refused. Moreover after a series of rows on my part their condition had materially improved. The news of bad treatment leaked out through other channels, but the Bulgars accused me of starting a press campaign against them though the only foundation was Newton's letter which put me in a very embarrassing light, for to have published it was grossly incorrect on his part. I told him I thought it would make my return to Sofia impossible, and his only reply was why should I wish to go back. He said the British Government was always being accused of secretiveness and they wanted to show they knew the facts, facts obtained from my confidential reports. At any rate the Bulgarian Government must have asked for my recall for three days ago I received a wire from the Department saying that in view of the delicate situation arising out of the protection of British interests it is deemed inadvisable for me to return. So I am discharged with less notice than one would give a servant and for having done the work I was sent out to do. I am privately thanked for 'valuable services' and publicly dismissed to oblige a semi-barbarous Government who were forced by dint of pressure to mend their ways. The thing is laughable if it were less what it is. Even Page,[35] the Ambassador here who has a keen mind, spoke to me yesterday in connection with it of the lack of experience and tradition of Washington, which sounded odd from a political appointee. I have reached the end of my tether.

My homages to Mrs. Holmes.

Ever yours,

L. E.

Beverly Farms, Massachusetts

July 11, 1916

My dear Einstein :

Have you thought me faithless or neglectful? My lad, if you write letters indicating that you are on the move and

[35] Walter Hines Page (1855–1918); American writer and diplomat who worked for an early entry of the United States into the war.

don't tell one where to send an answer silence necessarily ensues. I begin this not yet clear whether I shall send it to the State Department or try some other address.

I have been here about a fortnight seeking repose and a chance to get a fine edge to my intelligence by reading a little, though I have not yet quite divorced my reading from law.

At the moment I am in '*An Economic Interpretation of the Constitution of the United States*' [36] intended, I take it, to show that the Constitution embodies the point of view of the property-owning class etc., and to that end burrowing like a mole into the unindexed records of U.S. and States to find out just what the possessions of the framers of the Constitution were. So far as I have read it looks to me rather a futile job. One does not need an inventory to show that Washington, Madison, Hamilton, Gouverneur Morris, or Wilson belonged to and presumably had the prejudices of the property-owning classes, while it would need a good deal more evidence than the author can produce to show that the leaders were governed by sinister or self-seeking motives. So far it does not compare with Patten's book (not mentioned) on *The Development of English Thought*, which in a very ingenious way searches biographies from Hobbes to Darwin to show that some economic change was the starting point of an *aperçu* afterwards worked into a system for the sake of conformity. But these things don't interest you much and I apologize. It is merely telling you what I happen to be thinking about. I read aloud, translating French slang by guess, as best I could, *Gaspard* by René Benjamin, an admirable picture of going to the war, battle, return wounded, hospital, back to the front etc. touched everywhere by the entirely credible wit of Gaspard. But as yet any incursions into literature are limited.

We had a visit from two young Jews who hit me where I live : Frankfurter,[37] an old friend, Professor in the Law School, and Harold Laski,[38] twenty-three, a young prodigy in know-

---

[36] *An Economic Interpretation of the Constitution* by Charles Austin Beard (1913).

[37] Felix Frankfurter (1882–); professor at the Harvard Law School, Associate Justice of the Supreme Court of the United States 1939–62.

[38] Harold Joseph Laski (1893–1950); English political theorist, taught at Harvard University from 1916 to 1920; his extensive correspondence with Holmes edited by Mark DeWolfe Howe was published in two volumes in 1953.

ledge and intelligence. He read to me a letter to him from Morley that touched in such a pretty way the mixture of flattered vanity and real love for the young that makes meeting them so delightful. The young lawyers give me my share, and I respond with the same mixture.

I don't know whether I told you, it is so long since I have written, of the April *Harvard Law Review* dedicated to me apropos of my seventyfifth birthday with some articles that made me feel pretty happy. The *Illinois Law Review* under Wigmore's lead did something similar. Of course, one can't live *on*, and I don't at all live *in*, the past; but it gives one a kind of support in the battle of the present to believe that the past has been a success.

I do hope that your next letter will bring good news of you and yours. You have been having such a hard time that you deserve it.

This letter was interrupted, and it is now the 12th. which brings a lot of letters to be answered and things to be done. That is my bother. I don't get two hours a day for reading there are so many demands on my time. Of course I spend some hours out of doors; but to be able to sit down with nothing on my mind still seems a distant dream. Therefore I come to an end of this, but I shouldn't if I felt less uncertain whether it would reach you. But writing or silent I am always the same.

My very kindest remembrances to your wife and the Marchioness.

Yours ever,

O. W. Holmes

Easby House, Richmond, Yorkshire

31 July 1916

Dear Justice Holmes:

I purposely refrained from adding an address last time not knowing where I would be. But a variety of indications will always find me (not this one), at 27 Montagu Square, London W. My brother-in-law is always there. Even the

State Department is in touch, though I am no longer an official.

Early last month the Bulgarian Government did me the honour of asking for my recall and the State Department with that characteristic courtesy which consists in following the lines of least resistance at once acceded. I was privately thanked and publicly, so to speak, dismissed from one day to the other, and when I asked what I had done to merit such rebuke, for I had carried out the purpose of my mission in the face of difficulties, I could obtain no satisfaction. Here they have been charming about it especially as it is in great measure their fault, one of the Under-Secretaries, Lord Newton, attaching my name publicly to confidential statements regarding the illtreatment of the prisoners. Grey expressed at Washington his regret at my recall etc. etc., but I feel rather sore at the way my own people have grovelled before semi-barbarians, though it is more through ignorance and natural bad manners. In other respects it has suited me for my wife is only now convalescent and I could not cheerfully have left her in her present state. Just now we are a little family party staying with the Tweeddales — for Gifford is provisionally quartered here. I had grown sick of London pavements and for that matter of London temptations in the shape of lacquer furniture. The season, however, which I loathe, was rendered nicer by the war. It lacked its corpulence and was broken into fractions of interest which are all I have ever been able to consume; no more fat squashes but agreeable dinners and luncheons never exceeding ten or twelve. Shortly before leaving I went to Eton to give a talk to the boys in the school library and met with a very responsive reception. They may not acquire much learning but at least they are taught manners.

Now we are here for a few weeks before going to Schifanoia. Helen has a wild wish to see her villa again, and I have not been there in almost two years. I don't know how long I shall stay, I thought of returning home for the election but was advised to keep away. If Hughes is returned there may be a chance for me, especially as he censures Wilson for turning over the diplomatic service for his spoils. If it is Wilson I shall try to return to the English mind in the XVIth century if I can screw attention during the war. I still feel a bit unhinged and

my heart leaping with every ghost of news. But people here
are optimists again after the black spell of May.

Ever yours,
Lewis Einstein.

Beverly Farms, Massachusetts

August 12, 1916

Dear Einstein :

Even more you leave it doubtful between Montagu
Square and Schifanoia, but I will take my chance to thank
you for yours of July 31 and its enclosures. If our Government
has no manners, you certainly have your reward in English
appreciation of what you have done.

I really have nothing to write to one going through such
vicissitudes as have befallen you for the last year. I read books
mainly on themes you don't specially care for, and wonder
whether I haven't got overstrained and stale. I find it hard
not to feel as if I were wasting time when I read a novel, and
when I settle down into a book as into a green meadow straight-
way it becomes a dusty road the only function of which is to
lead you to the end. I think something indecent would do me
good. But the usual channels, I fear, wouldn't show much
now if I went to the foreign booksellers. I did get a few hours
of simple entertainment, unblighted so far as I see by any
improving tendency, in Cunninghame Graham's *Life of Bernal
Diaz*, a companion of Cervantes, largely in his own words. And
after finishing the *Oedipus Tyrannus* and at the same time a
Choix de Poésies by Verlaine I amuse myself as I sometimes do
by matching disparates and comparing the fate of Oedipus with
that of Verlaine. The healthy moralist, of course, would
repudiate such a comparison and say Verlaine was to blame ;
it lay with him to avoid his miseries. But being a sophist I pity
Verlaine the more. The other fate was external and left the
soul of Oedipus untouched. With Verlaine it was no less fate,
but attacking him within and interstitially destroying his
personality. Not that I care much for his own howls.

L

Do you see the *New Republic*? [39]   It is rather solemn for my taste; but the young men who write in it are, some of them, friends of mine, which doesn't prevent an occasional, flattering reference to this old man, and I get great pleasure from our occasional talks.   They put me on to books that they think will be good for me, and please me by their latent or expressed enthusiasm, and their talent.   But I fear they would be empty names to you.   Frankfurter (Professor at Harvard Law School), Walter Lippmann, Croly, Laski, etc.

I hope for good news from you.   All kind things to the two ladies.

Yours ever,
O. W. Holmes

Ritz Hotel, Piccadilly, London

31 Aug. 1916

Dear Justice Holmes:

I have as many addresses as a pickpocket and your letters I am glad to say always reach me.   But 27 Montagu Square, London W. is as good as any these days when I dare not prophesy more than forty-eight hours ahead.

Just now I am on the point of leaving for Lausanne for my wife's medical treatment.   She has had a bad time of it these last six months and physicians have chased her ailments through every corner of the body till at last the Xrays have localized their origin.   But it is disheartening not to have begun where we have ended and spared much anxious time and suffering.   The doctors tried to send her to another home in the north of Scotland, but those perpetual grey skies (for we have had no summer) have depressed her and she needs sunlight to regain health and spirit.   Yet we do not leave here without keen regret.   The background of war is a hideous thing and Marguerite's nervousness about Gifford, even though for the present he is in no danger, is intense.   I dare say we shall be back in January, and if Hughes is elected I will put in an early

---

[39] A weekly magazine of liberal tone founded in 1914 by Willard Dickerman Straight with Herbert D. Croly as editor.

appearance at Washington and look forward to nothing more than to seeing you. But will he be? Frankly, I am not proud of my country during this war. If Wilson takes immense credit for keeping out of it I prefer the President of Switzerland.

Yes I read the 'New Republic' and like it, though it is a bit Evening Posty passed through a college settlement. Lippmann writes well, although his diplomatic opinions are somewhat amateurish. I liked better his account of the conventions. But the paper has a good and encouraging atmosphere in spite of its indecisions, and it is a relief to get away from the war.

I am sorry you feel stale. I am sending you two 'shockers' by Buchan which carried me along to the finish, and after all one can ask little more of a story. But I have become scatterbrained as a semi-sickness in an atmosphere of London, war, and illness. If I reach Schifanoia after Lausanne I hope once again to find calm of soul. For the present it lives on war rations and I jog along counting the days and longing to settle down to something. Diplomacy with me has been a wretched will-o'-the-wisp and has led me away from my own mastery in scholarship — and half way houses are not good shelter while with the world aflame books become dust. I fear this wretched war will go on not less than another year and not unlikely two. The worst is that this war to end war will breed new war and the only way to defeat Germany will be to copy her. The real German victory will be the Prussianizing of the rest of the world. Will lotus eating be left to America?

Ever yours,
L. E.

Beverly Farms

Sept. 10, 1916

My dear Einstein :

Your letter comes this morning and gives me hope that now the trouble is discovered better days are in store for your wife. Do remember me to her and also to the young one, whom I still fail to realize in her state of wife and mother.

Things look so much more promising in these days that I am hopeful all round. I have been at my usual vacation employments, now nearly over. I expect my next letter to you will be from Washington, where, again I hope, I shall see you.

The news from Maine this morning is good for Hughes.[40]

I have just been endeavouring to make up for not reading the newspapers by reading Belloc's account of the *Battle of the Marne*. He argues it like a jury lawyer recurring to and repeating, with repeated simple diagrams, the main facts so that whether his conclusions are right or not you have a coherent notion left in your mind. I took another excursion away from my usual themes by rereading the *Woman in White*.[41] It has the quality that makes the work of those whom I call the Unknown Illustrious succeed. I mean the books that have the largest circulation and that we never have heard of. In other words, with almost as little character painting as they, and with only a little keener observation of life, it appeals to our primal desire for a story. Why bother about a character for the hero? The reader is hero and villain, if things only keep moving. Wilkie Collins knew what he was about, although the texture of his discourse is rather soft and naïf for our days. Presently I am going to try Hazlitt, in whom Birrell has interested me to my surprise; but first I must finish Faguet's *Le Libéralisme*, a sort of French parallel to H. Spencer's *Social Statics* as I remember it. I don't care much for theoretic limits to government activity, though on practical grounds I have little sympathy with the present tendency to increase its roles. But Faguet is amusing as literature, and in these latter days of my vacation I am trying to chuck all thought of improvement and to aim at simple pleasure.

With that end I interrupted this letter at eleven a.m. to go off with my wife for an impromptu two hours motoring inland among the estates of the rich and over windswept downs until my eyes were filled with the vision of September at its best.

[40] Charles Evans Hughes (1862–1948); Associate Justice of the Supreme Court of the United States from 1910 to 1916 when he resigned to run as republican candidate in the presidential election against Woodrow Wilson. Hughes served as Secretary of State from 1921 to 1925 and was later appointed Chief Justice of the Supreme Court of the United States, 1930–1941.

[41] *The Woman in White* by Wilkie Collins (1860).

Usually we toddle round behind a single horse jawing with the driver who is a cousin of Lucy Larcom,[42] authoress of certain locally known poems not without merit.   This country has my earliest associations and they largely affect if they don't control our deepest loves and reverences.   Among the foundations of my soul are granite rocks and barberry bushes, and the steps in Boston leading down from Montgomery Place, now Bosworth Street, in the rear of the Parker House in Province Street.   I could rhapsodize as does Balzac about *tours* in the *Contes drôlatiques*.

Yours ever,
O. W. Holmes

Supreme Court of the United States, Washington, D.C.

Jan. 17, 1917

Dear Einstein :

Your letter came to me yesterday, a breath from the outside world after I had been shut up for a week with the grippe ; the first time, as far so I remember, that I ever have missed being present in Court.   Everything has gone its normal way, and the doctor promises me that I may go on duty on Monday.   But it is queer how quickly one's horizon limits itself to the sick room, and what seemed an opportunity for a thousand rambles during one's enforced leisure is filled with no profounder interest than victuals.

I have read *Appreciations of Poetry* by Lafcadio Hearn, which was just about good enough for my condition.   He made me admit merits in Dante Rossetti, which I always regret to do, though perhaps my prejudice against Burne Jones is greater.   I remember how grieved I was when I read Nordau's book, (*Degeneration*) to have to admit that on a critical comparison Nordau did not make out his case against *The Blessed Damozel*. I think the short point was that the scene wasn't really visualized and did not hang together.   I hoped he was right, but on going

---

[42] Lucy Larcom (1824–93) ;   American poetess, teacher, and collaborator with John Greenleaf Whittier.

over it thought it failed. Before I was ill I had a book on Art, that ought to make you prick up your ears, but it was Pre-historic Art, and I fear your aesthetic spirit would rebel.

Now I think is the moment for a chapter of Casanova. Ordinarily I have no time for him, but now, with every fibre languid and no duty pressing, and my intelligence at a mini-mum, decidedly it is his hour. I leave you for the lounge and him.

Alas, slumbers prevailed over scandalous literature, or I rather should say *great*. The war interrupted a hope that had been kept along for years of an authentic copy in the original form being published.[43] I should like to have it definitely proved that the original exists, and to see an exact transcript. His is one of the few books that lasts. I don't see but he is as interesting and alive as ever. A fellow once said that Roosevelt would never be extinct, that he was a temperament, like Casanova and George Sand. So now I may say Casanova is like Roosevelt.

With reference to the peace (and other) utterances of the present head of the Government, though I read very few of them, they so exquisitely encounter every human and moral feeling, literary and other taste, and convictions of policy on my part that either his public or I have a very mistaken idea of his personality.[44] As I *really* don't know, and nevertheless have deep prejudices, it is better for me to shut up.

It seems as if my horizon was closing in pretty fast in these latter days. The last blow was a letter saying that Lady Castletown has had a slight stroke, not affecting her mind, but affecting her side. It is lucky for me that most of the time I have too much work to do to realize my own sadness, not to speak of the world's.

I hope your next will bring good news of your wife's health. You say nothing of Lady Tweeddale. I think charming thoughts of both and send my best remembrances. This little,

---

[43] For the first time since it was purchased over one hundred and forty years ago by the German publishing house of Brockhaus the manuscript of Casanova's autobiography has been published in its original state. *Histoire de ma vie* par Jacques Casanova de Seingalt, Vénitien, F. A. Brockhaus, Wiesbaden-Librairie Plon, Paris, 6 vols. (1960–62).

[44] President Wilson's remark in a speech in 1916 that 'there was such a thing as being too proud to fight' particularly vexed Holmes.

personal bulletin is all that I am up to now, but I don't think
the period of ideas has gone wholly by.

> Yours ever,
> O. W. Holmes

Supreme Court of the United States, Washington, D.C.

> May 19, 1917

Dear Einstein:

Your letter came the day before yesterday and was very
welcome, including the news that your wife's health is improving; but this is primarily an immediate reply.

I had a chance to see Phillips [45] yesterday and opened your
matter. I was beginning to expound your merits but he said
he knew all about you, expressed the highest opinion of your
abilities, and yet threw cold water on my hopes. He was host
and I could not take more than a moment of his time, but the
impression I got was so discouraging as to my present chances
that after hesitating somewhat I decided that it was better not
to write to him at the present moment. I am very sorry.

After being a messenger of bad news I can't go on and talk
about things in general. Indeed the only thing I could tell
just now is that I have been at work about up to my limit and
have not yet had time to relax, though for the moment all my
work is done. In a short time I go to a Conference of the
judges. On Monday we ponder some decisions, hear one last
case, and on June 11 I expect we shall adjourn and my wife
and I go to Beverly Farms.

I have had no time for books, though at odd moments I am
reading the MS life of Canon Sheehan of Doneraile [46] who
was a dear friend of mine, odd as it seems that a Saint and a
Catholic should take up with a heathen like me.

Tell me what you decide to do, and if you want me to do
anything more, though as to this last I am sadly convinced I
can do nothing.

> Yours ever,
> O. W. Holmes

[45] William Phillips (1878–   ); American diplomat. Assistant Secretary of
State, January 1917 to March 1920.
[46] *Canon Sheehan of Doneraile* by Herman J. Heuser (1917).

Beverly Farms, Massachusetts

June 27, 1917

Dear Einstein :

Your good letter met me here on my arrival Monday evening. It relieved me to know that my last, if it reaches you, will not be the first message of disappointment. In it I mentioned seeing Phillips and getting no hope.

I am so glad to hear good accounts of your wife. Please give her and the young one my warmest remembrances.

Coming on I had the almost forgotten pleasure of reading a book : Romain Rolland, *Some Musicians of Former Days*. It would have been better if I had had the French, but even in a translation it struck me as superlative, combining technical knowledge, so far as an outsider could judge, learning, philosophic grasp, and charm. One of those rare and delightful works that make you feel the world movement in a lot of personal details.

I remember when I was young thinking that the Goncourts' *Maîtresses de Louis Quinze* gave you the pleasure of backstairs gossip that improved your mind. Now I am hoping to do some quiet reading with that end (of improvement) in view. For I take advantage of my age and try to remain serene, I won't say detached, in the midst of war. I used to dream of a final calm under old trees, possibly, no — impossibly, in England or the East. But my life began and seems likely to end in war, and one must grow one's trees in one's soul. It seems silly to bother any longer about improvement. I remember at different times John Gray and Harry James thanking God they had got rid of that preoccupation ; but I can't. If I should pursue simpler amusement for a week I should feel as if I had eaten too many chocolates. I must have a *pièce de résistance*, and one that in some way buttresses some of the walls.

Perhaps a word on *The Value of Money* just sent to me. Two years ago I was rather pleased with myself about a statement, in a decision, of the meaning of value apropos of an absurd statute punishing combinations to enhance the price of goods above their 'real value'. 'Value is the effect on exchange of the relative social desire for compared objects expressed in terms of a common denominator.' Of course there is nothing except the form of the statement, which I thought compact.

I am expecting in two days to get the bound volume of my decisions that I have made up annually. I don't feel that the term is over until I get it, index it, and, strictly speaking, until I put the book into my shelves at Washington. I suppose perhaps people would say that I ought to be ashamed to be interested in such trifles; but I am not.

I hope this will survive the sea successfully and bear you my greetings.

Yours ever,
O. W. Holmes

Beverly Farms, Massachusetts

July 20, 1917

Dear Einstein:

A letter from you came a little while ago with news of your arrival in Scotland. You don't tell me whether to address my letter there.

I have got settled down here for the summer, at first having various chores to attend to in the way of paying bills, sending a schedule and valuation of property for taxation to the District of Columbia, and reading a big book on *The Value of Money* which was sent to me, I suppose, because it contained some quotations from opinions of mine. Now I have attained as much leisure as I ever have and am amusing myself while seeking a little instruction. I was impressed in reading Faguet's *Rousseau Penseur* by the fact that both R. and F. seemed to think the passion for equality founded on cosmic justice, and that the universe itself was wrong in creating men with different degrees of gifts. I think it rot not only because it postulates a *point d'appui* outside of the universe from which to criticize it, but because the so-called passion for equality really is a passion for superiority which denies the dogma. I was much pleased with myself yesterday when this occurred to me, until I bethought me that it was implied in the tale of the Irishman who answered the remark that one man was as good as another, 'Yes, and a damned sight better'. Now I am just finishing a volume of Brunetière's essays with interesting discourses on Descartes, Pascal, Rousseau, etc., and rather down on Voltaire, as I should suppose Faguet to be also. B. seems to be a man of learning and ability but without any personal cachet to his writing to give it charm. I learn from him but don't care about him. I also am renewing a sensation of youth by re-reading aloud (translation) Fromentin's *Dominique*. It seems like the rather dim impression I have of his painting and like the characters it depicts which, one conjectures, may resemble himself in having distinction without much force. After these I shall turn to a volume of Gyp.[47]

I generally do a little bit of Greek, but I don't know what it will be unless I try a part of the New Testament!

I really am bothered as I write with the wonder where to send this. I think I shall try 27 Montagu Square, and yet I don't know. Your letter says Yester, Gifford, *Edinburgh*; my note of addresses says Gifford, *Haddington*. What with doubts whether this will reach the other side and whether it will go right if it gets there I am inclined to shut up. Hoping that you will get this expression of friendship and will give my re-membrances, most vivid, to the ladies.

Yours ever,
O. W. Holmes

I have decided to send to Scotland as I am not sure to whose care I should direct at 27 Montagu Sq.

Beverly Farms, Massachusetts

August 6, 1917

My dear Einstein :

Your letter of July 15 makes me sorry, by what you say about your inability to concentrate. I think that you will re-gain the power to occupy yourself continuously before long. The only hint of criticism that I have heard was the suggestion by someone in conversation that you did not get along well with your associates, which surprised me, and seemed to me improbable. Well, short of generals, the wars have to be fought by younger men even than you. I try to practise serenity.

My last experience in the way of books was Edouard Berth

---

[47] Pseudonym of Sibylle de Riqueti de Mirabeau, Comtesse de Martel (1849–1932) ; French authoress.

Les Méfaits des Intellectuels, a royalist, syndicalist work written before the war and sounding a little old on that account. But I thought the author, as a result of sucking the candy of Hegel, Bergson, Sorel, Marx, and Freud, had simply drooled. I won't go into details as you probably won't read it; but I felt a certain interest in view of the ominous predictions of great, social changes after the war. I don't take great stock in them as I think we are too far along for the chaos suggested by Russia and have too many small property owners for anything more socialistic than stringent regulations of one sort or another, or state ownership of this and that. But I have too profound a contempt for the bases of all socialisms not prepared to begin with life rather than with property and to kill everyone below the standard, for me to prophesy what it may accomplish in the actual state of the world.

Solemn themes be blowed. I saw in one of our rooms among the cheap summer books some translations of Boisgobey.[48] I think I will go back to him instead of to Kant. It is not a good symptom that I find myself indisposed to read novels. As no doubt I have said before he who makes the most of himself doesn't make much, and I am haunted by the apprehension that I am industrious. The abdominal repose, like the abdominal laughter of the Englishman, is a mark of strength.

I wish I knew the rights and wrongs of Austen Chamberlain's [49] resignation as his sister [50] is a friend of mine.

My homage and warm remembrances to Madam,

Ever sincerely yours,

O. W. Holmes

[48] Fortuné Abraham de Boisgobey (1824–91); famous French writer of police stories.

[49] Sir Joseph Austen Chamberlain (1863–1937); British statesman, son of Joseph Chamberlain, and half brother of Arthur Neville Chamberlain. Joseph Chamberlain resigned as Secretary of State for India in 1917 as a result of the Government's decision to submit to judicial investigation certain charges arising out of the break-down of hospital arrangements during the Middle East campaign. 'In his view the public interest and his personal honour alike required his resignation, though not one of the charges referred to him. The official responsibilities for the horrible break-down of the hospital arrangements during the first advance on Baghdad were incurred without his personal knowledge. His insistence on resignation was over-scrupulous, but showed that his views of what principle and loyalty demand were stricter than the normal.' *Encyclopaedia Britannica* (1957), Vol. 5, p. 201.

[50] Miss Beatrice Chamberlain (1862–1918); intimate friend and correspondent of Holmes.

Beverly Farms, Massachusetts

August 27, 1917

Dear Einstein :

Your letter, August 12, comes this morning and sets me writing at once.

You make me feel so sorry at your lack of employment and inability to take up your old work. The war covers the whole sky now, but you will live until it becomes a distant memory. Beauty is not destroyed from the face of the earth, and nature has a longer wind than men. If nothing more immediate turns up, tasks that seem remote and unreal are ultimate contributions and sometimes better than more immediate ones. I lived for years on George Herbert's 'Who sweeps a room as for Thy laws makes that and the action fine', and Browning's, *Grammarian's Funeral*. So unless some other chance offers I say make yourself tackle the XVIth Century and go at your old studies.

Next as to Brunetière. My estimate of him probably is not very different from yours. A young fellow sent me a particular volume of his essays that dealt with subjects that were akin to those handled in other books that I had been reading, and B. showed knowledge and some ability and gave me some information. He and the others set me to reading Pascal's *Provinciales*, which I did with pleasure unexpected, little as I believe the declaration of Bergh, Catholic ?, royalist, syndicalist in *Les Méfaits des Intellectuels* that Pascal has conquered Descartes. Now my peaceful odd minutes are given to Virgil. I have read the *Eclogues* and am on the last *Georgic*. The recollection of school days does not destroy the mild enjoyment of writing every other line of which is quotable if not a familiar quotation.

But though I don't read the papers the war makes it hard for me too not to be unhappy, anxious, sad to be out of it. I could dilate upon the theme but won't. It somewhat recalls the mixed emotions I felt when our regiment went over with the first brigade to cross at Fredericksburg. I had nearly died of dysentery brought on by the frightful cold, and the doctor said I was not to go. We lost half our number in a few minutes in the street, and I lay in hospital the other side of a little hill listening to firing. I cried, and yet knew that my hide was safe. So I try to be philosophical, and even while I should encourage hatred for the Germans, meaning thereby their regime and their objects and ideals, I feel free to do them justice and ask myself (no one else, but my wife,) whether the destruction of a cathedral in war is worse than the deliberate swamping of Phylae,[51] but this is between ourselves.

Well, this is but an expression of sympathy and anxious good wishes. My homage to your ladies, a happy issue to you. It will come.

Yours ever,
O. W. Holmes

We go to Washington in the later part of September.

I don't believe Wilson is a great man and he has qualities that I do not admire; but I can't doubt he is doing his best in the war and I think we all should back him up as far as we possibly can.

Beverly Farms

Sept. 17, 1917

Dear Einstein :

Your letter of August 28 comes this morning, welcome as ever. It is the last that I shall answer from here as we leave in a week, the Term having been set forward. After I get to Washington I am afraid I shall be a bad correspondent as it is very hard to write in the midst of absorbing work.

In view of your many accomplishments I am pleased to think that you do not shine as a shot. To a nonexpert like me I think that having a gun that fits you makes all the difference. In my first experience in Scotland I surprised myself by my (very modest) achievements. At the next place I went to I couldn't hit anything.

You speak of the Wemyss. I wonder if you know Evan Charteris,[52] whom I have met often at the Desboroughs [53] and

---

[51] Islet in the Nile above the First Cataract which has attracted travelers and artists since the Roman period on account of the splendor of its temples and natural setting. Phylae is periodically submerged since completion of the Assuan dam in 1902.

[52] Sir Evan Charteris (1864–1940) ; sixth son of 10th Earl of Wemyss, barrister, author, devoted student and patron of art.

[53] William Henry Grenfell (1855–1952) and Ethel Fane Grenfell (1867–1952) ; 1st Baron and Baroness Desborough.

elsewhere, and whom I like? I often have wondered whether all was well with him. I remember his telling me, years before, that he thought the war was bound to come. My serenity, such as it is, is based on the conviction that worry is a futile waste of energy and the knowledge that I can do nothing but pay [*sic*] and do my work.

I shall look forward to your Diary,[54] (in Washington).

Also, on account of my friendship for Miss Chamberlain, I am very glad at what you say about Austen.

My life has continued its quiet course. I have had an occasional visit from some younger man with jawing late into the night, and I have read a few more books. I forget whether I was in Virgil when I last wrote. Before I got through with him I thought (to my surprise) that Dante was quite right in taking him for a guide. At first he seemed to me for the world what Pope has been for the English, a source of familiar quotations, but after the 4th *Georgic* and the 6th book of the *Aeneid* I saw the poet.

Latterly I have been rereading, or rather am, if I don't drop it, Goethe's *Faust*. Literary German troubles me with its vocabulary more than law and the only translation I have is by Miss Swanwick; a fine example of British bluntness, flabby adjectives interjected to help out the metre, soft periphrases to save her piety, and a general confidence in improving afar the old man that satisfies all the most exigent requirements of Philistia. As to the play it seems to me that it wobbles between the implications of the scene in heaven and the old tradition with which it began and which it embodies in the text, and I have a vague impression that a critic bent on tearing it to pieces as a work of art could make out a pretty good case. I doubt if I shall have time to finish it this week.

Please give my kindest regards to your wife and your stepdaughter.

Yours ever,
O. W. Holmes

My paper is giving out and I can't find an envelope to fit this.

[54] *Inside Constantinople* by Lewis Einstein (1917).

5 Lower Berkeley Street, London, W.

7 Oct. 1917

Dear Justice Holmes:

We returned to London just in time for the air-raids which have been causing a certain exodus. We were at Claridges Hotel and felt reasonably secure under its concrete roof. But the anticipations and the warnings and the fire of the anti-aircraft guns were almost as impressive as a good war play on the stage. The raids have brought the war home to London and next spring they may become serious. Meanwhile the 'tube' stations attract the more nervous. But both of us loathed hotel life and instead we have found this house which is by no means bad. I have a room to myself and a broad table desk which is luxury and can revert to the Renaissance with the feeling of habit if not of keenness. Scholarship seems remote in times like these yet the other day at the London library I saw a recent number of '*Englische Studien*' with an article on middle English phonetics! I don't suppose that the war has altered human psychology, but the violent change of occupations has had effect on some. There is a mad rush for amusement on the part of one group here and generally speaking theatres and restaurants have never been so full.

I recall your description of Washington in Civil War days. It will seem different now, and I admire your serenity without being able to share it. I try to read recent American books like Beer's *The English Speaking Peoples* and Weyl's *American World Politics*, but care little for either — both full of commonplaces. Anyone writing today along such lines ought to take the cinematograph as a model and project evolutionary currents, which would land the writer into another kind of nonsense. Yet it is odd that the war has been as little favourable to writers as to generals. Here they think it has produced only two great men — Falkenhayn and Kerensky!

I only know Evan Charteris by name but believe that all is well with him. One sees little of anyone now, for entertaining there is none in the American sense of the word. The winter for the first time will be a hard one. Though London at night is far less dark than during the first year of the war taxis are almost unobtainable and sugar cards are scheduled. Yet even inactive I prefer it here to Tuscan apathy and all the beauties of Florence. At least there is real throbbing pulse here while in Florence life is taken up by external details which are little satisfying at a time when one yearns for something more in relation with the age.

I am deep in the councils of the Armenians just at present who came to me most unexpectedly. But I am pleased to render these unfortunates any poor services I can. My diary which has a good deal to say about the massacres is slated for this week, so John Murray tells me. Do you know the latter? He is far more the old-fashioned publisher than any of our American manufacturers of books. With his five generations behind him he showed me the Byron and Scott relics the other day and the other accumulations of former John Murrays. He is trying to find a publisher for it in America, but there is little interest in such things at home and I doubt if he succeeds.

My compliments to Mrs. Holmes and tell her not to forget me altogether.

Ever sincerely yours,
Lewis Einstein

Supreme Court of the United States, Washington, D.C.

Oct. 14, 1917

Dear Einstein :
        Such a nice letter from you (Sept. 16) came last week. I can reply but inadequately because, even more than I expected when I got back here, there was a pile of stuff or rather came in a pile as soon as we took our seats. The war had nothing to do with it. It was just an unprecedented number of cases to be examined to see whether in our discretion we would allow them to be argued in our Court. In addition to the regular Court business it was a considerable burden. Most of that was disposed of yesterday but now the regular work is sufficient to keep my hands full. I shall be a poor correspondent during the term I fear.

It is a loathly business to try to make up your mind with
no more familiarity with such affairs than I have, whether an
ordinance establishing dollar gas is confiscatory and contrary
to the Constitution, and to that end, what is a proper valuation
of the plant, what proper allowance for depreciation, what the
probable return, etc. When such things come up I want to sit
down and cry or tell them to ask Brandeis. However, I always
say, I think truly, that no case is hard when you understand
it. My difficulties are with words that convey at best a vague
meaning to my mind, and with the unnecessary obscurities
caused by men rarely representing their case in a lucid and
logical way. Words are the worst thing. Every speciality has
its lingo from philosophy to railroads or art. I remember when
a clever man had painted my portrait and asked in an aesthetic
dame whom I met hard by to look at it. She thought there
should be a shadow under the moustache. He called her attention to the fact that she was sitting down and that he painted
standing ; but as she left saying, 'Very interesting, but I think
it would have more *brio* if you put in the shadow' after a
little silence he turned to me and said, 'What the hell is *brio*?'
and then, wherein I agreed with him, 'Damn a person who says
interesting !'

I am so pleased to hear that Madam Marguerite re-
members me. Tell her you know an old feller who will
remember her while this machine is together. My warmest
regards to her and to your wife who I hope will find the London
compromise agrees with her.

You are very loose about giving your address. I shall try
27 Montagu Square, but I wish I knew who lived there for
greater security.[55]

You make a comparison between now and 1861. I suppose there is less excitement, but I should think that everything
was much more businesslike and intelligent. The young men
of today still are quite as good as, if not better than, the men of
my time. Probably there is not much difference ; and I feel
better about my country when I see what tidy looking chaps
they are in khaki. I have heard amusing reflections from
those who remember '61 on the comfort with which the youth

---

[55] 27 Montagu Square was the home of Lewis Einstein's brother-in-law the
Honorable Edward Stonor.

M

who are supposed to be getting ready for hardships are surrounded here. I know not whether justified. I know I expected dysentery to begin every time I went back; but I have known every form of bellyache recognized by the law, except asiatic cholera, I think.

I cannot be intelligent outside the law in these days. So take good wishes in place of thoughts.

Yours ever,
O. W. Holmes

Washington

Oct. 30, 1917

Dear Einstein :

Your most pleasant letter finds me in the idleness of work done, fever, and a cold in the head. I got it, I suppose, by going last night to the Cosmos Club for a reception to the Officers of the Allies who were here, being very hot, and walking home. I tried to do my modest bit of welcoming and talked a little with French, Italians, and Britons before leaving. I don't attempt to speak of the Italian disaster.[56] Indeed I don't know how far it will affect the prognostics. At odd minutes I am reading what the French officers and others seem to consider the best war book, *Le Feu* (Barbusse). Much of it seems generically familiar to me, though different in detail and greater in degree. The sufferings from cold can't be greater than I know for I nearly died of dysentery brought on by about all that I could stand and live; *per quod* I was kept out of the battle of Fredericksburg when our regiment lost half its number in killed and wounded in a very short time. But I shall do devilish little reading in the next six months I imagine.

You will sympathize with me, though I fear you don't share my hobby for engravings, when I mention that yesterday evening at an attractive print shop opposite the British Embassy I gave way to my uneconomic tendencies so far as to purchase a charming portrait by Nanteuil, the King of portrait engravers, just as last year I got two of Vandyck's portrait etchings,

---

[56] In October 1917 the Austro-German victory at Caporetto inflicted losses of 320,000 men in killed, wounded, and missing upon the Italian armies and threatened to knock Italy out of the war.

both examples that when I was younger I wished but never expected to possess. It is odd, but these great masters of the past hardly cost as much as my ordinary specimens of second rate work of the day and not nearly so much as the people in fashion, alive or lately dead. I remember when I was a boy I used to read the cautions of the Reverend William Gilpin (dear old British parson *circa* 1800) against being governed by fashion in print collecting. However I don't collect. I merely have a few good ones and a few more not so good.

But, my dear lad, I am too sneezy to go on. I have a hurricane which I trust will blow off as swiftly as it came, but which bids me cut it short now. Present my most devoted homages to the ladies and believe me as,

Ever yours,
O. W. Holmes

Why don't you *say in terms*, 'This is my address'? I don't know if and how long you are or will be at 5 L B St.

5 Lower Berkeley Street, London, W.

6 Nov. 1917

Dear Justice Holmes:

Your letter of October 14th reached me in defiance of U boats, and the Montagu Square address is the best, for this is only a furnished house and I may leave at any time if a new offer of service with the Red Cross in France is accepted. I still go on offering and feeling about it somewhat like a miniature T.R.

Otherwise there is nothing new not even the air raids which kill a few people and frighten a good many more. One receives a warning usually a half hour or more before the raiders arrive. Everyone huddles in the cellar where one is safe from all save a direct hit and one waits greatly bored for the all clear signals to come. The other night it was not given till five in the morning. The raid itself means a terrific racket of guns, an occasional bit of shrapnel, breaking glass, complete silence, and a monotonous repetition when a new group of raiders appear, for they come in waves and lately we had six or seven servings of the same sauce. So much for warfare in London which promises to be more serious in the Spring. Otherwise we have few reminders, and if there is scarcity of food in the country there are certainly no signs of it in the shops. Future historians aided by contemporary journalists may talk about the heroic temper of the population. Personally I see very little change. Everyone responds more or less to necessity, but with an indiarubber rebound on the first occasion.

We are depressed over Italy though apparently the '*coup*' has long been expected by English military men. At least so they say now it is over. Helen's Italian maid summed up the disaster with a '*Mia patria a il corno*' (horns in the Shakesperian manner). Italian patriotism is still supposedly the property of the rich and the small people feel it rather in the Chinese sense of non resistance. But I am sorry for those who did their best and who were overwhelmed when the others let them down.

My other letters from home are full of the 'thank God we are living in this age making history' spirit and wondering why I don't join Colonel House [57] in the intensive training our statesmen are now receiving in diplomacy. Does he impress you as a Talleyrand or a Bismarck? I know nothing about him not even his face, which shows commendable restraint from the picture papers. The new expanded Washington must be an interesting city, and I imagine you must enjoy meeting some of the business talent who are managing things and who, after all, are our equivalents to the Prussian generals with quite as much efficiency and quite as little tact. If anything can save the situation it must be us. There is plenty of grit and determination here but neither the imagination nor the elasticity to conceive of anything new if that is possible. The bombast and swagger have gone and only the homely reality of pegging away keeps on. Without us I fancy there would be utter pessimism. The whole question now turns on whether we can do the trick in time, and a French colleague speaking to me the other day thought that peace would come long before our army would be ready and that Russia would pay the wreckage.

I hope my Constantinople diary will reach you. It was posted about three weeks ago. I believe — most material of

---

[57] Edward Mandell House (1858–1938); political confidant of President Wilson. Colonel House in the autumn of 1917 was named chief of the American mission to co-ordinate the war needs of the Allies.

tests — it is having a very fair sale, though to my disgust I found it was being used by some papers to criticize British diplomacy which I had 'unwittingly' exposed. I really published it because of the Armenian massacres. Our own diplomatic record in the matter is not one I feel proud of though I say nothing about that side of it.

My compliments to Mrs. Holmes.

Ever yours,
Lewis Einstein

Supreme Court of the United States, Washington, D.C.

Dec. 1, 1917

Dear Einstein :

Your letter of Nov. 6 came, welcome as usual, but giving me some apprehension as you say your Diary was posted to me and as yet I have seen nothing of it. I am in my chronic state of having my hands filled, though I hope for a day or two of leisure next week.

I have ventured outside the strictly economic once more and bought two more of Van Dyck's etchings and portraits at moderate cost. It surprised me that these works of one of the original men in etching should sell for less than many modern things not in the first rank. These are third state impressions and on comparison with productions of the first proofs I can see no change in the heads or abatement in the freshness of the lines. In one some details have been finished a little further and I think the ink is a little heavier but that is all. Of course the thorough going collector wants first proof irrespective of any aesthetic superiority, but I think that a weakness. I also am trembling on the verge of a more expensive Whistler, but I hesitate. These are unusual excursions for me — to make up for years of fasting and prayer. Whistler is another original man, and it is interesting and rather amusing in the print shop to see the echoes of him in later men. Indeed one sees lots of delightful little landscapes and what not of which one says that would be a masterpiece if it were the first, but Rembrandt or Meryon or Whistler had done it all before. One doesn't complain that a man of any time profits by what has been done before him; he must, of course, if he is to count. But there must be a new personality added.

If I do get any time my table is loaded with books — including a life of my old friend, (did you know him?) Canon Sheehan of Doneraile. I read it in the proofs and have looked through it in the published form with much emotion. I had a number of letters from him which the writer made some use of. He was a beautiful spirit, though I could never get over my surprise at his admitting a rank outsider like me to his friendship. A Catholic must think that except for some exceptions not to be looked for outsiders will go to Hell. And, as Dante reminded himself when feeling a moment of pity, those in Hell God hates or at least so feels to them that the business of a believer is to hate them. But, as the Chief Justice once replied to me, (he is a Catholic) none of us are logical.

I believe as you say that there is a lot of business talent here now, but I meet hardly anyone outside my job. Dinners are rare, and I am not very keen to go to them when I have the chance. We have even given up being at home on Monday after the official usage. One man who came here before the war I have met two or three times with great pleasure, Paul Warburg the banker, but with half a year between times.

The end of the sheet and of my time prevents my running on. My warmest remembrances to the two ladies.

Yours ever,
O. W. Holmes

Supreme Court of the United States, Washington, D.C.

Dec. 20, 1917

Dear Einstein :

The Censors know a good thing when they see it and generally open your letters. A very pleasant brief one from Yester comes today. In reply to which I plead my privilege to write short or cut it out while the term is on as I hardly have time to do more than hear arguments, write decisions, take my victuals, and breathe.

Please renew my assurances to the Marchioness whom I ever shall adore. Alas, it grows increasingly uncertain whether I shall see her again. The death of one of my last classmates, a man getting up to offer his seat in a car, my teeth, a thousand trifles, give me each a little sting of a reminder that, as one of the last of the Twentieth men wrote to me a few days ago, we are getting near the end. But moralize as I may I can't believe it, and most of the time feel as I did fifty years ago except that I am much happier.

No, I have not yet seen the illegible author's [58] *Quatre Cavaliers de l'Apocalypse*. It sounds less remote from my range than Morley's reminiscences. I did read *Le Problème de Jésus* [59] the other day which gave a good account of the myth theory; all a little extravagant I should think. Though granted the leader of a small sect I should think it plain that myth had shaped the religion that has been founded on him. Most of my latter reading here is on legal themes and the like. Le Roy's *La Loi*, Duguit, etc. I don't get much nourishment from the Mussoos on that theme. But their histories and handbooks of the law, so far as I know them, are the best in the world.

We are in the outskirts of war conditions; hard to get any coal, or sugar, or (I think) white flour etc. I have no belief in the democratic administration, except that we all will back any administration that is in to win the war if we can, and that I don't doubt the politician at the top is sincerely desirous among other things to put the war through in shape. I believe there are a lot of able men gathered here, but I see few except the lawyers and the young. There still are some young people who will play with us.

Every good wish to your wife and you.

Ever yours,

O. W. Holmes

5 Lower Berkeley Street, London, W.

30 Dec. 1917

Dear Justice Holmes:

Yesterday at lunch came a phone message from my sister-in-law to announce a letter for me at her house marked

---

[58] Vicente Blasco-Ibáñez (1867–1928).
[59] *Le Problème de Jésus* by Charles Guignebert (1914).

'urgent' and from the State Department. I did not anticipate anything in particular for such communications never come by mail, but Helen's heart fluttered at the dread of my having to cross the Atlantic till the letter turned out to be yours, with inscription misread, of Dec. 1. — four weeks on the road.

I too used to collect engravings as a boy and have one or two Vandyck portraits and also a couple of Whistlers bought ages ago when he was still alive and prices were less dizzy. But now many other things tempt my limited purse more. Since we entered the war I try to resist and only succumb with some of the remorse which ladies feel in French novels after their first *rendez-vous*.

I was pleased, however, to pick up in a small shop near Gray's Inn an original Tintoretto drawing of the Last Supper for thirty shillings. But as a rule things to be stuck away in drawers are more fit for bachelors, and I admire Mrs. Holmes's tolerance.

Marguerite has paid us a brief visit here — prettier than ever though almost too thin, and interested as always in you. She has now returned to Gifford over the holidays for the doctor will not let him come to London. It is rough for a keen soldier to be invalided out of the army, but he finds real interest now in raising poultry and painting lacquer. The babies, Helen and Georgina, are with us and the first is now in this room interrupting my letter. They are here rather on sufferance and if the air raids continue are to be packed off, for shivering in the cellar from three to six in the morning is not delectable even for grown ups. Fortunately most raids are at more reasonable hours.

We shall probably leave London in February to return to Florence where I shall look for some kind of work. Nothing has come of my offer of service to our Red Cross in France and I have found little to occupy me here. There is still one possibility left. Certain organizations here whom I have been trying to assist are anxious to have me act as adviser over Near Eastern matters, for my point of view is different from the one hitherto prevailing at Washington. The idea is entirely theirs and not mine and I know very little of what they are doing to bring this about but understand they have written to Brandeis on the subject who is interested in the East from

the Zionist end.   If anything comes of it is another matter.
Please regard this as confidential except of course with regard
to Brandeis.   I should naturally be overjoyed if it came off, for
it concerns a part of the world I am tolerably familiar with
and there is no more important question in this war than its
future.   It's the sewer which will make the house clean or
befoul it.

The war is dragging on in hideous monotony with little to
raise our spirits save the determination of America.   I feel
proud of my country though I hope the distributors of our
national energy will work as well as the accumulators.   Here
all confidence is centered in us though the issue seems to hang
on tonnage.   One of the lady *'Chauffeuses'* was reproved the
other day by an American General who told her she was three
minutes late.   'Oh that's nothing.   You are three years late!'

Have you read Locke's *Red Planet*?   A good war book I
enjoyed.

Helen Hay is at my elbow and keeps me from further
writing, but I am at the end of my paper with only place
enough to send warm wishes for the New Year to you both.

Ever yours,
Lewis Einstein

Jan. 23, 1918

Dear Einstein :

A delightful letter from you deserves a better answer
than it will or can get.   Not only am I always short of time,
(as well as of coal with the rest of the world), but it is making
bricks without straw to try to take one's part in agreeable
conversation when one can read no books but has to think
law all the time.

I admire and revere the eye that enabled you to spot the
Tintoret.   But let me protest that I don't buy things to be
stuck into portfolios.   I have had all my purchases framed
and they are in my library and dressing room ; in the latter
in place of some hideous memorials of friendship, a photograph
of C. J. Terry with huge projecting boots, a large portrait of
Chancellor Kent whose valet I was for three years (the time
spent in annotating his Commentaries) etc.

I will say a word to Brandeis on one theme in your letter, and as to another please give my unabated homage to the charming Marchioness as well as to your wife who I hope and rather infer is better than she has been. As usual you leave a hovering doubt as to the proper direction for this letter. I shall send to Montagu Square being sure, as the Swedish Chancellor said, that whichever I do I shall repent it.

Ah, my lad, your buying engravings in your youth was different from mine! I had no money to speak of, though when I was in the army my pay enabled me to make the last purchases before the present, and I think the careful reflection about some infinitesimal outlay probably lent an intensity to the joy of any acquisition that could not be felt if it came easy. In those days I hoped for some of the series of portraits started by Vandyck and engraved by the pupils of Rubens; but the possession of one by Vandyck himself surpassed my dreams. Now I am beginning to be aware of the collector's feeling, and to wish that my Jan Lutma (Rembrandt) was the second state instead of the third. I don't agree with Hamerton that one should look preferably at the first, (Four copies known; one sold for five thousand dollars and one for ten thousand dollars). It only became a finished work, and, I think, improved, in the second state. However this is only the occupation of rare half hours of a Saturday afternoon.

It is the time for me to scrabble for Court and no longer to scribble for you. Wherefore *adieu* with every good wish.

Yours ever,
O. W. Holmes

Washington, D.C.

Feb. 10, 1918

Dear Einstein:

Your letter of Jan. 15 (?) 18 (?) came yesterday, welcome as ever. I am proud that the charming young Marguerite should remember me for I have remained her slave.

I mentioned your matter to Brandeis in case he should have any voice, with my recommendation of course.

If you see Baron Moncheur again remember me to him.
I like him and have a sincere affection for his wife, from whom
I hear once in a year or six months. She has suffered much
since I last saw her, and I find it hard to write to one who has
been so up against the actualities when I have nothing worth
saying about them, and when other themes must seem if not
frivolous, at least remote.

As to the Bolsheviks I don't know much. I do know of
one or two men who seemed typical conservatives who have
come back converted. I don't worry much about possible
coordinated public changes, and I hardly think that chaos is to
be apprehended here. I do have a vague apprehension that
what you and I think the finest ideals and interests may be, I
won't say swept away, but dimmed and diminished by the
coarsely materialistic ones that are behind so much of what
presents itself with spiritual claims : socialism, pacifism, etc.
I take refuge in the irresponsibility of age, and do my work, as
all that I can do. I see ahead a few days of comparative
freedom.

I must read on irrigation as we have on hand a great case,
involving fundamental problems between States, but I hope
then to be able to turn to your book. As yet I have not a
single volume to put down on my list of books since the beginning of 1918.

I have looked into a volume that I got by some effort lately
on the great painter etchers from Rembrandt to Whistler with
admirable reproductions. Sometimes first states do not seem
to be so interesting or effective pictorially as later ones. I
have a little Ostade that I bought when a boy on Youth ;
an indefinitely late impression such as you are warned against
that seems to me to give more of his poetry of light than the
earlier ones or the photogravures, and to have lost nothing of
the drawing. Ah, my lad, in victuals and in engravings it is
well not to have had luxuries come easy in youth ; to have
gone through the time when some fishy slip from a neglected
portfolio in a print shop was an achievement and a bottle of
Burgundy a celebration. But let me not exult, for I have no
doubt that you acquired knowledge on a higher plane and
think not that I do not bow to you as connoisseur.

I think you would have been amused had you been with

me at my printsellers yesterday p.m. when there was a St. Louis man with aesthetic speech and seemingly with enviable possessions in the way of Rembrandt etc.   He pointed to a drawing that seemed to us evidently a modern copy of a Holbein or something inferior of that general type, and spoke of it as supposed to be a Leonardo.   (I don't mean that he thought it an original, as to that I can't say; but it seemed to me amazing that one could have given it that source.)

I still allow myself to think of prints though Paul Warburg pricked my conscience by saying that it was wrong to spend money for them at this time.   My crimes in any event are very modest.

My compliments to your wife and to the Marchioness, for I take no liberties with her name except in private talk with you.

Yours ever,
O. W. Holmes

Supreme Court of the United States, Washington, D.C.

March 10, 1918

My dear Einstein :
      This delightful letter of yours (Feb. 12) arrives just after I have sneaked a base — or, less metaphorically, turned seventy-seven without too much noise ; it finds me with work on hand so that I shall make but an inadequate return.   But you provoke replies.   The law is not a *chose matérielle* to a philosopher.   It is the great anthropological document and a door to all theories, ethics, economies, sociology, theology or atheology, and in short your view of life and the world.

No Mezzotints for me.   I am a stout old fogey ; etchings and a few line engravings.   Dürer, Nanteuil, and a very few others.   And there are not very many etchings that make me itch for them.   After Rembrandt, Vandyck, and a Whistler or two, and a Seymour Haden or two, I am hankering for Ostade. I bought a famous little landscape by him in fair condition the other day, but could not get the one I most desire.   Others spur me to buy a Zorn, but he seems to me to have mighty little poetry about him, and to be in most of his work an academic peasant whose naked women, though half wonderful for the most part, do not excite my desire (for their presentments).

Since I began this my little Ostade has come home and been hung in my library to the enhancement of my joy. A nervous dame slightly inclined to futile fidgeting reproached me for spending any money for such things and for my detached attitude. As to the former I told her that of course war gradually stripped away everything until nothing but victuals and soldiers were left, that it was a gradual and successive process, and before you reach the extreme is a question of values; that personally I consider art one of the last things to let go as it gives us spiritual food. As to the latter I said that I saw no good in unproductive emotion that merely detracts from one's working force; that I hoped I would go out and be shot in an hour for the cause, but that I wouldn't lie awake for it if I could help it, and I could. I hope you will think me right.

A chap has sent to me for perusal *Les Sentiments de Critias* by Julien Benda. I haven't had time to read it yet. In a recess I did read the two vols. of Merz, *Hist. of Thought in 19th. Cent.* that deal with philosophy, and since have reread Patten's *Development of English Thought*; the latter with renewed amusement, but I have time only to mention them.

I present my homage to the ladies, and say goodbye for the moment.

Yours ever,
O. W. Holmes

Supreme Court of the United States, Washington, D.C.

April 26, 1918

Dear Einstein:

A letter came from you sometime ago, but apart from work, which has been fairly hard, I have little heart to write when not thinking law because of the ever overhanging anxiety of these days. It is a great blessing to be able to forget it and feel that one is doing one's duty in doing so.

I am glad you liked Frankfurter. Most people do. And I am very fond of him. I believe him to have been very useful in work for the Government as he has been in the Law School.

You say your wife finds solace in bridge. I give up in advance all games that require intelligence. I am sure I never could do them well just as I am almost equally sure I never could have been a good fencer, and at least doubt if I ever could have been a good dancer. I was greatly pleased once in talking with Lord Rayleigh,[60] the scientific swell, at the way in which he brought the gifts required for bridge on to our plane, and said, 'I can do this. I can't do that'. When one is talking of capacities it is the rational way, and the results achieved have little or nothing to do with it. I often think of the tremendous ability shown in commercial transactions that leave no mark in history, except in some occasional case like that of Jim Hill with his railroad. I once as a young man was the penman for an agreement on half a sheet of foolscap by which the Atchison and the Denver and Rio Grande ended a private war and divided an empire, and as my partner who was the lawyer on the Atchison side and I walked away I spoke of the big thing that had been done and how it would be forgotten in the years, as it was, while Rob Roy remains a feature in the recollection of men. It teaches one not to accept literary valuations which go on the size of the letters on the posters.

I don't talk of the war. It's of no use, and I have nothing to say worth saying. All the money I can spare that won't be wanted next month for taxes I have put into U.S. bonds according to duty, and naturally I have no new development of my hobby.

I forget whether I ever have mentioned Ostade. I have had a late but charming impression of one of his things since youth and it now hangs here. I bought another little one some time ago. The one I should like is reproduced in Hind's *Short History of Engraving and Etching*, page 189. He had a sweet soul. He interprets the poor with a sympathy the more delightful that it is unconscious. No touch of discreet melo-

[60] John William Strutt, 3rd Baron Rayleigh (1842–1919); distinguished English scientist.

drama and Michael Angelo as with Millet, (whom Heaven forbid that I should undervalue.) He, in Jane Addams' phrase, is good *with* the poor not *to* them. The etching I refer to is a family saying grace over their bowl of porridge. The line of devotion in the little boy's back is as tenderly given as in the Angelus, and the whole thing makes me want to cry. I pity the people who only saw ugly boors in his work.

I read no books at present. A clever man who put up here the other night carried off to his room your book and was deeply interested by it. But most inlets to new ideas are closed to me for the present.

It is time for me to be getting ready to go to Court and I must shut up.

By exception, for I avoid dining out when I can, I dined last night in company with the Lord Chief Justice [61] and Ambassador. He is easy going and rather pleasant to talk to. His wife, I should suppose, would be ditto, if she were not very deaf. He has an intellectual face, methinks, but I don't know the scope of his interests.

My best remembrances to your wife and the young charmer. Would that some day she might realize her thought of writing to me.

Yours ever,
O. W. Holmes

Supreme Court of the United States, Washington, D.C.

May 25, 1918

Dear Einstein:

Your last letter had lain unanswered for some days in the press of work that has been upon me, harder than ever this week, when today your *Prophecy of the War* [62] came. This morning I sent off my last lucubration and got some cigars

---

[61] Rufus Daniel Isaacs, Marquis of Reading (1860–1930); served as English Ambassador to the United States from January 1918 to May 1919 while acting as Lord Chief Justice of England.

[62] *Prophecy of the War* by Lewis Einstein (1918) contained a preface by Theodore Roosevelt and reprinted two articles that had appeared in the January 1913 and November 1914 issues of the *National Review* of London foretelling the war and United States intervention.

(Porto Ricans; I keep Havanas for my friends.) and so I opened the book with an expectation that was not disappointed. I am proud of you for the fine, cool, statesmanlike forecast and the statement of our interests, which by this time I believe the country realizes. I hope and believe too that we are improving in our work, even if the President has not abandoned the notion embodied by Bryan that a phrase is a dud. I don't doubt that he is doing his best, and I am assured that those under him are trying to substitute science for guess and hard fact for moral aphorisms.

I was struck when a French Major here the other night put sentimentality along with a desire for results as a characteristic of our people. I hope that the war will knock it in the head for a long time. My secretary [63] of last year was a pacifist and a socialist, and it was so distinctly a religion with him that counter considerations only made him uncomfortable. Since then he has become engaged to one of the Evartses and perhaps the different milieu will affect him. He was physically unfit for the field or perhaps contagion would have done what reason couldn't.

I have done almost no reading, though I did find time for McIlwain's *High Court of Parliament*; an excellent piece of work, near enough to my subjects to have actuality for me. And I received the other day from Felix Adler [64] his *Ethical Philosophy of Life* in the middle of which I was interrupted by new jobs. It is interesting and moving to me to read works of hyper-aetherial piety, whether from an emancipated few or from a convinced Catholic like my late friend Canon Sheehan of Doneraile. I can imagine a man's being possessed by the ideal of saintliness, but, unfortunately, I can imagine one's being possessed with quite other ideals and can think him equally justified. I should have no criticism for a man who to paint the greatest picture ever painted filled his whole soul with that and never thought of morals. I should have little if any for one who said I would rather be Jim Hill or Rockefeller than

[63] Mr. Shelton Hale was Holmes's secretary 1916–17.
[64] Felix Adler (1851–1933); Professor of Hebrew and Oriental literature at Cornell University from 1874 to 1876. Adler founded the Society for Ethical Culture in New York City in 1876 and became Professor of political and social ethics at Columbia University in 1902. His *An Ethical Philosophy of Life* appeared in 1918.

any saint, and none very certain for one who would sacrifice a million lives for Empire (although I probably should want to kill him.)   So I am afraid my friend Adler will find my answer disappointing, although probably he won't care for it.

I hear the steps of my wife coming for me and must wind up suddenly — being a well trained husband.   My homage to the ladies, and thanks for the pleasure that your writing, MS, or print always gives.

Yours ever,
O. W. Holmes

Supreme Court of the United States, Washington, D.C.

June 13, 1918

Dear Einstein :

A hurried reply only to your letter of May 26.   I grieve over your troubles and can but hope that things will take a turn for the better.

The hurry means that we have adjourned, that we leave for Beverly Farms via New York, in a leisurely way, on Sunday, that one feels as if the bottom had dropped out when work stops, and that, as I am a bad case of train fever, I spend a good deal of time in futile fidgeting (as the accent is not on the last syllable I assume that one T is enough).   I have ready a note to inquire in New York for your *Quatre Cavaliers de l'Apocalypse* by an illegible author.[65]   I have no time or almost none to read down here.

I did reread Santayana's *Egotism in German Philosophy*, which a fellow sent to me the other day, with much more appreciation than the first time.   I don't think it the best of his books, but he always hits me where I live with his prose.   On his poetry I can't recite.   Also some time ago, I forget whether I mentioned it, Felix Adler's, *An Ethical Philosophy of Life* ; a strange quintessence of the Hebrew Scriptures and German philosophy by a man outside the churches ; the *ut de poitrine* of holiness.   He sent it to me, and I wrote to him that I hoped I could understand a man's making an ideal of holiness, (I have a feeling that I have written this to you before), but I also could

<hr>

[65] Vicente Blasco-Ibáñez (1867–1928).

N

understand a man's saying, 'I would rather be Jim Hill than all the saints', or never thinking of ethics but putting his soul into painting a picture. The main thing is that on which one concentrates the energies of one's being. Such things may be quite various and leave ethics a good deal in the background, so far as I am concerned.

Apropos of which I am glad you have turned back a little to the XVIth. Century. I don't remember what you refer to when you say I disparage literary effort. I repudiate the thought allegation. It must have been from some special angle. But I don't quite sympathize with your scorn of Rockefeller. I don't enjoy that kind of society, but I believe him (typically, I don't know much about him personally) to be a great man, and I think we should do justice to those who do big things however little we want to dine with them. I made an apologue with which I still am pleased of a man like Rockefeller coming up for the Day of Judgment forty years ago. Probably I have fired it off to you as my friends all have to hear it.

Do give my ever renewed admiration to the two ladies, and believe me as ever,

Yours,
O. W. Holmes.

Beverly Farms, Massachusetts

July 11, 1918

Dear Einstein :

Your letter telling of your wife's illness comes this morning and gives me a real pang. I readily believe what you say of her and hate to think of her as ill. I hope with all my heart that your next letter will tell that it is all right with her again. My love to her and to her delightful daughter.

As you see I am in my summer retreat, and after a fortnight of the emptiness and collapse that comes upon stopping work I have reached the happy state when I can resort to a lounge and alternate between a book and slumber. I had some work on accounts etc. to be done first. When they were done I took up some reminiscences of Léon Daudet whom I don't fancy as he seemed to be a man who, if his interlocutor differed

from him on important questions, slapped his face. I agree
that the logical result of a fundamental difference is for one
side to kill the other, and that persecution has much to be
said for it; but in private life we think it more comfortable for
disagreement to end in discussion or silence. However I took
another book of L.D.'s, *La Guerre Totale*, and inferred that in
that matter his bellicose propensities had served his country
well as he seems to have been active when others were inert
or afraid in hunting down German machinations in France. It
had something of the interest of a detective story.

Then under Laski's impulse I read or have nearly finished
Mark Pattison's *Life of Casaubon*; an interesting picture of a
poor, real scholar which, however, leaves me with rather a
moderate conception of Mark Pattison whom the echo of
tradition had led me to suppose a more considerable man than
he seems to be here. How can a clergyman of the Church of
England be a considerable man? Or at least can he fail to
show some intellectual or moral soft spot? However, it is
astonishing what people can take for granted if they have been
brought up in it. Somehow I find it easier to swallow in the
Catholics; perhaps because they are so much farther away
from the pretence of rationality. But so far as respect stands
on venerable tradition I don't see but a believing Jew has the
better of the whole Christian crowd. I never shall forget how
a Catholic Mass that I had just heard paled as I heard one
stand up and say, 'Brethren, twenty (and I forget what
hundred) years ago Queen Esther ordered us to celebrate this
day with charity and feasting, and for twenty hundred odd
years we have obeyed this command.' It thrilled me.

I must take this to the post.

Yours ever,
O. W. Holmes

Beverly Farms, Massachusetts

Aug. 16, 1918

Dear Einstein :

It is hard to get time when one is at leisure. Impossible
to get enough to make worthy answers to your so good letters.

Yours of July 2 has lain before me for several days, and what with guests to attend to and business to be done even now I can do no more than begin. In a small house like this you can't leave people staying with you to their own resources.

Thank the Lord, however, my business now is done. I have filed an account which drove me nearly mad, I have read all the improving works on social themes that I mean to bother with, and, but for the people that I must go forth with and talk to, the world would be left to Jules Lemaître and you, for I am reading or rereading some of his *Contemporaries*. I do not share his sympathy with the despair, revolt, pessimism, and disdain dear to French sceptics of his time on the departure of their old beliefs. It seems to me a mixture of melodrama and a remnant of theology. The big God had gone but the little ones remained, and they thought of themselves as spiritual centres outside of the universe and entitled to criticize and look down upon it. One who believes that he is *in*side of it and produced by it is at once more modest and more serene. But J.L. is so kind and generous in his appreciation of points of view, interests, and faculties that he does not share or greatly care for that I find him a very pleasant companion.

I have met pleasant companions in the flesh now and then for an hour or a day and had jaws with them. So many of these younger men overwhelm me with their knowledge that it keeps me modest. Of course the force of the reaction on what a man knows is the main thing; but for the moment I am impressed and depressed at the narrowness of the sphere within which I reach and the worlds of which I know little more than that they exist. I think the philosophers excite my query. I got an article this morning (Aug. 17) from Morris Cohen [66] that digs into the roots of things with the spade of mathematics in a way that causes equal pleasure and despair. However, in the main it favors my general way of looking at things, and does not discourage my bettabilitarian formula of the universe as a spontaneity taking an irrational pleasure in a moment of rational sequence. (Bettabilitarian means one who thinks he don't know anything but can bet with some confidence.)

[66] Morris Raphael Cohen (1880–1947) ; American philosopher whose writings greatly appealed to Holmes. An interesting correspondence between Holmes and Cohen was published in 1948 in 9 *Journal of the History of Ideas*, p. 3 ff.

Enough of this. Give my admiring homage to the two ladies. I do hope that things are still going better with your wife, and that you are straightening out the XVIth Century.

Yours ever,

O. W. Holmes

Beverly Farms

Sept. 28, 1918

Dear Einstein :

Frankfurter was with us for a Sunday after your letter came asking me to speak to him. He said he had written to the right man, I forget his name, and that when he heard he would let me know. But he is a very busy man and may have forgotten to write to me ; at all events I have not heard. I gathered that he had recommended you strongly. I have delayed my answer in the hope for news, but now we are on the verge of leaving for Washington unless we are stopped by an epidemic of grippe, which I hope will not happen. I intend to get there next Wednesday. After I do you must be lenient to my shortcomings as a correspondent for I expect that the work will be hard, as usual.

The vacation has been satisfactory, but ends just as it seemed beginning. I wonder if the reason why time goes more quickly as age advances is not partly that it does so when it is filled with thoughts and more slowly when filled with events, as in youth it is, and partly too no doubt because it goes more rapidly with what we are accustomed to than with what is new. Going out over a new road seems much longer than the return. The terms, of course, did the same before I was accustomed to the work. Well, I consecrated my leisure to improving my mind until the latter part of the time when I said, 'To hell with improvement !' — which I suppose showed that the vacation was doing its proper work.

In all the books that touch on social themes I noticed the same assumption, expressed or implied, that ownership means consumption of the products, that the ever repeated ownership of 9/10 by 1/10 means that 1/10 of the people consume 9/10 of the products — the emptiest humbug that ever served as a red flag. As no doubt I have said many times before I believe that the drain on the public resources by the consumption of the few is an insignificant item. This is an issue of fact upon which I am confirmed by all the information that I have been able to get.

Another theme on which I incline away from the majority is about the calling of our Western Civilization the triumph of Christianity. After reading in and about Virgil and Cicero and noticing how much nearer our real beliefs about life are to theirs than to those of the New Testament it seems to me that really it is Roman Civilization that has triumphed, clothed in what Miss Kingsley (*alio intuitu*) called an oriental misfit. No doubt, however, the New Testament has given to the poor and unhappy the feeling that more than their sorrows had been known to one before, and that he gave them all his sympathy from his throne.

Latterly we have been immensely amused by *The Irish R.M.*[67] and other books by the same authors. We are late in the day but the books are not dead yet. Now that the time is no more I am ready for all the amusement that many of the books down here offer. Earlier I would not look at them, and I still shrink from long novels which formerly I should have devoured. Did you ever hear of (Francis?) Grierson, a writer of a number of small books, *Parisian Portraits* etc. etc.? He seems to have come from the west and to have seen everybody from Dumas *père* to *duchesses* — without letters. I infer that it was by way of singing. The books seemed to me to be rather ordinary though they have been praised by eminent persons, and my curiosity is only as to how he comes to have seen the people he did.

Adieu for the time. I don't know where you are and shall direct to Montagu Square as your permanent address.

My homage to the ladies.

Yours ever,
O. W. Holmes

[67] Possibly *Some Experiences of an Irish R.M.* by Somerville and Ross (1903), a then popular humorous book describing the adventures of an Irish Resident Magistrate.

Supreme Court of the United States, Washington, D.C.

Oct. 31, 1918

Dear Einstein :

　　You will get but a dull and short answer to yours from the Villa Schifanoia. Not that I am not well. I am. The epidemic of influenza, which has killed a good many here and made it necessary for us to adjourn, has not touched me so far. But I am in that unsatisfactory intellectual condition that comes from having had leisure enough to finish up various details that required attention and not enough to read anything considerable or to venture into fresh fields. My highest flight has been to reread a few chapters in the *Education of Henry Adams* (queer combination of power and pompous futility) and half of Lord Charnwood's *Life of Lincoln*. The latter was fresh to me and I had to go into it and was glad to admit the author to be an artist. But I hate to read about those days, and should praise God if I had finished the book or someone stole it.

　　I hope the next news of your wife will be better. I confess I have some difficulty in imagining her happy in New York or here, but you know better than I. Indeed I should have thought that you were transplanted and would miss the atmosphere of the old world.

　　Meantime here the face of the world has changed for us with the changes of the war. I wish I didn't always feel an element of the uncertain about the President. I don't know how much remains of his psalm singing and belief that phrases were things, but I hope highly ; and I don't forget, as some seem to, that the Germans are not conquered yet.

　　My homage to your ladies.

Yours as ever,

O. W. Holmes

Supreme Court of the United States, Washington, D.C.

Nov. 30, 1918

Dear Einstein :

　　Your letter of 3 Nov. came last night. You never need be afraid of being as autobiographical as you like, for you always speak to an interested and sympathetic ear. I am inclined to be glad that you cannot gratify your wish to come back here. Sentimentally, it is natural, but I fear that you would find that you missed the amenities of Europe more than you realize. You have lived abroad so long that you must have become shaped to expectations and demands that would not be satisfied here. I should like to see you settle down and write a book. I am on your wife's side. Expatriation is a misfortune; but a scholar and thinker is his own home, and the opportunities for your work are better in Europe than here. I should have thought H. James a stronger man if he had been able to turn his native atmosphere and surroundings into poetry as, to take a modest example, I thought it a merit in James Whitcomb Riley to do; but your material is more nearly at hand where you are, and I incline to believe that you will get more out of life if you stay there. I am pretty sure that for a time at any rate there would be a reaction of disappointment if you came back. But the opinion of a third person is not worth much and I hold mine modestly.

I have just finished a spasm of work that lasted a few days until I got my cases written and now am looking forward to a few days break of relative leisure — introduced by an hour at the dentist's in forty minutes from now.

I have suffered a great loss in the death of Miss Beatrice Chamberlain who was a constant correspondent and intimate friend of mine in spite of a running quarrel over her belief that England always was right and the best ever. I cannot realize or truly believe that I shall see her no more. It always is hard with a strong vitality. But age accustoms a man to being stripped. It began with the Civil War, and now all my oldest intimates except my wife are gone. Yet one always has some goal ahead. Apart from the possibility of seeing England once more I hope now to keep at work till eighty, and if I reach that (in a little over two years) no doubt I shall fix another time to be climbed to. Life is functioning, and an end in itself. To function healthily even in the least mentionable ways is a pleasure. To do so in the exercise of one's best faculties is the joy of life. An ancient morality, but one to which I recur at every moment.

The dentist is over, praise the Lord, bar a half hour's

finishing on Monday. My telephone also has been restored to health, and I am hoping for a serene moment. Such moments are hard to get and more often dreamed of than accomplished.

I will first polish off a little book on Mysticism in English Literature, a theme that always interests me. I think the first adult book of the reflective sort that I read as a boy was *Hours with the Mystics*, and little as I believe in their private conversations with God, little as I can conceive that the way to get nearest to the centre of things is to abolish all the activities implanted in us and to get into a state of yearning receptivity, they interest me. My own beliefs are mystic in a different way. I see myself only as an intelligible moment of the unintelligible and unimaginable. I suppose I have written pretty much all this before — but if you can't repeat, why talk? Now I will sally forth to see some war pictures and feel free if I can. I always am haunted by the thought that I am neglecting some duty.

My homage to your wife. I am so glad to hear that Florence agrees with her so well.

Yours ever,
O. W. Holmes

THE HONORABLE LEWIS EINSTEIN
from a photograph taken December 1960

PART THREE
1919–31

Supreme Court of the United States, Washington, D.C.

Jan. 5, 1919

Dear Einstein :

A welcome letter from you. But you must not say that I think you unfitted to take a place in American life. I hardly can judge or should undertake to judge about that. It was how you would like it when the first glow was over that I had in mind. I fear that you would miss much that you now take for granted; just as we don't think about health when we are well. Henry James seemed to detest it, though I admit that he is not an example to be argued from. Your wife naturally would find it even harder. I should think New York would be disagreeable unless one were rich or beginning a career. And yet where would you find what you need outside of New York? But my practicalities are confined within my narrow limits, and I am the least fitted of men to talk about the subject. Don't forget that for it is literally true.

I rejoice at the thought of seeing you again. According to the schedule before me we have recesses from March 31 to April 14 and from May 5 to 19; but I rarely work at night at any time.

A recess is just ending now in which, after finishing my opinions, I have had a little time to read a little law; a book by Brandeis about Business (impressive) and also off my beat, Strachey's very clear *Eminent Victorians*, which convinces you that you see the men, the people I should say, as Florence Nightingale, a demon, is one of them. Lord, how I should have disliked a Christian English Gentleman brought out on his pattern by Dr. Arnold! Brave, of good form, and with a serene dogmatism, too deep to be conscious of itself, that excluded even recognition of the existence of most of the things I care for and believe. I will include with this a little article [1] that tells some of these things written to relieve my

---

[1] 'Natural Law', *32 Harvard Law Review*, 40-48 (1918).

mind one morning last summer and seized for the Harvard Law Review by Laski to whom I read it while the fit was on.

I also read with no little feeling a book on ' *The Ideals of the East with special reference to the Art of Japan* ' by Okakura, an authority, and, I think, a man who had charge of the collection in the Boston Art Museum for a time. There is much detail that I don't follow in the names of places, sects, and persons, but he gives you a great feeling of the continuous reaction of religious thought upon Eastern Art, of the unity of the East, (He begins : The East is one) of its haughty conviction that it is the centre and source of the greatest thought, and that it must look to its own past for its future. It seemed to me a big, little book. But all the beliefs of the different peoples that they are It, that they represent the *ne plus ultra* of the Cosmos, English, French, German, Japanese etc. make me smile when they don't irritate me as I said the Christian English Gentleman would. The volume happened to come on top of a little discussion with Brandeis the other day in which he affirmed much the same superiority for the Oriental mind. I said, 'Produce the documents. I can show you a hundred, I dare say many hundred Western books that seem to me to touch life and the world at more points and in a profounder way than anything I know of the East.' But Brandeis would claim men like Heine as characteristically Oriental, and I suppose if I should mention Zimmern's *Greek Commonwealth* would reply that that also was written by a Jew. I must admit that a large proportion of my later friends from Paul Warburg to Frankfurter and Laski are Jews. Herewith I close.

I suppose you have a better chance than I to judge whether the President's European trip is likely to prove useful. I have the scepticism of ignorance about the League to enforce peace, but am too conscious of ignorance not to leave open in my mind whether it is the great possibility to be snatched before it is too late.

My best regards to your wife.

Yours ever,

O. W. Holmes

Villa Schifanoia, Via Boccaccio, Florence

2 February 1919

Dear Justice Holmes:

I am certain that some accordeon minded student will one day stretch out your pearls into a long necklace, and you who thought to live as a jurist will for future ages have become mainly a philosopher — but that will be long hereafter for we are entering into an age of faith and collective energy and barbarism, and I think of you as one of the last of the great pagans, a Symmachus [2] living in a world of Goths.

For myself I see things as you do though more from the historical than the philosophical point of view, and try to find satisfaction in the humbler contentments of life without any belief in my messianic purpose. I have little belief in my ability to move the smallest fraction of mankind and less in the utility of so doing if applying the drill sergeant's methods to conduct. One slips back easily here into the local temperament of skepticism and the contentment of a life without struggle. Only the other day my wife was remarking that the unreality of our existence here seems to her the only reality. To play about in the garden, supervise workmen, write a little, read a little, play bridge a little are its landmarks. Her health allows her feverish energy no great field while my own resolution is sicklied o'er by many a pale cast. Her health, Roosevelt's death, and your letters have been three factors which have led me to delay my journey home until the autumn. I shall miss not seeing you sooner but hope you will not then be too occupied to spare me an occasional hour. I have no plans but shall venture over for a general 'look see' as one says in pidgin English. Will there be any chance of seeing you in England in the summer? I suppose we shall spend it in Scotland. Marguerite is expecting in April and we all hope it will be a boy after her two girls. How important hereditary absurdities still are! She often asks after you and I know it would give her real pleasure to see you again.

[2] Quintus Aurelius Symmachus (c. 345–410); Pontifex Maximus, Pro-Consul for Africa, and Consul in 391, Symmachus was the brilliant champion of the pagan Senate against the Christian Emperors of Rome.

I must try to get hold of Okakura's book though my own superficial impression of the East after some years of contact is that it is living on its reputation, has lost its virtues, and hasn't been able as yet to replace them by our own mechanically pedestrian progress. I never could see much orientalism, or, for that matter, much genius in Heine (though I love him), and think the orientalism of Western Jews about as far fetched as the Aryan theory. I never could see why people or races needed fictitious pedigrees or couldn't admit that acquired traits weren't comparatively recent innovations due to natural circumstance. To wit, love of liberty and love of the sea, were both about as foreign to England during most of the XVIth century as dialectics is to the Fiji Islands. I am just writing a lecture on the character of Henry VIII for the British Institute here where I think I can show that he was a great moral innovator and his own bad example led to an improvement in family relations. You have preached often enough that things are not necessarily what they are labelled and Jews and for that matter orientals should be reduced to a surprising commonplaceness of level if they are not made to play antics for the crowd's benefit.

I can hardly judge as yet of the effects of the President's visit. Here in Italy he had a very real welcome and did what Poincaré could not have done without arousing anger. In France for national reasons he is less popular. As Clémenceau remarked to a French friend of mine 'Ce Wilson m'embête'.

Ever yours,
L. E.

Washington, D.C.

Feb. 23, 1919

Dear Einstein :

Your letter is welcome as usual, Jan. 11 ; it arrived this last week and took its time.

As to growing older I made this poem to myself as I walked a few days ago :

> I will sit in the seats of the mighty
> If I can, until I am eighty (pronounce 'ity)

And what I'll do then
In the following ten
I leave to the Lord God Almighty.

But your centenarian is encouraging.

I have had a week of quasi leisure and devoted more than a day to a very interesting book by Coppier about the etchings of Rembrandt. He studies them as a connoisseur, a historian, and a forged note detective all in one, and I feel really instructed by the brief debauch. Comparison with his reproduction satisfied me that my Dr. Faustus, (he says it isn't Faust but another man of nearly the same name living and well known in R's time) that my copy was a very good impression. I have some other etchings of his in later states. I told you of my purchase of Jan Lutma.

I read a book by Parodi, *Traditionalisme et Démocratie*, which nicely smacked the Royalist and Catholic reactionaries like Bourget. But how before the flood a book on such subjects printed in 1909 seems!

There are various other excursions and alarums in my mind, but I shall have little time, and it will depend somewhat on what I can get without too much trouble. What a pity that one can't set a mechanical half of oneself to reading dull books that one ought to have read before dying and meanwhile think about actualities. You would say I never did if you knew how ignorant I am of the League of Nations and all that everyone talks about. I get my Secretary to pump a few rudiments into me once in a while, but in the main live as remote as Archimedes in his siege. Don't think I pride myself in it. I regret it, but can't help it. As the French justify themselves by generalizing their infirmities so do I. *Je suis comme ça.*

I was interrupted in the last sentence by a call from a returned officer looking very military and handsome; a chap who some years ago when I was talking scepticism about improvements by law stuck me under the fifth rib with the retort, 'You would found legislation on regrets rather than on hopes'. What an improvement khaki and a military bearing are! This chap has earned it at the front; but I know some spurred jurists who have almost frightened me by their smartness without even having left Washington. If a hoplite ($\delta\pi\lambda\iota\tau\eta s$) were not a foot soldier I should like to apply the adjective hyperhoplitic.

o

Well, my lad, I haven't talked much sense this time, but this will remind you of me and carry my homage to your wife. I hope that Florence is agreeing with her.

Yours ever,

O. W. Holmes

Washington, D.C.

April 5, 1919

My dear Einstein :

This must be an apology for a letter in answer to your amusing one of March 16 containing what I hope was apocrypha as to Miss Margaret Wilson [3] *et al.*   Also to your articles in the *Rassegna Italo Britannica*,[4] which I read with my usual deference for your learning and with interest of course.   Also I have had it in my mind that I never acknowledged a letter of the beginning of February which arrived just after I had sent off one. It deserved a special statement of accord, so far as my unsufficient knowledge goes, with your scepticism as to the talk about the Oriental mind, labels, and supposed pedigree.   I used to say similar things about the American novel.   There is no such thing.   We have world standards ; and a novel or a legal opinion or a picture must be good by them or it doesn't count.

Just now I am receiving some singularly ignorant protests against a decision [5] that I wrote sustaining a conviction of Debs, a labor agitator, for obstructing the recruiting service. They make me want to write a letter to ease my mind and shoot off my mouth ; but of course I keep a judicial silence.

Early in life I saw much of the abolitionists in whom I believed devoutly, but it gave me a lasting disgust for Comeouters.   They are so cocksure on the strength of semi-education. They may be one of the disagreeable necessities of progress, but I wonder how many of them could give an intelligent statement of what progress is — or even what they mean by it.   I

[3] The unmarried eldest daughter of President Woodrow Wilson.
[4] 'The League of Nations in the Renaissance and Vita Britannici' in the February, November, and December 1918 numbers respectively of the *Rassegna Italo Britannis*.
[5] *Debs* v. *United States*, 249 U.S. 211 (1919).

asked my secretary what it was and he said increasing complexity. I thought that good for a starter. I was inclined to doubt whether I could confidently call any step one toward progress unless it were to get broader napes to our necks. That we could help and it would be progress to help it along, but the only way I know of to do so would strike horror to the breasts of my fellow citizens including those who regard me as an old fogey to be got rid of as soon as may be.

Did I mention a good study of Rembrandt's etchings by Coppier? That gave me pleasure as did also, contrary to my expectation as I hate to read about the time, Rhodes's *History of the Civil War*. It's quite off my line but his sister, Mrs. Mark Hanna, sent it to me. Now I must go at my friend Laski's *Authority in the Modern State* dedicated to Frankfurter and me. He is a mysterious young man from Oxford. The most learned for his years I have ever met and a great pleasure to me, but, I am told, viewed by Boston as dangerous — (as I used to be) I don't know why.

Homage to your ladies. I hope the expected event was as decreed?

Yours ever,
O. W. Holmes

Villa Schifanoia, Via Boccaccio, Florence

5 May 1919

Dear Justice Holmes:

I am writing you a brief note to say how shocked we are to hear of the outrageous attempt made on you [6] and how thankful that it was frustrated. But it is incredible that you of all people should have been the butt for such a crime. Where all reason fails one can only express oneself emotionally and inarticulately while one's indignation boils over. My wife was wildly furious about it and there is little judicial in my judgment whatever else may remain — *noblesse oblige!* I can sympathize

[6] A bomb mailed to Holmes's address was detected and stopped at the Post Office in the end of April 1919.

with Mrs. Holmes though I am sure she remained imperturbable and would keep cool in the crater of Vesuvius.

These lines are just a short and informal thanksgiving service. I cut them short to leave for a joyride to celebrate it more adequately.

Ever yours,
L. E.

Supreme Court of the United States, Washington, D.C.

May 22, 1919

Dear Einstein :

Your letter of April 27 came a few days ago and this morning that of May 5 with its kind expressions as to the bomb incident. I haven't thought much about it except when reminded by letters, for, as I said to my wife, if I worried over all the bullets that have missed me I should have a job. As you say or intimate if the senders knew how I think and feel perhaps they wouldn't have wanted to blow me up. I have said several times it brought home to me what, if we don't read into it what is not there, seems to me the greatest saying of antiquity — the words on the Cross : 'They know not what they do.' That seems to have in it the recognition of the inevitables, of the mechanical nature of what seems the spontaneity of man, the condemnation of all the condemnations that since have been launched in the name of the utterer. It is the one suggestion of the modern man I know of from classic days. For the classics generally are as first intentioned as the bark of a dog. At least so they seem to me. I daresay I may have remarked before that the manners of a Greek chorus are those of our poor. They say what they think without polite qualification. 'Yes you are looking awful thin'. 'Yes you were very high and now you are down and out'. 'God keep *you* from pride of heart.' etc.

Please give my love and thanks to your wife for her kind thought. I do hope she is getting better. By the by, in looking into the Revised Version to get a rather belated verification of the phrases quoted by her I see a note 'Some ancient authorities omit' the passage. The most dramatic and impressive thing in the whole. I should like to see the MSS. I agree with you on that theme, though I have seen few in my life.

Dear boy, I was hoping to expatiate on things in general and at length, but the C.J. has asked me to write a case that involves difficulties and distracts my mind. I must stop *in medias* or else let this letter lie by unfinished which I abhor.

That diabolical Brandeis has skewered my heart by speaking thus as to vacation : 'You talk about improving your mind. You only exercise it dealing with the subjects familiar to you. You should do something new — take an excursion into some domain of unfamiliar fact, e.g. the textile industry in Massachusetts, and, after reading the reports etc., go to Lawrence and see with your own eyes what it means.' I hate facts, and I feel as if it might be a solemn call to duty. We shall see. It has made me squirm within anyhow.

Goodbye for the moment my friend, and do not blame my sudden collapse herein.

My compliments to the Marchioness. I remember what old Fitzroy Kelly [7] said to my wife : '*Le bon temps viendra.*'

Yours ever,
O. W. Holmes

Yester, Gifford, Edinburgh

6 July 1919

Dear Justice Holmes :
Just a line to acknowledge your letter which was forwarded here from Florence. For we have been here since mid June to see Marguerite and her now three babies, and to shiver in what is only a summer by almanac. I dare say I shall soon regret this cold as I expect to sail for New York on the 22nd with the 'Mauretania'. A wire asking me to report to the Chairman of the Republican National Committee has hastened my departure, and I now look forward with very mixed feelings of regret at leaving Helen, who has in her the stuff of the Hindoo widow, and pleasure at seeing my own country once more with the prospect of activity, and also I hope I shall see Mrs. Holmes and you. Will you be passing

---

[7] Sir Fitzroy Kelly (1798–1880) ; Lord Chief Baron of the Exchequer, 1866–80.

through New York? A line to the Farmers Loan and Trust Co., William Street, will reach me, for I have as yet little notion of where I will be, but somewhere or other I shall see you.

I have just come back from a walk with Marguerite to Goblin Hall in the old Castle — a fine old family ruin vastly improved by the trees grown upon its decay.

The days roll by leisurely here and it is hard to realize the swifter rhythm of life beyond. I should enjoy the calm peace of Yester as of Schifanoia more if the war had not left me morally groggy. I feel as if I had lost my pins and had to find them again. Even peace here has caused little rejoicing, and when Gifford was asked to plant a tree to commemorate it he said he would only plant a monkey puzzle.[8] Up on your heights you remain an Olympian, but I feel very perplexed and little certain of anything except Wilson's mistakes. Yet like the old Sicilian woman who prayed for the tyrant's life I feel that those of tomorrow will be worse than those of today. So much for optimism! Apart from that whatever one's ideas I find it is possible to pursue a number of the minor interests of life with considerable satisfaction, and that one's immortal soul occupies a very small part in a mortal body. Here golf, tennis, bridge, and babies take up an infinite time, and I must not be ungrateful to the cook. The cream is rich, the fruit is ripe, the air is good. What more can one wish, and were I wiser I should not wish more.

Marguerite inquires with interest after you, and my wife sends her love to you both. The teabell has rung its curfew on my lines.

Ever yours,

L. E.

Beverly Farms, Massachusetts

July 23, 1919

Dear Einstein:

Welcome home. But, alas for my chances, my wife has been ill and, though much better, the house here is still in such

---

[8] *Araucaria imbricata*: a Chilean nut-bearing evergreen with intertwined branches and spiky leaves.

condition that I can't put you up, if otherwise you could be tempted to this very quiet spot. I shall wait to hear from you on your arrival, and we will see whether anything is then possible.

Yours ever,

O. W. Holmes

Beverly Farms

Sept. 19, 1919

Dear Einstein:

Your letter relieves me from anxiety about you, but finds me still in a quandary as to our meeting. My wife is much better but so far has seen no callers, partly I think from shrinking and partly because she still is very easily tired. We intend to go straight through to Washington on October 1. I have taken a state room so that she can lie down. The servants go with us, but we shall go to the Shoreham for a few days until the house is comfortable for her. That is all that I can say as it is all that I can foresee.

Naturally I have been very quiet, and I have taken the opportunity to put in a few of the many stories that have been missing from my foundations, in the way of books.

I do hope that we may soon talk together, but I see no chance of it unless you should be called to Washington again. I can't offer to put you up in the present state of my wife's health, although the doctor said yesterday that her only trouble now was *anno domini*. We both have kept so well up to now that I find it hard to believe. I still hope to see eighty in harness.

Yours ever,

O. W. Holmes

Dec. 29, 1919

Dear Einstein:

Many thanks for your letter and for the earlier Nation.[9] I have every disposition to agree with what you write but not knowledge enough to entitle me to judgment.

---

[9] The December 6, 1919, number of the *Nation* contained an article by Lewis Einstein on the proposed mandate for Constantinople.

You give me much pleasure by what you say of your evenings here. As you know you always are welcome and I highly value your friendship. I hope I may see you again before you go home.

Yours ever,
O. W. Holmes

15 Jan. 1920

Dear Justice Holmes :

One word of goodbye before sailing on Saturday for Italy. Though it is only *Au Revoir* for I expect to be back in three months this time with Helen. On my return I am to be appointed on the Republican Advisory Platform Committee in charge of foreign policy — though this is still private. I don't know if it will amount to anything, but it is a matter of intense satisfaction for me to get back into any kind of 'functioning' connected with my own land and to feel other ties here than those of sentiment. After these years of homeless depression abroad I have felt that pure beauty and even the utmost devotion a man can have are insufficient substitutes for natural roots.

I can't tell you how much I enjoyed seeing you both in Washington or what a privilege I regard it to have your friendship.

Ever yours,
L. E.

Beverly Farms, Massachusetts

Sept. 10, 1920

Dear Einstein :

Your letter dated 5th arrived here last night. It gives me great pleasure for I didn't know where you were or what you were about, otherwise I should have written.

At the moment I am a little below par, after having had a pull down usual to me at this season, aggravated by going to town and sitting in a case on Tuesday. However it is nothing to howl about and I am on the up grade.

I am sorry to say that there is no chance of seeing you in New York as we go slam through on the 29th., and I am afraid that it is too late to hope to see you here. The last part of the time here the house is not in shape for guests, and I suppose you are kept pretty steadily at your job. But you will be in Washington, I expect, later.

I have spent a very quiet summer seeing very few people and taking in a certain amount of mental improvement; mostly dull books that I didn't believe, but one masterpiece, Tourtoulon, (Professor at Lausanne) *Principes Philosophiques de l'Histoire de Droit*, a wise sceptic who knows how little we know. Also I think my friend Harold Laski's book on *Political Thought in England from Locke to Bentham* is pretty masterly — the introduction A.1. (Home University Library Series, Henry Holt & Co.).

In my present slightly enfeebled condition I have got rid of the sense of duty and take up any little piddling thing that I happen to see in the shelves. I have just grasped Cranford! I have read one or two of Conrad's novels, of course with absorption. Any novel absorbs me while I am in it, but without the superlative delight that many feel. And one day, for one day, an itinerant motor van came to anchor (so to speak, it was a land craft) by the side of the beach, having inside a little book shop and run by two rather pleasing young women. Under the aegis of my wife I ventured in and the first thing I saw was *The Moon and Sixpence*. Remembering your recommendation I nabbed it and read it, perhaps not quite with your enthusiasm but with a good deal, and was glad of the venture.

In short I have allowed myself sufficient distractions, and still read stories with gusto although rather more shy of beginning them than I used to be. The books on social themes published nowadays seem generally astraddle of some formula for bliss, and as I don't believe any formula except to tackle your job and do your damnedest they leave me cold or hostile. The world longs for some cheap and agreeable substitute for hard work and welcomes every promise. So humbug has the most friends.

You certainly do know how to write good letters, and your Senator with his Louie tickles me.[10]

I hope your wife gets some compensating pleasures, but fear that the summer has been a trying one for you both.

Please give my kindest remembrances to her. I hope you will get credit for your work. You don't tell me where to direct my letter so hesitatingly I follow the heading on yours.

Yours ever,

O. W. Holmes

Washington, D.C.

October 3, 1920

Dear Einstein :

It was a disappointment to miss the chance of seeing you and your wife, but we have to consider what on the whole causes the least wear and tear and latterly have believed that on the whole it is best to slam through. It isn't as if we were twenty years younger. To my infinite relief after one day of rest my wife came out smiling and the transit has been a success. Also there was less than usual to do in getting into shape (on my part) in the way of disposing of the mass of books and pamphlets that accumulate in summer and all the other things necessary to clear the decks for action. The storm will break tomorrow or next day and I expect to be mad with the effort to dispose of the work to be done. We shall see you later, which is a consolation, but I don't expect to do any reading for sometime after today. Indeed even today I have my hands full of last preparations notwithstanding what I have said as to the decks being cleared.

I have found time to tuck in R. Rolland's *Liluli* sent by a dame. (I hate to have books lent to me and am worried until they have been returned). It has a lot of knowing touches, but the general implied moral, as if war were a swindle on the laborer perpetuated by various humbugs, I regard as empty bosh. I don't invest largely in *illuminés*, upward and on-

---

[10] Einstein's letter containing this reference is missing. See Appendix, page 366.

warders, or inventors of schemes for bliss without hard work. To file in and do your damnedest remains now as heretofore the only solution, to my mind.   One thing that you say reminds me of what I told a chap the other day, that he was repining because Chaos elected the other man God.

I must turn aside from this without expatiating on things in general as I should like to, just repeating my regrets and hopes, and sending homages to your wife.

Yours ever,
O. W. Holmes

Supreme Court of the United States, Washington, D.C.

Oct. 10, 1920

Dear Einstein :

A delightful letter from you for which I can make no adequate return.   I have been mad with work and must go back to it anon.   There are times during the term when it is impossible to get the freedom of mind necessary to write a pleasant letter.   Indeed I am afraid that it will be so during most of our sitting.

I sympathize with your difficulties about speaking.   The uneducated have an advantage in not being critical and in more easily getting rid of the self consciousness that is the root of the advantages of the modern over the ancient.   But if one has something to say one can transcend the troubles.

Your friend Sforza [11] was echoing *quam parva sapientia regitur mundus*.   I always tell my secretaries that they will have a chance to realize it.

I dined last night with our neighbours the Johnsons [12] whose pictures you may have seen.   They handed me a critical account of those which he gave to the National Museum by Rose of Arkansas which is a very good piece of writing of a somewhat old fashioned sort, in *Art and Archaeology* (published in Washington.)   It makes me want to go and look at them when the chance comes though I suppose that I saw them in former days in his house.   According to the account they are

[11] Count Carlo Sforza (1873–1952) ; Italian antifascist statesman.
[12] Mr. and Mrs. Ralph Cross Johnson.

very fine, although I observe that the writer professes incompetence in the matter of attribution. But this is about the only distraction that I have had from work lasting from after breakfast until dinner time, and I have no other matter to talk about.

Before we got started, as I may have mentioned, Brandeis lent me Haldane's [13] account of his part in preparation for the war which struck me as very noble and candid and as making the impression of a great man, which I am the more glad to believe as Haldane has always from an early date said kind things to and of me, a circumstance that influences most of us egotists. I believe there are about three survivors who do not castrate that last word by leaving out the *t*. I am one of them. All our tendencies are to be apologetic and soft and to give an infusion of sentiment where it does not belong, as in home for house in the rancid English of the reporters.

Well, dear boy, I must shut up and turn to applications for *certiorari* of which I suppose I must be ready to recite on about fifty by next Saturday. If you ask what a *certiorari* is I must answer with Jeremiah Mason to a client: 'That is something that your Heavenly Father never meant you to know.'

Warmest remembrances to your wife.

Yours ever,

O. W. Holmes

Supreme Court of the United States, Washington, D.C.

Oct. 21, 1920

Dear Einstein :

While the work is on here I can't write letters worth reading, if I ever can. This is merely a memorandum therefore to explain silence.

I will add an item, however, from a book that I have looked

[13] Richard Burdon Haldane, 1st Viscount of Cloan (1856–1928); British statesman and philosopher, Lord High Chancellor of Great Britain 1912–15 and again 1924. Enthusiastic student of German philosophy and life he is credited as Secretary of State for War (1905–12) with carrying out reorganization of the British army and introducing the concept of the General Staff on an imperial scale. Ignorantly accused of being pro-German by irresponsible elements of the press, he spent the war out of public service devoted to philosophical studies the fruits of which appeared in his *The Reign of Relativity* (1921). The book referred to by Holmes in his letter is *Before the War* by R. B. Haldane (1919).

into, James Huneker's autobiographical recollections,[14] I forget the title.   A friend speaking of one exhibition by a songster the night before said it was obscene but not heard, which tickles me.

I hope you both are well.   My homage to Madame.

Yours ever,

O. W. Holmes

Supreme Court of the United States, Washington, D.C.

March 8, 1921

Dear Mrs. Einstein:

You radiate beauty and beautiful things, and I thank you for turning your light on me.   I have not been able to thank you in person and am so tied up with engagements that I fear that I may delay unduly in paying my respects.   But I hope you will know how pleased I am that you should have remembered me.

Sincerely yours,

O. W. Holmes

Supreme Court of the United States, Washington, D.C.

May 20, 1921

Dear Einstein:

Your letter really moves me from the true kindness and friendship that it shows.

The cost to me is not so great as it might seem.   For a year the Chief [15] has been laboring against infirmities and pain, and, I think, could not have looked forward to much else. So that for him death must have been a release, little as he desired it.   Since he was Chief Justice I have seen much less of him than I used to, and, although there were points of keen mutual understanding, the close companionship that at one time seemed possible or probable did not exist.   But he had

[14] Possibly *Painted Veils* by James Huneker (1920).
[15] Chief Justice White died on May 19, 1921.   William Howard Taft was appointed Chief Justice in June of the same year.

qualities that always appealed to one's affections and there never was any alienation or coldness. I shall miss him a good deal personally, but speaking between ourselves I doubt if he could have been very useful to the Court if he had recovered. Still he was a big figure and will leave a great blank. I am talking intimately to your private ear. I can say no more as I am pressed until after the funeral tomorrow.

Do tell your wife that the plant that she gave us on my birthday has been a continuous delight to my wife until within a week. The way in which after the flower was gone it formed a seed vessel was watched by her with rapture day by day, and often I was taken by the ear to see and admire when I was struggling to get upstairs to a case. I thank you again.

Yours as always,
O. W. Holmes

Beverly Farms

Aug. 9, 1921

Dear Einstein :

It is good to hear from you. I had no notion where you were. My affectionate homage to the ladies.

I am or have been until yesterday evening, when I finished Aristotle's *Metaphysics*, (in a translation), pursuing a quiet philosophic debauch begun by Haldane on Relativity. Dear man, he wrote a most pleasing notice of my book and sent me his'n. Then fired by him I read the strikingest book in the world for the mixture of prophetic insight and charlatan word juggling (as I think) : Hegel's *Logic*, Wallace's translation. Oh damn him ! As I have observed before I repeat he cannot persuade me that he can make a syllogism wag its tail, or, less metaphorically, that he can get from logic into time and create the universe out of nothing. Aristotle always surprises me by the extent to which he has made the world for two thousand years think in his terms. The book also is a compound of profound verities and the discussion of sophisms no longer worth understanding and to which a sufficient answer is pooh. It seems to have been the foundation of the Christian conception of God, and but for it and its influence I doubt if Hegel would have selected *Being* for tight rope dancing. Oh how it bores me to read books that long since have ceased to be revelations and that are now important only in the history of thought. Yet I should have been unwilling to die leaving their rotten bones ungnawed.

Once in a while one allows oneself pleasure. I had it in Thomson's *Greeks and Barbarians* and still more in Taylor's *The Medieval Mind*, learned and delightful at once, also my instruction in tracing the process from the Latin fathers to a living appropriation and new product. In the light way I thought Shaw's *Back to Methuselah* a failure in spite of his wit. And I do detest the bringing of literary experience to back up dogmatic utterances when you are convinced that the speaker is not entitled to dogmatize, in fact don't care what he thinks. In *Greeks and Barbarians* Ruskin was quoted for what seemed to me another case. He says, and marks as deliberate, that the condition of Adam Smith's mind was damned; which only convinces me that the Good Ruskin could be an ass.

Well, this will I hope reach a hand across the Atlantic.

Yours ever,

O. W. Holmes

Presumably your book [16] has been sent to Washington and I shall not see it till I get there. Much to my regrets.

Beverly Farms

Aug. 25, 1921

Dear Einstein:

Your book (*Tudor Ideals*) [17] has come and has been swallowed with gluttonous pleasure. I was deeply interested from start to finish; instinctively also, of course, as I am not learned upon the theme. Were you here I should make some criticism in matters of style, but those are subordinate. You

---

[16] *Tudor Ideals* by Lewis Einstein (1921).

[17] A historical study of English life in the sixteenth century written 'because of the hope that an interest in ideals, and not in events, in currents of opinion, and not in annals, may, perhaps, stimulate a closer inquiry into a period embracing the formative elements in the life of all English speaking nations'. *Tudor Ideals*, p. vi.

had to deal with impalpables and those you made me feel. I wrote an answer to your letter a few days ago.

Yours ever,

O. W. Holmes

Beverly Farms

Sept. 12, 1921

Dear Einstein :

Your letter of the 25th crossed one from me thanking you for your book and the pleasure it had given me. As I am just a little pallid today and am expecting the Bryces [18] to-morrow for two nights I shall write but a line.

I am living as heretofore putting in a little improvement against the time when I must give it, or what the bar has to take for it, and under those imperatives to which you advert and from which you are so happily free. I view a tendency toward industry as one of my most sinister traits, having long said that those who make the most of themselves don't make much. But I am worried if I don't take in something every day or two. At this moment I am in the middle of Bradley's *Shakespearean Tragedy*, a perhaps excessively thorough piece of criticism and study of Hamlet, Othello, King Lear, and Macbeth. But it always impresses one to see reverence and loyalty leading to such devout scrutiny of what anyone else has written. I find it hard to care enough for any written word, and I am afraid that I should have the same trouble with other forms of art. Which suggests : Did you see that account of a doubtful Leonardo being authenticated by the finger prints in the paint? An amazing and delightful tale if true.

I infer that you haven't heard from the shrines of diplomacy as yet? We expect to go to Washington on the 28th. to begin work.

My most devoted homage to your ladies.

Yours ever,

O. W. Holmes

[18] James Bryce, Viscount Bryce (1838–1922) ; British jurist, historian, politician, Ambassador in Washington from 1907 to 1913, and recipient of degrees from thirty-one Universities of which fifteen were in the United States. Bryce's *American Commonwealth* (1888) was a standard authority on the American political system in the United States for many years.

Supreme Court of the United States, Washington, D.C.

Oct. 18, 1921

Dear Einstein :
Your letter divides me between you and Casanova. The other day I heard that you had been appointed Minister to — I am afraid to venture the name.[19] Before this you know. So I doubt if you receive this letter, at least for some time.

As to Casanova I tremble for the fate of one of the great books of the world. I like what I have read of Croce (in translation), but I couldn't recite on him. As to the book on Italian gardens I suppose diplomacy will head it off. I can't put my hand on what Laski wrote to me in praise of your *Tudor Ideals*. He contemplated writing to you, and I hope he did. I should think that your success there would tempt you further into the same field.

In view of my uncertainty as to reaching you and of the fact that I have been a little seedy for a day or two although on the upgrade now and nearly all right I shall leave this a note, not a letter.

My wife is curious to know the fate of the marmoset. We both send all remembrances to you both.

Yours ever,

O. W. Holmes

Supreme Court of the United States, Washington, D.C.

Dec. 26, 1921

My dear Einstein :
Your last letter left us in doubt where you would be and so I waited developments. I still don't know but shall try the State Department. Meanwhile this will tell you that on Christmas morning I was wishing you and yours a merry one. It is the first of many years that one has dared to say it. Your wife sent to F. such a pretty memento ; it gave us both a pleasure that I hope you will express to her. F. asked me to tell you it was very dear of her to think of it.

[19] Lewis Einstein served as United States Minister to Czechoslovakia from 1921 to 1930.

P

I should have been excused for silence by the work I have had on hand which has kept me busy as usual. (I pause to note a growing phenomenon: as one writes a word the next word is in one's mind and sometimes gets hold of one's hand. I started to end the *me*, supra, with the y of busy.) I read almost nothing, and the chief relief from absorption in the law is an occasional paradox, that takes the scum off one's mind. I told an unknown dame who was here with others last Monday afternoon that abuses were the parents of the exquisite — which disappeared from this country with wine, that I loathed most of the things I decided in favor of, etc. It's lucky for me that she (probably) was not a female reporter. I should have seen headlines CYNICISM IN HIGH PLACES, what a Justice of the Supreme Court really thinks etc.

Another mitigation is catalogues of secondhand books. Thanks partly to Laski I get a good many and they are better reading than Shakespeare. I mark things that I want and then don't send for them, reflecting that it is foolish at my age to buy books except for immediate needs or amusement.

I haven't even bought a print since I got back here, though once in a great while I hobnob with Rice,[20] the boss of the Print Department at the Congressional Library. He is younger than I am, but he beat me the other day. My grandmother, who didn't die till I was in the Peninsula in '62, remembered moving out of Boston when the British troops came in. He said that his grandmother, with whom he had talked, remembered and was in the old French War. I have a tomahawk inscribed by my grandfather, 'brought back by my father from the old French War', but my grandfather died before I was born. Younger men could beat or equal me in all my best reminiscences. I almost think that you might have seen Barry Cornwall — who was a friend of Charles Lamb and went to school with Byron.

But here comes an incursion of Christmas people and Christmas things and I must bid you *adieu* till next time. Give my homage and thanks to your charmer.

Yours ever,
O. W. Holmes

[20] Richard Austin Rice (1846–1925).

American Legation, Prague

26 Jan. 1922

Dear Justice Holmes:

I have thought of you far more often than I have written. Moving into a new house is rather like transplanting a tree, and I have not yet felt sufficiently at my ease to have the composure for letter writing. I must have been born with the smell of a Chancery in my nostrils but outside it I want a comfortable desk and a number of stupid details before I can sit down to write.

Here we are living in a Palace. The merit is not mine. It belonged originally to General Count Colloredo Mansfeld who built it after the Thirty Years War, and in second instance to the Acme plumbing whose heir (my predecessor) bought it and rents it to me. The Palace has over ninety rooms of which I occupy a dozen and the Chancery as many more. The other tenants vary from Countesses to stable boys. Its ceilings have the height of skyscrapers, its windows are sixteen feet high, it is majestic and terribly uncomfortable.

Having described my habitat, I have perhaps little to say. One detail will interest you. I remembered your anecdotes about your old Virginian friend, Col. McCabe. Well his son [21] is here as Military Attaché and we are very good friends. He spoke to me one day about his father and mentioned you in connection with him, and then I realized who it was and your anecdote about his darkie servant in the presence of the deity.

We had quite a lot of the deity this morning at a Requiem mass for the Pope. There were four Bishops and an Archbishop about the catafalque where they seemed to dance a kind of quadrille for one stood at every corner while the priests danced around them. The Archbishop lives in the most beautiful XVIIIth Century apartment I have ever seen, with tapestries, woodwork, and chandeliers intact like the setting for Madame de Pompadour. But here there is an odd mixture of Pre-Revolution and Modernism. The city is filled with old palaces and people who are still called 'aristocrats' and ignore

[21] General E. R. Warner McCabe (1876–1959).

the government and, worse still, modern conveniences. The Czech officials tell one gravely that the Hapsburgs didn't know the use of W.C.s. As they have seized quite a few Hapsburg palaces and have even offered me my choice of half a dozen as a shooting box they ought to know. I went to one shooting estate in Slovakia where the Archduke Joseph had simply enclosed twenty-five thousand acres for stags and other big game. The castle was decorated with Saints and horns, for praying and shooting were their main pursuits.

Prague is taking the place of Vienna politically but has not yet acquired its amenities, though Vienna is now a sorry spectacle with ten thousand crowns to one dollar instead of five before the war. So one reasons in millions and gets the impression of wealth out of nothing. Of course more serious purchases are made in foreign currency. We succumbed to a large tapestry of the end of the XVIIth Century representing 'America' with oddly enough a huge eagle flapping its wings over that word.[22] Below with some allegorical figures is an Indian lady counting her pearls on the future Fifth Avenue while an alligator close by suggests Palm Beach. The Dutch ships ride in the background. I saw some nice engravings in Vienna but thought them luxuries while tapestries are a necessity for a diplomat.

My wife joins me in warm messages to you both.

Ever yours,
L. E.

Supreme Court of the United States, Washington, D.C.

Feb. 13, 1922

Dear Einstein :

Probably your letter (Jan. 26) crossed one from me. Your uncomfortable palatiality amused me. I wish I had anything equally entertaining to tell. But I have little. A pause in my work, which is finished before the adjournment is over ; past joys of subtle expression ; past anxieties whether the laws

---

[22] This tapestry was subsequently given to the United States Government and now hangs in the Banqueting Hall of the new State Department Building in Washington, D.C.

would back me up in what I thought God's word more or less; some present dittoes; a look around for books to improve my mind interrupted by business, by efforts to clear up my table and shelves, and by the need of reporting to the dentist. That's about all.

I went to the last sitting of the Conference,[23] and without having followed it or estimated the achievement I was moved. I had more or less casual talks with people who came to Washington as parts of or attendants upon the show. Balfour was here for an hour and very pleasant. Wells for an evening and stimulating. Nevinson, (Manchester Guardian), several evenings, and we all roared delight, etc., etc. But I am getting old for I am thankful when I am let alone to read, write, be read to, and play solitaire.

I suppose that at or about this moment Mrs. Asquith [24] is here. This being Monday I was called down at this point and heard from some of those who looked in that she was here and had delivered her lectures this week. So if she hasn't thrown me over I probably shall see her. I am afraid her venture has been a mistake except from the point of view of money. People seem to speak rather slightingly of her talks, but she seems to fill her rooms none the less. I suppose they like to hear firsthand anecdotes of fashion from one who has dug a King in the ribs. I have a real (ancient) affection and respect for her and am sorry for these later manifestations.

I do get the rummiest books. Within a short time *The Master's World Union Scheme* by a servant of Alakamendra Mahabarata with a letter, which by Jove as I now look at it I discover to be signed by that Saviour in person. *The Destiny of America* by the Road Builder, which seems to be based on

[23] The Washington Conference of 1921–22 which resulted in the five-power Washington Treaty for the Limitations of Naval Armaments signed by the United States, Great Britain, France, Italy, and Japan, February 6, 1922.

[24] Margot Asquith, Countess of Oxford and Asquith (1864–1945); second wife of Herbert Henry Asquith, Prime Minister of Britain from 1908 to 1916, politician, writer, and celebrated hostess who made a deep impression upon the taste and fashion of her day. After fox hunting her greatest pleasure was intellectual and endearing conversation. Her lectures in America were not remarkable for their discretion. After her memoirs appeared under the motto 'Prudence is a rich ugly old maid wooed by incapacity', her friend Lord Reading, then Lord Chief Justice, remarked to her jocosely when visiting her in her country house that he expected to spend the rest of his life trying libel cases arising out of the publication of her book.

Scripture interpretative — as the former is an Indian revelation, this also with a letter expecting an appreciation. Brer Tarrypin's lying low and not saying nuffin. Instead of reading them and a lot of others less empty I will turn to the learned Pound's [25] *Spirit of the Common Law* and improve my mind.

My homage to the princess of your palace and salutations to yourself.

Sincerely yours,
O. W. Holmes

Supreme Court of the United States, Washington, D.C.

March 31, 1922

Dear Einstein :

Your letter of the 11th arrives at this moment. I owe you one for your, 'Balfour who left a blue stocking returns a garter'. It reminds me of, 'Did I say that?' 'No, but you will'. I will get it off to somebody, but native honesty or vanity will make me give you credit.

Your account of your life there and your wife's recalls similar experiences with mine. In house matters I simply have got out of the way and let the simoom pass, after going through the form of a consultation and approval. When we first went into a house, nearly forty years ago when I was made a Judge, after looking at one house and jointly condemning it, she suggested that I leave it to her, and the next thing I heard was an enquiry if I would dine that night at No. 9 Chestnut Street. After I gave my august consent to this house she sent me to Europe and spent her summer in altering and getting it into shape, determining what should be my library and even the color of the shelves against the will of the architect and coming out clearly right.

I have been and still am more or less absorbed in my regular business though I have a glimpse of a possible few days leisure in an adjournment through next week. I passed my eighty-first milestone on the 8th. We didn't mark the point, but I got a lot of letters, flowers and even some puffs in the

[25] Roscoe Pound (1870–   ); American jurist, educator, and Dean of Harvard Law School 1916 to 1936.

newspapers, two or three of which were really gratifying; a marked contrast to the notices at the time of my appointment, which, though very friendly, made me very blue because of the total absence of any critical intelligence. But I always say that one's brethren save one from any danger of a swelled head.

The details of my interests would not interest you as they turn on cases and questions of law. I am thinking however of the chance of a morning at the print department of the Congressional Library with my friend Professor Rice, and perhaps of the purchase of some duplicates that they want to get rid of. Also I look yearningly at various books that have been sent to me, especially Walter Lippmann's *Public Opinion*, which opens most bitingly. He is a born writer. But just now I ought to be searching the briefs and records in a great labor case that will be up for discussion tomorrow at our Conference. It reminds me of many years ago when we used to go to Mattapoisett with a *pro hac vice* cook, sometimes a rough customer. Once he was arranging with my wife for dinner and went on in a perfectly level voice, 'Yes, Madam, roast beef, potatoes, peas, God damn them flies I wish they was to Hell, carrots' . . . and I know not what.

Of course I shall be glad to see McCabe. I wonder if I don't know him already. I am a little mixed. One son I certainly know.

I am pleased at what you say of *American Civilization*. I shan't send it, but Mrs. Parson's contribution sounds interesting.

The telephone rings and tells me that a woman, her own counsel, is coming here at once to apply for a writ of error and I must prepare to resist cavalry or feminine blandishments. So fare thee well for the time.

My admiring homage to your two charmers.

Ever yours,
O. W. Holmes

Washington, D.C.

May 3, 1922

Dear Einstein;

A letter from you came a day or two ago. I think it was an extra because of seeing my birthday mentioned. The New

York Herald to which you refer was amiable, but some others were charming, e.g. the Springfield Republican and especially the New York World. A belated review of my book written in a March California Law Review really hit me where I lived.

But that is ancient history. I have not read *American Civilization*. *A priori* I don't care a damn for eternally pulling up the bean to see if the roots have sprouted, as I did when a little boy. But I hesitate to accept the absence of critical ability as a mark of virility. Many years ago a Philistine quasi-friend of mine, now happily dead and damned, used to say that the poets were degenerates and we know that line of thought. But a man may not be hairy or stink and yet may be able to beget a boy on occasion.

You interest me about your tapestry but I should think it was rather a white elephant for size. I had to look up Capercailzie [26] which I knew only as a literary expression. I guessed that it was a black cock but it seems to be some rarer and more magnificent bird. I am rather glad he escaped. As I grow older I would rather have a bird in the woods than in my bag.

If I could get any time I should like to rival you in a modest way with regard to prints, and get some desirable duplicates from the Print Department of the Congressional Library. But thus far I have been very busy, rather tired, have had a touch of asthma, and have had people staying here when I felt as if it was almost impossible to sit up and be polite. However the trouble is going down. We have heard our last argument. I have nothing more to write unless given something at the last minute, and my unfinished work is a portentous job of trying to make up my mind where lies the line of the South Bank of the Red River in a case that we took up to prevent private war between Oklahoma and Texas.

---

[26] *Tetrao Urogallus*; largest grouse in Europe sometimes attaining to a length of thirty-four inches and a weight of twelve or more pounds. The cock, black with red about the face and displaying a shaggy 'beard' and swelling iridescent green breast, mounts to the pinnacle of a tall tree during the breeding season to challenge all-comers with strident, retching calls and threatening gestures while his flock of mottled hens attend below the outcome of savage duels. Oblivious to their surroundings while performing their prenuptial rites the cocks are approached by gunners who move only during the repetition of a beautiful song of love, which commences with a quiet tick tock motion accelerating rapidly until it ends in a loud pop followed by a short phase of hissing whispering. When the gunner has taken his position directly under the bird it requires little skill to shoot him dead.

Later I hope to expatiate on the realms of cultivation, but not now.

Yours ever,

O. W. Holmes

My affectionate homage to the ladies.

Beverly Farms, Massachusetts

June 19, 1922

Dear Einstein :

Your letter is as delightful as usual, but I can't answer it adequately as for the moment I am on my back, except the short instant of writing a letter or two.[27] The misfortunes of age — discomfort rather than pain and I hope and believe with no very serious threat for the future, but knocking me out for now. I read Pepys's diary, sleep, am bored. I suppose I got too tired with my work and coming on etc. etc.

Pity the aged and keep young.

Yours as always,

O. W. Holmes

Supreme Court of the United States, Washington, D.C.

Jan. 4, 1923

Dear Einstein :

It is such a pleasure to receive your letter card. I had it in mind to write, the silence had been so long. I still spare myself in various ways, don't go about etc. etc.; but I have done my share of the work of the Court and am in pretty good shape, gradually getting stronger, though still a little stiff in the joints.

I had a few days leisure in a recent adjournment and read, more with reference to the Day of Judgment than now, the one-volume edition of Frazer's *Golden Bough*. The ideas are familiar through Salomon Reinach and others, but still I suppose that they were more or less original with Frazer. The book as a whole suggests a covert intent to show that every great doctrine

---

[27] Holmes underwent a prostate operation in Boston in June 1922.

of Christianity, the death, descent to hell, and resurrection of
the God, the periodical eating of hens etc., is a survival from
the most primitive superstitions. He accumulates multi-
tudinous facts that I forgot as fast as I read them, but they are
impressive even to one who has learnt to be sceptical of
generalizations derived from travellers' tales. Also fired by
the promise of improprieties and the statement that the author
had written two good philosophy books, I read May Sinclair's,
Anna Severn and the Fieldings, but got no thrill. It sounds a
little rum to hear a dame, unmarried, adverting with gusto to
fleshy contacts ; but why not if she likes ?

Now I am sitting again and shall be hard driven I expect
for four weeks. The new Judge, Pierce Butler, was so much
abused beforehand that I feared, but he appears well at
meeting and has rather a strong face. There is still another
appointment to be made, *vice* Pitney.

Do you feel, as I have heard it said, that the Czecho-
slovakians still show the impress of John Huss — and have a
kind of veiled protestant superiority to their neighbours ?

Interrupted here. I begin again by directing the envelope
and doubly doubt :

1) Whether the affixes to your name as abbreviated are
    proper ;
2) Whether it is possible to say U.S. Legation rather than
    Legation of the U.S.

I hope all is going well with you. We have bought a few
more Japanese prints. We have a number of them ; not the
uniquities to which alone you would stoop but still good
enough to give pleasure, and I have them and my etchings in
drawers that make them comfortably accessible. The result
of putting in an elevator was to necessitate a certain amount
of clearing up.

Thank Heaven for fire ! I feel as if circulation was restored
to my extremities. The library feels more alive ; altogether
I am cheerful.

My homage to the charming Mrs., and to the daughter
when you see her or write. I feel that I never shall cross the
ocean again.

Yours ever,
O. W. Holmes

Supreme Court of the United States, Washington, D.C.

Feb. 5, 1923

Dear Einstein :

Many thanks for your letter, messages, and photographs. They do me good. I thought that I had written last, before my letter that you answer, and was wondering whether your work kept you from correspondence. Very likely I was wrong for my memories of last summer are somewhat mixed. I still use my illness as an excuse, my wife thinks a necessary one, for not going out and for not undertaking odd jobs that one is continuously asked to do.

I have just completed a letter to a young Chinaman [28] in Berlin who professes himself an admirer of my legal philosophy, explaining my inability to write an introduction to an essay of his on that subject which he says is to be published in Germany and here. A devilish clever young chap with the *Ding an Sich* in his pocket.

Much against my will, until it was done, I have written an introduction to a book that my friend Wigmore is going to publish ; [29] a collection of discourses on all sides concerning the foundations of the law, property, contract, discount, marriage. He had asked me for it before I was ill. I said I must see the proof before I could tell. And so at my busiest moment the galleys began to come in, and as soon as I was free from other duties I became a galley slave. I expect my proofs this afternoon, and when they are corrected and sent off, a very short matter, I shall try to improve my mind during the two weeks of adjournment remaining.

Life certainly is one damned thing after another, and the moment one hopes to draw a free breath the air is laden with coal smoke. One good thing about an adjournment is that I can write a letter. I get no time for it when we are sitting. I shall recur to Spinosa's *Ethics*, which was interrupted just as I begun it. And I have a thriller by, I don't remember

[28] John C. H. Wu (1899–   ) ; Chinese jurist and diplomat, Minister of the Republic of China accredited to the Holy See from 1947 to 1949. Wu described his friendship with Holmes and his own conversion to Roman Catholicism in his autobiographical volume *Beyond East and West* (1951).

[29] '*Law and the Social Factor*', in *Introduction to Rational Basis of Legal Institutions* (Modern Legal Philosophy Series), edited by John H. Wigmore (1923).

who, called, I don't remember what — the remarkable cove who beside official activities and editing or writing a history of the war has turned out a lot of exciting tales. I think *Greenmantle* was the title of one; not the best. My wife is reading *Bleak House* to me in the evenings while I play solitaire. I had forgotten how good it is. The uncertain Chesterton I think talked well about Dickens. He certainly did about Victorian literature in the Home University Library.

It will be delightful to see you if you turn up here. Be sure to give my affectionate homage to the two ladies who you say are kind enough to remember me.

We are undergoing changes in the Court. The last appointed, Butler,[30] (*vice* Clarke I think) abused before he came, strikes me very favorably so far. I have not yet seen his writing. And the latest nominated but in the Senate now, is well spoken of. [31] You are in world affairs, but I am like the Vicar of Wakefield — all my migrations from the blue bed to the brown. But you listen kindly to the short and simple scandals of the poor, as Mr. Dooley has it.

Yours ever,
O. W. Holmes

American Legation, Prague

28 Feb. 1923

Dear Justice Holmes :

If you have been ill your handwriting doesn't betray it for Battling Siki [32] himself couldn't write with a stronger hand. I am glad to think of you seated in your Areopagus even without Pauls and Phrynes [33] around you. I wish I could see you there but I propose and Hughes 'disposes' for he has telegraphed me to stay here and not to wander overseas just now in view of the Ruhr and other matters.

---

[30] Pierce Butler (1866–1939); succeeded Mr. Justice Day, taking his seat on the bench January 2, 1923.

[31] Edward Terry Sanford (1865–1930); succeeded Mr. Justice Pitney, taking his seat on the bench February 19, 1923.

[32] Sobriquet given to a notorious prize fighter as well as to a well-known London hostess of the period.

[33] A fourth-century B.C. hetaera said to have been the model for the Cnidian Aphrodite of Praxiteles.

Here for instance, we have had a Minister of Finance murdered by a boy of eighteen who didn't agree with his financial policy and then cremated at his own wish because cremation wasn't allowed under the Hapsburgs. The Nuncio, who is the Dean of the Diplomatic Body, first presented our united condolences to the Government and then abstained from the funeral because the Church believes in the resurrection of the body.

I advise Paléologue's *La Russie des Czars*, 3 Volumes. Paléologue, who was French Ambassador at Petrograd during the war, is also a man of letters and has drawn a wonderful picture of Byzantine faith at the Russian Court, an almost incredible picture of Raspoutine's influence on the Empress and the commercialism of new Saints.

On the whole, however, I have little time to read and find myself relapsing into the prevailing barbarism which is settling over Europe. We have a philosopher here as President,[34] but he is philosopher enough not to attempt the impossible although things are far better here than everywhere else. But scholarship, the arts, and learning cannot divorce themselves from the furious struggle over nationality and party which is everywhere going on. Only the other night the American soprano wife of a Czech opera singer told me she no longer was able to get an engagement at the National Opera House because they were not socialists.

I am trying to establish an American Institute [35] here where we can send exchange professors and learn Slav ways. Most of the Russian intellectual swells are living at Prague just now and going to seed here. It is rather like the dispersion of Hellenism after the Turks took Constantinople. But I have ceased to try to fathom the meaning of this wild mixup everywhere and never attempt to move more than six inches ahead of me. Statesmanship I think means short steps when there is a mist and the fog is heavy now.

Au Revoir,
L. E.

[34] Thomas Garrigue Masaryk (1850–1937); first President of Czechoslovakia.
[35] The American Institute, designed to enable the United States to develop expert opinion and foster personnel trained in Russian and Soviet culture, was not continued by the Department of State for reasons of its own after Einstein left Prague in 1930.

Supreme Court of the United States, Washington, D.C.

March 24, 1923

Dear Einstein :

Your letter has the double interest of vivid and impressive suggestion, and of the different stimulus incident to deciphering. 'Battling . . .' who? In Boston I think it used to be 'Battling Nelson'. Also a casual reader would think that you spoke of me as seated in my oesophagus. But I am only seeking to call the kettle black; not speaking seriously. Your parallel of the dispersion of Hellenism impresses me much.

I began today hoping that I was beginning two weeks of leisure except when I had to go to a conference of the Justices or to read their opinions. But it has been one damned thing after another, and not a word have I read — except that a letter from Miss Howells required me to look into my limited preserves to see if I had anything to send her for a *Life and Letters of William Dean Howells*. She asked for letters to my father, of which I had none as I sent all his (that I had) to the Congressional Library. I don't think there were any from H. of interest. But I found a lot written to me before the Civil War that I felt she ought to have.

A few days ago I got the for me belated volume four of Salomon Reinach's *Cultes, Mythes et Religions*. The first three delighted me. So I doubt not will this, but perhaps less as space seems to be given to controversies about his *Orpheus*. I had expected to wallow in it today, but the time is not yet.

I observe with regret that he speaks with respect of Andrew Lang,[36] who for all I know may deserve it on those themes, but whom I have found dull and not too wise in what I have read and whom I thought an ill mannered boor when once I met him. Our conversation was this: 'Are you the son of old Holmes?' 'Yes.' 'Well, I don't like him.' Exit. Oh how I have regretted that I was not quick enough with either dagger or bludgeon of speech to hit back before he was gone ! [37] With

---

[36] Andrew Lang (1844–1912); Scottish scholar and man of letters who wrote articles on crystal gazing, poltergeist, and totemism in the 9th edition of the *Encyclopædia Britannica*.

[37] Another version of this famous encounter has been recorded : 'He, [Lang], had been asked to meet Holmes, and on coming into the room went up to Holmes, looked him over with ineffable insolence, and said : "So you are the son of the

what pleasure once crossing the ocean did I read his *Joan of Arc* and think ill of it. But I am glad to say I thought lightly of him before our interview.

Well, the result is that I have nothing to tell except that I have been hard at work listening to arguments and writing decisions. How much more convincing and pleasing to me the latter than the former. I think I have slowly improved during the winter. Certainly I have done all my work; but still I take some precautions and go out nowhere. I was eighty-two on the 8th. and had some pleasant letters, telegrams, flowers, etc. Delightful indeed if one doesn't have to answer them.

So now receive, my young friend, the benediction of age.

Yours ever,
O. W. Holmes

Washington, D.C.

April 28, 1923

Dear Einstein :

Your delightful letter comes this evening and I begin my reply at once but with nothing of corresponding interest to tell. As to your wife's chiding you for having no roots I should think that the trouble was that you *have* them, only in a different place. I recur to my old formula, that property, friendship, and truth have a common root in time, and our early associations determine what we shall love and revere. My homage to the dear lady, but I think she should take your birthplace into account.

You make my heart ache in speaking of the approach to manufacturing towns in Germany when I recall the squalors through which one passes in entering an American city. We have our share of beauty, however, down here. The Japanese single flowering cherry trees around the Potomac basin introduce the spring and are a world show — worth coming from

celebrated Oliver Wendell Holmes." "No," replied Holmes promptly, "he was my father." And then, snatching the play from his momentarily abashed opponent, Holmes launched into a disquisition that left Lang completely on one side and with his nose seriously out of joint.' *See* Introduction by Sir John Pollock to *The Pollock–Holmes Letters* (1942), p. xxi.

far to see — and now, unless last night's rain has destroyed them, the double flowering ones along the river for a mile or two are a rival of the first *éblouissement*. I don't remember whether you have ever seen them, but they are a new rapture every year.

I have had no time to read since an adjournment in which I had a turn at Salomon Reinach, Andrew Lang *et al.*, and bought three or four prints as I may have mentioned. I forget whether I had come to the point where I took up Montaigne in a rarely recurring moment when I neither had duty nor self improvement on my mind. For the first time I struck him when I was in the right humour and read until I had to stop with much delight. What a reasonable bird he was! I don't know whether one would have liked him in the flesh. Probably we should have reserves about anyone of a different century and different belongings. But at present he is a mighty good companion. Emerson's Essay about him I thought also fine, much better than I expected from memory.

I don't think I have seen your chief since I have been in Washington, but I go out absolutely not at all so the public highway is my only chance. These are my simple annals and I must shut up and heave at the enemy.

My ever kind remembrances to the Marchioness also.

Yours ever,

O. W. Holmes

Supreme Court of the United States, Washington, D.C.

May 31, 1923

Dear Einstein :

Your letters are always good and this one is most pleasant; but I am bothered by the stamp which I enclose. Is it a man or a woman sitting uncomfortably on the heel of the further leg ? I understand the sheaf and the buried sword, (I call up school boy recollections : Εν μύρτου Κλαδί το ξίφος Φόρησις) but what is he or she doing with the large photograph album ? It gets me.

You see from this beginning that I haven't much to tell.

My work is mainly over, and I avoid or decline all extras and outside work on the ground that I can't tell how narrow my margin may be.   The doctor says it is a miracle that I was able to get through my regular job.   For this reason I have just declined to write an introduction although the request came from one to whom I hate to refuse anything.   We don't adjourn till June 11, and F. and I leave here on the 18th.   Meantime I have prepared a dissent or two, read opinions as they come in, prepared myself on the outside Court work, which sometimes is considerable, and in the interval read Montaigne — for there is a good deal in that Sieur's book and it won't be hurried. The animal seems to me to have known pretty much all that I do, bar later discoveries.   It is my second great literary experience of later years, Dante the first.   I never read him seriously before and I don't wonder that Schopenhauer, I think it was, deals with him as a serious philosophical figure.

The town is filling up with Shriners; some sort of masons, I believe.   Pennsylvania Avenue is decorated, seats are going up everywhere, and I expect there will be a great show which probably I shall not go out to see.

We drive about a little in an old buggy and horse that we have employed since before automobiles won, and then if we want to enlarge our boundaries hire a taxi.   The Washington languor is on one, and I am making very little of myself at present.   Probably I have repeated often to you my axiom that those who make the most of themselves don't make much, and Montaigne seems to think that an old man who studies new things is an ass.   So I am encouraged by my listlessness.   I expect the North Shore will put a bustle into me, and I may seek once more to improve my mind.

Be sure to give my most affectionate remembrances to the two ladies.   It is sad to think that probably I shall not cross the ocean again, but they will remain vivid to me till I crack.

How much of the picturesque has been taken out of life by the 18th. Amendment!   I drank very little before it was passed, but the possibility of a bottle of wine gave a glow to many occasions that want it now.   I hope and think it possible that the race may be better for it fifty years from now, but I feel no clear conviction even as to that, and meantime we have more and more standardized prose.   I never am tired of saying that people don't consider the bill to be paid when they introduce their improvements. However I will try to keep up my spirits even if they do keep down my wine.

Yours ever,

O. W. Holmes

Beverly Farms, Massachusetts

Aug. 4, 1923

Dear Einstein:

You must forgive this niggard sheet. I got it in the village as the only one that would go into a lot of envelopes I had on hand. What a reason! Your letter as usual gives me a delightful whiff of the old world and of cultivation. I truly regret that your wife didn't send hers also. A letter is not a composition but a talk, a breathing out of the casual contents of one's mind, and, in spite of Sainte-Beuve's criticism of expressions in some of his subjects, I think that it may be intelligent or strange or any other damned thing that gives the writer's thought or want of it.

I told you I think that in this vacation I had given up any duty of self improvement and bought Sainte-Beuve's *Causeries* to amuse my leisure. It is very pleasant to turn to literature and to be serious about form. Ste.-B. seems to me unnecessarily squeamish in the early volumes, for I began at the beginning and am only in volume two. One result was that in looking over the volume of my term's opinions, which I have had bound up as usual, I was forthwith disturbed by a phrase that but for the Mussoo I thought all right. I have written to see if it can't be changed. But Lord, what's the use? Every six months reveals some new pitfalls of speech. If you get yourself out it is all that most of us at least can hope for.

This is a bad moment for me to write in as all sorts of accounts and bills have to be attended to and my secretary like his predecessors has assumed that though on duty for pay he may go to Europe. I don't mean to blame a most faithful man, but I have been rather struck with the easy assumptions that they all make. *Per contra* an ex-secretary has pressed me to let him come over from Nahant and do my books; but naturally I don't like to accept much in that way.   Accounts drive me mad.   Do they the same to you?   However, if I could make a deduction of three cents fit into my probate account I should be on the verge of vacuity and bliss.

Sainte-Beuve is a rational joy, but he doesn't seem to me too good for plain mortals.

Please remember me to your wife and repeat to her my motto: When in doubt do it.   Also to the Marchioness.

Yours always,
O. W. Holmes

Beverly Farms

Aug. 13, 1923

Dear Einstein:

Your letter, welcome as ever, recalls what I recently read of Franklin saying to Volney and Cabanis, both young, when they called on him: '*A cet âge, l'âme est en dehors: au mien elle est en dedans, elle regarde par la fenêtre le bruit des passants sans prendre part à leurs querelles.*'   On public matters I listen without taking part.   I have done so for the most part of my life to be sure, but now I have the excuse of age.

Your account of the Secretary of Labor delights and that of Benes interests me.   I cannot but imagine that there was a bit of chaff in the suggestion of dividing the old garden into building lots etc.   I always am grateful to Ruskin for his statement that the most real capital of countries was in their works of art.   And while I admit, as I heard Royce the eminent philosopher assert with force, that the present always has a right to sacrifice the past to itself, I would rather that a million fellaheen or for the matter of that, Englishmen, should have been prevented from coming into being than that Phylae should have been submerged by their dam.   An average life is not worth, I take it, more than thirty thousand dollars.   It justly, even if not lawfully, might be destroyed to save a great reservoir of food, and that is only an estimable value.   When one thinks of the unique monuments and supreme works of art left by the past I confess that I would spare many of my countrymen sooner than them.

I am not wholly free from bothers.   As several of our

Justices are out of the United States people apply to me not only in my own circuit but from others for writs of error etc., which means a certain amount of time and energy, but not much. In the main I continue assiduously idle with nothing more serious at hand than Sainte-Beuve. (*Causeries*; not *Port Royal*). I begin to want a different field to browse in after eight volumes.

Since writing the last word I have been at Marblehead, zigzagged through its old streets, and visited its old burying ground at the top of everything with a wonderful outlook on the sea. There also is the charm of the (relatively) old, and one would loathe improvements. The old sea captains and some of the fighters of the revolution and sailors who were lost in the storms on the Banks are buried there. At the foot is a path leading to a well where I was told that the fair Agnes Surriage (if I see the name right) used to meet her lover Sir Harry Frankland in prerevolutionary days. My father used to talk about it and wrote a poem upon which I can't recite.

I am promised a murder story to mitigate the asperities of Sainte-Beuve, but it has not come yet and I took an excursion into Jane Austen (*Pride and Prejudice*) without the superlative admiration of some of my English friends. I don't think that she transfigures snobs, bores, and fools as Dickens does, for instance, and untransfigured they don't delight. These are the short and simple scandals of the poor, as Dooley says, and I can tell you no more.

I renew my homage to your ladies, and am as always,

Yours,

O. W. Holmes

Beverly Farms, Massachusetts

Sept. 20, 1923

Dear Einstein :

You will get a rotten letter this time, but it matters less if I am to see you, as you promise and I hope, a little later. We are on the verge of departure to Washington, and I have been spending the day at my table clearing up, attending to business — (business questions always come at the most inconvenient moments but then so does everything) answering letters, and God knows what. It is close to 4 p.m. and I must take a little walk before it is too late and refresh my weary brain. But it is unfair to speak of my brain as weary except in this momentary way. I have idled through the vacation — deliberately — that I might jump into my work next week rested.

All I can show in the way of cultivation are a dozen volumes of Sainte-Beuve, Carlyle's *French Revolution*, and a truly difficult volume of philosophy which I read under protest because it was sent to me. However it gave an edge to my mind for the moment. I don't count stories and other light stuff, although Sainte-Beuve is light enough. He has made me dislike more actively some French characteristics, especially this one : impression of *rules* as against spontaneity. A Frenchman said to a friend of mine : 'The first thing we teach our children is *tenue*.' But that means eternal self consciousness and all that makes the bogus feeling of XVIIIth Century art, and in short the opposite of the divine unconscious Greek Grace, or the poignancy that England does not have to go back to Shakespeare to find. A while ago the great glory of a French hero was his disdain. He must be disdainful — no matter of what. But I loathe and disdain disdain as a philosopher and as a gentleman — (if the two qualities could be united, which they can't. For a philosopher ultimates are fluid, and his self only a cosmic ganglion ; whereas a gentleman must really take himself seriously and sin against the Holy Ghost by thinking himself a little God whatever became of the big one.) But I must out into the air and not sit here scolding.

Convey to your ladies my most worshipping homage — and await our meeting for the message to you.

Yours ever,
O. W. Holmes

Supreme Court of the United States, Washington, D.C.

Jan. 31, 1924

My dear Einstein :

The sonnet seems to me excellent. My only criticism is that 'Stared' on palm trees etc. is reminiscent of Keats on

Chapman's Homer.   You interest me very much by all that you say, especially about Lady Tweeddale.   I don't wonder that she makes people do what she likes.   Writing a life of Cass [38] seems a rum business for you; but I daresay it is a good exercise.

We adjourned on Monday for three weeks.   All my work is done up to the moment and I am contemplating the use of leisure. I think that I shall drop from philosophy into literature. I am even thinking, for the lesson has just begun, of trying to see the difference between Corneille and Racine.   To an outsider all Chinamen look alike.   I remember once reading a book of interviews with the then young French *littérateurs*, who were savage about one another.   (Zola was quoted as saying that the young sharks having nothing else to eat devoured one another).   To me they were like herrings in a box; much of a muchness.

I have just been through a book that requires more careful reading to do it full justice; *The Old and the New Germany* by John F. Coar, to me previously unknown, though he is said in former days to have been a member of the Massachusetts bar. It stimulated and moved me, but it is off my beat.   I read it over because it was sent to me.   Earlier, as I may have mentioned, I got unusual pleasure from Aubrey's *Brief Lives* (two volumes, Clarendon Press).   Aubrey tells of all his contemporaries (between 1650 and near the end of the century), and has gossip about those who died a little too soon for him to see them e.g. Shakespeare and Raleigh.

I must try to go to the print department of the Congressional Library where I pick up a few trifles from my friend Professor Rice.   I fear that you would look down on my second, third, or later states; but I get a great deal of pleasure from them at odd moments, all the more when as usual they are not too precise and give me shabby company with the past in its shirt sleeves.   In the same way you know the old books in my library, usually not valuable enough to be a worry, but taking one back.   I like to think that this or that volume was standing in a bookcase before America was discovered, to give you a chance for poetry.

[38] *Lewis Cass and American Diplomacy under President Buchanan*, contributed by Lewis Einstein in *Lives of American Secretaries of State* (1927).

I shall not finish my paper but shall go out for a walk with my secretary. I got up late, and I like to finish and post my letters at once.

It was great to see you here. My homage to your ladies.

Ever yours,

O. W. Holmes

COLUMBUS

He dared to sail his ships from Palos port
And steer a course over uncharted seas
Westward from the pillars of Hercules,
To bring the Indies to the Spanish court.
In quest to seek the spices of Cathay,
A glorious vision of the New World fell
Before his gaze when from the caravel
He stared on palm trees round an island bay.
Then as he stepped upon the reef of sand
Raised on his sword the pennant of Castile
The sunrays glistened on its burnished steel.
As he knelt down upon the coralled strand
In the dark forest shrieked the wild macaw
And naked Caribs stared at him in awe.

Supreme Court of the United States, Washington, D.C.

March 8, 1924

Dear Einstein:

This must be a word of acknowledgment for your letter, *Character of Henry VIII*, and speech as this is my birthday (83) and I am somewhat distracted. The speech and *Character* are both to your credit, *sub judice*, all the more if you, as I, have large reserves with regard to Wilson. I can't think him a great intellect, and while I still await light on his character I am ungenerously inclined to read his idealism as largely egotism.

It is a good touch in your letter by which you distinguish Corneille and Racine. Possibly I feel it a little, but I shan't get to heaven on that discrimination.

I am interested in your noticing the growth of a Wilson myth. Perhaps I have told you that until I reached middle age I believed that I was watching the growth of a myth about Lincoln. In the war time like other Bostonians I believed him a second rate politician. But later I saw and read things that convinced me that I was wrong. When I was leaving the army talking with General Lowell (soon after killed in the Valley) as to who would be remembered, he mentioned Lincoln, but I think we both smiled. Perhaps I am as wrong about Wilson now, and should like to see a rational statement of his claims to greatness, other than his being President at a great moment which I fully admit as a claim. Philosophically, being there, then, was part of his personality.

I shall read nothing more till we adjourn, though I hear some entertaining things while playing solitaire. Forgive my brevity.

Give my undying homage to the ladies and remember me as,

Yours ever,

O. W. Holmes

Supreme Court of the United States, Washington, D.C.

May 4, 1924

My dear Einstein :

This must be but a poor return for your, as ever, interesting letter. We are just at the end of our regular sittings although we don't finally adjourn till June 9, soon after which date my wife and I shall head north for Beverly Farms. At the present moment, therefore, my hands are full, the last week having been a hard one and giving new jobs of writing. I have paid my dearest compliments to the writings that you have sent me in earlier letters unless I am mistaken. No reading — no general reflections. I am full of law for the moment, among other things trying to soften and make swallowable an opinion for my brethren who couldn't down the victuals I offered yesterday. Things always come in a bunch and I hardly know which way to turn.

I am not surprised at the impression made on you by Mrs. Asquith although she is an old friend of mine and I am sincerely attached to her. A portrait of her when she was Margot Tennant has always hung in my library here, behind my back as I write, though you wouldn't remember it.

Your remark on Coolidge as having 'avoided rhetoric' strikes me as hitting on the secret of his popularity. The letters and speeches I have seen are in marked contrast to the meaningless polysyllabic adjectives and adverbs of which his predecessors were fond. Even Roosevelt would be 'inexpressibly surprised and shocked' at events that hardly called for an exclamation mark.

I wish I could have seen your ball, and hope that your wife has recovered from the fatigue. My love to her.

You know my general ignorance and won't be surprised that I don't know much about the scandal and investigations now on hand.[39] I have the impression that poor old Harding does not escape — because of the company he kept, not because of any more personal charge. His rhetoric had a full share of what Coolidge avoids. But the pleasure that our people take in swelling phrases regardless of facts is an eternal wonder to me. Yet I wonder if this country is not making a sincere effort to improve and see things as they are. A good many are, I am confident. Would that I could shake off the law and say something worth saying.

Yours ever,

O. W. Holmes

American Legation, Prague

24 May 1924

My dear Justice Holmes:

I am glad that when these lines reach Washington you will be soon exchanging your watch on the Constitution for that of the North Shore. Yet if I were a graphologist (I hope that's the word) I should say that you hardly needed rest.

I have taken a little one myself for we motored with the Tweeddales from here to Holland. I am enclosing a couple of billion marks as a souvenir of my trip through Germany which I send you as an economist. They represent about one and one half cents and were the change I received when buying a loaf of bread. Inflation has made Germany one of the most

---

[39] In the spring of 1924 the Teapot Dome oil lease scandal threatened to involve members of the Cabinet of Calvin Coolidge who had succeeded to the Presidency upon the death of President Harding on August 3, 1923.

expensive countries in the world, and I had to pay thirty five cents for a small cup of coffee and three dollars for a portion of boiled salmon. However, enough of such sordid details. I was disappointed by the absence of visible atrocities in motoring through the occupied region in Germany. French, English, Belgians, even Moroccans seemed little out of place on the Rhine, though doubtless had I been a German they would seem otherwise. Yet we passed a German motorcycle race near Bonn and saw a German crowd lining the streets of Dusseldorf when the French cavalry marched through. I liked best in Germany the new film of the *Niebelungen Lied* which gives one a different idea of the artistic possibilities of the Movie. If, as I suppose, it reaches America I strongly recommend it.

At The Hague Helen was taken ill with what the doctor called appendicitis and advised an operation. Returning here the leading surgeon declared there was no appendicitis and no need for an operation to our immense relief, and remarked to me that if surgery were gratuitous there would be far fewer operations in the world.

I join with you in admiring Coolidge's English. It speaks well for the Massachusetts tradition. I wonder if our one hundred ten millions can ever attain more than a spasmodic emotional unity in times of stress and if Coolidge's clear reason is popular. We have left Cincinnatus and haven't yet reached the Antonines, and between the two there were a devil of a lot of demagogues.

I am vegetating peacefully here with occasional excursions into more active realms. But there is not enough to keep me busy and too many distractions to allow for anything serious.

I throw another sonnet on your indulgence and with many messages to Mrs. Holmes subscribe myself as ever,

L. E.

BEFORE THE BUST OF HOMER AT NAPLES

And have you seen great Homer's vacant eyes
For whom the glimpse of day was as the night?
Despite the sunburst in the Grecian skies
He walked in darkness with an inner light.

Led by a barefoot child, he sang the lay
Of Gods and heroes in the fight at Troy.
He called Achilles from his tent to slay
And left Andromaché clutching her boy.
He told how the wise wanderer returned
Unknown, save to the dog that licked his hand,
And found the faithful one for whom he yearned
While still a prisoner in Calypso's land.
Before the hearth he chanted to a throng
Of goatherds raptured by the blind bard's song.

Prague, April 1924.

Supreme Court of the United States, Washington, D.C.

June 4, 1924

Dear Einstein :
    Your letter comes today, in good time. On the 9th the
Court adjourns and on the 11th I hope to go to Beverly Farms
via Boston for a day or two's rest.
    I enclose, from yesterday's evening paper the last stage of
the White House performance, being photographed at the
rear of that building.[40] You will recognize the President, Root,
and Mr. Hughes, over my head, turned away. Lodge in the
middle, sideface. I think it must be Roosevelt's son just above
Root's head and the Secretary of War above and to your left
of him, me. I should think there were twenty machines
clicking away as we got into place. I don't know whether it is
that the President hates being photographed, but after he had
presented the medals he said the show was not yet over as this
remained to be done. He said it was the third time that day
and that it hadn't been much of a day for photographers !
    I gathered that one was to say a few words on receiving

[40] On June 2, 1924 President Calvin Coolidge presented three awards of the
Theodore Roosevelt Memorial Association to their respective recipients. One of
the three medals went to Holmes, for distinguished service in the development of
public law, one to Charles W. Eliot, President Emeritus of Harvard University,
for service to the nation's youth and for his contributions to the development of
American character, and one to Elihu Root, for service in the administration of
public office.

the medal. *Entre nous*, this is what I said : 'For five minutes, Mr. President, you make the dream of a life seem true. But one who is still on the firing line cannot dream long. I hope that the short time that is left to me will not dim the honor of today.' I meant what I said, for the dream of my life has been to accomplish an intellectual achievement, and office has seemed valuable mainly if not only as evidence and opportunity. Forgive so much egotism. I have not talked so much about the affair elsewhere.

I haven't read much since last writing to you. Part of the time I was under the weather and there are always a lot of odd jobs at the end. Also one always feels tired at this season in this climate. I have at my elbow the Πέρσαι of Aeschylus which I started to reread at odd minutes. It must have stirred up the Greeks when the messenger enumerates the Persian losses and tells how the Greeks smashed them. I think I mentioned a previous excursion into the *Chanson de Roland*, a curious contrast to the Greek fighting poetry. I won't catalogue the rest of my mild experiences, except to mention that if you ever read the *Legacy of Greece*, Clarendon Press, it will pay you to do it ; essays by a lot of crack Englishmen.

I am pretty glad that your wife escaped the operation for appendicitis. I had it repeatedly over twenty years ago and also escaped, thanks to my doctors, on condition of accepting a regime. But in those days the operation was far worse than now. I thank you for the sonnet, which is of more value than the German treasures also enclosed.

I find that old men get tired quicker than young ones, but I have nothing to complain of. My homage to your wife and the Marchioness.

Yours ever,
O. W. Holmes

Beverly Farms, Massachusetts

July 6, 1924

Dear Einstein :

Such a nice letter from you. It gives me great pleasure and interests me much in what you say about Buchanan. Even n my ignorance occasional hints have indicated that he was a considerable man.

I meantime am not wearing myself thin by intellectual efforts. The greatest one is to get sums done correctly in my accounts. The only other is slowly working along in Spengler, *Der Untergang des Abendlandes*. I have to use the dictionary, and look up the same word twice in an hour. Also his easy reference to Arabian, Chinese, or Egyptian Art, and a thousand details on as many subjects that I know not doesn't help to diminish the difficulties that begin with the language. The man is suggestive but not to be followed, I still think, very far. He presents his ideas as what damned fools never have thought of hitherto but that will put things in their true light. The war hasn't licked the German out of him. I shall praise God if I ever finish the book, and if I could feel sure that I had got the substance of all he has to say I could gladly see him slowly ground into fish bait. What a stinking business it is to postpone the amusement of literary browsing to a task that you dare not neglect for fear that you miss some idea essential to salvation, although you know you won't and don't. But I am nearing injustice to a remarkable work. How glad I should be if I heard the author was dead.

I hope for time for trifling and possibly finding something amusing to tell you — which you see that I haven't done.

My love and homage to the ladies.

Ever yours,
O. W. Holmes

Beverly Farms, Massachusetts

Aug. 3, 1924

Dear Einstein:

Your letter this moment received raises many thoughts as to the Turkish 'Keif'.[41] Formerly I thought that anyone who didn't realize that the chief pleasure of life was to use all one's faculties to the limit simply didn't understand himself. Now I have come to the counter realization that different

---

[41] See page 44, note 71.

crowds have different fundamental emotions, and that the
matter lies too deep for argument, although I can't but think
that *my* fundamental gets more from life than the Turk's
Differences of that sort, if not eternally at least for a long time
will be the justification of war. If the Turk wants to make one
kind of a world and I another in particulars that we both care
very much about I don't see anything left except for one to
kill the other. Spengler fortified a conclusion that later years
had brought me to. But Spengler be damned. His dogmatic
announcement of a lot of things that I don't in the least believe
did not make me love him or his crowd. Yet it was worth
the trouble of reading him perhaps for the stimulating side
suggestions. I wish I had seen Croce's review, though I should
need a translation. I thought of Croce as I read Spengler and
as a better man of a race that Spengler dismisses with contempt
I gather that the Germans even in their downfall are showing
great intellectual activity which I hear has extended to the
law, but I have not seen the product. I think I read their
books (when I can with effort) without prejudice, but there are
few things that I more dislike and despise than arrogance,
intellectual or social. The Germans carry the intellectual to
the highest point, and it is not so long ago that one of the chief
glories of a French hero of romance was Disdain. I should
like to see all such taken to a latrine and spanked till they
howled.

I am nearer to being able to take pleasure in doing nothing
in agreeable surroundings, as you put it, than I often have
been, but I am busy all day even if it is with amusement. I
find, or have reason to suspect, that my two hours motor drive
of a morning is too much for me and have cut it down, but
there are many things to fill the extra hours. Among others
my last Day of Judgment book, I believe, Thucydides. I never
had read more than what I did at school, and the time seemed
to have come — with a translation to smooth the way. I don't
find the Greek difficult and am as near getting my money's
worth for the trouble as one often is with a classic. It is
interesting to see the same thing said when a war is threatened,
or on, two thousand years ago and now, and there are many
sentences that would make good texts for modern discourse.
But I must admit that this *pièce de résistance* becomes a task and

a duty to be finished rather than an entertainment. So the days go quietly and swiftly by, and I see no present reason to fear that I shan't be good for another year's work.

An anonymous correspondent a few days ago wrote that La Follette was going to be President, that he hated the Supreme Court, and that I should deserve execration if I gave him a chance to appoint a Judge, which my wife pointed out to my stupidity meant : Resign now. Not to please one who dared not sign his name.

My love to the ladies.

Yours ever,

O. W. Holmes

Beverly Farms, Massachusetts

Sept. 6, 1924

Dear Einstein :

You talk of the atmosphere from which I write. Yours excites my envy.

Your American business man is reproached for want of other resources, often no doubt truly ; but I think that there may be another less discreditable element. When the mind has become accustomed to a certain tension it is uneasy at any relaxation beyond a short rest. I enjoy irresponsible browsing as I do a portfolio of prints, but before long I feel the need of more effort. To that extent I am subdued to what I work in. But I try to believe that idling is good for one and latterly have idled more or less, more rather than less from any serious point of view. Just now I have relaxed so far as to take up another book of philosophy just to make myself feel right. But I do like to stretch upon a lounge with half a dozen easy books about me, and sip, now an essay of Hazlitt's, now a few pages of a French caricaturist, and now an ode of Horace or a chapter of George Borrow, with happy slumber as a release. When one is moving about these worries disappear, but I can't move very far without being the worse for it. Your recommendation of a *Passage to India* [42] comes on top of so many

<hr>

[42] *A Passage to India* by E. M. Forster (1924).

from England and here that though I have resisted thus far I think I must yield and send for it to the Old Corner Book Store, Boston's principal dispensing agent.

As you give me that glad promise of being here (i.e. in Washington) in two months i.e. by the latter part of October I feel doubts of this reaching you and shall cut it short.

A friend of ours sending us a card to tell us that she had a little daughter dated it Labor Day.

My love to the two ladies.

Yours ever,
O. W. Holmes

Supreme Court of the United States, Washington, D.C.

Jan. 27, 1925

Dear Einstein :

Your letter was welcome and full of entertainment. Somehow I don't think of you as killing boars and cock pheasants, but I daresay that like the hero of the French novel, *Le Bossu* (Paul Féval),[43] I forget the name, that gave rise to *The Duke's Motto*, a play we used to see, you develop a new talent with each new exigency of life. You intrigue me about books. You say 'As Harry Higgins described it'. Harry Higginson [44] was a cousin of mine and some one, in his day. But who is Harry Higgins? But to go on, who was Mrs. Jack Gardner's venerable lover? I heard of her affairs in earlier days and knew her fairly well, but I didn't know that she had devotees in later years. You seem primed with gossip. You excite my curiosity as to London. Item. I don't know what 'Dollar Diplomacy' is.

I have nothing to tell because I go nowhere. I have an intellectual spasm at the beginning of some weeks until the case assigned to me is written and then settle to comparative repose in the latter part. But sitting always is fatiguing. When the adjournment comes, however, I shall be the only one with no cases to con except what may be given me on that day.

---

[43] These four words are inserted above the line in Holmes's writing.

[44] Henry Lee Higginson (1834–1919) ; founder and benefactor of the Boston Symphony Orchestra.

Against that day I have got a volume of F. H. Bradley, *Essays on Truth and Reality*. I hear him called the only English philosopher since Hume. I always have shied at him, not believing he would say much to me, and from a glance I still don't believe it, but I don't want to die without a notion of him. At present I can read nothing though I listen to light things at night.

I am afraid that the sketch you sent to my wife missed its destination in some way. Please tell the adorable Marchioness that I hate Salomon Reinach for destroying my last hope of a joint to my nose.

I don't know but I think that to find you absorbed in Lewis Cass odder than to see you destroying boars. Are you gaining a senatorial post from your intimacy with him or from diplomacy?

Hughes' resignation may have been the cause of a remark in the paper that I was going to resign on my birthday in March, as Hughes and I used to be confounded not infrequently when he was on the bench. I keep getting letters about it which add to the bores who beset me, others are elaborately genealogical to show relationship, others require a photograph for a school and what not. When I can I chuck them into the basket. I genuinely regret not being able to say: 'Sir or Madam, I don't care a damn about your descent. I don't believe we are cousins and I hope not.' One dame called on me to resign my office and the Roosevelt Medal because I don't show interest in the name of Wendell and take steps to save her from a conspiracy to interfere with her mail and literary reputation. Brandeis says that it is a pity that the Post Office is so cheap.

I must stop, dear boy, and rest a bit after a hard day.

Give my love to your wife.

Yours ever,
O. W. Holmes

American Legation, Prague

17 Feb. 1925

Dear Justice Holmes:

Ten thousand more birthdays I'll wish you in good oriental style, and may your wisdom and your personality

R

continue for many years to grace Washington and ornament the land. My own birthday a week after yours will remind me that I am deep in middle age with slight achievement, slight ambition, and even slighter regret. But I envy you for the pride of having been wounded three times in the service of the country.

Please do not marvel too much at Cass. He was a gallant fellow who had some really picturesque Indian adventures. His character I have described as being not unlike the painted Grecian columns which, hollow inside, supported the upper stories of some houses built in that time. But my Cass is a misnomer and a fraud. What I have tried to do is really to relate the history of our foreign intercourse in the four years preceding the Civil War — when the real Secretary of State was President Buchanan — and a mighty good one too, although unscrupulous and a bit headstrong. I have just finished my work and it will go to form a section of the twelve volume history of American Diplomacy which J. B. Scott is editing under the alluring title of *Lives of Secretaries of State*.

I fancied you knew Harry Higgins. He is a London lawyer who is married to an American, a former Mrs. Breese ; a charming fellow and a real wit. He was formerly Director of Covent Garden, and when Cavalieri had asked him some huge price for appearing there he remarked, 'It's only for singing.'

Here we have had a tempest or rather a series of them in a teapot. My wife has given a ball preceded by an entertainment one of the features of which was a Revue where there was gentle fun made of the diplomats beginning with ourselves. Unfortunately standards of humor are not the same and two of my colleagues felt aggrieved. One threatened to challenge to a duel the French *Chargé d'Affaires*, who had written the verses, for having said that he was '*très chic et portait un prénom*'. There was a public explosion followed by long and delicate negotiations which ended in a reconciliation. The other, the Dutch Minister, has declared war on me. He is a Dickensian gentleman ; very obese and with a particular fondness for decorations and for asking indiscreet questions. He came to dinner here wearing a Liberian order to be closer, as he explained, to America. He always introduces himself as The Dutch Minister on the theory that no one save another Minister is exalted enough to do so. He asks ladies if they are married and if not he inquires, '*Alors vous êtes vierge?*' He now regards the dignity of the Netherlands injured because the couplet sung about him said that he liked decorations. In vain my wife and I have tried to assure him that no offence was meant. He remains unpacified and as irreconcilable as a Senator till at last my own dander has risen and I have demanded an apology for his rudeness toward my wife. I have only one fear and that is for a reconciliation.

My wife joins me in warm messages to you both. Again our congratulations.

Ever yours,
L. E.

Supreme Court of the United States, Washington, D.C.

March 7, 1925

Dear Einstein :

First, my thanks for your remembering my anniversary and your ever faithful friendship, and my counter-wishes of every good to you, who I believe are a week younger than I. In spite of your discoveries I think you will want to fill the time before you catch up with some satisfactory form of life, as you are filling it now. There are many forms.

I am much interested and I am pleased that you find Buchanan so considerable a man. In the old days I blindly followed the abolitionist superstition about him, and I like to have it corrected. I was reminded of the Abolitionists in quite another way a few days ago when we were adjourned and I had a chance to read a few books. One of them was *A Prince of Modern Art* by a man who thought that the people worth talking about in the past were El Greco and, a little, Michaelangelo, and the real ones began with Cézanne. The same dogmatic extremism that I became familiar with as a very young man came up again. It made me think of one of Browning's plays, when the observer at the beginning says : 'I have seen thirty-nine revolutions', and at the end : 'I have seen forty revolutions.' I could talk for half an hour on what seemed to me the humbugs and fallacies of the creed. It made me think of skirt dancing, which I took to be an invention of those who wouldn't take the trouble to learn the art of the real *danseuses* but found a cheap and agreeable substitute in a kick and the suggestion of a hope that you would see more than you were going to.

I got more nourishment out of Hind's book on engraving and etching, but it enhanced my sense of loss in the death of my friend Rice who was head of the Print Department of the Congressional Library. That shut one of the few vistas still open to me from the Law.

I was amused by *Anatole France en Pantoufles*, which though slight seemed to me probably a fair sketch of Anatole France's more familiar talk. I think I should have liked him better than Sainte-Beuve whom I ended by rather disliking after reading his *Causeries*. A few pages of Pierre Loti's *Diary* and *l'Illustration* led me to take up again the *Pêcheur d'Islande* though I don't finish it before we begin to sit again. Pierre Loti's prose seems to me to have more charm than that of any other Frenchman — I don't know but more than any other in the world. I believe he was simple to the core (as he says himself) with all manner of outer layers, that make him a real person (in a good sense.) He reminds of what I have sometimes thought, that unless one can think like a devil one does not know the deepest thrills of the intellect (I won't say, of life.)

We have got through the Inauguration and I hope I have escaped without a cold, as the weather was fine. We have to sit in the open air during the President's address without a hat (but with a skull cap.) Such things always bore me, but this as little as well might be. Dawes [45] was grotesque, but he had an idea (not very new) if the place and manner had been appropriate.

Now I am balled up again with duties. I hope your rusty moment with the Dutchman has smoothed out.

Please give affectionate messages to your wife and the Marchioness.

Yours as ever,
O. W. Holmes

[45] Charles Gates Dawes (1865–1951); American statesman and philanthropist whose name is associated with a plan for the payment of German war reparations in 1923. Elected Vice-President of the United States Dawes called in his inaugural speech on March 4, 1925 for a revision of the rules of procedure in the Senate permitting a majority vote to apply the closure to debate.

Supreme Court of the United States, Washington, D.C.

April 12, 1925

Dear Einstein:

A delightful letter from you that made me long to share your dream of beauty in Florence; but nature has done pretty well for us here. The cherry trees around the Potomac basin are worth coming hundreds of miles to see, and the nature show has been hardly less. Magnolias in town, and in the country white masses of pearblossoms, and around Fairfax Court House (a dear little old relic with Lord Fairfax over the Judge's desk and Washington, John Tyler etc. on the sides) around Fairfax Court House the seed vessels of the maples glowing like masses of rubies in the sunlight.

A word more about *Anatole France en Pantoufles.* Of course that form of industry, which seems familiar to the French, excites one's prejudices. In this case at first I thought it had the last sin of belittling its subject; but as I read it I thought the writer really means no or not much malice, but to tell how his boss talked — and I thought it had a slight interest. A.F. himself does not interest me enormously as you know.

I shall hope to read of your discovery of China in St. Mark's.[46] Also I am sorry not to have seen McCabe.

You suggest that in America we are living in an age of faith. Certainly one is struck by the faith in contentless generalities and the readiness for extremes, which I knew in college among the Abolitionists. I think I learned a lesson then, (I think I referred to it apropos of the modern art people) and in the Civil War I formulated to myself the value of prejudice and being cocksure for achievement. Only you and I don't care to achieve in that way. As to unexpected results that is the general lesson of history. Great improvements, as they are believed to be, always are liable to show holes in fifty years. I always have remembered going to the Political Economy Club with J. S. Mill and listening to discussions whether the financial policy of England should be shaped with reference to the exhaustion of coal (for commercial purposes)

---

[46] 'A Chinese Design in Saint Mark's at Venice' by Lewis Einstein in the *Revue Archéologique* (1926) in which his discovery of twelfth-century Chinese decoration on a door in St. Mark's cathedral is described.

in ninety years just then predicted in a book by Jevons (?). I ventured to whisper that a good deal happens in that time and to ask if it wasn't attempting to look too far ahead. Mankind is like a juggler I once saw with burning alcohol on his hands; he wiped it from one hand to the other and wasn't hurt. That's about all we can do.

We have been adjourned for three weeks and come back to Court tomorrow. I have done my work and some slight extras, had a few days when I was no good, with coughing at night etc., read a little legal history, philosophy (minimum), and literature. Just now a play or two of Shakespeare's which I am enjoying, if only for the song of the words. How much depends on the mood. I reread the whole works of the bard when I came from the hospital with mighty little profit, and one tired half hour I walked through the National Gallery to feel that I was looking at bogus gestures and rather a pitiful result of the passion of man. One must be in tune, and can't be always. Growing old reconciles one to the notion that man may not be quite so damned important as he is wont to feel or as at least a good many of his brethren are.

My affectionate homage to your two charmers.

Yours ever,
O. W. Holmes

Prague

6 May 1925

Dear Justice Holmes:

Your letter always gives me pleasure, and I am glad that your small ailments have disappeared and that now you can go on reconciling XXth Century life to an XVIIIth Century constitution. I love the continuity of the past only when I am not conscious of its mummification. Otherwise it seems a glass case in a museum.

Last week I went to Vienna to meet my wife back from Florence. The great palace of the Hapsburgs is an odd case in point of what the past may be used for. It no longer fits in with a somewhat ramshackle republic which has no use for it, so the court ballroom hung with beautiful tapestries has been turned into a public theatre where I saw a Mozart ballet charmingly given. But there was something incongruous in it all which left me with the feeling that I was an adventurer trespassing. Mozart is a tradition here, for *Don Juan* was first produced at Prague in a theatre which is still utilized today; and here too Lorenzo da Ponte,[47] Mozart's librettist, met Casanova and by neglecting his advice (not to gamble in London) was forced to become a grocer in New York!

Have you read *Martin Arrowsmith*? I enjoyed it thoroughly with its exposure of university and uplift bunk. The writer, Sinclair Lewis of *Main Street* fame, passed through here only the other day, gay and mellowed by success and no longer thinking that people wished to patronize him.

Otherwise I am deep in Nicolay and Hay's *Abraham Lincoln*. It is splendid in a way, though the North is too magnificent and the South too villainous and unredeemed. It has the 1880 quality of success built on the Civil War when people still thought that a Romanesque cathedral applied to domestic architecture indicated substantial respectability.

Otherwise my deeds are few. I bought two smallish Venetian early XVIIIth Century consoles in Vienna, where the support is a carved American Indian. I possess a couple of old Dresden porcelain Indians and one in silver in addition to the large tapestry of Indians. So far as I collect anything except livable old furniture I like to pick up our Indians in art at a time when the exotic entered into decoration. Vienna was full of objects which I would be told came from the King of Saxony or the King of this (or that) or the Duke of Cumberland who had sold I forget how many tons of his family silver. With eight hundred dozen plates he had some to spare. My own tastes are unluckily ruinous and my wife's no less so, but she would starve to buy. As it is we walked away with a few objects which fit in with our taste better than with our means.

Our garden is a delight now. We have seven acres in the center of Prague, and as a good citizen you will rejoice that since I began this letter I've had a cable to say that the Government has acquired this property. So the United States own

---

[47] Lorenzo da Ponte (1749–1838); Italian adventurer, theatrical writer, and Professor of Italian at Columbia College in New York. A fine portrait of da Ponte by S. F. B. Morse hangs in the Union Club in New York.

a *palazzo* of a hundred rooms, mainly a slum, which dates from XVIIth Century.[48]

Helen joins me in love to you both. Midge would if she were here, for often she talks of you, and your little book is one which never leaves her.

Ever yours,

L. E.

Supreme Court of the United States, Washington, D.C.

May 6, 1925

My dear Marchioness :

It is short and, as you say, long since a direct word has passed between us, and I am truly rejoiced that the silence is broken. In the meantime you have married and have children whom I never have seen and I have become an old man. An anonymous letter a day or two ago said superannuated, but, as it embraced the whole Court except perhaps two dissenting judges because of a judgment that probably made the writer pay more taxes, I do not take it as a serious warning.

Turning to what you write about, of course you have to take a hand, and I think it futile to ask what does it all amount to. One may ask that about all human activities ; and to one who thinks as I do, there is no answer except that it is not our business to enquire. It is a question of the significance of the universe, when we do not know even whether that is only a human ultimate quite inadequate to the I-know-not-what of which we are a part. It is enough for us that it has intelligence and significance inside of it, for it has produced us, and that our manifest destiny is to do our damnedest because we want to and because we have to let off our superfluous energy just as the puppies you speak of have to chase their tails. It satisfies our superlatives and it seems to me unnecessary to demand of the Cosmos an assurance that to it also our best is superlative. It is so in our world and that is as far as we can go. So I accept

[48] The Schönborn Palace in Prague. A splendid example of Baroque architecture purchased on behalf of the State Department by Lewis Einstein in 1924, the Schönborn Palace today houses the United States Embassy together with the Chancery. It is one of the rapidly disappearing examples of fine local architecture the United States Government owns and still uses for its representation abroad.

the motives of vanity, ambition, altruism, or whatever moves us as fact, only reserving the right to smile on half-holidays at the obvious *dureté* of nature to get our work out of us.   One of my old formulas is to be an enthusiast in the front part of your heart and ironical in the back.   It is true that many people can't do their best, or think they can't, unless they are cocksure.

As long ago as when I was in the Army I realized the power that prejudice gives a man ; but I don't think it necessary to believe that the enemy is a knave in order to do one's best to kill him.   However, I am now a spectator in everything except my judicial duties.   I don't read the papers and am not what the reporters call abreast of the time.   I read and try to enrich my mind when I am not turning out stuff that other people have to read ; but in the main I read books not periodicals ; though I pick up some things from my wife's reading while I play solitaire of an evening.   I read a little of the old, but one can't read the old with much profit until one is mature.   What the old can tell us is better said and more clearly understood in modern books.   An idea becomes part of the common stock in twenty years (the common stock of the civilized that is, for the humbugs that Malthus killed a hundred years ago are alive and kicking today).   So when I read the classics or anything of that sort it is more to enlarge my historical understanding than for themselves, bar, of course, the aesthetic pleasures one can laboriously pick out here and there.

My work for this term is mainly done and so I have spent a part of this forenoon in driving in Rock Creek Park, (Do you remember it ?) by the side of the stream through all manner of tender greens with the white of the dogwood blossoms flashing out on one.   It always makes me remember 'to haunt, to startle and waylay' — which seems written for it as much as for a woman.   Also agreeable zoological possibilities roundabout one from wolves and lions to a swan setting on her nest between the road and the creek laughing regardless of automobiles.

If now I could have a talk with you it would put the *comble* to my felicity.   But indeed I have vivid thoughts and affectionate recollections of you, and am delighted that you have remembered me enough to write.

Ever sincerely yours,

O. W. Holmes

Supreme Court of the United States, Washington, D.C.

May 16, 1925

Dear Einstein :

Your letter comes at a most opportune moment, for I crossed the divide this morning, so to speak ; that is I finished all work on hand and can't have much more as arguments are over. And much to my pleasure I had the long suggested letter from your Marchioness a few days ago, and answered her at once with an exposition of my views of life which I hope she won't think a bore. I really am deeply pleased to think that she remembered me.

As yet I have not had much leisure beyond some morning drives with my wife. She read to me Francis Hackett's *That Nice Young Couple*. I used to think he had more than anyone the power to utter the unutterable. Perhaps I was too enthusiastic, but this has marked felicities of that sort, and scenes of vivid observation. I wonder if a tendency to mention things usually omitted from tales or literature is Irish. I think of Joyce who wrote unspeakable things in his first book, I have read no others, and George Moore. I had taken up just before your letter came in *La Petite Illustration, Madelon,* by Jean Garmont. It opens amusingly.

With your letter comes your tantalizing hints at enchantment. The photographs of course speak for themselves, but I can't read Italian without a translation alongside, though I am surprised to see how much I can guess at. I wonder if I should do any work in such surroundings. My usual melancholy thought that the modern world would like to destroy these things has been mitigated today by reading two or three speeches of Baldwin, the Premier, in which he seems to think that the labor people have been learning what he quoted from Sidney Webb, the inevitability of gradualness. (Crib phrase but valuable thought to realize). If I could rid my mind of the desire to keep on producing as long as it can and with that of the duty to seek selfimprovement it seems to me that the happiest leisure would be the drinking in of the loveliness of the past. But with me I fear that such a joy will be confined to picking up an occasional old print ! Well, I think selfimprovement a better aim than the improvement of one's neighbour, an unfashionable thought nowadays, but I think it would be good for uplifters in general. You seem to resent continuity with (not of) the past. As I once remarked, originally to a man from Prague, Augustus Pulizky, (whom I met in London. Do you know whatever became of him?) it is not a duty it is only a necessity. I don't rebel at the necessities of nature; it is like damning the weather, as I believe I wrote to the Marchioness the other day. A good deal of new wine goes into the old bottles and some of the XVIIIth Century precautions put into bills of rights I think are more in danger of being undervalued than over sanctified. The whole tendency of uplift is to be tyrannical and to disregard the individual.

I fear that I have written rather jerkily from interruption, but this will carry my thanks for a glimpse of beauty and my love to your ladies.

Yours ever,
O. W. Holmes

Beverly Farms, Massachusetts

June 1, 1925

Dear Einstein:

A delightful letter has come from you, forwarded to me here, when we arrived last Saturday pretty tired by the journey and the frightful heat of Washington which took everything out of you except what you wouldn't part with. I tucked in all lower ends before I left, and, except the daily mosquito bites from unknown letter writers who have to be answered and occasional bills, I am seeking to forget duty and my immortal soul and to rest in contemplation and leisure.

I wish indeed that I could do some of the contemplation with you, but I am very content with green grass and blue sea. I shall browse a little among books but try not to bother too much about improving my mind. Perhaps you will think I am bothering when I mention that by Laski's recommendation I have begun Sainte-Beuve's *Port Royal*. I am afraid I hardly shall satisfy his enthusiasm. I don't like Saint-Beuve. I may be wrong as I don't know what he believed or didn't, but his smug pious tattle sounds to me like hypocrisy, and although anyone interests who is interested in literature I don't care so much for the time of Louis XIV. It takes a Mussoo or one who has had a Frenchman's training to thrill as they do over Racine. Even Molière has his limits for me although I feel his bigness. Pascal wrote magnificent sentences, but I think Montaigne was a more profound philosopher notwithstanding Pascal's propensity for spiritual passion which didn't trouble Montaigne. As I don't believe most things that those of that time mostly believed, the limits of my delight are natural.

I am so glad and also relieved to know that the Marchioness liked my letter, and I am charmed by your picture of her as by her. Also I rejoice with you in the purchase by the Government of your headquarters. My, wouldn't I like to achieve complete laziness for a month, to waste time and my cares! Nothing could be more enriching and nothing is harder for me to achieve. Industry is a thing of evil, and I always say that those who make the most of themselves don't make much. However, this last year has brought in my share of superlatives. If I were naïf I should be intolerable. Scepticism is a saving grace if it takes in enough of oneself.

My affectionate homage to your ladies.

Yours as ever,
O. W. Holmes

American Legation, Prague

2 June 1925

Dear Justice Holmes:

Your vacation begins with the summer though I don't know how much of the *recubans sub tegmine fagi* there is at Beverly. For me the summer means American tourists and parties and my conversion into an information bureau plus a restaurant. But there is also the garden to be lazy in, and today is a red letter day for the U.S. Government actually buys this place. Fancy a palace with a hundred rooms and three great court yards and a covered entrance through which two trams can pass and a garden of over seven acres which climbs up a hill in the heart of the city and commands a

wonderful view.   How I regret you cannot see this place.
Nothing I would have enjoyed more than to have had you and
Mrs. Holmes here.

Instead I have been living through an age of Congresses.
First an international musical festival where a Czech sonata
called 'Half Time' which reproduced the emotions of the
football field was triumphantly played.   It is modern enough
though not quite up to the productions of a new French genius
who for the first violin substitutes the click of four typewriters.
And now we are in the throes of a great Olympic Congress —
forty-five nations representing the sportsmen of the world, and
those who serve their cause have now grown old and hardly
give the impression of great athletes.   Instead they seem to be
wonderfully successful in the race for decorations.   Never have
I seen so many human Christmas trees assembled.   Colonel
Robert M. Thompson, whom you probably know, is our chief
delegate ; a nice old man who dined here last night.   I had
the French general, Mittelhausser, who is Chief of the Czech
Staff here, and he seemed a bit aghast at all our military titles
so lavishly distributed i.e. General S——.

Midget was delighted with your letter which she sent on to
me to read.   She is now at Yester with a large house party.
But death duties and jointures have weighed heavily on them
and they must let the place for the shooting months.   I hope
they'll come here then.   She is an intelligent little creature
with immense natural charm and a somewhat unfortunate
taste for the grand manner which more and more is of the past.
Yet I have a clinging fondness for its survival.

My love to dear Mrs. Holmes.   I see her now sitting in
her armchair knitting.   Helen joins me.

Ever yours,
L. E.

Beverly Farms, Massachusetts

July 11, 1925

Dear Einstein :
Your letter, just arrived, gives me the usual pleasure.
What you quote from Dizzy comes in apropos as I was just

writing a day or two ago to a friend who repeated a criticism of my opinions that they might be literature but were not the proper form of judicial exposition. My notion was that long winded expositions of the obvious were as out of place in opinions as elsewhere. This however is not intended as a hit at the judgment of the majority in the Gitlow case.[49] I had my whack on free speech some years ago in the case of one Abrams,[50] and therefore did no more than lean to that and add that an idea is always an incitement. To show the ardor of the writer is not a sufficient reason for judging him. I regarded my view as simply upholding the right of a donkey to drool. But the usual notion is that you are free to say what you like if you don't shock *me*. Of course the value of the constitutional right is only when you do shock people.

I am not yet free from Sainte-Beuve's *Port Royal* though drawing to an end. Louis XIV and the spirit of his Court seem to me detestable ; and the postulates of the time are so removed from mine that I don't care what they thought. I wonder if our views of life will seem to some future generations equally arbitrary and unfounded. I don't believe it. But the reason why imbecilities last so long is that if, as usual, people have followed a certain line of thought unquestioning up to maturity, you attack them in their life if you try to make a change. Man is like any other organism and shapes himself

---

[49] *Gitlow* v. *New York*, 268 U.S. 652 (1925) upheld the constitutionality of the New York Criminal Anarchy Statute punishing the publication of a manifesto advocating the forcible overthrow of the government. Holmes filed a dissent in which Brandeis concurred. See page 249.

[50] *Abrams* v. *United States*, 250 U.S. 616 (1919) upheld the defendants' conviction under the Espionage Act for a conspiracy to publish language intended to encourage resistance to the United States' war effort against Germany. A portion of Holmes's dissent merits attention as exemplifying his 'bettabilitarian' philosophy : '. . . when men have realized that time has upset many fighting faiths, they may come to believe even more than they believe the very foundation of their own conduct that the ultimate good desired is better reached by free trade in ideas — that the best test of truth is the power of the thought to get itself accepted in the competition of the market, and that truth is the only ground upon which their wishes safely can be carried out. That at any rate is the theory of our Constitution. It is an experiment, as all life is an experiment. Every year if not every day we have to wager our salvation upon some prophecy based upon imperfect knowledge. While that experiment is part of our system I think that we should be eternally vigilant against attempts to check the expression of opinions that we loathe and believe to be fraught with death, unless they so imminently threaten immediate interference with the lawful and pressing purposes of the law that an immediate check is required to save the country.'

to his environment; when he is grown up a change is like
pulling a tree from the crevice of a rock in which it has aged
and hardened.

People mention books to me, but none that I can hope will
call a blush to my cheek, so I postpone them. The women
seem to do their share in the fleshly, but I am pretty tough and
brazen. I see but few and then rarely. One dame with whom
I have glad discourse is a warm admirer of your *Italian Renaissance in England,* if I get the title right.

You never were here, were you? Nature does pretty well
for us in the way of sea and shore, not to speak of an occasional
rose garden constructed by the same lady who bosses our two
modest beds. The old houses, although not old on the Continental scale, take us back to the local past which was as
different from now as Port Royal. Indeed I read a little in
Mather's *Magnalia* [51] last winter, and I should think that apart
from the sacraments Mather and Arnould would have agreed
very well. But I hope that each would have thought the other
damned.

Now I will turn to my daily stint of Sainte-Beuve. I seem
to get very little time to read though ostensibly at leisure.
After this no more improvement I hope.

My homage and admiration to the ladies. I took this
paper because notepaper cramps me. The photographs are
charming.

Yours ever,
O. W. Holmes

Beverly Farms, Massachusetts

Aug. 8, 1925

Dear Einstein :

By an oversight that I did not discover till too late I
put only a two-cent stamp on my last letter to you, I hope you
got it; therefore I am not sure that this morning's letter is an
answer to that or the one before. You can collect what you
had to pay when next we meet.

It isn't the formalities of the XVIIth century that disgust

---

[51] *Magnalia Christi Americana* by Cotton Mather (1702).

me, though the idolizing of Louis XIV does, but the brutality, servility, and cruelty that I seem to see under the forms. I have, however, just been reading Racine with Lemaître's little book [52] as an eye opener. Result: after allowing so far as I can for my failure adequately to feel the exquisiteness of his verse and for fundamental differences of national tastes, I don't believe that he was one of the four or five great poets of the world, as the Faguetzians and Lemaîtrians do vainly talk. I put it in conversation that Racine makes intelligent statements of love. I do not think he gets the great cry.

The Dayton trial [53] I didn't follow; it seemed to me hardly to touch any intellectual interest though Bryan's death makes it dramatic. I should not suppose, however, that any of the actors was entitled to the consideration of educated men. I suppose that the population concerned are most ignorant; but when I was young and Cabot Lodge a boy we passed a few days at a little settlement on the R.R. in the middle of Illinois (shooting), and I realized that Cotton Mather would not have seemed out of place there. The Minister impressed me more than any other clergyman ever did. I said to him, 'I should not think life would be happy with your beliefs'. He answered, 'It is not.' And his face had deep lines.

This afternoon I turn to the second part of Don Quixote. Fitzgerald [54] (friend of Thackeray and Tennyson) in his delightful letters (do you know them?) says that it cannot be read except in Spanish if you are to do it justice. But I must content myself with the translation by Motteux — I suppose the same who translated Rabelais and years ago seemed to me to find Rabelais as an inventor of words. In general the fun of the past is rocky reading. Practical jokes and dirty words pleased down to the time of Theodore Hook [55] but now please only little boys. I suspect that slumber will dispute the palm with Cervantes great as I believe him to be.

---

[52] *Jean Racine* by Jules Lemaître (1908).

[53] In July 1925 John T. Scopes was tried and found guilty in Dayton, Tennessee, of violation of a State law prohibiting the teaching in schools supported by the State of theories to the effect that man is descended from the lower animals. Clarence Darrow was counsel for the defense while the prosecution had the support of William Jennings Bryan who died a few days after the trial.

[54] Edward Fitzgerald (1809–83); translator of *The Rubáiyát of Omar Khayyám* (1st edition 1859).

[55] Theodore Hook (1788–1841); English novelist, dramatist, and improvisator.

You speak of the neighbourliness of the North Shore, but I see hardly anyone.   My most frequent converse outside of the house is with the keeper of the railroad crossing hard by. In my short walks I pause and tip him a twister on books on the Cosmos.   He had a poetess for a cousin and is open to a thought more or less.   We drive about for two hours nearly every day much to my delight.   I love this region.   It is my earliest memory, and it is all granite which ensures noble contours, with wind swept spaces inland that delight me when I turn from the sea.   And so the vacation is rushing by.   I hate to have it go so fast, and yet I shall go back to work with pleasure.

I am amused by your tale of the Nuncio and do not pretend to fathom the constitutional difficulties of the solicitor of the State Department.

My best remembrances to your wife and the Marchioness, and may you gain in favor with God and woman as you lose in flesh.

Yours ever,
O. W. Holmes

Beverly Farms

Sept. 21, 1925

Dear Einstein :

This is the last letter from Beverly Farms and is likely to be a poor one, as not withstanding the fact that our departure is a week off I am bothered and distracted with a thousand matters incident to the end of vacation.   Yet I had promised myself that the last fortnight should be *bona fide* idleness.   You may say the whole vacation has been that, but the books I read converted themselves into duties until now. Now, that is last week, I am or was dawdling through Pliny's letters, so modern as everyone knows, and redipping at random into George Moore's *Ave-Atque-Vale*.   My events are as limited as ever, nothing more exciting than going to see a house that has been built out of newspapers, literally ; the newspapers pasted together to make boards, varnished, and set up.   The

s

man who built it and lived in it said that his own was dry when his neighbours' houses were letting in the rain. I expect when I get to Washington to leap into work up to my ears and I may prove a bad correspondent; but there won't be time for much shortcoming if you make good the hopes you hold out to me of seeing you in November or soon after. Be sure to give my love to your wife and the Marchioness, delightful creatures. I wish I might see them again.

Did you ever read any of Synge's plays? (Irish). I remember thinking that I never had read such lovemaking. As I see that Moore cracks up one that I haven't read I shall turn to it (*The Well of the Saints*), but reading soon must come to an end. I have had a few thoughts as the result of the *Odyssey*, my last serious venture, but if I haven't told them they must wait. I think I may have talked about Racine and Pascal.

Our latest adventure was going to a County Fair, seeing the horses, hearing the fakers all about, buying popcorn, and my wife professing to have been cruelly stopped by me from mounting a horse on a merry-go-round. But her stock of fiction has increased in this last month. The dentist having supplied me with some extras to make up for some teeth that time has taken, she says that I come back from calling on a lady, put in my teeth, and bite her. It is well to be able to get some sport out of the ravage of time. It gives me malignant pleasure to see George Moore pitch into Newman's style.

Fare thee well for a while, as I said in a day of my youth.

Yours ever,

O. W. Holmes

Prague

17 Feb. 1926

Dear Justice Holmes :

It is ages and ages since I have written you for I have been prevented by a number of vicissitudes. And I do so now both to inquire how you are and to send you my warmest congratulations on your birthday and couple this with the wish for ten thousand more. I feel you are becoming fast such an Olympian that nothing short of the sacrifice of a sheep answers the purpose, but remain in doubt as to transmitting the orders from here.

I spent a happy fortnight at Yester in a modernly patriarchal atmosphere where three young ladies who address me as grandpa made me realize my years, then on to London where my good lady descending from a car fell and broke her ankle. This was very early in January and I delayed there a month hoping she would be able to accompany me. But the stretcher on which she was to travel proved too great an undertaking for her strength and I have had to return here alone to mark time like a night watchman. As soon as she is well enough to travel I go to fetch her, for she has the weakness to miss me.

I took advantage of my enforced stay in London to write to Laski and he came to lunch with me. I found him most attractive and able, and my only criticism is that he seems a bit over omniscient which I suppose is a grace of youth. Needless to say we discoursed over a subject of common friend-ship in admiration.

Lord Buckmaster [56] was greatly pleased with your opinion about the Gitlow case [57] etc. which coincided with his own. I gave him your address so I presume he has written you. But he has resigned from the Judicial Committee of the Lords which ended by boring him, has chucked his Chancellor's pension, and accepted the Chairmanship of a large Oil Company where he disconcerted the stockholders by saying that the quotation of the shares was completely indifferent to him. I am sorry he never met you for I think you would have found much in common with his ingenuous, clean cut mind hating all sham and yet responsive to the really fine.

Now I am back in the drudgery of this place with nothing very much to look forward to for long to come except a change in the weather. I read, I walk, I sleep, and reduce life to its animal functions, for I live here in moral isolation and remain

[56] Stanley Owen Buckmaster, first Viscount Buckmaster (1861–1934); English statesman, orator, judge, and Lord High Chancellor of England 1915–16.
[57] *Gitlow* v. *New York*, 268 U.S. 652 (1925). '. . . A dissent (in which Brandeis joined) in favor of the rights of an anarchist (so-called) to talk drool in favor of the proletarian dictatorship.' Holmes to Pollock, letter of June 18, 1925, see *The Holmes–Pollock Letters*, Vol. II, p. 163.

without the stimulus of a good talk or the charm of an agreeable house to frequent.   And so I live inwardly and yet in memories outside, and you are one of the great ones.

My warmest devotion to Mrs. Holmes.

Ever yours,

L. E.

Supreme Court of the United States, Washington, D.C.

March 6, 1926

My dear Einstein :

Your letter goes to my heart. I know your kindness, but this new expression of it gives me joy. I hope that your wife will have recovered before this reaches you or at any rate will be on the high road to doing so. My best regards to her. I was truly sorry to hear of the accident. I have been in such a whirl this last week that I hardly have known which way to turn. An unusually high pressure of law, the dentist in the background to make it gloomy, and people turning up when it seemed as if I couldn't spare the time.

Reporters have been about seeking interviews which I have declined, but I yielded to the request for a chance to take a snap shot this morning — from a young fellow who was punctual for the five minutes plus, that I allowed him, did his job, and cleared out. I was very glad afterwards for he told my driver that this was his first chance for some newspaper and that he felt that it had started him on his career. Poor little devil, had I known that, I would have been more considerate. However he got some clicks at me here in my library and again when I came out to get into my automobile. I hope for his sake they will succeed. Another cove made a drawing for which I gave him an hour and again he kept to the time. Also I am beginning to receive letters although the anniversary doesn't come till Monday. Rum business growing old ! One little withdrawal, by time, after another, but as yet nothing that I mind though my walking is much curtailed, and I get up and sit down like an old man.

A flash of pleasure this morning from Laski. You know

what an eye he has for books. I told him that if he ever got the chance I should much like Richardson's note on Milton,[58] and it came this morning. In the beginning is an etching by Richardson, who was a portrait painter, of Milton, which his daughter seems to have thought the best, (or at least Richardson's crayon from which I suppose he made his print) and De Quincey says it is the best likeness he knows of Wordsworth ! There is a note in pencil on my copy 'portrait etched by Richardson but a perfect likeness of Wordsworth'. Whether it is independent testimony I do not know. I am too old to collect, but little things like this give one a real pleasure and make me feel young.

I should have liked to see Lord Buckmaster, but I am afraid that I never met him. I am glad to hear that he has agreed with my view.

Now it is Sunday morning. *The New York Times* has the drawing I spoke of and a long article that I have not read. There are few who could write anything that I should care about. From time to time competent men have spoken. My wife doesn't like the drawing. I think it pretty good. It looks as if he had taken to heart a remark I made that people didn't get the potential ferocity hidden in a man. Oh dear, how much I have talked about myself.

Of books at present I see nothing. A while ago I began Horace Walpole's letters with much pleasure. He was ahead of his time in humanity, and the different emphasis of a different time always is interesting. I guess he wrote the best letters there are in English, taking them all round. Also I returned to my youth with a different (Symond's) translation of Benvenuto Cellini. I don't think he was specially a liar. He only told things in Continental fashion. He reminds me of a French servant of one of our officers who after Ball's Bluff, our first engagement, wrote, 'It was sublime to see those young heroes advancing at the head of their battalion'. He couldn't have seen the action, but that was a natural mode of speech for a mussoo. The things that I listen to of an evening are amusing and varied, but I fear that you would think some of them unworthy of a learned jurist. And so, *adieu pro tem.*

---

[58] *Explanatory Notes on Paradise Lost* by Jonathan Richardson (1734).

My homage to the Marchioness, to whom I wrote with thanks for a letter and photographs.

Yours ever,

O. W. Holmes

Supreme Court of the United States, Washington, D.C.

April 28, 1926

Dear Einstein :

You grieve me that you should have to give up Florence, and yet I daresay it will be for the good of your immortal soul. I don't dilate upon the theme, as in these days my thought is apt to be that men have taken themselves too seriously, and also because it is one of my old sayings that a man who makes the most of himself doesn't make much.   Aesthetic effect demands a certain waste, and yet we are told that Goethe and some other great men were industrious, although I always have feared the fact as of ill omen for myself.   To sum up I shan't be sorry if the more strenuous atmosphere forces you into a routine of study and achievement while I don't believe them quite as necessary as I did when I was younger.

The advertising that I got by the talk on the occasion of my birthday leads to an accession of letters from fools of various character that bother one and take time.   I regret the absence of a large machine by which they could be ground into fish bait.

I know not why but the last five or six weeks have kept me tense all the time without relaxation and I feel a little tired. I have no chance to read though I have a *History of Political Science from Plato to the Present* on my table ; interesting, I judge, but written, by a parson, R. H. Murray, who doesn't quite disguise his cloth (to my disgust) and who quotes Emerson's line, 'He buildeth better than he knew' as 'the old saw'.   Also it gives me pleasure to notice a seemingly selfsatisfied clerical gent writing badly as this chap does.

For my hour of solitaire my wife last night read to me from some book by a forgotten authoress who was popular thirty years or more ago ; very good Yankee talk of the old orthodox

period. It is astonishing what good things the world willingly
lets die, quite rightly, as they can't hit the *ut de poitrine*. Perhaps
you would turn up your lordly nose at things that give me
pleasure. I am such intellectual pulp at the end of the day
(which now is) that pap is kindred to me.

I do hope that your dear wife is better and all right again.
I envy your going to the movies. I wanted this week to see
one on the theme of *Moby Dick*, (I think you have never read
that. It has dullish spots, but it has greatness to my mind,
and thrilled me as an old Yankee). But I am not allowed to
go to public shows. I obey my boss who has kept me wondrous
well.

My love to both your ladies.

Ever yours,
O. W. Holmes

Supreme Court of the United States, Washington, D.C.

May 26, 1926

My dear Einstein :

Your phrase 'the real humility of the skeptic' hits me
where I live. I always insist and believe that the skeptic is
more humble than all the other devotees of the sects. He does
not look at himself as a little God but recognizes that his only
significance is as a part of the I-know-not-what.

I pass from what no doubt I have said a dozen times before
to the statement that I have read or listened to the greater
part of *Gentlemen Prefer Blondes*.[59] It was borrowed before I
quite reached the end ; amusement short of ecstacy.

As to what you say of Henry Adams I should think it
was too severe, but all that I remember is that I was impressed
by the opening description of the *Times* which you agree in
praising. I felt real respect and gratitude to Adams. When
he gave up teaching he handed on to me a collection of German
and other books on the history of the law that was really a
noble present, though subsequent events have caused me to use
it too little. And yet I take a discreditable pleasure in hearing

[59] *Gentlemen Prefer Blondes* by Anita Loos (1925).

him criticized because his Education of H.A.[60] seems to me futile and pretentious, which is all the worse because it is so interesting. He was very keen and a thinker, but seems to me to have allowed himself to be satisfied too easily that there was no instruction for him in the branches in which he dabbed. When I would step in at his house on the way back from Court and found him playing the old Cardinal, he would spend his energy in pointing out that everything was dust and ashes. Of course one did not yield to the disenchantment, but it required so much counter energy in a man tired with his day's work that I didn't call often. And yet meet him casually on the street and often he was a delightful creation. He was kind, sad, and defeated, although another man would have thought the same life a success. Did I ever tell you of his reply to some one who said he had been travelling with Charles Adams and found him delightful? 'You found Charles delightful? You interest me'. He had many fine things in his house, yet it left you cold.

The *Odyssey*, that last theme you mention, I finished last summer. I never have found Homer's Greek as easy as it is reputed to be. There are too many words that I don't know, the same trouble that I find in discourses on Railroads, Values, Admiralty, and I may say in everything that has become a specialty. There was much, or considerable, that moved me in the Odyssey; but I don't spend much time in extracting small bits of edible matter with a nutpicker when I can get it by the slice in modern books.

Speaking of last summer I forget whether I told you of the moderate joy I got from Racine — probably I did. I recount my emancipating formula that I have no doubt that I have uttered at least once before. The literature of the past is a bore. Having said that you can make your own exceptions. They will not be very many for most people who don't tell lies.

Apropos of the strike,[61] I was delighted by the British homeliness and avoidance of superlatives in a letter written in the middle of it. 'So we are all very grumpy'. Solid lot that take things that way.

[60] *The Education of Henry Adams* by Henry Adams (1918, privately printed 1906).
[61] The great general strike in England called by the Trade Union Congress began May 3 and terminated May 12, 1926.

My love to your wife, who I hope is still getting better, and to the Marchioness.

Yours ever,
O. W. Holmes

Prague

8 June 1926

Dear Justice Holmes:

Once more a letter from you reaches me to bring welcome news from a philosopher and a friend. And I am glad to think that these lines will find you enjoying a rest from the grind of Rhadamanthine decisions, and an opportunity, which of course you will neglect, to indulge in frivolities. I hardly know the NORTH SHORE though a brief visit there gave me the idea that everyone could look into everyone else's windows. Perhaps this was due to the visit being in the late Autumn when there were no leaves on the trees.

I was keenly interested in all you say about Henry Adams. I had found his 'Education' interesting but almost vulgar in its selfconsciousness. Is it not true that the law of demand and supply operates even with 'historic' families? We have so few that their importance becomes inflated at least in their own estimation. Over here they are more often taught the grace to conceal such advantages, though it used to be said of the late Duke of Atholl that he would daily gaze at himself in the mirror and repeat 'I'm the Duke of Atholl'. Yet we are going toward a new set of values. Fancy the joy of being able to point to Jackie Coogan [62] as an ancestor. But I wonder if we will be able ever to fund our fame in the way that titles of feudalism coupled with the transmission of landed estates have done in Europe.

I give up all idea of looking for a rational purpose in history. I take it this means only interpreting the world in the terms of one's particular vision. If I were really a philosopher I should like to write a treatise on the theory and technique of accident in modifying history and try to arrive at some actuarial result. But more and more I feel that I haven't the remotest idea

[62] Jackie Coogan (1919–   ); American child actor who was one of the early prodigies that emanated from Hollywood.

what it all means and it really doesn't make much difference. Therefore why be proud? I try to play the game according to Hoyle just so long as Hoyle exists and he will probably outlive me. But for the rest I've ceased to wonder.

Outside the birds are chirping merrily, and I hear from Midget that her eldest daughter — aged 12 — shot in one day a hare, four rabbits, and a wood pigeon. So the education of others than Henry Adams is proceeding. My wife also is picking up again; so much that she wants to accompany me to Paris in a couple of days to bring back a new car. She joins me in many greetings to you both.

Ever yours,
L. E.

I enclose a brief preface for a new picture book on Baroque Prague.

Beverly Farms, Massachusetts

June 21, 1926

My dear Einstein :

A nice letter from you this morning enclosing your admirable introduction. It filled me with interest and pleasure. I remember last summer Spengler, *Der Untergang des Abendlandes* Vol. 1, had some discourse on the Baroque. As I remember it marked the transition from sculpture to painting as a more adequate mode of expression, *en route* for music, which culminated in *Parsifal*, and then the end. I don't swear to my synopsis, but that is the way it remains in my mind. Spengler can wait, but what you say is stimulating and makes me believe you.

I have been here now a week, and am gradually getting idleness into focus. I suppose that by and by I shall get some *pièce de résistance* but at present I am not bothering beyond having sent for a book on French law that I don't believe I shall get. I did bring down with me, read, return, and write a letter to the author, Carver, about *The Present Economic Revolution in the United States* which pleased me much, especially by its contempt for class war and all the fashionable twaddle. He says the revolution consists in the fact that labor is becoming

capitalist, as shown by labor banks, increased deposits, purchases of stocks by laborers, etc., and believes, I gather, in our
policy of limiting immigration. But that was an episode.
Otherwise I have read stories, and have fallen back on Pepys's
Diary of which I found a cheap edition in the house. I think
that the two best books for irresponsible moments when you
don't require ideas but don't want rot, the two best, at least
that I think of, are Pepys's, and Horace Walpole's letters.
Apropos of the latter, there is a very good article by Lytton
Strachey called *The XVIIIth Century* in a late *New Republic*,
June 16th. I think.

I was naming that thrice accursed Spengler over whom I
labored with a dictionary. He mentions as a great etcher,
Leibl, of whom I never heard. Did you? Leibl, I rewrite
that you may be sure of the spelling. I believe Spengler to
be a bore who talks stimulating humbug. Can you recite
upon him? You see that as yet I have got into no current of
thought or interest, but I have done a number of odd jobs
that wouldn't interest you though they satisfy me to have done
them. So I will shut up *pro tem.*

My best remembrances to the two ladies.

Yours ever,

O. W. Holmes

Beverly Farms, Massachusetts

July 16, 1926

My dear Einstein :

The ocean breezes that you wish us are rather too cool
this season, but a good deal better than the heat of Washington,
which kills. We all feel well under them.

I have little to tell. All our migrations from the blue bed
to the brown. Yesterday we went again to the House of the
Seven Gables, which now has had added to its neighbourhood,
I believe by moving, two other old houses that make a charming little enclosure with it that looks old world. Antiquity is
relative and these are enough to make you feel that you have
roots in the past.

A small boy offered his services as guide to Gallows Hill

'where they hanged the witches' etc., and my wife bid him hop in. We hadn't time for Gallows Hill, but we took in a charming old burying ground that I didn't know in the middle of the town, where were interred my ancestor Governor Bradstreet *et al*, and the boy imparting his ambition to go to Harvard College and the Law School got five dollars and our blessing.

The other day, again under the energetic impulse of my wife, we stopped on our way through Salem on the occasion of its tercentenary, pushed through the crowd to the Court House, where to my surprise I was promptly recognized by a young man who rushed to get us chairs and put us in the best place to see a procession celebrating the town, *now* and *then*. The old houses were opened and the whole business was done with taste and dignity though I saw no more. I will not go on with our small adventures but they are pleasant.

My neighbour Beveridge submits to me chapters of his *Life of Lincoln* [63] which I think will be *the* life when it is finished. He takes infinite pains over every detail, knows how to subordinate them to the story, and I should think has every quality for a first rate life except that he is not a remarkably good writer — not a master of English style. He takes criticism as if he were a disinterested judge, his only interest being that the work shall be done well.

I don't read a great deal; some stories, and *Pepys's Diary*, alas drawing to an end, and slowly plodding through Declareuil, *Histoire Générale du Droit Français*. A daily drive, a daily nap, a daily walk, and solitaire every evening leaves not too much time for improvement! I hope for a little before the vacation ends. With which summary *adieu* for the moment.

My homage to the ladies.

Yours ever,
O. W. Holmes

Prague

6 August 1926

Dear Justice Holmes :

I find your letter from the Shore on my return from a forty-eight hour jaunt to England whither I had gone to

[63] *Abraham Lincoln, 1809–1858* by Albert J. Beveridge (1928).

deposit my wife who wishes to be with Midge. She is expecting, and after three girls hopes to produce a son. I hope so with her, and yet the whole thing seems such a joke of nature. Still even in a pack of cards we like to hold kings. I suppose we must judge life by its conventions, and I cordially wish for an Earl of Gifford.

I found the flavor of the past in your account of the visit to Salem. I too enjoyed it. For me at least the past has always seemed the memory of man as I myself know him and not merely as he existed. I could never find anything human in the cave dweller and very little for that matter in Tutunkhamen though I admire the art of that time. But I love the white porches of Salem and the respectability of wealth built on slaves and opium. Our own generation seems more indulgent though I don't think that the fibre has weakened. But long may the small towns of New England live to remind America that its conception was not immaculate.

I have been immensely busy as usual doing nothing. Even the houses of Prague require a priestlike devotion. Two hundred American doctors pass through who require to be fed; then come our champion tennis players for whom all conversation is a despised art; then forty Kansas farmers who have converted their wheat into the dynamic force of a joyride through Europe; and last and best of all Douglas Fairbanks and Mary Pickford have honored us. They were hardly here before a dozen operators crept up to film us, while in the street outside there gathered a large and enthusiastic crowd which made me realize what popularity really was. I liked Fairbanks. He had always made me proud I was an American as if vicariously I shared in his agility. But I found him brimming over to meet, a magnificent, healthy person with an odd interest in history (for movie purposes) and a somewhat simple interpretation of the role of 'the barons' in the XVIIth Century. He has come from Moscow. He was on his way to Paris and then China — treated where he went as a kind of super royalty, for the entire world are his admiring subjects! I wish Mrs. Holmes had been there.

My devoted homages to her and to you.

As always,

L. E.

Beverly Farms, Massachusetts

Aug. 22, 1926

My dear Einstein :

Your news as to the Marchioness reminds me of some friends of mine here who after having had four or five girls took medical advice as to the possibility of affecting the result, and following the advice now rejoice in a boy.

I am delighted with your suggestion that the conception of the New England towns was not immaculate, but you hardly do them justice. I imagine Salem was built up, unless I am mistaken, mainly by commerce that would call for no blush even on the cheeks of one who did not look on world events as inevitable stages in an organic movement.

Your account of your occupations pleases me hugely. I have been quietly reading and forgetting a *History of Modern Philosophy* (Höffding), and chuckling over, what seems to me, the drool they all let out over the 'Problem of Evil'. I don't see that there is any problem until you come to the ultimate mystery of the Universe and the illusion of separateness with which it inspires its fractions when it gives them a separate consciousness. But I won't bore you as I have been bored, although far less by a good book on philosophy than previously by law.

Sitting in for amusement yesterday and the day before I read Guedalla's *Fathers of the Revolution*. The briskness of his writing led me to expect something, but he seemed to me a Jazz Carlyle. His appreciations are worth reading perhaps, but his skepticism as to great men makes him almost blind to their great qualities. You hardly would know that Burke was anything but a tongue. However, as I have Guedalla's *Second Empire* I think I should read that this afternoon. The calibre of the events there I should think would make them a better field for him.

Incidentally, I have looked over some forty cases (applications for leave to come up to our Court) so as to diminish the pressure of work when the next term begins. It will make all the difference between worry and calm when we start in.

My reading of history did me one good thing. I had been

inclined to rebel a little at Marshall's long-winded establishment
of the almost obvious, when I was reminded that not much
more than two hundred years before they had burned Bruno
for upholding what probably we should think still more
obvious. And it made me realize that the man who was called
on to make a new institution work could not be too careful
and too laborious in making all the great premises free from
doubt. As I have said in decisions, great affairs bring such
hydraulic pressure to bear that they can make every past
principle seem questionable. So let us honor Marshall and
leave others to read him.

I hope that all will go well with your ladies, to both of
whom my love, and now I will lie upon a lounge with a book
and read or sleep.

Yours ever,
O. W. Holmes

Beverly Farms, Massachusetts

Sept. 20, 1926

My dear Einstein :

Your letter arrives as I am in the first (very slight)
spasms of departure. We leave for Boston on Saturday 25th
and for Washington on Tuesday the 28th, where I suppose I
shall drop at once into the deep water of work. However I
took the precaution to get enough done here this summer to
make the start easier. We have to look over a great number of
cases to decide whether they should be allowed to come up in
the numerous instances in which an appeal is left to our discretion — (a wise means that saves much time). I have
examined forty or so which is more than we shall have to
recite on at the end of the first week.

My first act on arrival is to put the bound volumes of my
last term's decisions with the others, and then the last term
is finished. Next, do my very little unpacking, for we leave
most things here, then copy from the back of my check book
the list of books read in the summer for the permanent list I
have kept I know not how long, then pay any bills and answer

any letters that require attention, and then begin business. My secretary always has orders to appear on Friday at 11 a.m., so as to give me a day or two free, and to start on that day with the morning squared. He will go to work opening and sorting the books and pamphlets that have accumulated during the summer, and then I will set him to work to find out how it is that the bank credits me with two or three hundred dollars more than my check book shows — an agreeable mistake and the bank assures me that their figures are right. What a lot of trouble about insignificant details.

But last week I read a Greek play (the *Antigone*) so I am not wholly lost in trifles. Did you ever read Leacock's account of a college presentation of a Greek play? It is very funny. (In *'Over the Footlights'* I believe.) I don't know that I have made any startling discoveries this summer. A fact occurs to me that seems to me a sort of epitome of life, my life at least. My first book ended with the word 'explained' (intentionally chosen) my last, with the word 'unknown'. After all our explanations we end with a mystery.

Now I must turn to first considerations and finish packing my trunk for the express. From Saturday to Wednesday I shall live on a handbag and feel free.

My homage to the ladies. You have not told me the result.

Yours ever,
O. W. Holmes

Supreme Court of the United States, Washington, D.C.

Jan. 8, 1927

My dear Einstein :

Your New Year's good wishes have come and with them two interesting papers. I thank you for all and reciprocate the former. I am afraid that two recent opinions hardly would maintain the balance for the latter, each of which gives me real pleasure.

We are sitting now, and I am a worm gnawing in darkness until we adjourn again. The work keeps everybody breathless for the time. I have read a few things of which I should like to talk but have not the energy to write after a fairly strenuous conference of the Judges this afternoon and a succession of things to be done after it until now, 6.30 p.m.

Do you know Redlich [64] of Vienna? Clever man, great talker as I remember him, and author of some important work on matters concerning the history of Austria, I don't know exactly what. He is coming here for a few days at the end of next week, he writes, and I expect he will pass an evening with us. He writes from the Harvard Law School and I believe has been lecturing there. Some years ago, before the late war, he wrote an excellent report on American law schools.

Other news have I none, and after a conference with my brethren no ideas; an agreeably insolent suggestion but it only means that I am too tired to think further. So fare you well.

My loving homage to the dames.

Yours ever,
O. W. Holmes

Supreme Court of the United States, Washington, D.C.

Feb. 1, 1927

My dear Einstein :

Your letters always interest me, and this one does even a little more than usual. Not because of your going on boar hunts, although that is impressive, nor because of your *mot* about the men, women, and Pilsen of your land, but because of the criticism of Henry Adams's history. It is long since I read it, and I retain no impression except of a brilliant account of the society of that time. But what you say seems to fit the man, e.g. 'painstaking yet superficial'. That seems to me what he was to the different candidates for his interest, such as science or ultimate conceptions. He had a right to pronounce himself a failure if so minded (although I should not call him one) as his brother Charles called himself; but he wrote nothing that I ever read that entitled him to pronounce science

[64] Joseph Redlich (1869–1936) ; Austrian historian, professor, politician, and student of English government. Redlich was Professor of Comparative Law at the Harvard Law School from 1926 to 1935.

T

a failure and speculation futile. He had a lot of intelligence and sense and knowledge, but I think he also covered ignorance with a pontifical manner. They all had it, and Brooks, who has just died, would be equally august whether what he had to say meant real thoughts of his own or what another feller or even I myself had told him within half an hour. The lot always gave me a kind of intellectual irritation at being put to discover what was real flesh and blood and what *papier mâché*. Haven't you found people or writers who have bothered you to decide whether they were great men or humbugs? I have. Hegel, Walt Whitman, Karl Marx, Langdell; all gave me troubles now long set to rest. To prove it I should go on and characterize them except that it would not interest you much.

I believe I have mentioned a piece of philosophizing far more profound to my mind than Hegel's rotten system that I have read twice; Dewey's *Experience ánd Nature*. But Hegel while a humbug as a system maker was a man of genuine *aperçus*. You could gather enough sayings of profound thought I daresay to cover three sheets, and that is about as much as a first rate thinker can expect to contribute.

As to your Frenchman and his books to prove what man would be but for men, who is the *man*? The type of the few thousands who, as Bourget says, constitute the civilized world? Or the millions who are only animals? Or any of the second grade between the two? It seems to me that the sceptic well may be the most truly religious as well as the most philosophical of men. I would undertake to defend that thesis.

I have had a few days of irresponsible leisure — broken in upon by new work but renewed — when I could dine in the midday and snooze in the afternoon, without a scruple, and I set the Idles of the Judge against the *Idylls of the King*, but that is interrupted every minute with the day.

Tomorrow Conference. Monday, after shooting off our decisions, arguments again, and no more chance to read about fishing. Between the last sentence and this there comes a long opinion from the C.J. on which I must be ready to recite in the morning, wherefore *adieu*.

My best remembrances to your wife and the Marchioness.

Yours ever,

O. W. Holmes

Supreme Court of the United States, Washington, D.C.

March 25, 1927

My dear Einstein :

You have given me three pleasures : your message on my birthday, your letter, and the third, in anticipation, as it has just come, your *Tuscan Gardens*.[65]

I don't know whether what you say about the Red danger in the U.S. is serious or is wrote sarcastic (as A. Ward used to say). I don't believe there is any such danger.

As to leisure here — I have not known it for a long time and my birthday which you rightly dated the 8th added to my already hard work a lot of letters and telegrams to be acknowledged. The papers to my surprise made considerable talk about it. Mostly the usual reporters' stuff, but every once in a while something that showed thought and gave me pleasure. I don't care as much as I thought I should before it came for the *digito monstrari*, but when a man who knows what he is talking about says something good about me it sets me up. One is always ready to suspect that one's desert is small, even on the human scale and apart from a more general surmise that mankind is not so important a phenomenon as with the help of the priests it has come to think itself. So praise from the competent encourages. When Roosevelt nominated me the papers made a good deal of talk of a friendly sort, but it made me very blue. For I said to myself that for twenty years and more I had been doing my best to produce the first rate and only one article so far as I remember showed the slightest discrimination or notion, favorable or unfavorable, of what my work had amounted to. But, as my papa used to say, our self estimate is a stock of fancy goods which if they are put up to auction fetch mighty little. The foregoing though personal is not primarily egotism but philosophizing.

I have had no time to read serious books, though I have listened to some light things while at solitaire. Jerome K. Jerome's *My Life and Times* is pleasant. Perhaps you have known him as an amusing writer. And I have listened to

[65] 'The Tuscan Garden' by Lewis Einstein appeared in *The Architectural Review* (February 1927).

Pickwick at intervals. They had a play here that revived it, it is said very prettily, and that suggested a recurrence. Lord, how the atmosphere changes. I like the simple old past, because I can remember something like it, but I doubt if many young people do. Indeed I suppose Dickens generally is out of fashion. Yet I don't believe there has been any genius comparable to him writing in English since his day. And how constantly one sees in art as in law the recurring effort to discover a cheap and agreeable substitute for knowing one's business, for imagination, and intellect. However, I suppose that advertising now in its turn is at least philosophized about, which reminds me of what you say about the President. I wonder if you are right and he is an artist as you say. I don't follow things and don't know. It is a nice idea I should think.

Since the last word I have been to look at the cherry trees around the Potomac basin. They are worth coming hundreds of miles to see. For once one really has enough, such endless billows of white and pink. Nature does some other pretty good things here without the aid of importation.

But I am very languid and a chap is coming to see me very shortly who I expect will jaw, not shortly, and I want to lay me down for a minute or two before he comes.

I have an expectation, or rather a hope, of a week or two of leisure after today or tomorrow, which I shall be glad of. A letter is like an instantaneous photograph; the subject moves while the photograph remains the same. The mood in which one writes is forgotten before the letter is received. I am in very good shape and the collapsed feeling is simply of the moment.

My love to the dames.

Yours ever,
O. W. Holmes

Supreme Court of the United States, Washington, D.C.

May 19, 1927

My dear Einstein:

Your letter in its turn has lain by for a (very) few days, as yesterday and today have been my first glimpses of leisure for a considerable time. Decisions to write, opinions of others to examine, and above all, just when quiet seemed to dawn, a damned great pile of records in cases where there were applications for *certiorari*, i.e. for leave to come to our Court when the parties could not come up as of course. There has been a great improvement in submitting an increased number of appeals to our discretion, to determine whether they should be allowed or not; but it puts a great labor on us. We have examined about six hundred cases this term in this way. Not of course so thoroughly as to decide them in our minds, but fully enough to decide whether they ought to be brought before us; and of course, I should say, in most cases incidentally to have an opinion whether the judgment below is right or wrong. One decision that I wrote gave me pleasure, establishing the constitutionality of a law permitting the sterilization of imbeciles.[66]

I think I can somewhat dimly imagine your feeling as to Italy, but the charms must be hard to give up, and I at least feel a pang at the separation. Also I am envious of your phrase that you do too little to have much time for reading. *Pereant qui ante nos postea dixerunt.*

My little scraps enlarged yesterday and today I have read Lawrence's *Revolt in the Desert*, a vivid book, that leaves me rather wondering why he thought it worth while to take so much trouble, but giving a vivid picture of the Arabs and of tremendous hardship borne without special emphasis because they were his. They say he is now a private in the English army. A devil of a fellow. It reminds me of Clarence Day's *This Simian World*, which says that being super-monkeys when we get through fighting we have to do a lot of chattering. Had we been super-cats we simply should have stopped and walked away. Lawrence, although he was collared for a book, seems simply to have stopped and walked away.

Also I have read most of a little volume by Laski on Communism which seems to state the pros and cons in an interesting

---

[66] *Buck* v. *Bell*, 274 U.S. 200 (1927) where Holmes wrote: 'It is better for all the world if, instead of waiting to execute degenerate offspring for crime or to let them starve for their imbecility, society can prevent those who are manifestly unfit from continuing their own kind. The principle that sustains compulsory vaccination is broad enough to cover cutting the Fallopian tubes. Three generations of imbeciles are enough.' P. 207.

way, although he seems to believe in the fundamental thesis that the rich exploit the poor and the ideal of equality, both of which (with some slight explanation) I believe to be drool. Indeed they provoke me out of intellectual indifference into a fiercely contemptuous wrath. But perhaps I don't know enough to be entitled to it.

I believe *Elmer Gantry* is outlawed in Boston on some fool action. I suppose really because it pitched into the clergy. I haven't read it, but am tempted to. *Arrowsmith* began by boring me and ended by leaving the impression of a great book. I think *great* is not too strong though I could not recite now. I am told that Boston also is down on Mencken, and when we add the row that has been kicked up, Frankfurter potently abetting, over the trial of Sacco & Vanzetti [67] some years ago, I feel as if I was going to a perturbed teapot when I turn North in June.

My friends die daily. You will have heard long before this of Lady Castletown's death, and probably of my summer neighbour, Beveridge. I shall miss him; and he was cut off when half way through a labor that no one can continue on the life of Lincoln. I do not desire immortality, but one always wants a few years more for one's friends and oneself.

My love to the ladies.

Yours ever,
O. W. Holmes

Beverly Farms, Massachusetts

June 14, 1927

My dear Einstein :

Such a pleasant letter from you arrived here just about the same time as we did. Vacation has begun ; and although I have not yet seriously perpended what should be done to

---

[67] Nicola Sacco and Bartolomeo Vanzetti were executed for murder August 23, 1927, after a short trial and seven years' subsequent proceedings, the conduct of which was widely criticized in the United States and abroad as being prejudicial and unjust with respect to the defendants. See *The Case of Sacco and Vanzetti* by Felix Frankfurter (1927).

improve my mind, and although there are always some distracting details when one moves, I have whiffs of leisure, little as I believe that such critters really exist. I brought down with me the *Life of Liszt* by Pourtalès. I doubt if I should share the enchantment of the ladies over him, or perhaps over music and fame. The portrait of him as a young man *d'après un dessin de Nancy Mériesnes, 1836*, seems to present a rather loathly being. But the contents as far as I've got and a sentence of Wagner's has the great note : '*J'ai tâté le pouls de notre art moderne, et je sais qu'il mourra. Mais, loin de m'en attrister, cela me remplit de joie parceque je sais aussi que ce n'est pas l'art qui périra mais seulement notre art à nous*'. I suppose art was a religion to those two, and I don't know that the feeling is very different from that of people in other times who put an ideal into their work.

I am struck by your criticism of Lawrence, which I daresay is just. Our rival hero, Lindbergh, seems to have kept the right tone, as also his mother. Everyone seems to unite in unmixed praise with unmixed pleasure. People may envy and belittle talents but they are called to admire a man who quietly bets his life on his own courage and skill.

Since the last words I have read the letters of Liszt to Wagner when Liszt brought out *Tannhäuser* in 1849. They certainly are fine, and Liszt appears in a very noble light. I will wait till I have finished the book before really making up my mind. Owen Wister [68] talked with him I believe, and when Wister returns to this country I shall try to get some firsthand impressions from him. Liszt and Wagner seem each to have discovered himself? / themselves? in the other.

You may see by this paper that I have not yet got settled with conveniences, though if I had more distinguished stationery I still might prefer the comfort of writing on a block. But you will also see that I cannot write at such length because the moment I settle down there is something to be done.

Again I sympathize in your giving up Florence, and yet believe that you know what is for your own good. Give my love to the dear ladies.

---

[68] Owen Wister (1860–1938) ; American lawyer, novelist, and intimate friend of Holmes.

The term just adjourned has been very encouraging to me. I have enjoyed it and have felt up to the mark.

Yours ever,

O. W. Holmes

Beverly Farms, Massachusetts

July 12, 1927

My dear Einstein :

Another delightful letter from you finds me in the full routine of my life here. *Pièce de résistance* two hours in the automobile. As you know I never tire of this region, my earliest recollection of the country and the ocean. Then the crevices filled with a little reading, some letter writing mostly to bores, a short walk, a sleep, and solitaire. I have just finished a volume that only the absence of others, the pressure of this, and personal recommendation would have persuaded me to read. *The Story of Philosophy*, by Will Durant. Fancy a book on philosophy by a man deliberately calling himself *Will* ! Yet it is very good — I thought especially in pointing out in Plato the anticipation of future isms — the criticisms tinged with the writer's personal preferences, as when he treats the desire for immortality as one of the profoundest in man. I don't believe it though most men are brought up to it. Also I should not have given a large (or any) place to Voltaire in a history of philosophy however large a one he deserves in the history of human thought. But the book is good, easy, and instructive reading. Now I am in the middle of a short life of Disraeli by Maurois, in the same series as *La Vie de Franz Liszt*, which probably I have mentioned. Maurois as probably you know wrote *Les Silences du Colonel Bramble* and *Ariel* ; an effective writer. Waiting for me to finish this is *Coningsby* which also I have begun (to reread). But as you see I have shied off from any very solid work, so far. I have been somewhat troubled at my inarticulate pleasures. Living as I do it seems as if improvement consisted only in accessions of things said, either by others or myself. Yet I am sure that really one is enriched by impressions that lose their form as soon as one turns one's back.   What a Philistine a painter would think me for even feeling a doubt!   But to him such *im*pressions are on the way to *ex*pression, whereas it is not so obvious though perhaps true with regard to a dry as dust judge. Expression is life, and it is lawful to suspect anything that does not lead to it.

I suppose that now you are at Yester and in company that I grieve to think that I never shall share again.   My love to the two charming ladies.

As a rational man I make as short plans as possible.   As the natural man I picture keeping on and turning out decisions with an eye to ninety, only three years and eight months, but alas!, not that I shall grumble at the fury with the abhorred shears — I have had my whack, and do not appreciate the longing for immortality — but I am somewhat like a relation of mine many years back who said she didn't see why people wanted to be rich as long as she could have five dollars in her pocket.   She was all right.   One may not want eternity; but one wants a little more.

This paper is detestable to fold and is sold with a horrid name 'Gentleman's Club'; but it is good to write on and sets the hand, arm, and thoughts free.   I shall not use the huge envelopes sent with it but resort to the prosaic offering of the United States.

Yours ever,
O. W. Holmes

Beverly Farms, Massachusetts

Aug. 14, 1927

Dear Einstein :

The picture of your pageant charms me, and your contact with royalty amuses and touches my sympathy.   It has befallen me to sit by royalties often times and I have found it a dull business.

I find the summer, as you do, disinclining me to consider the welfare of my immortal soul very much.   The most valuable result of such philosophy, as I have said, has been to add one article to my Bill of Rights, viz., 'No man shall be held to master any system of philosophy that is fifty years old'. The great philosophers have had a fine insight that could be stated in two minutes. They then have constructed systems that posterity willingly forgets, but in which their insights are tucked away. The latter are all that we want, and if we read their damned books it is only to get the *aperçus*, which probably we know already.

Just now I have reread *The Sentimental Journey* and *Tristram Shandy* and put them among the exceptions to my rule that the literature of the past is a bore. Now I have nothing on hand except some Court business which I shall take up when I feel like it to cut down the work for next term. To that extent I am willing to bet on my survival to October.

You probably have heard of the row kicked up all over the world on Sacco and Vanzetti convicted of murder in Massachusetts a number of years ago. Their counsel came to me last week with something of a crowd, and applied for a writ of *habeas corpus*. I heard them for two hours and half and denied the writ, stating my opinion that I had no power to take the prisoners from the custody of the State that had jurisdiction of the offence and the persons. If the prisoners had been held without jurisdiction it would have been different. And, by a decision that I wrote, the writ would lie when, although there was the form of a trial, the Court room and those in it were under the domination of an angry mob ready to lynch all concerned if there was not a prompt conviction. In this case the only ground was the alleged prejudice of the Judge. If justice was what the world is after, this case is not half so bad as those that are more or less familiar in the South. But this world cares more for red than for black. In the evening a cousin by marriage came and wanted to spend the night on my piazza against the chance of some violence being attempted. I declined, but was much touched by the generous and gallant offer; all the more that we found it came from a man nearly worn out with four bad nights in sleepers which are too short for him so that he cannot sleep.

No other events worth chronicling. I reserve the right to seek improvement if anything stimulating enough comes my way or if conscience kicks too hard. Golf! I should say not.

I play no games that require intelligence (Bridge) or skill.
Solitaire (with my own rules) and a short toddle are enough
for me now.

My affectionate homage to the two ladies.

Yours ever,

O. W. H.

Beverly Farms, Massachusetts

Sept. 11, 1927

Dear Einstein :

Probably this is the last letter from Beverly Farms, as on
the 26th we expect to leave here and after a day in Boston to
go to Washington the night of the 28th. The journey is a
fatiguing business, but I think we have arranged to make it as
little so as possible.

As to the Sacco and Vanzetti affair: I see no reason for
commutation and the time elapsed, as I suppose it all was due
to successive attempts on their part to rip up the sentence —
not to the State. The world does not seem to realize that the
whole thing was a State matter with which the U.S. had
nothing to do and in which the Courts of the U.S. had no
power except in circumstances that I thought very plainly did
not exist. However they came at me three times, the last at
9 p.m. on the eve of the execution. I won't go over the
matter now, but a lot of nonsense has been talked here and
abroad and I have received many letters hortatory or abusive,
agreeing, however, in ignorance of the limit of my powers and,
I should think, of the case.

I have just received Ludwig's other book, *Wilhelm Hohen-
zollern*, which I expect to be much more interested by than I
was by his *Napoleon*. I am curious to know more about the
Kaiser as he was, and my malevolence is gratified by the
picture as far as I have got.

I have spent some time on work in anticipation to make the
beginning of the Term easier and therefore haven't read much
latterly. I have had some sensations and made some reflections
as I went along, but the chances are that I have told you at
least some of them. Just now the broomstick is not blossoming

very much. This is the trying season of the year for me and I am coolest if I can keep tolerably well, and, yes, a daily drive.

Your letter is delightful. You must have grown into Prague and the people pretty well, I should think, by this time, so that they at least would be sorry to part with you; and, however you may feel, I know that you have at least occasional hankerings for America as an abiding place; but I fear that you would tire of it and miss the old world in which most of your life has been spent. Associations determine our loves. No doubt I have repeated often truisms as to the part played by time in our affections and beliefs. We could not account for the stronghold of current religions otherwise. I have little doubt that there is something in England that is to you what to me are the granite rocks and barberry bushes of this Coast. There is a little ledge in the ocean hard by here to which are anchored my first feelings of romance. By that I swung in a dory when very little and fished for small fish and watched the seaweed swinging from the broken barnacles. There I saw Charley Lowell, afterwards the great General Lowell killed in the Valley, shoot two peep [69] and thought him greater than I ever did in after years.

My love to the ladies and their master.

Yours ever,

O. W. H.

Supreme Court of the United States, Washington, D.C.

Oct. 10, 1927

My dear Einstein :

This is just a line to say that I can't write. Ever since I've got here the work has been so constant that I haven't had a breathing moment until this afternoon; and have it now only because my secretary by mistake returned to Court the papers in a case assigned to me last night.

I have read nothing but endless records of cases, and heard nothing but arguments. Do give my love to the two charming ladies, and tell the Marchioness that her foot is on my neck.

[69] A name given in the United States to several species of small sandpiper.

Ah, my boy, it is harder work to live at eighty six than it is at twenty six, sixty six, or seventy six; but it is a great advantage to have gaiety on top of melancholy. I suppose it is the thyroid gland. I had a call from a judge who has done fine work but was caved in and said that it was the defeat of his thyroid. I should think that living in a corner of Dakota or Idaho or some such State might help to exhaust a gland.

Please keep on writing and don't bear malice when it is physically impossible for me to give you *quid pro quo*.

Yours ever,
O. W. H.

I haven't seen or heard of *Mother India*, and I don't want to read Beard.

Supreme Court of the United States, Washington, D.C.

December 8, 1927

My dear Einstein :

If I had nothing to do but to make sure of another pleasant letter from you by answering the last one I should be a very certain correspondent. But when my head is crowded with bothering questions of law on which I must be ready with an opinion each Saturday it is more difficult. This week seems to have perplexed me more than usual and, although I always say that there is no such thing as a hard case that presupposes that one is locked in with the seeming lion and has time enough to see the ass's ear sticking out from under the hide, which one has not when another case begins as soon as that one is finished. So today I have not the gusto I like to have when I start to *parcourir* the Universe, as a girl said to me once.

Today I may mention is the 25th anniversary of my taking my seat here, a happy event as it turned out, though I doubted it at the time.

The booklets came even before your letter. I have read one before and am glad to have it. I shall soon read the others, and I thank you. I doubt if Lord Buckmaster quite knew the facts as to the trial of Sacco & Vanzetti; [70] but as I know them only partially I will not talk. It was rather a lamentable case, but I don't think it deserved the notice it has received, largely it seems to me because it gave the reds a chance to howl.

Some place in England seems rather your destiny now that you have left Italy. Your wife would not be happy in America, and I doubt if you would after so many years in Europe. Also it would divide you from the adorable Marchioness. But no doubt you will visit U.S., and may I be here to see.

Apropos of early Chinese do you know Mrs. Meyer or her book? I bowed to her authority, but felt as if she were more or less subject to the illusions that come from too continued contemplation. I remember when a boy I sat for hours over my father's microscope and began to see considerable things which I drew for his admiration : they were air bubbles that had come into the preparation.

9th This inadequate reply must come to an end as I must turn to legal records and try to clear my mind on matters that left me doubtful at the argument. Tomorrow I must be ready to recite, but on Monday we adjourn for two or three weeks and I shall breathe again although I fear that the dentist will get hold of me. I suppose that Time may be one of the limiting illusions to the finite, but within that realm it gnaws away silently but steadily.

My devoted homage to the ladies.

Yours ever,
O. W. Holmes

Supreme Court of the United States, Washington, D.C.

Jan. 17, 1928

My dear Einstein :

Fate is cruel in not letting me meet the lovely Princess whom you mention. I lay at her feet the devotion of an ever faithful heart.

---

[70] Lord Buckmaster's opinion of the Sacco–Vanzetti Case given to Einstein was that one and possibly both the defendants were innocent and that their defense had been badly handled.

You surprise me by your great interest in Roosevelt; not that he is not an interesting and striking figure but because I think he was entirely right in regarding his intellect as ordinary. I don't doubt that it had some extraordinary qualities, especially memory, but his reactions on what he knew seemed to me to be commonplaces, to be sure I did not follow his political utterances. I remember too that Joe Cannon spoke to me of his wonderful way of getting out of any misstep that he made. And I told him (Roosevelt) that he made [*sic*] a Yale lock for every individual he met in a procession and gave him the feeling of being his special personal relation. Still, delightful as he was, I don't think you ever would have felt that deep stimulus so necessary to make a man count. Of course, our relations were chilled after I didn't go the way he wanted in the *Northern Securities Case*, but I don't think that has affected my judgment at all. I took his modesty of expression regarding himself as genuine and right, though amusingly irreconcilable with his attitude to anyone who didn't do what he wanted. Even in the law, as to which he knew nothing, I remember hearing a Senator quoted as saying, 'The reason the boys like Roosevelt is that he don't care a damn for the Law'. Having made these remarks I have little more to add.

I found your piece interesting and had hardly any criticism to make upon it.[71] Those that I had were matters of language. On page 1 '*None* of the seven generation ... offe*r*'. None is singular and should have 'offer*s*'. On page 2 you refer to forbears. I don't greatly admire the word and once would do no harm; you, however, repeat it again and again on later pages. On page 7 'His democracy was not the democracy of Lincoln swapping stories ... and who could concern' etc. Either: 'and able to concern' or 'who would swap etc. and who could' — have a uniform construction. Page 9: Why R. 'was unwilling to convey ... the impression of early prodigy'? query instead 'of having been an'. Page 10: 'He does not mention *if*' — query *whether*? 'like the reading of Plutarch influenced' etc. This use of *like* sets my back on edge. I observe, however, that Fowler in his dictionary of *Modern English Usage*, who generally sanctions all my prejudices, seems

[71] *Roosevelt, His Mind in Action* by Lewis Einstein (1930), advance proofs of which Einstein had forwarded to Holmes for comment.

to more than tolerate it.   I repeat more strongly that I thought
your pages very interesting, and I ought not to do more than
wonder a little at your choice of subject.

I have been pretty hard at work as usual but look for
something of a let up next Monday when we adjourn for a
time and I may read a book.   I even think at times of abating
the feeling of duty and relapsing into such things as biographies
for a change.   I have felt that I hadn't time for them and must
keep to more abstract or at least more general themes.   Just
now I have nothing pressing on hand of that sort.   I know that
they exist but don't know what they are.

My homage to the ladies.

Yours ever,

O. W. H.

Supreme Court of the United States, Washington, D.C.

Feb. 16, 1928

My dear Einstein :

The second instalment has come and been perused.   It
seems to me good ; but it is very vain to try to work me up to
great enthusiasm on a belief in hidden powers wilfully belittled
in the interest of political success.   On p. 21 there is ambiguity
in 'its' at the place marked.   I should say 'Tammany's' there,
cutting it out if you like earlier.   On the same page you call
R. the greatest of reformers.   I am too ignorant to deny it, but
I am far from knowing how or in what ways he was.   I am
so busy these next days preceding our sitting next Monday that
I just send this line — with my blessing on your young head.

Yours ever,

O. W. H.

Supreme Court of the United States, Washington, D.C.

April 1, 1928

My dear Einstein :

As I was about to begin this letter and looked at the
calendar for the date I interrupted my intention to go down-

stairs and practise a little sin on my wife by way of an April
Fool. It was fairly successful, enough so to make her try to
box my ears. My duty done I resume. There has been
devilish little except duty during the period of my leisure that
ends with this week. What with *certioraris*, opinions of other
judges to be examined, dissents, (I have three to deliver a week
from tomorrow), business, etc., I have had little time for anything else except delightful two hour drives in the mornings
and finishing the reading of a French lawbook that was most
excellent but that told me almost nothing that I didn't know
or disbelieve and yet that I didn't have the moral force to leave
unfinished. How much time one spends in finding that
fortresses that one doesn't dare to leave in one's rear are empty
and the guns dummies!

I am interested by your interest in Roosevelt, which you
explain admirably, and I should say that you are right about
Lodge. Perhaps you have come to the place when he was
uneasy about appointing me because he thought I didn't
appreciate Marshall? I thought it rather comic. I have no
doubt that later he heartily repented over his choice when I
didn't do what he wanted in the *Northern Securities Case*. I
believe I have told you what a Senator said about him: What
the boys like about Roosevelt is that he doesn't care a damn
for the law. Long afterwards, at a dinner at the White House
to some labor leaders, I said to one of them who had been
spouting about the judges: What you want is favor not justice;
but when I am on my job I don't care a damn what you want or
what Roosevelt wants, and then repeated my remarks to him.
You may think that a trifle crude, but I didn't like to say it
behind his back and not to his face, and the fact had justified
it I thought and think.

My birthday, March 8, added to the difficulties of the time.
There was a rage of letters and telegrams to be answered, some
very pleasing, and now I am so old that the newspapers are
always amusing about me. One special activity of my secretary
was declining interviews. But that's over now.

One morning I went over to Anacostia and saw Lindbergh
come down with a load and start off with another. Result a
telephone invitation from the boss of the show to go up with
him; but what with unwillingness to take the trouble to turn

U

out and the fact that I had just escaped from being kept in the house by the doctor because of my recurring bother of a cough I declined, and fell back on my formula that the joy of life consists in the neglect of opportunities.   No other event has occurred to me.

I think what you tell me about your wife and her influence for fusion is fine.   My homage to her.

It was a surprise to hear you speak of 'this hate ridden city'. I didn't realize that that was an element in the situation.   I am so out of everything that I hardly know what the Black Bottom is.

This week also has old tasks.   One pleasant one, too long deferred because of that infernal French book, is to read a typewritten volume by Morris Cohen,[72] a real thinker, who I should think disputes with John Dewey the leading place in American philosophy.   The work is to be published and dedicated to me, of which I am proud.   Also a new lot of thirty cases to be examined to decide whether they should be allowed to come before us — (certioraris).   Certainly, as it has been said, this life is one damn thing after another.

Please give my love to the Marchioness when you see her.

Ever yours,

O. W. Holmes

Supreme Court of the United States, Washington, D.C.

May 16, 1928

My dear Einstein :

Your account of your journey to Spain and flight to Scotland (it says) entertains me and stirs my envy.   But when you tell me that you have just sent back the corrected proofs of your Cass [73] etc. it is only after meditation and prayer that I find that you are not saying that you have just sent back

---

[72] Morris Raphael Cohen (1880–1947) ;   American teacher and philosopher and friend of Holmes to whom he dedicated his *Reason and Nature* (1931), an essay on the meaning of scientific method.

[73] *Lewis Cass* by Lewis Einstein appeared in the series entitled *The American Secretaries of State and Their Diplomacy*, Vol. VI (1928).

arrested people of my Cass, and who the devil they might be I wonder. What you say about Roosevelt is deuced good, though there also I had to rival Champollion,[74] and there are people who profess to have difficulty with my handwriting.

I meantime have been thinking of nothing but the law, assenting and dissenting, the latter with some gusto. The only thing I have read by myself is Walter Lippmann's short book, *American Inquisitors*, talking most justly and wisely I think about the difficulties between fundamentalism (which you and I are apt to think of with a pitying smile) and Rationalism or Modernism. He is a born writer, and when I take him up I can't lay him down until I have finished his book. Pending solitaire, however, I have half heard some rather thrilling things about flying. Commander Byrd, etc. Also *The Marsh Arab*, to which Miss Gertrude Bell [75] was to have written an introduction and including two excerpts (from) her letters — which recalled the time when occasionally she wrote to me, especially during her exploits in Switzerland.

I don't know whether when I get to Beverly Farms (our tickets for Boston are taken for June 6th) I shall be able to get hold of cultivation again, but I need a good draught of something solid and stimulating. Things are getting to seem too transitory and unimportant. I must regild the illusions of life. Not that there is not always a sort of animal interest in what one is doing, and not that the inner calm of reason prevents one's never getting on edge with worries, mostly superfluous.

My love to the two ladies.

Yours ever,
O. W. Holmes

[74] Jean-François Champollion (1790–1832); French orientalist who, profiting from the work of an English physician Thomas Young (1773–1829), succeeded in deciphering the Rosetta Stone and establishing the principles necessary to read Egyptian hieroglyphic inscriptions.

[75] Gertrude Margaret Lowthian Bell (1868–1926); English traveller, orientalist, archaeologist, and government servant who contributed much to the movement for Arab independence through her sympathies and great influence in the creation of the state of Iraq. An intrepid mountain climber, Miss Bell was the first woman to attempt the north-east face of the Finsteraarhorn in Switzerland where she was forced to spend forty-eight hours of bad weather on the rope before she completed her descent.

Prague

22 May 1928

Dear Justice Holmes :

I can't resist sending you an article by Emil Ludwig [76] on Washington where he describes you as the best man he met in America. I am not surprised at the conclusion but at his meeting you. Ludwig, you may recall, knows how to make biography readable and has produced some excellent lives of Napoléon and Bismarck etc. I am glad you were there to efface the impression of the sky-scraper. By the bye did you hear the tale of that exalted philosopher Arthur Balfour when in New York all the sky-scrapers were paraded before his gaze and their economic, architectural, sanitary etc. merits explained at great length ? His invariable comment was, 'Indeed !' At last when he was told that like the pyramids they were eternal he said, 'Pity !'

I too am steeped in a morass of biography. I'm in the heart of Roosevelt in his ante Caesarian period — for like Gaul he divides himself in three parts and I am still in the first. But I have to lay him on the shelf to do a quick Hoover for the *Revue des Deux Mondes* — and that pantheon of literary respectability wants it as personal and intimate as possible. So I must scurry about for anecdotage. My *Cass* appears in July and I trust may be a little less dull than it sounds and at least bring out the merits of Buchanan who, strange as it may seem, was a good deal of a man.

Otherwise I mark time here. We had a marvellous show the other day which you would have relished, a meeting of the agrarian party. Several hundred thousand peasants came to Prague, tens of thousands of them in their national costumes which vary from village to village. It was a magnificent display of color and taste. They danced and they rode and they sang, and I thought of the pity of peasants having to go through the mill of modern industrialism and forgetting their native sense of picturesque beauty in order that they may ride in Fords and own radios !

I'm glad you'll soon have a rest and exchange bench for shore.

[76] Emil Ludwig (1881–1948) ; popular German-born author and biographer.

Do give our love to dear Mrs. Holmes and tell her not to be too critical of the nonsense I write.

Ever yours,
L. E.

Supreme Court of the United States, Washington, D.C.

June 5, 1928
Tuesday

My dear Einstein :

Tomorrow we turn Northward (for Beverly Farms by the end of the week) so I can write but a line to thank you for the article by Ludwig. Something similar had taken me by surprise in an American paper. I had a very pleasant talk with him, but scarcely could believe my eyes when I read. I can only say Hooray for Ludwig. All your impressions and remarks about Roosevelt interest me very much. Good luck to your studies.

We all are somewhat tired at the end of the term, but not extremely so. I have been somewhat active in dissent, which I regret, but regret more the position of the Court on some important questions.[77] But today that is finished for the time, and I am hoping to find some culture stuff that will give me an edge. I have nothing very definite in view except to drive about Cape Ann and see the cliffs, the beaches, the old towns, and the occasional old Yankees. I am too old to start into any new field. I still want to keep on a little longer in the law. Perhaps one always wants a little more, but my grounds are somewhat more specific. I am so nearly old (ninety is old) that people are kind to me. I think I have told you how impressed I was as a boy to see carried in civic procession a barge full of survivors, I don't know exactly from what, the revolutionary men were almost all dead. I seem to see a role for myself in that way. The boys will come and poke up the

[77] Holmes wrote dissenting opinions during the term in the following cases : *Black & White Taxicab Co.* v. *Brown and Yellow Taxicab Co.,* 276 U.S. 518 (1928) ; *Untermeyer* v. *Anderson,* 276 U.S. 440 (1928) ; *Long* v. *Rockwood,* 277 U.S. 142 (1928) ; *Springer* v. *Philippine Islands,* 277 U.S. 189 (1928) ; *Panhandle Oil Co.* v. *Knox,* 277 U.S. 218 (1928) ; *Olmstead* v. *United States,* 277 U.S. 438 (1928). See *The Holmes–Pollock Letters,* Vol. II, p. 215 ff.

old man and I will growl a little, mention some remote fact, and send them off with something to tell.

But as I said I can but a line now.   My affectionate homage to the ladies.

Yours ever,
O. W. Holmes

Beverly Farms, Massachusetts

June 17, 1928

My dear Einstein :

Your letter finds me here as near to leisure and bliss as I am likely ever to be.   There is not much Amaryllis in it, only semioccasional literary discourse with a respectable dame, unless you count a call last night from a well contoured party who wanted me to stay the entering of a decree of divorce against her until she could prosecute with a writ of error to our Court, which I told her I could not do.   She thanked me and I quoted to her that you never must thank a judge, he only does his duty.

I have brought down a book or two : Bertrand Russell's *Philosophy*, Parrington's *Main Currents in American Thought*, deuced good so far as I have read, not to speak of *But Gentlemen Marry Brunettes*, handed to me by the literary dame.

I don't envy you your Wilson task [78] unless you make your oration like some of the welcomes to the French Academy, a vehicle for latent malice.   I never could see more than second rate in him.   Hoover, now the nominee, I don't know much about, but suppose on faith to be a considerable person.   As to your formula of greatness I think it right for political greatness, for the politician has to advertise ; in other forms, not.

I can't read the name as to whom the Englishman wrote a skit.   It looks like Butler, but I don't suppose it means the late Ben, and I hadn't supposed any holder of that name would attract foreign attention, but I am very ignorant.

Rum business, this growing older.   Nature withdraws here a raisin and there a plum from your pudding, until one doubts

[78] Address delivered by Einstein on the occasion of the unveiling of a statue of Woodrow Wilson in Prague.

if anything is left but sodden dough. I am afraid that I mention this too often, but it obtrudes itself in a hundred little ways and so makes me conscious and apprehensive that one ought to get into a corner.

What you tell me of your Italian friend reminds me that the first translation of my work was into Italian and resulted in the sending to me of one or two legal brochures with inscriptions in the Italian superlative. Which again reminds me of a call with Lady Pollock on George Meredith, who had just received something inscribed to the *illustrissimo poeta*, at which he snorted, his attendant, however, remarking, (he being very deaf) 'He liked it all the same'. I can't quite get back his phrase, 'to me a —— novelist and puny wiffmajig poet'.

I must now leave you to walk about an inch and quarter; I didn't walk in Washington and I am relearning the art. I shall go to the railroad crossing and talk with the flagman who has a touch of poetry in his make up, a cousin of Lucy Larcom who had some reputation in that way, and then return and get on to a lounge with a book and see what it offers. One needs to go to bed at 11 — 12 A.M. to recompense the fatigue of getting up.

Your letter is delightful. Would I had equally interesting things to tell. My love to the ladies.

Yours ever,
O. W. Holmes

Beverly Farms, Massachusetts

July 1, 1928

My dear Einstein :

This will not interfere long with your lucubrations on Hoover, Wilson, Roosevelt, and whatever other illustrious keep you busy. I haven't much to tell since my last in which I imagine myself to have stated such preoccupations as I have had in the latter days. Perhaps I didn't for I don't keep past letters in my head. I must have mentioned Parrington's *Main Currents of American Thought* which instructed and interested me, in spite of convictions (implied in the ever recurring word exploitation) which I think humbug. I am finishing Bertrand Russell's *Philosophy*. Somehow I never find his theorizing as nutritious as I should expect from the one very agreeable talk I have had with him. Much that he labors I am ready to take for granted. Probably part I miss, and do not fully understand. There is more sentiment in his opinions than I like. I don't want sugar in my coffee. As soon as I am able to read the few remaining pages, after manifold interruptions, I expect to be rather at a loss for a *pièce de résistance*. I dare say a few days browsing will be as good for me as anything.

I imagine your Cabot to be an aeronautical neighbour of mine. He always meets with a smile, but I don't know him well. I forget if I have mentioned that a dame with whom I talk on literary themes always twinkles up when your name is mentioned and repeats her admiration for your early book, *The Italian Renaissance in England*, and comes near enough to the letter to show what she is talking about.

My most important events just now are the daily drives. I don't expect to get so fat as to hang down in collops on the two sides of my chair, but I dare say there is no harm in not thinking very hard about anything for a time.

My love to the ladies. May the expectation fulfil hopes.

Yours ever,

O. W. Holmes

Beverly Farms, Massachusetts

July 28, 1928

Dear Einstein:

A good letter and a mighty good address on Wilson extricating yourself with skill from the great difficulties that beset you.

I haven't much to report. Some law cases to be attended to, drives, and a little reading. After some history (the last Morison's *Oxford History of the United States*, just and admirable with a bare hint at prejudice that I don't share), and a little philosophy. Bertrand Russell's which doesn't nourish me and *Human Values* by H. Osborn Taylor, a writer of good books on the Middle Ages, which seemed to me more or less truthful twaddle. I have just read a book about Villon which seems to give one all there is (by Wyndham Lewis); but I don't like the writer very well. He has a Catholic swagger that seems to me like a literary flavor rather than devotion, he pads, and, while he affects Urquhart's Rabelaisian English, the minute he comes to a straight stout word in Villon that calls a cock a cock he dodges and gives some flat generality instead. I shouldn't mind if he wasn't so damned Rabelaisian when it costs nothing. Also a book by a young American living in Paris (Hemingway), *The Sun Still* [sic] *Rises*, which excites some interest in others and in me. No events greater than going to a bull fight, much conversation without an idea in it, characterizing phrases replaced by damn and hell, no marked character, the chief interest of the parties food and drink with a discreet hint of fornication, and most of them drunk nearly every evening. I think of rereading the book to try to find out why it interests and why I suspect it to be a work of art. I should think that the chances were that the author of such a book living in Paris would go to the devil, but he may leave the swill pail and rise.

To return to Wilson, I rather wondered that you found it in your heart to speak so highly of his eloquence. He never moved me either heard or read. To be sure I was prejudiced against him by talk of White C.J., which later I was led to doubt, but still he never got an emotion out of me. The other aspect of him I am content to leave to you.

I feel those cases waiting to be examined, (they have just come) and I turn to them.

You gave no news of the Marchioness who was expectant in an earlier report.

My love to the ladies both.

Yours ever,
O. W. H.

Beverly Farms

Aug. 15, 1928

My dear Einstein :

Can one interrupt the reading of a detective story long enough to write, even to you? That is the question.

I have been dragged upon by duties in a way that interrupted the full vacation feeling, and the last one disappeared this morning, for the time being at least, when I disposed of an application to me to order a stay of an execution for murder in California. So I plunged into *The Mystery of the Blue Train*, but I faltered in that a letter from you came a day or two ago and I pause, but gravitation is always at work. Also there are several books waiting, one that came from England this morning, I know not what the second was. Mallock's *Memories of Life and Literature* looks interesting. But although I have done a little history and philosophy I feel as if the real reading time was just going to begin, the heavenly time when you may even say to yourself, what the devil shall I do now? — instead of having something that is or makes itself a duty waiting for the first vacant moment. But when I get a good dull improving book of six hundred closely printed crown octavo pages I am apt to make it a duty.

How universally the 'mountainous me' takes the first place in a letter or a talk! I was thinking of all you had told me and yet the first words were about my occupations.

I am very sorry for the disappointment, but I thought they had one boy. Am I wrong? I know here one couple that had a lot of girls and being anxious for a boy set themselves carefully to following scientific advice in order to accomplish the end, and they did it. I know not what the prescription was.

Your reception of the Americans was part of the day's work, so I didn't condole upon that. I think you have more leisure than I do. Your letter has two mysteries, one who the 'unknown warrior' (if I read it right) is, and the other the ribald joke about the nature of hash. Apropos of art here I heard from Laski of some Belgian artist thinking that American architecture (with I believe that of Holland) led the world, with reasons that I won't try to repeat. It is wonderful to see the crowds on the beaches on one of these hot days. I shouldn't think it would be pleasant to be in a close packed crowd in the sea. But they seem to like it. In view of the present costumes or lack of them it might make some difference who was your neighbour.

Now, my boy, I leave for '*I ask myself why a Mr. Papopoloas suddenly came to Nice?*' — a question stated by the detective that may be a clue to the murder. We shall see.

My love to the ladies.

Ever yours,
O. W. Holmes

Beverly Farms, Massachusetts

Aug. 31, 1928

My dear Einstein :

A letter from you, good, as usual, but making me very sorry for the disappointment of the Marchioness. Once at dinner in England old Sir Fitzroy Kelly on hearing that we had no children said, '*Le bon temps viendra.*' But I am so far abnormal that I am glad I have none. It might be said that to have them is part of the manifest destiny of man, as of other creatures, and that he should accept it as he accepts his destiny to strive ; but the latter he can't help and part of his destiny is to choose. I might say some sad things but I won't. Whatever I may think of life, the last years of mine have been happy and are so now. Of course, if I should break down before dying it would be awkward, as there is no one to look after me as a child would. But I daresay my nephew and my friends would cook up something.

What you say with doubtful legibility from Lord Blanes-borough [79] gives me pleasure, and I wish I could reciprocate ; but it shows how little I keep up with affairs that I do not know the name. I may have known his name before he took the title, but probably not. I read the reports in these days only as necessary for decision. If he was a judge before he was a Lord I should be more likely to know him ; if he were a Scrutton [80] for instance, a good man.

I read *War and Peace* a few years ago, it having been interrupted much earlier, but the long panorama rather bored me, and I found it hard to keep the people distinct. I believe, at any rate I concluded, that my time for reading long stories was over. Yet this minute I am just beginning *Moby Dick* which I believed great on a former inadequate reading.

I have read a fair lot of books this vacation besides examining one hundred and twenty-five cases to decide whether they should be allowed to come up to our Court, but nothing that has made a very deep mark. Dill's dull *Roman Society from Nero to Marcus Aurelius* led me to read Petronius, which paid

[79] Robert Younger, Baron Blanesborough (1861–1946) ; Judge of the High Court of Justice, Lord Justice of Appeal, and Lord of Appeal in Ordinary.
[80] Sir Thomas Edward Scrutton (1856–1934) ; famous English judge considered to be possibly the only Englishman of his time who never shaved in his life.

for the few hours it cost. The fun is dead, of course, and boorish as it was meant to be, but generically was akin to all the practical jokes of later days, and there are a wonderful lot of quotable and happy sayings which a more economic person than I would have made a note of. I find in Petronius's pages that fear first created the Gods, which I thought was Lucretius, perhaps it was, and merely was echoed by Petronius. Do you remember Emerson's verses about *The Days*? [81] I can't quite recall them but as the Day made its offerings he took a few nuts and berries —

I under her solemn fillets saw the scorn.

If I write more I shall drool, so my love to the ladies.

Yours ever,
O. W. Holmes

Beverly Farms

September 16, 1928

Dear Einstein :

This will be the last letter from Beverly Farms as we expect to go to Washington on the 26th and leave this place on the 24th.

I am afraid that I shall have no or very little time to write at the beginning of the term, but if your good news prophesies truly there will be no need of letters before we see you and, I hope, your wife to whom my joyful homage. There is nothing to tell of here. I continue to lead an unusual life of open air dawdling, driving, and sleeping during most of the daytime knowing that in less than two weeks the simoom will be upon us, about one hundred more *certioraris* over the one hundred and twenty-five that I have done to be examined outside the sitting in Court.

[81] *The Days*

> Daughters of Time, the hypocritic Days
> Muffled and dumb like barefoot dervishes
> And marching single in an endless file,
> Bring diadems and fagots in their hands.
> To each they offer gifts after his will,
> Bread, kingdoms, stars, and sky that holds them all.
> I, in my pleached garden, watched the pomp,
> Forgot my morning wishes, hastily
> Took a few herbs and apples, and the Day
> Turned and departed silent. I, too late,
> Under her solemn fillet saw the scorn.

By the by, you speak of the warmth of our hearth. It is a convenient phrase for alas, as you know, the wood fire that used to glow there has given way to unpoetic electricity. My library alone continues the wood. I have reread *Moby Dick* and again have been immensely impressed by it. The characters all talk Melville just as Richard II and Macbeth talk Shakespeare, but just as I would rather hear Shakespeare than Richard II or Macbeth in person I would rather hear Melville than Captain Ahab. I also have read a little in a book that I mean to buy when I get to Washington, a *History of English Literature* by Legouis and Cazamian, the second volume which I have here by Cazamian translated from the French by W. D. MacInnes and the author. The parts that I have read seem to me unparalleled for grasp of all the influences that wrought a change from classical to romantic, and for critical discernment. It really freshens a faded mind to read the few chapters that I have picked out and it makes one want to read the whole; though in a form that I dislike, crown 8vo with smallish type closely filling too long a page and trying the eyes. I recently went through another work in this form with tribulation but was partially rewarded by being led to read Petronius, as I may have mentioned; not that ancient fun seems funny but because it suggests reflections, and Petronius when speaking for himself says many things that would be good to quote. But I don't keep a commonplace book or diary and so I barely remember that if in search of a spicy sentence I know where to look, if ever I were willing to take the trouble.

You do not speak of the Marchioness in your last. Do give her my love. I close in view of your approach.

Yours ever,
O. W. Holmes

1720 I (Eye) Street, N.W. Washington, D.C.

January 3, 1929

My dear Einstein:

A happy New Year to you and yours and thanks for a delightful letter just received. As the miseries of the voyage and the attendant anxieties are over I will not speak of them

except to be glad they are ended. I was disappointed not to
see more of you but a glimpse was better than nothing. I
know not the mysteries of your job or whether you did or
could do anything to secure its continuance, but I hope that
all will turn out as you desire. The house in London sounds
attractive. What you say of purity of taste has my sympathy.
Do you remember a remark of Santayana about the lady who
is careful to have everything of one period and does not per-
ceive that she is the greatest of anachronisms?

I haven't much to tell. My wife has been having a hard
time with a cold, or whatever it was, but is pretty nearly all
right again now I am happy to say. Our sittings have begun
again and my hands will be full for some time to come. One
or two great cases to start off with. I hate great cases. They
rarely have anything very interesting except that a lot of money
is involved, which as I once said brings a hydraulic pressure to
bear to cast doubt on the obvious. I have had a little time for
reading, not much. It is queer that one should so want to
read, when reading generally is a bore. One does want to
know; but it is a pity one can't get knowledge through the
pores or in the way a child learns such lots of things.

I must be off to Court in a minute. My love to the ladies
who are both I hope now recovered. I wish I could see your
London house. How hard it is to realize the never again.

Yours ever,
O. W. Holmes

1720 I Street, N.W.

January 30, 1929

My dear Einstein:

Yours as always most pleasant letter coupled with
another fact makes me begin an answer within a few hours
from its arrival. I have been so far off my beat as just to have
finished Redlich's: *Life of the Emperor Francis Joseph of Austria,*
and although his familiarity with the atmosphere leads him at
times to take things for granted that I don't understand I feel
as if I had got my first glimmerings of matters hitherto to me
unknown. I know and like Redlich very much. He is very

intelligent and widely informed and he sent me the book. Hence my divergence from my track. It is extraordinary to be led to realize the state of mind of a man who had not one of the ideas that to me make life worth living. Not only that, but one whose ideas and beliefs seem to me hopelessly thin and wholly detestable, and yet, in a sense, a hero, one who would have died for his cause. He wonderfully illustrates my axiom that a gentleman can't be a philosopher or a philosopher a gentleman.

Did you ever read anything of Hemingway: *Men without Women, The Sun also Rises*? They would lend themselves to some remarks, but I mention them now for a sort of indifference to the customary morality that I found again in a short poem (so called) that you are not likely to see. The last two also at home in a slang that was more or less new to me. It is comparatively new also in English to see a picture of a debauch of blackguards and whores given without reserve and if with any feeling with an animal sympathy. I read anything of course, but I rather think such performances best dropped in the fire. What I am wondering is whether these books represent an eddy in current literature or an expression of a minority wish to upset current morality or merely themselves. Of course many of us would be willing to see the prevailing codes considerably revised, but these gents are not reformers with a high purpose.

You speak of leisured sloth. I regard it as a gift to be capable of it as I regard my own industriousness as a thing to be suspected and distrusted. I haven't read Bishop,[82] but I dare say the truth was told about Roosevelt's letter to me. There were no directions to show it, I think, but I read it to Chamberlain. I can't read who the man was for whom a ball was given and who you believed might have been (it looks like) the next president of Harvard.

My love to the ladies.

Yours ever,

O. W. Holmes

[82] See letter of Theodore Roosevelt to Holmes dated July 25, 1908, reproduced on p. 259, Vol. 1, of *Theodore Roosevelt and His Time* by Joseph Bucklin Bishop (1920). The interest of this letter lies less in the Alaska boundary dispute, which was settled amicably by a mixed Commission, than in the roundabout way used by Roosevelt to attain his purpose. In this case it was very successful. It would be interesting to know what became of Holmes's reply.

Washington, D.C.

February 28, 1929

My dear Einstein:

This will only be an acknowledgment of a delightful letter from you because you say nothing as to your address and I don't know whether to direct to Prague or to London, and if to London to the Ritz Hotel which sounds transitory. I hope that the new President will know a good thing when he has it, and that the *status quo* will remain.

My wife had a tumble which left her very uncomfortable just after recovering from a long and trying pull down that I suppose was the grippe. But no serious harm was done. I am in good shape sitting daily in Court.

My homage to the ladies. You tell an amusing thing about the doctor and the jaundice and other matters. Please don't forget to tell me your address.

Yours ever,
O. W. Holmes

March 6, 1929

My dear Einstein :

You are so secretive about your address that I cannot answer your telegram and thank you as I wished to in words until a day or two ago informed us that you were going back to Prague. I do hope that the President will do the sensible thing. I am ignorant of the ways, works, and machinery in the State Department, but it seems to me as if rudimentary intelligence would keep a good thing when it had got it.

I have been working hard, sitting in Court, writing opinions, doing other work outside the Court, having a birthday and writing sixty or seventy answers to felicitations. Today sees me at the end for the moment and ready for a little leisure if not too cramped to give way to it. I reread today an odious tale, *Dieu protège le Tsar* by Louis Dumur, which represents incredible doings of Rasputine in high society with ladies up to the top. I couldn't but believe it a delirious dream of a writer seeking a sensation. Do you know anything about it? I shan't write more now till solemnly notified of your address.

Please give my love to the ladies.

Yours ever,
O. W. Holmes

Many thanks for the enclosures from *The Times* and the Countess of Oxford. This is scurvy paper to write on and its size invites a scurvy envelope, but I have not yet got better blocks from the Capitol where they furnish us, and a block is so comfortable.

1720 I Street, N.W.

April 7, 1929

My dear Einstein:

You will get but a word from me this time again, because it is hot and I am languid and tired and have to resume work in Court tomorrow. (Early too — the Chief wanting to confer with us on a special matter and having required our presence three quarters of an hour earlier than usual, which I loathe.)

I have little to tell. After some hours with philosophy rereading John Dewey, *Experience and Nature*, I have had but small chance to read. I think I may have mentioned a dirty French story *Dieu Protège le Tsar*. It led me to read a more dispassionate book about Rasputine. Of course I am indifferent to his character, but the picture I got of his influence, of the ignorance, superstition, and corruption of the *milieu*, made me think that, though one shudders at the name of it, the welfare of mankind was promoted by the removal of such persons as the Tsar and Tsar(itsa?) and the extinction of Rasputine. It intensified the feeling I had when I read the life of Francis Joseph by Redlich. It is paying too high for *distinction* to have such people able to ruin an Empire, not to speak of the individuals in it.

Last night I took up a *Life of Herman Melville* by Lewis
x

Mumford. Melville interests me much by his Moby Dick etc. and a shadowy memory of him, but the biographer slightly riles me. He has all the perhaps unconscious superiority of a modern aesthete, and talks about actualities in a way that makes me doubt if he ever experienced them and about art as if it were a world in which he lives withdrawn from you and me. Perhaps I am unjust, but he has rather roused my prejudice, so that I have gone back over what I have read in the vain effort to find a passage, it is there somewhere, that shows he is not at home in the differences between *shall* and *will* However he admires his hero, and I am with him there.

In course of time you will no doubt give me your address in London. At present I know only Prague, which may be enough so long as I last. But I have howled to you before on this theme.

My love and homage to the ladies.

Yours ever,
O. W. Holmes

Prague

31 May 1929

Dear Justice Holmes:
By accident I opened an old paper and by accident my glance fell on the news of dear Mrs. Holmes's death [83] and I felt the shock for the loss of a very old friend. I see her before me knitting in her armchair by the fire while you were playing at patience, and I hate to think of the void she has left in your life. I know it is irreplaceable, and I know that any poor words I can say are meaningless. And yet I would have you feel that I realize the depth of the loss of one who has been a life companion. Also to me something has gone out which made life richer. I recall on one or two occasions the real warmth of her heart which she did her best to hide, and there was true generosity in her sympathy for those who needed it. I find it now hard to believe that she is gone for she seemed to with-

---

[83] Mrs. Holmes died April 30, 1929, after a fall which broke her hip bone.

tand the march of time, and especially I find it hard to express
o you the depths of my own affectionate feeling.   There are
hings one can hardly say.   I think of you these days for I fear
ou remain lonely.   I only hope that your work will make the
ours less heavy.

My wife sends you her warmest sympathy.   You know
my own.

L. E.

Beverly Farms, Massachusetts

June ?, 1929

My dear Einstein :

My affectionate thanks for your kind and feeling letter.
t was better that my wife should die than live in suffering
and pain which I am sure was the alternative.   I think too that
t was better that she should die before I do ; she was of the
ame age as I, and I think would have been more at a loss
han I am if left alone.   I like solitude with intermissions, but
he was almost a recluse.   I have my work and a fair number
of people whom I like to see.   She shocked Gifford Pinchot
once by saying, 'I have no friends' ; and it was true that there
was no one except me with whom she was very intimate.
Things hurt her that I didn't mind.   We have a lovely spot
at Arlington where she lies.

I may last even a year or two; but my work is done, though
merely as a *jeu d'esprit*.   I shouldn't mind writing decisions in
my ninetieth year and still better at ninety.   I have had my
reward, especially in these last years in the form of letters and
articles.   I wrote to a man yesterday, who had said super-
superlative things, that if the devil came round the corner and
said : You and I know that that isn't true, I should believe
him.   Still so long as he didn't appear in person, such letters
kept alive my hope that I had lived my dream.

I am quietly settled here for the summer and expect my
usual routine.   I have just finished Walter Lippmann's *Preface
to Morals*, a book that hits the time and, I rejoice to hear, is
having a great sale.   Also (what a fall was there !) Isadora
Duncan's *My Life*.   Her raptures don't quite carry me, but it

is interesting, written with the quaint innocence of one who did whatever she wanted to do, without bothering. She didn't believe in marriage and took up with various men each of whom seems to have inspired her with passion, and I don't doubt had a passion for her art of dancing that was deeper than vanity. *Requiescat.*

I haven't got far in books yet, but I may do better. I love this region and hope for a rest. You say nothing as to whether you are to continue at Prague. Perhaps no news is good news.

Please give my love to the two ladies.

Gratefully ever,

O. W. Holmes

Beverly Farms, Massachusetts

July 27, 1929

My dear Einstein :

A letter from you this week, pleasant as always. While you amuse or bore yourself with Kings I see nothing more exciting than scenery and legs on the beach.

My secretary is here and we pass a good part of the time in going over applications for leave to come up to our Court, a task that we always have with us. I expect about one hundred and fifty before this vacation is over. A great many are wholly unwarranted and I suppose are brought some for delays, some from inexcusable ignorance, and some, I expect, merely to give the lawyer a chance to make another charge in his bill. So just now I have little chance to read. Some light stuff, *Magie Noire* by Paul Morand, poems by women who are just able to flutter into the aether but not to stay there, and especially *Saki's* stories which are amusing, very amusing when not cruel. For a *pièce de résistance* I have had a German book on Trusts, which quotes me a good deal in the historical part and is a good piece of work. But I have to use a dictionary and I doubt if I shall finish the modern part which probably wouldn't tell me very much. I am promised a philosophical book that sounds interesting, but it hasn't come yet.

From time to time some friendly dame comes to luncheon with me or calls, and one of them made them promise I am not allowed to be lonely — hardly as much as I wish, for friends keep turning up. But I don't want them too often or more than one in a day. Two hours jaw is enough to tire me, though I don't mind writing all day. The other day a chap came well before supper (7 p.m.) and stayed till after 10 p.m.; first rate conversation for four hours etc. Too much for me.

Have you had any news as to the interest of the powers that be to retain you at your post? I hope they will be sensible. I have no notion that they could replace you.

I hear funny stories and think I will tell them to you and then I forget them, and as this must go to the postoffice I can't sit and meditate.

Yours ever,
O. W. Holmes

Supreme Court of the United States, Washington, D.C.

October 6, 1929

My dear Einstein:

Your letter is a relief to my mind so far as anxiety about your health is concerned but a disappointment in what you say about your prospects. Yet even that seems to admit the interpretation that the Government is so well pleased with your performance and your duties at Prague that it wants to keep you there. I am ignorant in these matters, but I don't see why it is not one of the most satisfactory places in our list. Mrs. Beveridge, when I was at Beverly Farms, rather startled me by the suggestion that with our modern appliances she didn't see the necessity for keeping up the old arrangement of Ministers etc. Is there anything in it?

I have just got here, and I have been struggling through the chaos of books, pamphlets, letters, bills, and cases, and have reached a letter or two, but am pretty busy. Before I left the Harvard Law School sent a most flattering request that I would pose for a full length portrait to hang as a pendant to John Marshall in the great reading room, five hundred feet

long, of their new building. I went to see it last Tuesday
and was overwhelmed by its magnificence. I rather think it
the best law library in the world ; an equity room with portraits
of the English Chancellors etc., another with ditto of all the
judges of our Court whose portraits could be got, another with
English judges gathered from English country homes etc.,
another with distinguished American state judges. Oh, I was
flabbergasted ! Without further cataloguing I should say, as
my father said to me about the Alps, it stretched your mind.
But one result of the portrait, which seems to me most successful, was that the idleness I had promised myself for the last
two weeks of my vacation was destroyed. However I am in
good shape and without further palaver with you must get to
work.

My love to the ladies. A dame expressed some hesitation
over coming to luncheon *tête à tête* with me, but I told her she
might as well scruple about visiting Bunker Hill Monument.

Yours ever,
O. W. Holmes

Supreme Court of the United States, Washington, D.C.

November 10, 1929

My dear Einstein :

It is pleasant to hear from you again. I am sorry that
you are kept pending in doubt. I should think that a man of
your ability and experience ought to be grappled with hooks
of steel. I am interested by what you say of the letters of T.R.,
Lodge, and H. Adams, especially the selfconsciousness etc. of
the last. I used to think he posed a little, perhaps unconsciously, and your touch about the assumptions of superiority,
at least through the inferiority of everyone else, seems to me
penetrating. He had remarkable abilities but never seemed
to me to get quite to the bottom of his subjects, unless it may
be in political history as to which I do not know. If he could
have been put on a pedestal, made a general without ever
having gone through the schools of lower grades I dare say

he would have been valuable. My friend Kaneko,[84] a Japanese of the Privy Council, thought him one of the three Americans who understood the Eastern question, and I think he touched nothing without adding something valuable. And yet I think he would have called himself a failure, with some truth, as his brother Charles called himself in so many words.

I have been hard at work here most of the time but just now have a few days of relative leisure, although as yet I have read very little. When I can I snatch two hours for a drive in the parks and adjoining country, and yesterday (Saturday) p.m. went to a *matinée* to see the supposed funniest men on the stage here. They made me laugh but not very much or very loudly. In spite of polite tradition I guffaw if anything hits my funnybone hard. Also yesterday I was shown a copy of a book not yet released for publication: *The Dissenting Opinions of Mr. Justice Holmes*.[85] Of course I had nothing to do with the publication except to write when written to that my assent was not necessary and that I should regret to see nothing but dissent. It is a very decent looking volume and has an amiable and flattering introduction by Kirchwey [86] (once Dean of the Columbia Law School). I couldn't imagine that more than three people would want to buy such a book, but I hope that the publisher knows his business.

I have on hand two books to read: (1) Whitehead's *Process and Reality*, which I should infer is intended to be a later Critique of Pure Reason and the language of which I find very difficult. Whitehead [87] himself when he came to see me last summer was as simple, intelligible, human, and delightful as possible. (2) Rueff, *From the Physical to the Social Sciences*, sent to me by a southern judge, of which I know nothing except that it is supposed to be good in some way. Then damned duties keep presenting themselves — when one wishes that one

---

[84] Viscount Kentaro Kaneko (1853–1942); Japanese lawyer, statesman, and historian. Kaneko graduated from the Harvard Law School in 1878 and later received an LLD from Harvard. As President of the American Friend Society he did much to promote friendship and understanding between the United States and Japan.

[85] *The Dissenting Opinions of Mr. Justice Holmes*, Alfred Lief, ed. (1929).

[86] George W. Kirchwey (1885–1942); American law professor and criminologist.

[87] Alfred North Whitehead (1861–1947); eminent English philosopher and mathematician who taught at Harvard University from 1924 to 1937.

could get the same improvement from amusing books. But as I used to say it is vain to say that this is the best of possible worlds — when it could be so improved if we could go to bed drunk and wake fitter than ever for achievement.

I turn the page simply to say goodbye for the moment. I am expecting a call from a Chinaman and must be ready for him.

My love to the ladies.

Yours ever,
O. W. Holmes

Supreme Court of the United States, Washington, D.C.

December 13, 1929

My dear Einstein :

Your Nuncio who sleeps all day and works all night is a valuable suggestion, but not wholly available to one who has to appear in Court.

I am proud that you should have looked into my Common Law. You ask if it was an original contribution. So far as I know, I made the thread, wove the cloth, and cut the pattern, and I have been more than satisfied with its effect.

I hate to think of you leaving your post, but it is a matter upon which I am incompetent to judge.

You overawe me by saying that you enjoyed Whitehead's *Modern Science & Philosophy* if that means *Science and the Modern World*. I read it and didn't understand it and hoped to read it again. I now am reading his *Process and Reality* and hardly have understood a sentence so far. I resolved that by the 150th page I should be in human relations with him. I have just got there, and there is a glimmer, a suggestion that this may be followed by another cosmic epoch to which, as I take him to hint, the terms may all be changed. Which seems to fall in with my old definition of the Cosmos as a spontaneity taking an irrational pleasure in a moment of rational sequence. I know no warrant for assuming that phenomena may not appear without phenomenal antecedents, what we should call effects without causes. But I am bettabilitarian — i.e. I think the Universe can be bet upon and I bet the sun will rise to-morrow, but if I weren't too scared I shouldn't be surprised if it didn't. Returning to Whitehead I don't believe the difficulty is in the ideas, but it is the darned words that get me. He talks all the time of entities and I have not yet gathered what he means, and as to such filthy things as the quantum theory my mind has never been bifurcated with such thoughts. It is simply an X in an equation that needs an a or b. He called on me last summer and was most pleasant and intelligible and an article in *The New Republic* on Education was ditto. I believe him to be a great and good man, but I wish he would send me, or rather someone else, for he would expound *obscurum per obscurius*, a Whitehead Dictionary.

I must stop to go to a Conference, but this brings every good wish for you and the admired ladies. Things are going quickly and well with me.

Yours ever,
O. W. Holmes

Supreme Court of the United States, Washington, D.C.

January 16, 1930

My dear Einstein:

The C.J. having gone first to the hospital (slight) and then South for a rest for some weeks, I am presiding and the result is that I am pretty constantly occupied and can write but a word. While we were adjourned, as I never go out, I persuaded Mrs. Hoover to take luncheon with me (This *entre nous*. I don't know whether she regularly goes out as she chooses.) and while she was here took occasion to let fall that I realized that the President was a great man after reading what had been written by my friend Einstein, the Minister to Czechoslovakia. The lady is very pleasant and has done some considerate and feeling things for me, but this was my only interview.

I have just finished sitting for a bust by an Italian sculptor, Simone, said to be patronized by Mussolini. I gathered that he wanted to do some prominent persons for his own purposes, and the British Ambassador put him on to me. What with this and having been painted full length for the Harvard Law School at the end of last vacation I feel quite important. Both picture and bust seem to me very successful, except that I fear the bust flattering and indicated the devil of a fellow. If I look like that I ain't afraid to die.

Evidently the Whitehead book that you read was an earlier one. That had its difficulties, but I spoke of a later one, *Process & Reality* that would squeeze your guts. I must stop.

Yours ever,
O. W. Holmes

Supreme Court of the United States, Washington, D.C.

February 1, 1930

My dear Einstein :

Your letter saddened me, but many years ago I realized that we are brutal in our way of dealing with public officials, and that men who in other countries would not be allowed to end a long and faithful service without some mark of recognition here are simply dropped. Your case is not peculiar ; it is, I think, what always happens. I always am shocked when I hear of it, so I can say nothing except that I am sorry. I had a faint, very faint, hope that I might do some good by a few words that I got a chance to let fall to Mrs. Hoover, but of course it was unfounded.

I sympathize with your wife. I had a mild case of the shingles and it is a hellish disease. Undoubtedly she knows that collodion over the surface of the places on the skin that itch is a great relief to that, but the intense pain I know no relief for. I hope that the trouble is over before this.

I have been kept extra busy by the absence of the Chief who was run down.[88] I have had to preside in his place, which means some additional work. We adjourned for three

---

[88] Chief Justice William Howard Taft resigned from the Supreme Court February 3, 1930, and died on March 8, 1930. He was succeeded as Chief Justice by Charles Evans Hughes whose appointment was confirmed by the Senate on February 14, 1930.

or four weeks last Monday, at which time I was kept in by a cold. Now I am out. My work is done for the moment, and I have visions, never realized, of culture. I use the odious word malevolently as I know my anticipations will be disappointed one way or another. But I may manage to read a book.

I hope that you will settle down to a regular occupation that absorbs you when you are through your political work.

Yours ever,

O. W. Holmes

Supreme Court of the United States, Washington, D.C.

Feb. 26, 1930

My dear Einstein:

The times have not been favourable for writing as I have been rather driven and unnecessarily nervous about some of my duties, now happily escaped from, that cost me a slight upset. It lasted but a moment and I am all right again.

I was glad to read what you say of Hughes. He is an old friend of mine and a very hard worker. He can tell a story and say a funny thing on occasion as well as do his job.

I forget whether I have mentioned my private activities or rather passivities, as I am thinking mainly of having had an Italian sculptor, Simone, up here in my library doing a bust of me, (not *for* me, but on his own.) I thought it devilish good. That coming on top of Hopkinson's full length picture of me taken last September makes me feel grand, though I should be happier if the picture had been hung in the Harvard Law School where it belongs. Until the painter lets it go one is afraid of some pottering change that will spoil or at least hurt a good thing.

I don't have much time for reading. Just purely accidentally I have been reading *L'homme blanc, souvenirs d'un pierrot* par le mime Séverin, which interested me by the seriousness with which the French take arts, and he his share in it. According to him others are characters, but the man with the whited face is humanity, being trained to express without words everything that man can feel. I should have liked a chance to see him with, if necessary, an expounder to make sure that I understood.

I really find it hard to write in these days. There is work that I ought to be doing almost all the time. I wind up now rather abruptly with my love to the ladies.

Yours ever,

O. W. Holmes

Supreme Court of the United States, Washington, D.C.

March 29, 1930

My dear Einstein :

It seems to have grown increasingly difficult for me to write. I think the duties really have increased, and I have so many demands upon my time that your letter looks reproachfully at me from my drawer or table but in vain. Well, I am free for half an hour and turn to you.

You make me writhe with envy when you speak of motoring down the valley of the Rhône and of your meal at the *Relais de l'Empereur*. I remember an amazingly good breakfast at a railway station, I rather think at Dijon. But after all I don't suppose I could enjoy what I envy if I had it. It wouldn't suit me to drink wine, and where are you if you leave that out? Wine is joy, though an adequate temperament doesn't need it for gusto. You speak of the provincial museums. Owen Wister was saying last Sunday how he liked to mouse around in them.

I am content with what I have, but the price has been to give up years in the old world that would have hit me where I lived.

I have ever before my mind that the order to pack up and move may come at any time and flatter myself that I am serene about it, and then suddenly I realize that I still am interested in life and shouldn't mind an extra piece. A week ago they had the ceremony of presenting my portrait to the Law School and there was a lot of palaver. I really am glad and proud to have it hang as I understand they arranged, as the pendant to John Marshall.

I have not read Maurois' *Byron*, but have had it recommended to me before. Perhaps I shall get round to it, but I am too busy now.

I will ask you in your turn if you have read Joyce's *Ulysses*? I haven't and don't intend to, but I have looked into it. A reputable critic in the New Republic calls him a great poet. He may be, but he has what seems to me an abnormal propensity for dirty words and disgusting images of the lesser sort. I should think he must be queer in the nob, and so, though I think it possible that I am laying a genius on one side, I shall not read on.

I have been busy on an important case and others too of less importance, all now written, with a huge mass of stuff that I have got to examine on the question whether the cases should be allowed to come to our Court. But then details are not interesting. It is more so to say that the white and pink magnolias were in flower a week ago, much too early, and after two or three days of beauty were blighted by the cold. I am hoping that the Jap. appletrees around the Potomac basin won't open too soon, but the trees are already pink. They are one of the events of the year and worth going two or three hundred miles to see. I try to get a motor drive of a morning while we are adjourned and let duty wait for two hours.

My love to the ladies. I haven't heard about the Marchioness lately.

Yours ever,
O. W. Holmes

Supreme Court of the United States, Washington, D.C.

April 15, 1930

My dear Einstein :
          This is merely a line interpolated between duties to tell you that talking with Hughes (C.J.) today, he said that you were not only one of the most accomplished but one of the most efficient and useful as well as popular of our foreign representatives and lamented the loss to the service. There was no qualification, but solid high appreciation that gave me great

pleasure.   He contrasted your reports with the run of those received.   I think you would have been satisfied had you heard him.   I have been a poor correspondent of late because I have had very little breathing time from work.

My love to the ladies.

Yours ever,
O. W. Holmes

Supreme Court of the United States, Washington, D.C.

May 7, 1930

My dear Einstein :

Your letter was most welcome.   My trouble has been, and still more or less is, to get time, I won't say to send a worthy answer, but to answer at all.   As I write these words proofs of opinions come in that demand immediate attention, so I suspend, and begin again in the afternoon having vainly expected my eminent friend, Morris Cohen, at luncheon.   He had agreed to come, but being a philosopher did not turn up. In view of his calling I waited half an hour, a quarter more than I should allow the normal man, but in vain.   He is a very remarkable chap and I have profited much from his talk and writing.

I had not noticed Joyce for pornography, but for scatography, to use a word that I didn't find in the dictionary.   It seems as if he never had outgrown the little boy's pleasure in dirty words.   Stevenson very prettily sees in their talk their beginning to take possession of life, but in a grown up I think it repulsive.   I hadn't heard of O'Flaherty.   My secretary is better up on the moderns and tells me a little about him.   *Farewell to Arms* moved me moderately, not to the superlative degree.   I have run through a few books of the moment but I don't remember their names very well.   *L'homme blanc*, a pretty striking account of the life of a mime, (I believe he is called) who has the traditional costume of our clown and who can express all that there is in life without the aid of words.   I was delighted with his contempt for the crazy successes of the drawing room as against the achievements that need a lot of hard work.   So many things recall to me the period of skirt dancing, when the suggestion that perhaps you will see a little more next time is the substitute for the severe gymnastic training that makes a *danseuse*. A good deal of the modernist art and literature strikes me the same way.

I am glad you know and like Laski. He is a very remarkable chap. He pours out books always interesting and sometimes admirable. In a volume of essays by him just received, *The Dangers of Obedience*, there is an account and appreciation of Rousseau that I think admirably good, and a very interesting one of Machiavelli. Then I should think his talk about endowments very wise, but am not quite with him in his passion for equality. There are few things that I value so much as meeting and being met on a simply human basis, without ulterior consciousness; but I take no stock in *a priori* human rights, see no injustice in our being made with different degrees of power, (I have seen it declared unjust and by an eminent Frenchman, who made me want to ask where he got his lever to criticize the Cosmos.) and I have not quite Laski's respect for the human soul as such; I suppose he would have the majority vote that I was wrong.

I am interested in what you say of Lord Castletown. If you hear more tell me more.

When the moment of relaxation comes there are few books that suit me so well as Horace Walpole's letters. I was interested to look at Macaulay's estimates; sweeping, forcible, sounding like a twister, and leaving in your mind the impression that he has missed all that was generous, delicate, and ahead of his time in Horace Walpole. I suspect that it was the same as to Boswell. But I must go to work.

Yours ever,
O. W. Holmes

Beverly Farms, Massachusetts

June 10, 1930

My dear Einstein :

First as to a detail. You have seen Robeson.[89] I forget the name as I always do nowadays, but he must be the same

[89] Paul Robeson (1898–   ); American actor and singer who acted the title role in Eugene O'Neill's play *Emperor Jones* in 1923.

negro that my wife and I saw in Washington years ago in a terrific piece.   A black man who has made himself King of a little island and whose subjects revolt — he has just time to fly to the woods, misses his mark, and wanders all night through visions of his past — always the tump, tump, tump, of the drums of the men who are out for him and kill him before morning.   It was an event in a lifetime to see it.

But to more serious matters.   I am worried at your idleness. You *must* get a *pièce de résistance* to work on.   If it merely gives you a regular occupation, good, if it results in a *magnum opus*, best.   Laski, who took great pleasure in meeting you, suggested a course of lectures over here.   I will pass the suggestion along if you desire, though I have no direct pull on the wires. That seems to me good as far as it goes, but I should like to see you committed to a longer, more laborious, and more ambitious task.

I interpolate here that a lady, a constant admirer of your early book on *The Italian Renaissance in England* (if I get the title right) told me that Cameron Forbes,[90] who was unhooked from the Philippines in the same brutal, unceremonious way that you experienced, made a row about it in some public way, but he doesn't seem to have done any good; and I told you that Hughes evidently regarded it as normal when he said unusually good things about you, as I wrote sometime ago.

This is Monday.   I got here Saturday night and am gradually getting settled from the upset of the journey on.   I have some angels for servants, and they look after me with a care that does not foster the illusion of youth to which my temperament is liable but that makes me very comfortable. The *certioraris* will not begin to come for some days, and I am nearer leisure than I thought possible a month ago.   My secretary reads to me as he did in Washington various light and entertaining things, and I have on hand as a serious piece Paul Warburg's big book on the Federal Reserve System, the narrative part of which (but not the appendices) I shall read, am reading, out of affection for him.   Also I get two hours in a motor, though the weather just now is coldish and so foggy that we can't see much.

[90] William Cameron Forbes (1870–   ); American banker and public servant.

It is time for me to go to my evening solitaire, so, with love to the ladies, I say farewell for the moment.

Yours ever,
O. W. Holmes

Beverly Farms, Massachusetts

July 2, 1930

My dear Einstein:

Your letter of June 20 comes this morning after having been opened by someone else. The envelope bears Beverly Farms and U.S.A. and I think Mass. in your handwriting, but I think another hand wrote General Sea Foods Corp., 5 Fish Pier, Boston — a mystery. You apologize for an 'outrageous infliction of my own woes'. What in hell is a letter for except to tell of the writer's feelings, condition, and experience? I am sure that I inflict my ups and downs on you. I expect an apology for the apology! So I proceed to my little affairs.

I am not wholly idle. A first instalment, a bag of fifty-one cases to be examined on the question whether they should be allowed to come to our Court, is with me now and many more will come. But I get a motor drive every day and people call and I read a little. My secretary is reading to me Trotsky's autobiography which promises to be interesting, perhaps exciting, now that I have got past his early youth. I don't read such things except on compulsion, because my time is limited, but this was imposed by Laski as a while ago the life of Lafayette, two volumes, was imposed by Owen Wister. That paid, though I didn't expect it, and I think this will. Various kinds of light stuff have filled in the crevices. I may have mentioned them before so I refrain, except perhaps to repeat one first class saying of Oscar Wilde in a play: 'A cynic is one who knows the price of everything and the value of nothing'. I don't know that I should choose the word cynic, but the phrase is admirable.

I do not reiterate my exhortations but I insist on them. You are too much of a man to be able to afford to be idle

Y

except as a vacation. My secretary is ready with a case, fifteen cases in one, of Indians, an eternal source of trouble, and I turn to duty.

My love to the ladies.

Yours ever,

O. W. Holmes

Beverly Farms, Massachusetts

July 28, 1930

My dear Einstein :

Your lectures I hope will materialize, but I don't know who or where Fred Keppel [91] is.

I am going on as quietly as I can but see rather more of people than I want to although I want to see each one. I get tired more easily than I used to. To make sure that I don't have too much vacation the Clerk's office has sent me a bag of seventy-four cases to be examined ; one before with fifty-three has been disposed of. So I am not idle.

I have read a fair list of books, one of philosophy which I understand less than anything I ever read, unless when in college I looked into Jacob Behmen (sic), if I get the name right. A very remarkable book by Willa Cather, *My Antonia*, which turns the most squalid life of early settlers on the prairies into poetry without leaving the facts ; a combination of good sense, imagination, and tenderness that went to my heart. I do like to see a poet tackle the facts that he has lived with no matter how unpromising and make them blossom. I call Miss Cather a poet though she writes in prose. I got a similar impression from four paintings of a haystack, by the famous French impressionist, I can't think of his name — Monet, it comes to me — I am old — which simply by the changes of light seemed to say : You want incident ? Isn't the infinite enough ? Other adventures with books I will not enunciate, but I should like more time for them.

When you write of the London Season I can't help longing

91 Frederick Paul Keppel (1875–1943); American educator and President of the Carnegie Corporation of New York from 1923 to 1941.

to see it again which I shall not. A dame who lunched with me today said that I reported my experience of one such as a tragedy and two sighs. I don't remember it. You remember — 'I can't think who the deuce it was gave me that forget-me-not'.

I hate to take up a letter cold and go on with it, and as I can no more tonight I stop, with my love to the ladies.

Yours ever,
O. W. Holmes

Grand Hotel Toplice, Bled, Jugoslavia

15 Aug. 1930

Dear Justice Holmes :

I hope you will be impressed by the unknown name on this letter paper. I am writing in Carniola which I think is the most beautiful land in the world with its low hills and snowy peaks and mountain lakes and forests. It is rugged and wild yet green and smiling. The people are Slovenes but all speak German, and this land which is next door to Italy is really a bit of old Austria which has now become Jugoslav. But I shall not proceed lest you find me professorial.

We came here in search of figs and sunshine which Helen missed after a polar July in London. So far we have had little of either and only downpours which made me look with confidence on the high peaks in case I needed an Ararat for my future Ark. I read of people grilling at home and hope you have been spared the tropical heat. We would have welcomed some of it in this place. Otherwise we lead the simplest of lives in clean though not over comfortable surroundings. This is really a summer capital of the country and the diplomats from Belgrade throng here — a somewhat self-inflated lot who make me wonder if I was ever as ridiculous and confirm me in my lack of desire ever to reenter diplomacy. The time idles by agreeably and I am ashamed of my own sloth when I read of you buried in your seventy-four cases.

At Lady Oxford's suggestion I gave a letter to you to Lionel

Cohen [92] who has gone to Chicago with the British Bar and I understand is a really eminent K.C. But I told him I was convinced you would not be there so I don't think he will trouble you. If he should you will find him intelligent and agreeable.

The night before I left London I dined with Margot O. at Lord Reading's to play bridge. The latter has now returned to the city where he first began. What an extraordinary career the man has had! He was very interesting in relating his experiences with Wilson particularly when he obtained his consent for our troops to be brigaded with the English which was really the turning point of the war, when Wilson assured him he would do his 'damnedest'. After he spoke of Wilson's big sides he spoke also of the smaller ones as when he refused to receive Grey because of the latter's social secretary. And he turned to Margot and said 'Fancy Henry [93] doing a thing like that'! I fancy that English political life is more nearly approaching our own and a rougher type of man is taking the place of former leaders who no longer can lead. The easy catchwords of the cheap press provide formulas which save a lot of reasoning.

We lunched yesterday with Prince Paul of Serbia, a highly cultivated fellow with a real taste and knowledge of art which is almost unique in this land. He is married to a beautiful Greek princess who with her two good looking cousins beside her gave a good last impression of Greek art. They live in a Swiss chalet by another mountain lake, but the chalet was adorned with a fine Nicolas Poussin and some ancient and rare Spanish rugs. Beyond his place extends a good chamois shoot to convince you that this land is really wild. We are planning a long deferred ambition to visit the Dalmatian coast after this place. I am rereading Finlay's *Greece under the Romans* with enormous interest and looking forward to seeing Diocletian's palace at Spalato to which he retired when fatigued with the imperial crown.

Helen sends her warmest messages.

Ever yours,
L. E.

[92] Lionel Leonard Cohen, Baron Cohen of Walmer (1888–   ); English judge and Lord of Appeal in Ordinary, 1951-60.
[93] Herbert Henry Asquith, 1st Earl of Oxford and Asquith (1852–1928).

Beverly Farms, Massachusetts

Sept. 5, 1930

My dear Einstein :

A charming letter from you has waited a week for an answer as I have been turning over another batch of cases, now all tied up in a postbag ready for return.

You say you are in the most beautiful land in the world, but I was inclined to read the words 'with its low hills and snowy peaks' — 'with its low bills and money peaks' until I remembered the canon that words must be read with reference to their surroundings. I couldn't forbear reading a part to my friend Mrs. Curtis who is an old time admirer of yours and who would have gratified you by her appreciation. Do not fear for my discretion. I should not dream of showing anything that had the least touch of privacy.

I suppose that by this time you are carrying out your future plans. I envy you and wonder if I have been foolish not to risk another trip abroad. I had my cousin John T. Morse at luncheon the other day who is a year and some months older than I and who has just returned from Algiers etc., a three months trip that seemed to have made him younger. But me — not.

Some dames come to luncheon with me, and when we have done a day's work and returned from our afternoon drive my secretary says, 'How about culture?' and I yield to the temptation and listen to light literature. Two books not heavy but not too light have given me great pleasure. Hall's *The Religious Background of American Culture* and Helen Waddell's *The Wandering Scholars*. The former insisting that the background was not the Puritans properly so called, who believed in a church governed State, but the Lollards (Wyklyf) who had no general organization, but conventicles and separate groups that went as they pleased and being the poor hated the splendour of the Church that recalled that of the rich. The second volume is a delightful study of the poetical products of the poor medieval scholar-priests without benefices. It recalled a book by Rémy de Gourmont dealing with the religious poetry of the same time, from the earliest to the late Middle Ages, I believe not very well thought of, but good enough for an outsider. Which reminds me that I read Rémy de Gourmont's *Une Nuit au Luxembourg*, but didn't care much for it.   There is something dirty about him, I think.   I used to read his fortnightly summaries in the *Mercure de France*; but some of the Mussoos have a queer streak that I don't admire, including Anatole France.

Well, dear boy, I suppose you will get this on your return, but it is hard to fire a shot at a will o' the wisp flitting one knows not where.

My love to the ladies and my thanks to you.

Yours ever,
O. W. Holmes

25, Great Cumberland Place, W.1

24 Sept. 1930

Dear Justice Holmes :

As you foresaw I found your letter to give me pleasure on my return from Dalmatia.

How I wish you could have enjoyed it with me.   You would have seen a coast line far rockier than the NORTH SHORE with great mountains behind and strung with hundreds of islands great and small.   I visited one island fifty miles long on which there was neither motor nor horse, but it contained beautiful marble palaces of the XVIth Century and fine Italian paintings and water so clean you could see the bottom at a hundred feet or more.   And I saw there an ancient theatre of the Renaissance and the prow of a galley which had fought at Lepanto.   The governor of this island was a doctor of law and a doctor of philosophy, but, as no one had been murdered in fifty years and theft was unknown, he spends his days fishing with an income of twenty dollars a month on which he lives happily.   And I saw Diocletian's palace at Spalato which now contains a city and which enthused me to write a sonnet I am bold enough to send you.   For the first time in many years I really felt freedom and enjoyed it, for my only responsibility was one of time.

I spent a week at Lausanne where Helen went to consult a famous Swiss doctor who has devised a new series of tests which seem to reduce diagnosis to mechanism.   My fondness for the imperfections of human observation leaves me a little skeptical of the value of such tests which threaten to Fordize the human body, but I suspend my judgment. The doctor was immensely conscientious and I'm convinced was no charlatan, yet I can't help feeling that even the human body contains some elusive ingredients.

I came back to find my *Roosevelt* out and wrote at once to Houghton Mifflin to send it to you. Please forget the garish jacket for which I'm not responsible. Like Galileo's *E pur si muove* I feel about Houghton Mifflin though wondering if the name is in the right direction? If you find time to dip into the book I'll value your impressions for I have put into it a certain amount of personal philosophy.

We went to Yester for a weekend visit to see Midge, fortunately much better in health, and I am now back here, trying to prepare lectures. They are bones to gnaw. I am glad to try to settle down for a bit before a new venture.

Have you read Siegfried Sassoon's *Memories of an Infantry Officer*? Admirably written I thought by a real poet who is also interesting.

Ever yours,
L. E.

Pray who is this Curtis,[94] I should love to know her?

DIOCLETIAN AT SPALATO

Fling off the purple and forget the camp,
Forget I once was Caesar in great Rome,
No more to hear the legions' mighty tramp
Now I plant cabbage in my childhood home.
Let others rule o'er Egypt, Gaul, and Spain,
And give the law and bear the mighty load
Of Empire, till they fall beneath the strain,
Henceforth I rest in my new-reared abode.
I, son of a poor scribe, tho' born a slave
I burst the shackles which had weighed me down,
With wit and sword I rose to highest fame,
Men trembled as I passed, yet did I crave
And longed for freedom, when I found the crown
Had merely changed for me the master's name.

[94] Mrs. Charles Pelham Curtis.

Supreme Court of the United States, Washington, D.C.

Oct. 1, 1930

My dear Einstein :

Your book [95] arrives today in the turmoil of my own arrival. All I can do at present is to thank you and say I will read it when I can. You remember I have read some preliminary portions (or I suppose such) some time ago, with much pleasure.

My love to the ladies.

Yours ever,
O. W. Holmes

Supreme Court of the United States, Washington, D.C.

October 17, 1930

My dear Einstein :

Your book with many others met me on my arrival here. The manifold activity was only one item in the duties by which I was beset, so that this is the first moment when I could write with sufficient acquaintance with the theme. My secretary [96] has read to me all but a few pages that I need not wait for him to finish. Well, I should think it ought to be a marked success. Your estimate and appreciation seem to me wisely and delicately formed. Perhaps you make rather a greater and more interesting figure of Roosevelt than he seems to me, but not more so than I can understand another thinking him. I wish I had made a note of the President's suggestive remarks to me but I didn't and I can't rake them up. I notice some foibles in your English, such as using 'forceful' when 'forcible' would have been enough and better, but there are not many. You have made a very interesting book about one who was not to me a very interesting man ; but he was to the Americans, and I wish you a large sale.

I have not read Sassoon's book that you mention, but I think he was the author of a letter from the trenches written

---

[95] *Roosevelt, His Mind in Action* by Lewis Einstein (1930).
[96] Alger Hiss was Holmes's secretary 1929–30.

during the War, I think to *The New Republic*, that was A.1.; but I think the author of that letter was killed or died soon after. So if Sassoon is still going I give him up.

The sonnet seems to me good enough, but not too good for human nature's daily food.

My lad, I have been at a Conference of the judges and I *guess* it has made me a little uncomfortable to deal with and I had better shut up. I get tired more easily than I once did. I am afraid my words seem a little cool but my appreciation of the writer is very warm.

My love to the ladies.

Yours ever,
O. W. Holmes

Supreme Court of the United States, Washington, D.C.

November 14, 1930

My dear Einstein :

Welcome. And you will be welcome next Monday the 17th at 7, unless you prefer to make it 7 : 30. I have so absolutely given up dinners that I shall allow myself not to dress.

Let us not forget to mention *The Moon and Sixpence* which I once read at your behest and which I believe was by the author of *Cakes and Ale* that I have just listened to.

I am delighted to expect you.

Yours ever,
O. W. Holmes

25, Great Cumberland Place, W.1

14 Dec. 1930

Dear Justice Holmes :

A scratchy pen kept me from writing you in New York, but I do so now to send you a multitude of affectionate wishes from Helen and myself for Xmas and the New Year. And I want also to mention the real pleasure it gave me to catch even a fleeting glimpse of you. I felt almost like plagiarizing Goethe's remark of, 'There is a man', though I missed sadly the friendly Madonna of the armchair in her seat by the fireplace. I enjoyed every minute of my stay in the land which is at once home and yet not a home to me. The American atmosphere has a kind of rejuvenating effect, a sort of national monkey gland which quickens the pulse and makes the blood stream faster. I saw some old friends and some new, I lectured at a few Universities, I dined and went to parties no longer befitting my years, and I returned here sooner than I would have liked, for Helen has the weakness to miss me badly and has a distressing way of being unwell as soon as I go, though she tries to conceal this not to spoil my pleasure.

It is my first December in London and the sky is terribly grey after our own. I have not yet made up my mind whether I feel depressed or merely comfortable. I still have some work to finish up after which my mind is misty as to what to take up. To bore into the past is to snatch the present, for the present moment seems to me to have a double quick and diversified stride and we are heading toward an unknown future the roughest boundaries of which I can hardly detect.

I was glad at home to find that our superiority complex had been rudely shaken, but with opinion still clinging to statistical demonstrations as the only proof of things. I find statistics myself a kind of legalism of the masses, if I make my meaning clear — namely a conventional, partial, and often distorted criterion of opinion which at its best affords a rough working test and at its worst throws a sanction over every stupidity. I can't help feeling that our fondness for broad avenues allows us to go ahead faster when all is well but keeps us from venturing into byways when there is an obstruction. Meanwhile I hear that Bryanism is to resurrect again and the tyranny of gold will be challenged. But I shall 'Let Euclid rest and Archimedes pause', and repeat once more only the affectionate wishes to which Helen, Midge, and myself subscribe.

Yours,
L. E.

I hope you liked Siegfried Sassoon's book.

Supreme Court of the United States, Washington, D.C.

Feb. 8, 1931

My dear Einstein :

It must be over a month since I have written. Lumbago, colds, and work are my excuses. I won't dilate upon it beyond saying that little burdens weigh heavier as one nears ninety. That is just four weeks off now. A fortnight ago when I had a cold I told the Doctor that I wanted to take every precaution to live until I rounded the cape. Not that it matters in any way except that one makes goals for oneself to reach and then wants to reach them. Solitaire seems always an epitome of life. One says to oneself why do I care whether I win the game or not, and then one answers, why do you care to live, or like beer (not that I ever drink it), or why do you work? I know no answer except that that's the way I'm made. As French-women in novels frequently justify their foibles by generalizing them, *Je suis comme ça.* One can take oneself solemnly or lightly. One has to be serious when at work. When at leisure one surmises that it will not matter much to the Cosmos whether one turns to the right or to the left, but one doesn't know. It may be that one's act is a cosmic necessity and has the whole weight of the universe behind it. It may be that there is no necessity, but that one's unimaginable spontaneity takes now this turn now that. We may be important. It may be that the universe would be in ruins were not this paper on the table now in front of me a nodus that has the illusion of personality and in its freaky moments fancies itself distinguish-able from the before and after of the stream of energies that for the moment is able to say : 'I'. I recur to my old formula. Having made up your mind that you are not God don't lie awake nights with cosmic worries. Here endeth the First Lesson.

Of events not much to tell since you left. The usual routine, made less comfortable by the above mentioned lumbago and colds and alleviated by my secretary reading to me when I was too tired to work. *Inter alia* he read *The Newcomes* to me, which I have been wanting to reread for ten years. At intervals I read *Medieval Latin Lyrics* by Helen Waddell whose *Wandering*

Scholars I read with much pleasure last summer. She writes with feminine enthusiasm but is a scholar and translates loosely but well into pretty verse. Also two amusing books that I can recommend : Hoffenstein's (I think) *Poems in praise of practically nothing*, some of them very good indeed, and D. B. Wyndham Lewis and Charles Lee *The Stuffed Owl*, an anthology of good, bad verse, showing the bathos, platitudes etc., of which our most highly gifted men have been capable with a few samples of the less highly gifted like the Sweet Singer of Michigan. Also a volume of essays from the *Spectator* by Addison & Steele showing where Thackeray got some of his pleasantness, although the hidden music of his style is his own, and counts for much. Style, I think, is sound, a matter of ear. I liked Siegfried Sassoon's book. No special comment to make.

My love to the two charming ladies.

Yours ever,

O. W. Holmes

Radiogram

London   March 7, 1931
Justice Holmes 1720 Eye Street, Washington

Our affectionate wishes for continued health and many more birthdays.

Helen and Lewis Einstein

Supreme Court of the United States, Washington, D.C.

April 4, 1931

My dear Marchioness :

You shall not turn my writing to you into a reproach for want of confidence. I wrote because of the vividness of my feeling for you and because I couldn't leave a word from you unanswered. I write again for the same reason and to say a word about discouragements. I often have quoted what a Russian said to me, it must be near fifty years ago : 'In our middle class we have many specialists. In our upper class we have civilized men'. The specialist is more likely to achieve fame, i.e. to be talked about in the newspapers, but the civilized man creates a new atmosphere that is one of the greatest gifts to mankind. It would be hard for you to be a specialist in your surroundings, I assume, but you are to me a civilized woman and so you make life better for the world. I used to say to my father that the literary men took deuced good care to get their names on the handbills in large letters, but that many of the great achievements of life pass unnoticed by print. Part of the greatness of a great life I think consists in leaving it unadvertised. A woman with your gifts who does not let her cultivation decay and doesn't worry over the chances of displaying it, seems to me to be living nobly, and to have a right to be content.

Some of the Law Schools started a radio discourse on the evening of my birthday and the Chief Justice spoke and I had to say a few words. I enclose them:

'In this symposium my part is only to sit in silence. To express one's feelings as the end draws near is too intimate a task.

But I may mention one thought that comes to me as a listener-in : The riders in a race do not stop short when they reach the goal. There is a little finishing canter before coming to a standstill. There is time to hear the kind voice of friends and to say to one's self: The work is done. But just as one says that, the answer comes : The race is over, but the work never is done while the power to work remains. The canter that brings you to a standstill need not be only coming to rest. It cannot be while you still live. For to live is to function. That is all there is in living.

And so I end with a line from a Latin poet who uttered the message more than fifteen hundred years ago : "Death plucks my ear and says, Live — I am coming." '

There were some touching things happened on the day, and though I can't believe much and am not much elated by the newspapers I found myself feeling more than I expected. Among the things that counted was the word from you.

Affectionately yours,
O. W. Holmes

Will you tell Einstein that I have been very hard at work and that all the crevices of time have been filled with acknowledging letters and therefore I have made a regular correspondent wait? I think he will forgive me.

Supreme Court of the United States, Washington, D.C.

May 7, 1931

My dear Einstein:

What a pleasure to hear from you again. Your letter comes just as I am beginning to breathe a little freely, though not quite. My two last opinions were circulated this morning, the final adjournment is announced for June 1, and I expect to turn northward on the 3rd. What with age, work, and the debilitating Washington weather I am tired and my elasticity seems gone for the time. Out of working hours my secretary has been reading to me G. F. Young, on the Medici, reprinted in The Modern Library, that I have found very interesting. He admires the family and is eulogistically inclined towards most of them, including Catherine de Medici. I had just as lief think well as ill of her, and am glad to get more definite notions than I had, even though confused by playing solitaire while I (more or less) listen.

How I should like to doff my serious interests like a garment and wander directed by an experienced boss so as to take in all that remains for Europe to convey, but I suppose it is too late. It would be a bore to be ill abroad and I suppose there would be a good chance of being so. I will cultivate my garden.

The town is full of eminent jurists today gathered for the *Restatement of the Law* on which they have been engaged for some years, a task that leaves me unenthusiastic. But this resulted in two judges at luncheon, another just after, and later an eminent leader of the Chicago Bar, who has just left. Others telephone their imminence. These little things tire me now. Perhaps when I get to the Beverly air I shall realize that the present languor and fatigue are climate not old age. At present I am wondering whether I have taken another step down.

Give my love and sincere homage to the ladies whom I wish I might see again.

Yours ever,

O. W. Holmes

Supreme Court of the United States, Washington, D.C.

May 29, 1931

My dear Einstein,

In your letter of May 17 you say, perhaps prophetically, that you are glad to think of me back on the North Shore. But not yet. We adjourn on Monday next, June 1, and June 3 I have taken tickets for the North. Meantime there has been pretty constant work. Last night a lot of stuff coming in for a wind up on which we had to be ready to recite at our conference today. However it is over now.

I shall go out to Arlington tomorrow, Memorial Day, and visit the gravestone with my name and my wife's on it, and be stirred by the military music, and, instead of bothering about the Unknown Soldier shall go to another stone that tells that beneath it are the bones of, I don't remember the number but, two or three thousand and odd, once soldiers gathered from the Virginia fields after the Civil War. I heard a woman say there once, 'They gave their all. They gave their very names'. Later perhaps some people will come in to say goodbye.

It is beginning to be very hot and if it goes further will take the life out of one. It is very different from the North. It is easier to live there in the summer. I like to live, but feel that it does not matter much.

My secretary has been very good in reading to me out of working hours, more serious matters finished. We began yesterday Wodehouse, *Very Good, Jeeves* which makes me roar. That chap is master of a light rather original slang that makes life joyous when all the carbonic acid gas seems to have fizzled out of it. Few benefactors can be compared with him.

Turning to what you say I respect laziness and probably have said to you more than once that those who make the most of themselves don't make much. I regret my limited capacity for it. A sinister sign, but not, I hope, conclusive.

You speak of the Americans in England at and after the Revolution, and among them Gilbert Stuart. I thought he was an Englishman. As to the spark of art, poetry, and philosophy being passed on and kept alive, I bet it will be, though when I wanted to be disagreeable to White and McKenna (Catholics) I used to suggest that perhaps in two hundred years Mongolian ideals would be in the ascendant.

Well, I am a rag now, but hope to be different in a fortnight. My love to the ladies. I hope the ball you speak of will be or has been a success.

> Ever yours,
> O. W. Holmes

Beverly Farms, Massachusetts

July 7, 1931

My dear Einstein :

A moment of freedom. Yesterday I finished the first batch of activities that try to spoil a vacation, and apart from dames coming to luncheon etc. I can draw breath. Not much to tell. Just now we are having the rainy days which encourage keeping indoors and will give me a chance to listen to my secretary reading *Our Mutual Friend* (a rare recurrence to Dickens) which swamps its many faults in its exuberance. I even hope to do some serious reading and have got the last edition of Plato's *Laws*, Greek and translation opposite, to that end. I suppose I shall find the book you speak of sending on my return to Washington.

I had nearly forgotten to say that I have been sitting for another portrait by Hopkinson, who did me a year ago. I think this like the last a great success. The former one was for the Harvard Law School. This is intended for the new Court House by my ex-secretaries if a full length of a live judge will be admitted. I should think it would not.

I have so little to tell that a sudden moment for sending this off coming I wind up abruptly.

> Yours ever,
> O. W. Holmes

Love to the ladies.

25, *Great Cumberland Place, W.1*

19 July 1931

Dear Justice Holmes:

I write you again as a semi-idler to interrupt your vacation with my chatter which will take you away from your briefs. At least your portrait painter will also help to do this. I wish Vandyck might have done you or even Copley. The latter I read yesterday died almost broken hearted because his Beacon Hill property which he sold for £7000 had risen to an enormous value. His philosophy was at fault!

Venizelos, who came to England nominally to make a speech on Byron, remarked aptly that if poets can no longer guide a great democracy yet a democracy without poets would be dreary. Oddly, there is a Byronic revival here and John Murray the publisher has an interesting exhibition of his relics which includes Clare Claremont's letter asking for an assignation which produced Perdita. The bill for £46 of soda water, when he threw the siphons at his wife, and a forgery of his handwriting by Lady Caroline Lamb which took in John Murray who sent her the Byron portrait she asked for. A friend of mine possesses the miniature Byron gave her with his motto '*Crede Byron*' before which she scratched a *ne* when he abandoned her.

Do you follow the politics of the time in an Olympian survey? They interest me enormously and I'm not displeased to have become a spectator rather than something less than a pawn. Hoover has suddenly made himself popular by completely reversing everything he ever said.[97] I don't know if he deserves more credit for his eleventh hour change, or blame for not having done this before. Will it always be necessary to wait until the last inhabitant of Squidunc understands what ought to be done? Frankly I should feel happier if there were a little more conviction about what he does and if his sympathy for Germany had somewhat less in mind the German vote. Apart from that he acted ably but insufficiently and too abruptly. A little friendly advice on his part in Berlin

---

[97] President Hoover had proposed on June 20, 1931, a year's moratorium on all intergovernmental debts in order to save Germany from immediate financial collapse.

z

would have made it easier for the Germans to meet the French. However, you will have a chance of skipping what I have written on this for the *North American Review*.

Apart from that my principal preoccupation lately has been Benjamin West [98] who died convinced of his own genius which he also had persuaded the British nation to acknowledge. You recall Byron's line 'the dotard West, Europe's greatest daub, poor England's best'. Do you consent that people may be as interesting by their deficiencies as by their merits? I should like to be the Plutarch of failures, but would probably fail even in that.

Ever yours,
L. E.

Beverly Farms, Massachusetts

August 10, 1931

My dear Einstein :

This is a postscript to a letter that I imagine myself to have written to you some time ago, but that may be a dream. I am dim in my memories of the Byron fornications but like to have them refreshed. An extreme admiration of him is not necessary for that.

I am going on with my routine. Rather more calls on my time than I like, but they keep me busy. I have dispatched the last (3rd.) bag of cases that I have had to examine, had a few dames to take luncheon with me, read a few books, too, Plato's *Laws* and a volume on the Mesta (a Spanish Association of merino wool growers that lasted from 1184 to 1838) for the Day of Judgment examination. Others for pleasure and mundane purpose. *Inter alia* the last adequate reading of *Vanity Fair*, a great story, though the mundane aims depicted there and in the *Newcomes* seem to command Thackeray's sympathy more fully than he admits and somewhat belittle him. I have just finished a detective story and am about to begin another and am reading a new tale by Willa Cather. She seems to me a very remarkable novelist. *My Antonia* especially

---

[98] Benjamin West (1738-1820); American artist who lived in England, history painter to George III, charter member and later President of the Royal Academy.

stirred me deeply.   She takes what she has seen and turns it
into poetry while keeping it fact.   I like to see a person realize
that poetry doesn't depend on going somewhere else but on
the power to 'make a broomstick blossom'.

In a few minutes Mrs. Beveridge, widow of the ex-senator,
author of the admirable *Life of Marshall* and the torso of a
Life of Lincoln, comes to luncheon.   Later my nephew and his
wife and someone else from the Art Museum come to supper,
I believe with things to show, and between I must go to Salem
to get my hair cut.   Simple joys, but they take time.

So much for a friendly bulletin.   Time every little while
gives me a fresh notice of its advance, but the dilapidations
are gradual and still consistent with life.

My love to the ladies.

Yours ever,
O. W. Holmes

Grand Hotel Majestic Palace et Pavillon Majestic,
Royat-les-Bains

24 Aug. 1931

Dear Justice Holmes :
Your letter discovers me here whither my wife has come
for the waters and I to keep her company.   We began our
vacation by a meteoric motor journey to Prague to see old
friends which would have been pleasant save for her catching
bronchitis.   She is over this now but still enfeebled here.   The
country, Auvergne, is pretty but the locality dull and the
weather abominable.   The local hero is Vercingétorix whose
statue on horseback brandishes a sword which he looks as if
he were trying to put through the silver ring in a carrousel.
The other speciality is liqueur chocolates which is an ingenious way of putting alcohol into sweets.   The country is
volcanic, but the volcano which is now rumbling is Europe
and I hope we shall get through the coming year without an
eruption.

I am not enthusiastic about Hoover's methods which
seem to me to consist of first doping opinion and when that
is no longer possible sidetracking it along alleys which offer

the minimum of political risk.   Banking credits are useful stopgaps but nothing more, and to try to divert opinion to disarmament is to my mind the most dangerous fallacy of all at a moment when Germany and other countries too have their 'bootleg' armies.   The remedy, I think, lies in a broader view of the situation by making it plain that we will not tolerate another way, but I fear the question is too shot through with politics and too little with diplomacy.

I have just finished the fourth and last volume of Bülow's memoirs which seems to me a terrible revelation of his petti- ness and his caddishness.   The Kaiser is supposed to have said after reading them that it is the first time he had heard of a man committing suicide after he was dead; but the remark sounds too apt to be true.   I met Bülow some years ago at dinner and found him a very agreeable talker.   His memoirs are inflated by the gossip and hearsay of a lifetime.   But what is pleasant to listen to at the dinner table is hardly what one would expect a serious statesman to leave as his life message. I think old John Adams was right when he refused to leave a testament of advice to the American people, for, as he said, if he extolled domestic virtues he would appear to glorify himself and cast aspersions on Hamilton.

I am in the midst of *Moll Flanders* [99] and find it enormously interesting, and I am amused by the magistrates she met in Virginia whose palms bore the brand of Newgate.

Have you read Hindus's *Humanity Uprooted*?   It is extremely well written and explanatory of much Bolshevik psychology in trying to create a new world.   Though I can never see how a purely materialistic philosophy can deny the material basis of life by the acquisition of the earned comforts of property.

Helen sends her love.

Ever yours,
L. E.

(Postmarked October 9, 1931)

My dear Einstein :

This will be but a feeble word.   I am not ill, but the Washington heat coming on top of a sort of cave in last summer

[99]   *The Fortunes and Misfortunes of the famous Moll Flanders* by Daniel Defoe (1722).

finds and makes me languid. I fear that I may depend on your indulgence this winter, if I survive, but I hope you will not stop writing to me. We begin to hear arguments on Monday (it is Friday now) and I expect to be all right for my work, but flabby.

My love to the two ladies.

Yours ever,
O. W. Holmes

PART FOUR
1932–35

Supreme Court of the United States, Washington, D.C.

January 3, 1932

My dear Einstein :

You write such interesting and entertaining letters that I blush not to do likewise, but I can't. I have not been very well and I find it difficult to write; difficult physically and mentally. I hope to get back to normal but at present life is hard. We begin our sittings again on Monday. I have but one opinion to deliver, another being held up for tinkering to meet a long dissent from Butler — agreed to by no one else I believe.

The last adjournment has given me a chance for some literature and several murder stories, averaging poorly. Actually my secretary has fallen back on Walter Scott's *Quentin Durward*, and very good it still seems to me.

The year has begun overcast and rainy, but as we have suffered from drought I am content.

My love and best wishes for a happy New Year to the ladies and yourself.

Yours ever,

O. W. Holmes

25, Great Cumberland Place, W.1

17 January 1932

Dear Justice Holmes :

Your letter caused me some anxiety, and then the same evening over the radio, which exceptionally I listened to, I heard the news of your resignation.[1] My feelings were extremely mixed for though I know the pang you feel at leaving the bench, yet I also thought, perhaps more than you, of the good sides and principally of your health with the feeling that you are no longer slave to the tyranny of your own decisions. And

[1] Holmes resigned from the Supreme Court of the United States on January 12, 1932.

I am glad also to think that you will now have leisure to seek expression in some other medium than that of the law. You poured the best into your decisions, but even the best like sonnets need to keep their structure.

Do you recall when a friend suggested to John Adams, then a very old man, to write his valedictory, and he answered he did not like to do so because if he spoke about the felicity of his married life it would be construed into a dig at Hamilton and if he mentioned his church attendance this would reflect on Jefferson?

I wonder if you still have in mind the memoirs of which you spoke to me many years ago. Their interest is far too obvious for me to dilate upon. You have been associated with a pretty important part of the nation's history. You have been a bridge between New England literary tradition and modern industrialism, and having enjoyed your early warlike fugue you were wise enough to skip the dreary decades which followed. Well, I wonder if you won't startle the country with your reminiscences. Lately I saw Minnie, Lady Hindlip, who is your age and three times your weight at luncheon relating scabrous tales.

There are glimmerings of optimism once more here which pierce through like snowdrops that precede the spring. The feeling that reparations will be swept away encourages hope and our own debt demands are to be ignored or placated. For we have become the villain in the piece and some of the cheaper press find it desirable to stir up sufficient feeling against us to justify what they propose to do. I have not a few misgivings about the future for it will lead to a good many harsh words, but I keep silent in my own little wilderness.

You write that you are rereading Walter Scott. A friend of mine who has married his descendant and lives at Abbotsford offers us her house in the South of France and thither we are going this week. I hope to write and to play golf — pastimes I put on the same level.

My ladies send affectionate messages.

Yours,
L. E.

If you wish amusement ask your secretary to read you '*Juan in America*' [2] which I sent you.

[2] *Juan in America* by Eric Linklater (1931).

25, Great Cumberland Place, W.1

Washington's Birthday
1932

Dear Justice Holmes:

It is Washington's Birthday and I think of yours in a fortnight's time with many affectionate wishes. And I hope that you may celebrate your century and that I shall be there to rejoice with you. It is after all an achievement, a kind of Olympian record on the road to immortality, and where mind is unclouded and health tolerable it is one to be envied. I recall your early admiration for some decrepit veterans dragged about in a procession. I wonder if you could have seen yourself today when you were a boy in the way Macduff saw his descendants if you would not have been proud. I know that I am to know you. Usually one needs some perspective, but I feel you are already a historic character, and if you had lived in Manchu China you would have run a real risk of being made a divinity. I think I once quoted Metchnikoff to you who came in one day saying that the first fifty years should be devoted to the passions and the emotions, the next fifty to the pursuit of some art or science, and the third fifty to the service of the State. Perhaps you have begun too early?

I lunched at Margot Oxford's the other day and we spoke of you. She was less convincing when she told me of the men who arrived at British ports in their own yachts to touch the dole. She is a bit mad which makes her all the more sympathetic.

London is a city of exhibitions now. A Persian exhibition where objects Sassanian and Sefavid are collected. But I dislike even the finest rugs when they are hung on walls, and books concealed in showcases mean little to me. It is unavoidable but spoils half my pleasure, though the exhibition has been a revelation to many thousands who were unfamiliar with Persian art. The Labor Government is giving a reception there which seems to me intelligent. I do not see Mr. Hoover as a patron of the arts.

Political animosities rage, but all parties are divided and there is yet no clear cut issue. There are some budding

Mussolinis who would enjoy a fling. I stayed with Lord Lloyd at Coton who was a candidate for Viceroy of India and who, I think, would like to be Viceroy of England — so would Moseley and I suspect Winston Churchill — but the talk of future dictatorship seems to be nonsense, though there may be some new political alignments. Everyone is sick of the old, but the alternative is not alluring. I have wearied you with these reflections.

Our affectionate wishes for ten thousand birthdays as our Oriental would say.

Ever yours,
L. E.

1720 Eye Street, N.W., Washington, D.C.

March 16, 1932

My dear Einstein :

You must forgive my long past and future silence. I don't know the reason, except ninety-one years, but I find it very hard to write, physically and more or less intellectually. I am trying to recover from old fatigue and some trouble in the way of health, and am much better than when I came down here. But my cure is idleness. I take a motor drive of one and a half hours in the morning after getting up late, then in the afternoon and evening listen to my secretary who reads philosophy and murder cases including rereading all of Sherlock Holmes, the best in that line since *The Moonstone* which I still think A.1. People call and I see them. I don't need to write my memoirs. Mr. Bent has just published a life of me.[3] I haven't read it but my impression is that the book is largely filled with extracts from me. My executors, John G. Palfrey of Boston and Felix Frankfurter (Harvard Law School), will take charge of any posthumous volumes that may be printed, but I doubt the need of one. I hope this won't stop your writing. You will not take silence for regret or indifference.

My love to the ladies.

Yours ever,
O. W. Holmes

---

[3] *Justice Oliver Wendell Holmes; a Biography* by Silas Bent (1932).

25, *Great Cumberland Place, W.1*

29 March 1932

Dear Justice Holmes :

The sight of your handwriting gave me real pleasure for I felt that you had picked up in health and strength. And I shall wait till you pass the century before again you speak of age.

Did you ever meet Count Greppi, a former Italian Ambassador who began his career as an Attaché of Metternich? He only died a few years ago, but on his hundredth birthday one hundred ladies in Rome gave him a tea. I am sure there are more in Washington who would like to do the same.

Oddly enough I dreamed the other night that as you were no more on the bench you were without a secretary and I was going to act as one, only I found I was expected by those around you to learn stenography, which filled me with horror.

We are just back after spending two months in a villa near Cannes where we had sunshine and blue sky and a panorama of olive trees. I put in a good deal of writing on my *Divided Loyalties*,[4] which includes a fairly wide range of spies, secret agents, and highly respectable Boston refugees who naturally felt all the more American as they lived in London. I thought I might discover some general law on the subject of patriotism and loyalty, but I think your adage that no generalization is worth a damn the right one.

Passing through Paris I saw Jusserand [5] who has recovered from a very serious operation and has the same agile mind as before even if his physical movements are a bit more sedate.

London is now the only merry place for everywhere else reigns black gloom and people are either ruined or certain they will be tomorrow. I don't like the looks of things ahead and particularly our relations to the rest of the world give me no little anxiety. I wish I could discern a little more character

---

[4] *Divided Loyalties — Americans in England during the War of Independence* by Lewis Einstein (1933).

[5] Jean Adrien Antoine Jules Jusserand (1855–1932); distinguished French author and diplomat. While serving as French Ambassador in Washington from 1903 to 1925 Jusserand completed his *Histoire littéraire du peuple anglais* in three volumes, was awarded the Pulitzer Prize in history for his *With Americans of Past and Present Days*, and became the only non-American ever to serve as President of the American Historical Association.

on the part of those at the helm, but that vile word of politics, which is only a synonym for egotistic ambition, seems to excuse the reticences and equivocations of those in power when a little unpopular frank speaking would be preferable. I have in mind such matters as the foreign debts and prohibition and even gangsterism, which I imagine needs a non-political magistracy and police rather than new laws.

I wonder if you have begun your memoirs, which you spoke of already many years ago. How do you spend your time? I wish mightily I could catch a glimpse of you and perhaps I may in the Fall, though I have little wish to be caught in a presidential election in which I feel no enthusiasm for either side.

My ladies send their love.

Ever yours,
L. E.

25, *Great Cumberland Place, W.1*

9 May 1932

Dear Justice Holmes:

I wish I could think of you coming over here for your London 'Season' as you did formerly, even if there is no more a 'Season'. A few 'débutantes' go to dances, and Midge is busy with her eldest daughter and her youngest monkey (for she has an uncanny fondness for these animals). But the great houses are no more and the great entertaining is over and people live more and more in service flats. The old London you knew before the war doesn't exist, and the few souvenirs of the Edwardian age prowl like Homer's heroes in the Elysian fields. Even the silk hat has disappeared except on state occasions, and Tory ministers wear soft collars on the front bench.

I hope you are enjoying your spring at Washington and preparing for Beverly. And I shall be very astonished if I don't hear that you have begun some new work. Didn't Titian paint his last great picture at ninety nine? Oddly enough he had previously retired to his native home and become a lumber merchant. As he had plenty of lawsuits with his customers he took to painting once more.

I have been working at the Record office lately and have now found all the proof I needed about the Reverend John

Vardill of Trinity Church, New York, whom George the Third made a Professor of Divinity because he arranged the successful theft of Franklin's correspondence. Do you like the association of theology and espionage for he was also that?

It is amazing the things one finds as soon as one rummages in archives. I discovered a letter [6] of John Adams written four months after Bunker Hill to say that in spite of what people believed in England no one in America had the slightest thought of independence, and not one of the Massachusetts leaders would dare to propose this as it would lead to dissension.

With nothing more to do about the history of today I concern myself with that of the past which is more satisfactory. Our own age is too disorderly and I am little in sympathy with Hoover's attitude toward affairs. I believe he is becoming once more a great man reconstructed like a miracle working saint by the Republicans who *faute de mieux* need him, even if they don't like him.

This morning I spent rummaging in the backstairs and small bedrooms of Windsor Castle looking at and for West's pictures. I saw numbers, and yet his monumental pictures on the *Triumph of Revealed Religion* have disappeared and none of the custodians of Windsor had so much as heard of a work which was to insure his immortal fame as well as that of George the Third! What an extraordinary place Windsor is with its Victorian feudalism, magnificent objects, and execrable taste. I think Walter Scott's inspiration is behind its sham medievalism, but I believe he was also responsible for the 'cavalier' element in Virginia and the southern chivalry. I read *Moll Flanders* the other day and she speaks of the magistrates she met in Virginia who were highly respected but had convicts' hands!

My ladies send their love.

Ever yours,
L. E.

[6] The text of the extract made by the Post Office, which intercepted the letter and recorded its contents in the Public Records Office, is given on p. 405 of Lewis Einstein's *Divided Loyalties*. Dr. Lyman H. Butterfield, an eminent authority, does not believe its author was the second President of the United States; but he is unable to account for the initials J.A. of the signature. Admiral Samuel E. Morison is, on the other hand, of the opinion that the author of the letter is the second President as it reads like his other letters of the time and he can think of no other prominent patriot having the initials J.A.

I use some old sheets.

~~Supreme Court~~ *of the United States, Washington, D.C.*

May 15, 1932

My dear Einstein :

A letter from you has been on my table for a month without an answer. I don't know what is the matter with me. I can't write. I listen to reading for hours though with doubts as to how much I get from it, but I am convinced that I am no good as a correspondent any longer. My handwriting has grown small and uncertain.

In short letters are gratefully received but whether they will be answered depends on powers beyond me. It is hard for I delight in your letters.

In the way of reading my secretary estimates that since we got here we have read about four million five hundred thousand words, which isn't bad, heavy and light, together.

I hope that I shall see you again before I die, and beg you to give my love to the two dear ladies.

Yours ever,
O. W. Holmes

25, Great Cumberland Place, W.1

3 June 1932

Dear Justice Holmes :

Your letter came as an agreeable surprise for I hardly ventured to expect it, which made it all the more welcome both as coming from you and as a presumption of good health. May the warm weather and the north shore breezes set you right once more. I wish I could feel as sanguine in other matters but the outlook fills me with apprehension and doubt as to the adjustability of our institutions to meet a crisis which does not call for a unified emotion. Eventually I suppose we will emerge from it by a kind of survival of the fittest, but it seems to me as if the cost of human suffering has been

immensely increased by omissions and commissions and mis-
representations and reticences all in the name of politics. If the
crisis will help to shake the country of belief in its gospel of
materialism (the full garage, and the new American philosophy)
the price may not be too high. Personally I am disgusted by
Hoover and disgusted with the Democrats.

Over here the outlook is even blacker in the long run; the
continent seems to be heading for a fall, and is sliding down
the hill very rapidly. Our economic philosophy under which
one part of the world gorges and another starves is not working
out very well though I'm convinced that socialism would be
even worse, and the prospect of our adopting a five or a
twenty-five year plan fills me with horror at the thought of
surrendering still more powers for cheap politicians to regulate
one's life.

I enclose some clippings regarding a recent judicial scrap
which may amuse you. McCardie [7] by the way, who is not
an enemy to publicity and delivers himself of opinions on birth
control and how much a lady ought to spend for her under-
wear, has since expressed his readiness to submit his notes.

My own manuscript of *Divided Loyalties* is approaching
completion. I have brought together I think some facts of
interest regarding the opinions and feelings of Americans in
England in the revolution. But of unity of thought I find
none and everyone had his own experience.

We are in the midst of the 'Season' which, except for
events imposed by tradition like races and statutory dinners, is
uncommonly like any other time of the year. People are
poorer and receive less and there is not so much hospitality
and no great houses. We are fast getting into a new world of
which the unit for all is bedroom, bath, motor car, and cocktail
parties provide the social solvent. Back to the dark ages again
with only the printing press between man and obscurity. I
don't relish the prospect though my prejudices will hardly affect
the result.

My poor wife suffers from acute arthritis which imposes the
prospect of some watering place. I rather hate them all, but
hate even worse to let her seek its benefit in solitude.

[7] Sir Henry Alfred McCardie (1869–1933); English judge whose prolix
opinions discussing current social issues achieved considerable notoriety.

2 A

What are your plans this summer, and when do you move northwards? I should be terribly disappointed in these days of conference if I were not to hear of you presiding over a conference of centenarians.

My ladies send their affectionate greetings and are glad to be remembered by you.

Ever yours,

L. E.

25, Great Cumberland Place, London W.1

22 June 1932

Dear Justice Holmes:

I am regretful we are so far apart and just because the 'Season' is no longer as gay you refuse to go to London. Doubtless you put this on another ground but I know better. I too was beginning to feel my years till I read in this morning's papers about Lord Halifax at 93 talking High Church for a whole hour. What can a poor agnostic do?

I have whiffs of the young world from Midget's girls who treat me almost with respect. The eldest is a sporting young lady of eighteen with the mind of a cavalry subaltern whose only intellectual distraction is treatises on war, and who shows her superiority over the Sandhurst cadets who call on her every Sunday by scoffing at their notions that communication trenches are built at right angles to the front line.

The other night we attended the Aldershot 'Tattoo' which a soldier friend describes as a military cabaret. It is really a very fine spectacle of stunts and pageantry carried out by various regimental detachments, for the artistic expressions of the English people are, to my mind, gardening and pageantry in which they really excel.

Lately I read the manuscript diary at the British Museum of your predecessor, Chief Justice Oliver [8] of Massachusetts (*tempus* George III), who remarked that English country

---

[8] Peter Oliver (1713–91); American colonist appointed Chief Justice of Massachusetts in 1771. Oliver remained loyal to the Crown, left Boston in 1776 for England where he was awarded the degree of DCL at Oxford, and lived modestly on a government pension in Birmingham until his death.

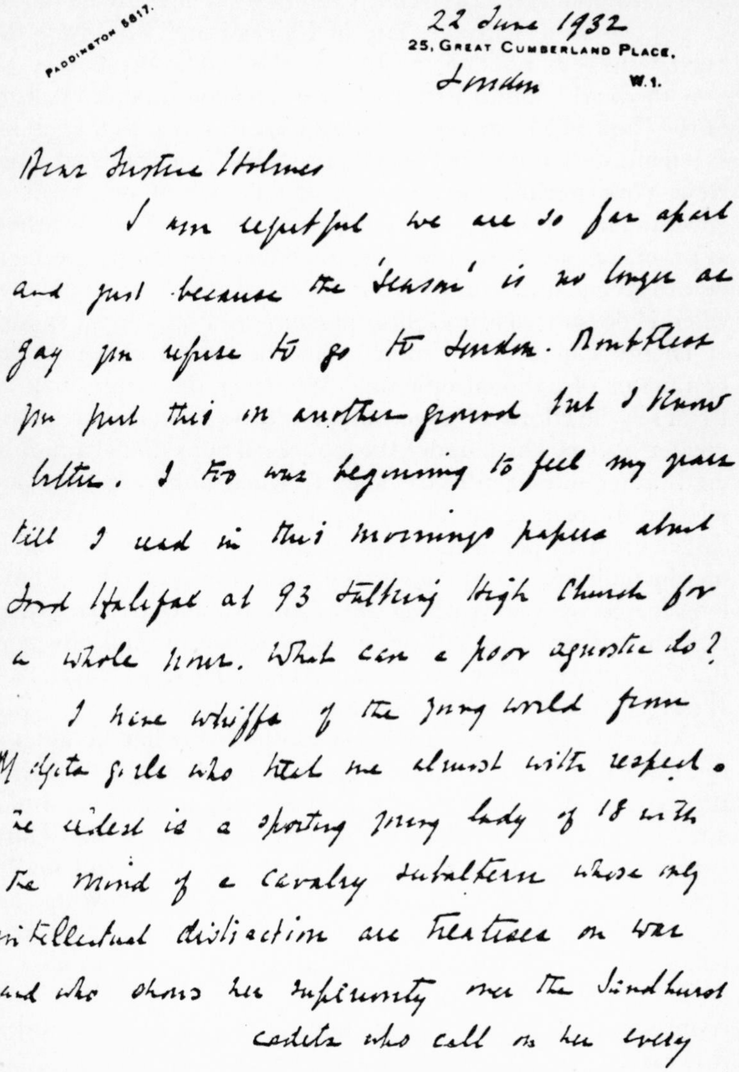

PADDINGTON 5817.

22 June 1932
25, GREAT CUMBERLAND PLACE,
London W.1.

Dear Justice Holmes

I am regretful we are so far apart and just because the 'season' is no longer as gay you refuse to go to London. Doubtless you put this on another ground but I know better. I too was beginning to feel my years till I read in this mornings papers about Lord Halifax at 93 talking High Church for a whole hour. What can a poor agnostic do?

I have whiffs of the young world from my sister's girls who treat me almost with respect. The eldest is a sporting young lady of 18 with the mind of a cavalry subaltern whose only intellectual distraction are treatises on war and who shows her superiority over the Sandhurst cadets who call on her every

Specimen of handwriting of Lewis Einstein

From a portion of Einstein's letter to Holmes of June 22, 1932 people had the same fondness for poetry that in Massachusetts they showed for the law — but I doubt if the first is true today.

Mr. Gordon Selfridge, late of Chicago and who owns the biggest store in London, prophesies the end of democracy all over the world, and my friend James Truslow Adams, exulting in the 'best seller' success of his *Epic of America* which contains excellent stuff imbedded in claptrap, has just returned from New York terribly gloomy over the failure of our form of government. I have little confidence in myself or in others as prophets, but I am rather disgusted just now by the spectacle we are giving, and wonder if our system of governmental inertia when it doesn't yield to selfish pressure and occasional spasms of energy can ever be more than the lowest common denominator of national opinion. Whatever the future may be I can see the efforts of governments always to concentrate still greater powers which under the jobbery of our system cannot be used either intelligently or honestly when public servants are selected for reasons entirely independent of the duties they are called upon to perform. The outlook is not cheerful, but to me the fault lies not in democracy but in our methods. I have long feared we were rushing ahead toward another barbarism though neither of us will be on hand to see the full effects of the new order. Have you read Aldous Huxley's *Brave New World* as a satire of what is in store?

My *Divided Loyalties* is almost finished and has taught me the history of our revolution from a different angle. Some of the material I found has been uncommonly interesting, and I am sure you will be pleased to learn that George the Third rewarded a New York clergyman for being a successful spy by appointing him a Regius Professor of Divinity! Now my job is to find a publisher which is no easy matter under present conditions though Houghton Mifflin have made me an offer.

I hope your old haunts on the NORTH SHORE may restore your strength. Please don't attempt to answer unless it is easy.

My ladies join in sending you their affectionate wishes.

Ever yours,

L. E.

Beverly Farms, Massachusetts

September 8, 1932

My dear Einstein :

It is ages since I have written to you. I believe I have explained that I find it very hard to write. This will carry my love to you and to the two ladies who have counted so much to me. I hope you will overlook what is not neglect and send me a line once in a while. I hope to go to Washington early in October. I am an idler now, but hear a good many books, with copious allowance of murder stories, take nearly daily drives, and receive a good many calls. I find the life of my old friend Beveridge [9] very interesting ; a pretty big fellow. His wife comes to see me when she is near, and some others, but most of my friends are dead and my time must be near.

Yours ever,

O. W. Holmes

25, Great Cumberland Place, W.1

September 18, 1932

Dear Justice Holmes :

It is so long since I have heard from you that I should love to have news, and I wonder if your secretary would be kind enough to write me a line in order to tell me how you are and if your summer was passed agreeably.

Yesterday at the London Library I saw your new biography.[10] Of course it is a great compliment and I hope gave you pleasure and yet, I can hardly say why, I resented it. Still as Mussolini and Al Capone have all had their biographers I'm sure I am ridiculous.

We have only just returned here after Helen took a cure for arthritis at Aix and half a cure for the heart at Royat, and now I am on my way to Yester. Midget's eldest daughter Helen has just got herself engaged to Lionel Berry, the son of

---

[9] *Beveridge and the Progressive Era* by Claude G. Bowers (1932).
[10] *Justice Oliver Wendell Holmes; a biography* by Silas Bent (1932).

a newspaper king and a nice boy. They are in love and well suited, but it is hard to realize that the infant is of marriageable age.

Apart from that I am putting the last touches on my *Divided Loyalties*. Books have gone the way of other commodities and Houghton Mifflin are not in a hurry to publish anything though they will undertake this. It has given me an interest in default of anything more active to do, and as I see little prospect ahead of the latter I suppose I had better settle down to historical writing for the rest of my days, though what I do hardly seems important when one lives on a volcano. I know that you with philosophic skepticism will see little that is new in events, but the world seems to me rather like a Sunday afternoon in Hyde Park when one hears soap box orators shouting the most contradictory opinions. One finds ideas for every taste, but somehow or other the surface of resistance against the backing of force appears to me to have considerably weakened. There are no longer the same structural bulkheads and the education of some huge aggregate to a single idea seems to me peculiarly dangerous. I enclose a few thoughts on the subject so far at least as concerns one question today.

England alone remains magnificently optimistic perhaps in contradiction with the rest of the world. But they show an ability and a will to pull together which I admire.

I went to the first night of Bernard Shaw's last play *Too True to be Good*, but found it feeble ; nothing new and much that seemed stale. Shaw goes on with an old momentum and I watched him after the performance laughing to himself.

My ladies send their love.

Ever yours,
L. E.

Beverly Farms, Massachusetts

September 30, 1932

My dear Einstein :

It is a great pleasure to hear from you again. One can't expect letters unless one writes and it is almost impossible for me to write these days, but I hope that your kindness and affection will lead you to spare me a word from time to time. You speak of my biography. I have not read it, but I should think it was harmless. I had nothing to do with it. Perhaps when I die my executor (John Palfrey and/or Felix Frankfurter) may do something, with more materials, but I have done my best to destroy illuminating documents. Your letter to the paper seems to me able and instructive, but I regard myself as out of the world and don't try to keep up with events, so I cannot criticize it. I can but admire and wish I had your knowledge. Give my love to your ladies. I don't know whether I shall have a chance to send another message, as I can't tell whether my time *ici bas* is long or short, but it seems as if the end was not approaching very swiftly and we may hob nob in future years. What there has been has been delightful. As I have said writing comes very hard to me now so I will say no more.

Yours ever,
O. W. Holmes

25, Great Cumberland Place, W.1

June 5, 1933

Dear Justice Holmes:

I have returned here once more and I write to express the pleasure it was for me to see you and to know that your interest in life was as keen as ever. And I was glad to find you looking so well. The body is an awkward drag on the mind, but the real things which count are always the same with you and I could detect no alteration in your glance or expression. We both shared the same aversion to saying goodbye which is an unpleasant ceremony where it is not perfunctory.

I had, however, a pleasant incident on the steamer which I must relate to you. There was a charming boy on board called Chauncey Stillman lately out of Harvard and now studying architecture at Columbia. With my inquisitiveness to learn the ideas of a younger generation I asked him who were the heroes of this age. He said he could not answer for another but for himself it was Justice Holmes. And this was said to me by a boy who had no idea that I knew you so you can judge of my pleasure. And when I told him you were a friend he wished to know much of your views of life. Were you a Chinese I should now forecast a temple in your honor. All the same I was glad to hear you spoken of as an example for youth.

My own family are scattered just now because of Whitsuntide. Helen alone is here immensely pleased at my return and full of affectionate enquiries about you. Also Midge to whom I have only talked over the phone, for she is in Scotland, was warmly interested in all that concerns you. Her eldest child marries in a fortnight which seems incredible to me though I am beginning to absorb the Einsteinian conceptions of space and time.

My book is just out and doubtless it will reach you at the same time as this letter. Typographically it seems to me creditable and rereading it I found it less turgid than I had feared. Perhaps the preeminence of some worthy and unworthy gentlemen from Massachusetts in its pages will add to your indulgence if you read it. Following your example I took up Zweig's *Marie Antoinette* on the steamer and thought it well written though somewhat oversexed in accordance with modern taste. It is rather like a play in many scenes than a continuous biography, but the writer brought out well how a commonplace character rose to greatness in the tragedy of events. Do you know the same author's *Fouché* in which he draws the portrait of a most accomplished scoundrel?

The London 'Season' goes on as per calendar and statute. The debutantes still debut and Ascot must still be run. But the interstitial living has shrunk with fortunes and an altered taste, and I doubt if you would find much to remind you of the past you knew. I don't think that people worry much about the political and economic chaos in the world. There is hardly enough pattern left to tie up any standard to. But the holiday makers will still go on up to the eve of the day of judgement, and why should they worry beyond? There is plenty of healthy virility left and, though we may all become barbarian once more, I don't think the world will perish from effeminacy.

Ever yours,

L. E.

25, Great Cumberland Place, W.1

June 14, 1933

Dear Justice Holmes:

I know that your course follows that of the swallows even though your flight comes later, and I like to think of you once more on the NORTH SHORE surveying humanity from your seaside Olympus. My own return was greeted like that of Ulysses though I had no occasion to look for a bow. Instead I attended the marriage of Midge's eldest girl, Helen, to Lionel Berry, the eldest son of Sir Gomer Berry who is the head of a vast newspaper syndicate. It is entirely a love match and so far as one can foresee they have all that should make for happiness. Helen (named after her grandmother) is a dear, healthy girl, fond of sport, and unafflicted by any intellectuality.

I hope you will have received my *Divided Loyalties*. It has met with an astonishingly good reception here where books are praised but never bought. Houghton Mifflin's are to bring it out at home and as it is in great parts concerned with gentlemen from Massachusetts this seems appropriate, but I have sent you the English edition. Now I feel somewhat between time and tide without any definite urge to begin something serious and yet bored to stay unoccupied for long.

The economic conference is in the background but it is a dissolving one for by various processes of exclusion it has been whittled down till the Leviathan became a gnat. Popular interest is more taken up by tennis and racing. I was amused the other day walking through the park when an elderly man with what seemed to me tragedy written in his eyes approached me. After the young beggars who accost one in every street of Washington and New York this one seemed deserving, but his only request was to ask me if Ballyhoo had won the Kempton Sweepstakes!

Yet the old London you know has gone, and more and more monstrous apartment houses now line Park Lane. There is hardly a great house left and these are doomed. But life passes pleasantly enough. No one has much to spend yet everyone seems to have a little and there is little gloom around. I hear that the economic delegates who have thronged here from every country in the world are mainly impressed by British cheerfulness. The great livery companies invited them to banquets but as they thought that the fishmongers etc. had asked them to advertise fish they declined! The old London dinner party is almost a thing of the past though we have one of eighteen tonight with your old friend Margot as a guest.

My ladies send affectionate greetings.

Ever yours,
L. E.

25, Great Cumberland Place, W.1

August 23, 1933

Dear Justice Holmes:

I am writing more to have news of you than because I have anything in particular to relate. And if you feel indisposed to send me a line perhaps your considerate secretary will be kind enough to do so. But you will find it hard to persuade me that any burden of years weighs heavy on your pen. We are just back from Hull where we had the visit of youthful Lady Hindlip. She is only ninety but a more alert, keen minded woman I have never seen, with one eye on the races and another on a series of house parties which she intends to grace. I live among the venerable whose activities put me to shame. Only lately we stayed at Campsea Ash with the Ullswaters whom you must have known as James Lowther when he was Speaker. They have almost the finest gardens I have ever seen and certainly the finest yew hedges. Lady Ullswater who is 80 does all the gardening herself and runs the farm while he has charge of the shrubbery.

I am ashamed to say how lazy I have been of late, and if I whispered that golf and bridge have taken up many of my hours you will of course despise me. Lately your friend Margot asked us to dine and play bridge with the Culbertsons. I hasten to add that they are the world's most famous bridge players and she the world's worst! But in this age of overproduction bridge at least provides a very necessary non-productive outlet. At least there is no glut of cards like of wheat.

Also it keeps one from more depressing thoughts of one's own impotence before the overwhelming imbecility of events. England is still an island of the blessed, but only a few miles away there is a tension which cannot be indefinitely prolonged and one hears the echoes of human suffering.

I hope you received my *Divided Loyalties* which I sent to Beverly. It has met here with an unexpectedly good reception and favorable reviews which is all one can expect for few Englishmen ever buy a book. Now that it is out of the way I feel like a dog without a bone and not quite ready to begin something afresh. It is hard to bury oneself in the past when the present is engaged in tumbling down our houses of cards which we took for castles. I admire your philosophy of skeptical humility, but I see a whole past disappearing and do not relish what is beyond the new watershed.

My lady wishes to be warmly remembered.

Ever yours,

L. E.

25, Great Cumberland Place, W.1

January 7, 1934

Dear Justice Holmes:

I was very glad to have news of you from your secretary,[11] and will you be good enough to thank him for his kindness. For I like to think of you enjoying life from an Olympian throne turned into an armchair, even if you don't quite realize the triumph of these venerable survivors of prehistoric wars who were once the objects of your greatest admiration.

Something even more venerable is now front page news over here, namely the Loch Ness monster — a still unidentified animal from twenty or thirty feet long which inhabits Loch Ness. As the Loch is landlocked no one knows how it got

---

[11] Mark DeWolfe Howe (1906–   ); Secretary to Holmes 1933–34, Professor at the Harvard Law School, and author of the definitive biography of Holmes, the first two volumes of which have been published; *The Shaping Years 1841–1870* (1957) and *The Proving Years 1870–1882* (1963).

there, but there seems to be no doubt that it exists. It has even been movied, and two nights ago just escaped being run down by a motorcyclist in the dark.[12]

Washington also seems to have its monster in the shape of a budget. An impoverished country is to squander its way back to prosperity and create wealth by shortening work and cutting down production. Yet in spite of such seeming economic absurdities I am for it and like Tertullian *credo quia impossibilum*. Modern economists seem to me like XVIth century theologians when Geneva and Rome had their little differences. At least Roosevelt talks with a refreshing semi-modesty. But the official Fascist creed declares that Mussolini is never wrong, and Hitler seems to me a dangerous mystic with a real gift for politics but in whose half educated brain general ideas work havoc.

I too, as you see, indulge in easy thoughts from my arm-chair and have shortened the hours of my work beyond the point even preached by the American Confederation of Labor. Now that such important occupations as shooting are nearly over, I shall go to my last tomorrow, I propose to take Helen to Madeira where the Tweeddales join us. I have taken a villa for I suppose the six weeks we will spend there in order to break the blackness of this London winter. For if I have to bask idly I like the idea of basking in sunshine, and I am past the illusion that my idleness makes any cosmic difference. Also I propose to take in Portugal on the way which is almost the only European country I have never seen.

The exhibition of British art opened here yesterday. They have tried, without much success, to establish a continuity of tradition from the Middle Ages. But really English art only begins in a true stream after Vandyck, Reynolds, and Gainsborough give distinction to the dining room, and a kind of unconscious compromise between art and native taste takes

[12] On the night of January 5, 1934, Mr. Arthur Grant, the first recorded person to observe the Loch Ness monster on land, reported having seen a beast twenty-five feet long with toes on its hind legs bound twice across the road in the beam of his headlight and then disappear down a steep slope leading to the loch. Maurice Burton, D.Sc., believes Mr. Grant could have seen an otter. In a recent article Dr. Burton explains how persistent probing of lake bottoms has led him to conclude that most aquatic appearances of the monster can be explained by the phenomenon of rising marsh gas. See *The Illustrated London News*, Vol. 238, May 27, 1961.

place in the sporting and nature pictures; so Stubbs [13] and Ben Hall are the new Gods who knew how a horse should look on canvas.   There are some splendid pictures, but they lack the continuous tradition of the Italian and French schools.

All good wishes for 1934 from Helen and I.

Ever yours,
L. E.

P.S.   I played bridge with Leo Everett the other day who told me you once paid him the compliment he prizes most in life and asked to be remembered.

25, Great Cumberland Place, London, W.1

July 1, 1934

Dear Justice Holmes:

It was a real disappointment for me not to see you.   If I had only known it in time I would have gone on a welcome pilgrimage to the North Shore to catch a glimpse of you. Instead I shall have to wait for this till next year.   Washington was so hot that I understood your exodus.   But I spent a most agreeable three quarters of an hour *tête à tête* with the President. Involuntarily one thinks of Theodore Roosevelt though there is not much in common, but the difference shaped itself in my mind by the feeling that I would gladly have followed T.R. to hell and would as cheerfully accompany Franklin Roosevelt.

Also I saw Hull [14] a couple of times and liked him exceedingly.   I share much of your skepticism on the subject of greatness (though now you've become a G.O.M.[15] you ought to revise your views), but Hull seemed to me to have a kind of moral bigness harking in the background and a simplicity which one associates with Lincoln.

[13] George Stubbs (1724–1806) ; English animal painter.
[14] Cordell Hull (1871–1955) ; American Secretary of State from March 1933 to November 1944.
[15] Grand Old Man was the name given to Civil War veterans after the First World War. It was also an affectionate nickname given to W. E. Gladstone in England about the same time.

The New Deal finds me neutral in the sense that I approve of any emergency measures while remaining skeptical as to their healing powers, but I am delighted to find that the capital of the United States is Washington. Keynes, the English economist, was immensely impressed by the earnestness of the New Dealers and the great liberal experiment, but his prophecies are so often wrong that I felt nervous. I met him at dinner at Butler's [16] in New York and next day was paraded for my medal.[17] Butler was magnificently pontifical when he entered followed by his college of Cardinals all in gorgeous array. Then came the investiture. Conant was on hand looking a small but sympathetic boy who was there to receive the canonical blessing. The deans of the different colleges produced rolls of parchment which the touch of Butler's finger converted into thousands of degrees. As a piece of show work it was excellent academic mass production to fit synthetic learning into the modern world.

Now I am back here once more as a rather nondescript and spasmodic participant of a season which exalts the debutante. Midge's second daughter, Georgina, who is an amusing young lady brimming over with verve and a sense of humor, is one of the season's crop and by no means the least appreciated. So I participate vicariously. We go to occasional parties — certain in the Edwardian style with artists to amuse some of the guests who have been imported from Paris and royalties to awe the others. But I feel in that half way house too old and too distant to catch the stride and not old enough to retire into philosophic calm.

May the North Shore breezes restore you. With many friendly messages from my ladies.

Ever yours,
L. E.

Please tell your sympathetic secretary to give me occasional news.

[16] Nicholas Murray Butler (1862–1947); American scholar and President of Columbia University from 1901 to 1945.

[17] Einstein was awarded the Columbia University Medal of Honor June 5, 1934.

Bellevue Palace and Bernerhof, Berne

March 4, 1934

Dear Justice Holmes:

I know that your birthday is approaching and these lines are to wish you, in Chinese fashion, ten thousand more and the immortality of the sage. Most of the celestial sages are represented in porcelain images nodding benevolently and somewhat whimsically. I will not go so far as to compare you to the followers of the Tao, but I think of you in your rocking chair as not altogether unlike an Oriental philosopher.

We have come here for Helen's medical treatment after having somewhat unexpectedly passed six weeks in Portugal. We were on our way to Madeira where I had taken a villa, but Helen's illness compelled us to remain at Lisbon and nearby. Save for her ill health the stay was pleasant in a wonderful climate, a beautiful land, and among people whom I found very sympathetic. They did not seem interested, and the struggle for life appeared less bitter than elsewhere. Also I saw something of country houses, and perhaps my impressions were mellowed by the 1840 Madeira and 1860 Port which was offered me. Portugal impressed me as having hid its vision of real greatness, which lasted little more than the span of two generations, and ever since with occasional flickers has passed into calm. But the tombs of her great Kings held up by marble elephants convey the image of the Indies which her mariners brought back to Europe.

Here at Berne all is dull order and life goes on with a placid efficiency which would end by turning me into an anarchist. But Swiss doctors are first class and give you a care and attention difficult to obtain in a larger capital. The real problem is what to do with one's time. I heard Maître Torres speak the other day in the Criminal Court. He is, as you know, one of the greatest of French lawyers, and if I had not known that I should have mistaken him for a great actor. His delivery was simple but perfect, and he spoke with humor and covered malice of other lawyers. I wish you could have been present.

I am in the midst of Caulaincourt's *Mémoires* [18] which have

[18] *Mémoires du Général de Caulaincourt, Duc de Vicence*, 3 vols., édition établie et annotée par Jean Hanotau, Paris (1933).

just seen the light after having been written over a century ago. He was with Napoleon at Moscow and returned with him in the same sleigh to France.   There is a good deal of realism and an absence of all rhetoric in his observations, and the portrait he draws of the great man shows how even genius suffers from self deception.   For Napoleon is far more vacillating than one commonly represents him.   Yet as he had placed himself so high he did not know how to climb down and therefore tumbled.   Caulaincourt who admired him enormously was yet never blind to his faults.

I am sorry to see the French are again in a bad way.   The murder of Prince [19] the day before he was to give his evidence is a horrible story, particularly as the truth is so carefully hidden that all kinds of surmises are made.   That something is rotten in Denmark is pretty evident, and if the present government is not able to get at the bottom the conditions will only get worse at a time when the whole of Europe is sinking into a worse mess.

Helen sends you her affectionate greetings to which I add my own.

L. E.

25, Great Cumberland Place, W.1

October 4, 1934

Dear Justice Holmes :
It is some time since I wrote you for I find that moving about on the Continent with the scratchy pens offered one is not conducive to a penmanship on which I recall you once cast aspersions.

But often I think of you wondering how you are, and your secretary's kind lines to tell me that you were enjoying Beverly were most welcome.   Will you thank him warmly from me. Lately I heard that you were to be the great triumph of the Harvard Tercentenary.   I almost resent your having become a G.O.M. for I don't like the implications, but of course it was unavoidable and popular recognition must seem something of a joke to the mind of a philosopher who has never sought it.

---

[19] Albert Prince, *Conseiller* of the Paris Court of Appeal, was found dead February 21, 1934, under circumstances suggesting his murder before giving evidence in an investigation connected with the notorious Stavisky scandals then causing considerable political unrest in France.

By way of pleasantry I must relate to you one of our mutual friend Lady Oxford's latest. Having met Jean Harlow (the original platinum blonde) at a party the latter exuberantly began to call her Margott stressing the final t. Margot (severely) — 'The final "t" in my christian name is silent, unlike your family name'.

We have just returned from a month passed agreeably in that south western corner of France next to Spain between Biarritz and St. Jean de Luz where I idled away my time with more beneficial results to my health than mind. I swam amid lovely nymphs attired like Conrad's South Sea heroines, I played golf and bridge, occasionally I even opened a book; but somehow the world of serious books seems remote while the barbarian is at the gates of Rome. I hear that the young no longer read history because it is developing before them. I try to follow a very limited field and discover even that is impossible till like an ostrich I bury my head in drifting sands.

I came back from the South of France by car and procured there aesthetic and gastronomic satisfactions. For after seeing the glories of XIIth century sculpture at Moissac I tasted the glories of XXth century cooking in a small restaurant at Poitiers adorned with the menus served to King Edward at Buckingham Palace. For his chef, when he had retired, opened a restaurant of his own in his home town which boasts a University but not a single permanent movie — so backward are the French.

Now after two weekends in the country I am back here splashing my morning ink more by habit than conviction and trying to relate diplomatic recollections with a creaking pen.

Midge who is ill with an inflamed appendix asks affectionately after you, also my lady. May you prosper long.

Vale,
L. E.

25, Great Cumberland Place, W.1

December 2, 1934

Dear Justice Holmes:

I wonder how you are passing your Sunday in that back library of yours, and fancy I can see you there sitting in an armchair while your very dutiful secretary reads aloud to you. But I wish you could have been with me last night at a performance of Hamlet by John Gielgud. He is still a young actor and his vintage ought to ripen, but even as it was I found him magnificent and original, his elocution admirable, and shifting his emphasis with extreme rapidity. Only the soliloquy was delivered unstressed and almost monotonously; but I talked to Margot and Somerset Maugham between scenes and both found this right.

Elizabeth Bibesco, (Margot's daughter) told me of an XVIIIth century epitaph in a London churchyard which I repeat for your amusement.

> 'Under this stone lies poor Charlotte
> Who was born a virgin and died a harlot,
> To the age of fifteen she retained her virginity
> Not a bad record for this vicinity.'

And Margot related the best retort courteous I ever heard. It concerns George IV who having been to inspect the fleet at Portsmouth remarked to Admiral Tryon: 'Are you still the greatest scoundrel in Portsmouth?' The Admiral: 'I hope, Sir, you haven't come down to take away my character.'

London forgot everything last week for the Royal wedding. Frankly Princess Marina [20] bored me, but the enthusiasm of the crowd for this modern Cinderella was amazing, and all the jaded kings of Asia and Europe came out of their cubby holes of exile to be the guests at Buckingham Palace. But to avoid wrangles of precedence between the 'Emperor of Russia' and other old and young Pretenders the King did the seating himself. I saw the procession of cantering Life Guards, crimson footmen, and state carriages from Carlton House Terrace. The crowd cheered wildly, but as I have a vulgar taste I should have fancied a brass band and a couple of elephants to add to the display.

By the bye when they launched the new Cunarder the other day, Lord Aberconway, whose company had built it, prepared a humorous speech in which he compared the vessel to the Loch Ness monster. Just as he was about to deliver it

---

[20] Princess Marina, daughter of Prince Nicholas of Greece, married the Duke of Kent in November 1934.

a friend addressed him that the ship was to be christened
'Queen Mary'.

I met Lady Desborough the other day at the French
Embassy who told me that she had heard from you which
sounded well for your health. I wonder if you miss or rejoice
having nothing to do with interpreting the New Deal?

I have been asked to appear in court by that strange
creature Gladys, Duchess of Marlborough. She is bringing
action against a paper which published a picture of intertwined rose trees with the caption underneath, 'I guess we
should not have planted the Duchess of Marlborough and the
Reverend H. Robertson Page in the same bed'. She considers
this a cruel libel which reflects on her moral character, but as
I regard it only as a vulgar and stupid joke I don't think she
will call me as a witness.

Well, I have babbled along principally because it seemed
like a Sunday chat with you, and if Howe has the leisure tell
him I would appreciate a line to know how you keep.

Ever yours,
L. E.

25, Great Cumberland Place, W.1

18 Dec. 1934

Dear Justice Holmes :

I am sending you an account of a scene in the Lords
which probably you have read about already. A friend
described it to me as something quite unparalleled to see the
Lord Chancellor shake his fist with rage at the Lord Chief
Justice, yet in the end they all made it up. Of course behind
it all is the feeling aroused by Lord Slesser's socialist convictions, and when I mentioned this to Helen she thought that
socialists had no business to be on the bench.

I attended Lord Buckmaster's funeral the other day. He
was glad to die for the world held out little to him and his
family life was unhappy. His views, as you may know, on
such topics as birth control and divorce were uncanonical,

and as he went into every cause with the ardor of a crusader there was no mystery about his opinions. Yet for some occult reason he was buried in a church so high that it seemed Roman, for the service was in Latin and they chanted the *Dies Irae*.

Yesterday, by an odd coincidence, they sold the Empress Joséphine's carriage at Christie's and three hundred of Napoléon's letters to Marie Louise at Sotheby's. The latter, which hitherto had been unknown, were bought by the French Government for £15,000. I think that the fascist fashion contributes to this vogue for Napoléon. Here at least there is still enough political sense to prevent fascism from making headway. The English are as usual rather pleased with themselves. They have never suffered from humility, but when they contrast their position with that of other countries they feel that they are endowed with some superior wisdom. Their great merit so far as I can see is never to try for the one hundred percent. But more than ever I find I am baffled by all that is going on in the world today.

I am engaged in doing badly what you ought to have done but wouldn't, namely to write down my memories — at least so far as they are diplomatic for I have neither the talent nor the wish to expose my own imperfections. But it amuses me to retrace former scenes and describe men and events in different capitals. I am not good at relating gossip and the book, if it sees the light, will not be popular, but it has given me an interest to write at a time when I have few others. Yet life in London is pleasant enough to make up for the want of something more active. I have not reached the stage where shooting is a pursuit in itself, but I find it amusing. The present Lord ———, who is a friend of mine, was disinherited by the late Earl because he had socialistic views. Also the second son was passed over because he had won several scholarships at Oxford. The fortune has gone to the third because he was fond of shooting!

We are leaving to spend the Christmas holidays at Yester, and may these lines bring you ever so many affectionate wishes from us both for your health and your enjoyment of life.

Ever yours,

L. E.

25, Great Cumberland Place, W.1

19 Feb. 1935

Dear Justice Holmes :

Your birthday is approaching and you will have many affectionate wishes from us three for your life and health. *Fortunate Senex* I almost feel like saying, only that people no longer quote Virgil. But if you had attained your present years at the time when you were born I suppose you would have been greeted with more Latin than English congratulations. The *Festschrift* never entered our traditions so you will be spared this, but I suppose that even at German Universities there is less of this since even learning has to bow before Nazi doctrines.

We have acquired a new physician who was a professor for thirty years in Berlin but had to bolt when Hitler came in though he tells me he could now return and by a slight recantation be received with open arms. Yet nothing will induce him to although he could get back valuable property which has been sequestrated. I hear many prophecies of what will take place in the Continent and no two are the same, but I foresee little that is good at least from our point of view.

Here, people still jog along sanely, and when someone like Winston gets excited over India he finds himself in a minority. But he has the gift of quick reply. Lately —————[21] remarked that there was no one he admired as much as Randolph Churchill (Winston's son) for being completely unspoiled by his numerous failures. He counted without Winston who expressed surprise at hearing this from ————— who was the greatest 'Miss' of the Century !

Today I have had a row with Helen who refuses to speak to me. It is all about your Court's gold decision. I applauded Hughes, but she is a female counterpart of McReynolds which is not unflattering to your late associate. I don't know if she also regards Roosevelt like Nero but she is pretty close to it. I fear that being without her convictions I find nothing theological about the law, and I think the country should be glad to have a man with the administrative and political experience

[21] A popular entertainer of the time.

of Hughes as C.J.   I should have hated to see a complete divorce between the Court and the country.

This has been our first winter here, and if I am to be unemployed I find London far pleasanter than Riviera hotels. At least one sees movement although one's own movements remain singularly unconvincing by their cosmic importance. The other day I went to see an old friend, Lady Paget, who lives in a magnificent garden at Coombe from which she never stirs.   She tells me she is perfectly happy gardening and barely seeing a soul.   I have not yet got so far for I enjoy a small bridge dinner and best of all an interesting chat, though I find few nowadays willing to talk, so I sit down and chat with you from time to time.

Ever yours,
L. E.

Mr. Justice Holmes died after a short illness in his home in Washington on March 6, 1935, two days before his ninety-fourth birthday.

'. . . he died as he lived, with unflinching gayety and rectitude.   And nothing that will ever be written or said of him will testify to his quality more than the strange deep discernment of the whole nation that the country's finest figure had departed.   From the point of view of the crowd Holmes was a recluse but the quality of him somehow or other broke through, to let all the millions who could not even remotely put into words his significance feel his glory as part of their own.'

Extract from a letter to Lewis Einstein written
by Felix Frankfurter, June 25, 1935.

APPENDIX

HISTORY OF THE HOLMES–EINSTEIN LETTERS

SHORTLY after Justice Holmes died on March 6, 1935, Mr. Einstein wrote to Professor Felix Frankfurter of the Harvard Law School, one of Holmes's literary executors, announcing his intention to give the Holmes letters to the nation in the form of a gift to the Library of Congress in Washington. Frankfurter replied on June 25, 1935, approving this decision and suggesting that Einstein forward the letters to him for perusal with such instructions for their eventual deposit in the Congressional Library as he might indicate in a letter addressed to Dr. Herbert Putnam, the Librarian. In accordance with this suggestion Einstein forwarded the letters through Frankfurter to Dr. Putnam under cover of the following letter:

25, Gt. Cumberland Place, London, W.1

November 27, 1935

Dear Dr. Putnam:

I am sending you through the courtesy of the Secretary of State, a collection of two hundred and six letters covering a period from 1903 to 1932 addressed to me by the late Justice Holmes, and which contain many interesting comments on the men and events of the day as well as on literature and his philosophy of life.

Believing that the Justice's memory will live in our national inheritance, I would wish these personal records of a long friendship with which he honoured me to be preserved in a public institution at Washington. But, until a decision has been made regarding the proposed Holmes Memorial, it seems to me premature to express an opinion as to where these letters ought most appropriately to be kept. I am therefore sending them to you with the understanding that failing any other

disposition on my part within the next three years the correspondence is to become the property of the Congressional
Library.

Regarding the use of these letters, I think that it is only
fitting that the public should be denied access to them until
the Justice's literary executors decide on the ones which they
may wish to publish. Beyond this, and in view of the personal
nature of certain of them, I would like to stipulate the
executors' consent to their literary use during the next ten years
though I would have no objection to anyone approved of by
you seeing the letters in the meantime.

Very sincerely yours,
Lewis Einstein

Dr. Herbert Putnam
Congressional Library
Washington

The Holmes letters are now located in the Manuscript Division
of the Library of Congress in Washington and are accessible to all
who wish to see them.

Einstein's letters to Holmes were found among the Justice's
private papers upon his death. Holmes, however, destroyed many
personal papers and even took comfort in the thought that he
had destroyed illuminating documents that might have otherwise
survived.[1] It seems highly probable that the missing Einstein
letters to Holmes were destroyed by the Justice himself and con-
sequently did not survive his death. The fifty-six letters published
in the present collection came into the possession of Holmes's
nephew and second literary executor, John G. Palfrey of Boston,
and upon his death were given by his widow to the President and
Fellows of Harvard College. They are now preserved in the
custody of the Harvard Law School Library.

Justice and Mrs. Frankfurter felt for many years that the
Holmes-Einstein correspondence should be published. Mrs. Frankfurter particularly appreciated their flavor and in 1943 she obtained
copies of the Einstein letters from Mr. Palfrey and had the Holmes
letters photostated by the Library of Congress, preparatory to
editing them for publication. Unfortunately Mrs. Frankfurter's

---

[1] See letter of Holmes to Einstein dated September 30, 1932, p. 349.

health interfered with her editorial work and, although her interest and wish to see the letters published never abated, after the end of World War II she found her strength did not permit her to continue editing the correspondence.

In 1959 the present editor, after perusing a bound typewritten copy of the Holmes letters on the shelves of Mr. Einstein's library in Paris, arranged for him to address the members of the Harvard Law School Association of France on February 10, 1960, on the subject of the correspondence. The interest elicited in the correspondence at this meeting caused Mr. Einstein to consent again to the preparing of the correspondence for publication. The editing has been done entirely from photostatic copies of the originals. It appears reasonably certain that all letters in existence between the two men, with certain minor exceptions mentioned in the preface, have been included in the present collection.

ACKNOWLEDGMENTS

MANY persons have assisted in preparing the Holmes–Einstein letters for publication. Mr. Einstein's consent to the publication of his letters to Justice Holmes provided the primary impetus which started the correspondence on its way to the reader. Subsequently he placed his fine library in Paris at the editor's disposal, and never failed to answer positively any questions relating to the letters, with the exception of several concerning his own handwriting which, with the best of intentions, he was unable to decipher.

Professor Mark DeWolfe Howe of the Harvard Law School was also most helpful. His recommendation to the President and Fellows of Harvard College that permission be granted to publish the Holmes letters was an essential step toward their publication. His kind help, which has never wavered, includes obtaining photostatic copies of the Einstein letters from the Widener Library, reading the manuscript, and giving many helpful suggestions at various times.

The editor is particularly grateful to Mr. Gerald H. Selous and Mr. David C. Mearns, Chief of the Manuscript Division of the Library of Congress, for their help in putting the manuscript into final form.

Mr. Henry Andrews, Mr. Elliott Nixon, and Mr. Hans Brecht have assisted the editor in more ways than he can properly express to see the manuscript through to publication.

It is a pleasure to acknowledge permission from the following for leave to quote from the works mentioned: Harvard University Press and Cambridge University Press, *The Holmes–Pollock Letters* (*The Pollock–Holmes Letters*) edited by Mark DeWolfe Howe; *The Encyclopaedia Britannica*; and Mr. Justice Frankfurter for permission to publish an extract from an unpublished letter to the Honorable Lewis Einstein dated June 25, 1935.

INDEX

Aaronsohn, Miss, xxiii
Aberconway, Lord, 360
Abrams v. *United States*, 244 n.
Adams, Brooks, 5, 14, 16, 18, 30, 62, 264
Adams, Charles Francis, 5, 90, 254, 263, 301
Adams, Henry, 11, 12, 253-4, 255, 256, 263, 300
Adams, James Truslow, 346
Adams, John, 99, 336, 341
Addison, Joseph, 322
Adler, Felix, 166-7
Aeschylus, 56, 226
Ainslee, Douglas, 129
Aldershot 'Tattoo', 344
Aldus Manutius, 6
Algeciras, 21
Alger, Horatio, vii
American Diplomacy 1900-50 (Einstein), viii n.
American Foreign Diplomacy by a Diplomatist (Einstein), viii n.
Anély, Max, 43
Anti-Trust Act, 38, 40
Aristotle, 24, 196
Arnold, Matthew, 41, 99
Asquith, Henry Herbert, 203, 314
Asquith, Margot, viii, 203, 222, 313, 314, 337, 352, 359, 360
Aubrey, John, 220
Austen, Jane, 218
Auvergne, 329

Bacon, Robert, 44 n., 130
Baldwin, Stanley, 240
Balfour, A. J., 203, 204, 282
Balletti, Manon, 89, 91-2
Ball's Bluff, xvi, 27, 64 n., 66, 251
Balzac, 35, 39, 139
Bancroft, George, 54
Barbusse, Henri, 152
Baring, Maurice, 28 n.
Barlow, Robert Shaw, 23-4, 25, 30-1
Battling Siki, 210
Beard, Charles Austin, 132 n.
Beer, George Louis, 149

'Before the Bust of Homer at Naples' (Einstein), 224-5
Behmen (*sic*), Jacob, 312
Bell, Gertrude, 281
Belloc, Hilaire, 138
Benda, Julien, 163
Benjamin, René, 132
Bent, Silas, 338 n., 347 n.
Bergson, Henri, 54, 55, 63, 98
Berkeley, Bishop, 99
Berry, Sir Gomer, 351
Berry, Helen (*née* Hay), 159, 347, 351
Berry, Lionel, 347, 351
Berth, Edouard, 144-5
Beveridge, Albert J., 118, 258, 268, 329, 347
Beveridge, Mrs., 299, 329
Bibesco, Elizabeth, 360
Biddle, Francis, xv
Birmingham, George A., 80
Birrell, Augustine, 138
Bishop, Joseph Bucklin, 293 n.
Blanesborough, Robert Younger, Baron, 289
Blasco-Ibáñez, Vicente, 157 n., 167 n.
Bloy, Léon, 46
Boigne, Comtesse de, 29
Boisgobey, Fortuné Abraham de, 145
Boissier, Gaston, 10
Bomb attempt, on Holmes, 185-6
Borrow, George, 229
Boucicault, Dion, 84
Boutmy, Émile, 19
Bowers, Claude G., 347 n.
Bradley, A. C., 198
Bradley, F. H., 17, 231
Bradstreet, Governor, 258
Brandeis, Louis Dembitz, 128, 151, 159, 160, 179, 180, 187, 194, 231, 249 n.
Bretonne, Restif de la, 113
Brieux, Eugène, 61
Browning, Robert, 146
Brunetière, Ferdinand, 146
Bryan, William Jennings, 77, 78, 99, 109, 117, 246 n.
Bryce, James, 65, 198
Buchan, John, 137

371

THE END

PRINTED BY R. & R. CLARK, LTD., EDINBURGH